T0207122

Praise for *Expert ASP.NET 2.0 Advanced Application Design*:

"Most intermediate to advanced developers will be familiar with the information presented and think of it as a good re-introduction/refresher to the topics. New ASP.NET developers will learn a ton of good internal information in only a few pages that will round out their knowledge quite nicely."

—David Hayden, .NET Developer (http://davidhayden.com)

Expert ASP.NET 2.0
Advanced Application Design

Dominic Selly
Andrew Troelsen
Tom Barnaby

Apress®

Expert ASP.NET 2.0 Advanced Application Design

Copyright © 2006 by Dominic Selly, Andrew Troelsen, and Tom Barnaby

Softcover re-print of the Hardcover 1st edition 2006

Lead Editor: Ewan Buckingham

Technical Reviewers: Robert Lair, Rakesh Rajan, Victor Garcia Aprea, Fernando Simonazzi, Hernan De Lahitte

Contributors: Dave Zimmerman, David Schueck, George Politis

Editorial Board: Steve Anglin, Dan Appleman, Ewan Buckingham, Gary Cornell, Tony Davis, Jason Gilmore, Jonathan Hassell, Chris Mills, Dominic Shakeshaft, Jim Sumser

Associate Publisher: Grace Wong

Project Manager: Beckie Stones

Copy Edit Manager: Nicole LeClerc

Copy Editor: Lauren Kennedy

Assistant Production Director: Kari Brooks-Copony

Production Editor: Kelly Winquist

Compositor: Dina Quan

Proofreader: Nancy Sixsmith

Indexer: Broccoli Information Management

Artist: Wordstop

Interior Designer: Van Winkle Design Group

Cover Designer: Kurt Krames

Manufacturing Manager: Tom Debolski

ISBN : 978-1-4842-2090-0
DOI : 10.1007/978-1-59059-522-0

ISBN : 978-1-4302-0073-4 (eBook)

Distributed to the book trade worldwide by Springer-Verlag New York, Inc., 233 Spring Street, 6th Floor, New York, NY 10013. Phone 1-800-SPRINGER, fax 201-348-4505, e-mail orders-ny@springer-sbm.com, or visit http://www.springeronline.com.

For information on translations, please contact Apress directly at 2560 Ninth Street, Suite 219, Berkeley, CA 94710. Phone 510-549-5930, fax 510-549-5939, e-mail info@apress.com, or visit http://www.apress.com.

The source code for this book is available to readers at http://www.apress.com in the Source Code section.

Patty made Lucy
while I made this book, and so
I give it to them.
—dws

Contents at a Glance

PART 1 ■ ■ ■ ASP.NET 2.0 Internals

PART 2 ■ ■ ■ .NET Middle Tier Solutions

PART 3 ■ ■ ■ Data Access Layer

Contents

PART 1 ▪▪▪ ASP.NET 2.0 Internals

PART 2 ■ ■ ■ .NET Middle Tier Solutions

PART 3 ▪▪▪ Data Access Layer

About the Authors

DOMINIC SELLY is an Intertech trainer and consultant. Dominic is a frequent presenter at developer conferences. He is also a coauthor of *Visual Basic .NET at Work* (Wiley, 2002). Dominic has been creating software for more than a dozen years.

Dominic has also been teaching developers for many years, in topics including ASP.NET, VB.NET, C#, XML, Visual Basic, ASP, and SQL Server.

He is the author of several of Intertech Training's courses, including Complete ASP.NET, .NET for Architects, and much of their Web Services curriculum. Dominic also co-created the Web Application Development Certificate program offered at George Washington University in Washington D.C.

Dominic spends his spare time trying to master the perfect determinism of the game of pocket billiards.

ANDREW TROELSEN is a Microsoft C# MVP and partner/vice president of Training and Technology at Intertech Training, where he has worked for more than eight years. He teaches and mentors America's leading organizations (including NASA, Microsoft Corporation, Honeywell, Lockheed Martin, Wells Fargo, and the Mayo Clinics) regarding the ways of .NET, and if duty calls, the Component Object Model (COM).

He is also the author of *Visual Basic .NET and the .NET Platform: An Advanced Guide* (Apress, 2001), *COM and .NET Interoperability* (Apress, 2002), and *Developer's Workshop to COM and ATL 3.0* (Wordware Publishing, 2002).

When he has a spare moment, he enjoys re-creating the games he once programmed for his Atari 400 using C# and the BCL, spending too much time with his XBox; cheering for the Timberwolves, Wild, and Vikings; and doing whatever possible to return to the Gunflint Trail.

TOM BARNABY is a Microsoft Consultant, C# MVP, national speaker, and author of several .NET books including *Distributed .NET Programming in C#* and *Applied .NET Attributes* (Apress, 2002). In his spare time, Tom enjoys playing with his two sons, watching movies in the family home theater room, and banging out power chords on his electric guitar with the volume turned to 11.

About the Technical Reviewers

ROBERT LAIR is the president and CEO of Intensity Software, Inc. (www.intensitysoftware.com), which specializes in offering Microsoft .NET solutions, including legacy migrations to ASP.NET. In addition to consulting services, Intensity offering .Kicks for .NET, a CICS to ASP.NET migration utility that automates the migration process while maintaining existing business-logic source code. Bob was one of the developers who created the original IBuySpy Store and WebPortal demo application as well as the NetCOBOL for .NET version of IBuySpy and the QuickStart samples. Bob has been a participating author in a number of books and has written numerous articles on topics related to Microsoft .NET. Bob's personal website is located at www.robertlair.com and his blog is located at www.robertlair.com/blogs/lair.

RAKESH RAJAN Rakesh Rajan is a software engineer from India working at Technopark, Trivandrum in Kerala. He is a Microsoft MVP in C# and an MCSD in .NET. He has been working in .NET for the past three years. You can find him posting at newsgroups, writing articles, working on his own projects, or speaking about .NET. Visit his blog at http://www.msmvps.com/rakeshrajan/ or drop him an e-mail at rakeshrajan@mvps.org.

VICTOR GARCIA APREA is founder of Clarius Consulting S.A., providing training, consulting, and development in Microsoft .NET technologies.

Victor has been involved with ASP.NET since its very early bits and has been awarded each year as a Microsoft MVP for ASP.NET since 2002. He has written books and articles and done lots of reviewing for Wrox Press, Apress, and Microsoft Press, and he is also a regular speaker at Microsoft Argentina (MSDN DevDays, Ask the Experts panel, etc), .NET Local User Groups, and international conferences like VSLive!.

You can read Victor's blog at http://clariusconsulting.net/vga.

FERNANDO SIMMONAZZI lives in Buenos Aires, Argentina, and is an associate of Clarius Consulting S.A. He has more than 10 years of experience in object-oriented technology projects. These projects involved both academic research at LIFIA (http://lifia.info.unlp.edu.ar) and industry projects for application domains such as financial trading support, sales support, and consumer behavior analysis, where he performed development, architecture, and project leading tasks. He complements a strong background in object-oriented theory with extensive in-the-field experience on applied object technologies in Smalltalk, Java, and lately .NET.

He's currently working as a consultant for the Patterns & Practices group in Microsoft Corporation as part of the team building the next version of the Enterprise Library.

HERNAN DE LAHITTE is an engineer and development consultant based in Argentina. He has more than 15 years of experience and has been helping enterprise customers build scalable component frameworks based on the .NET Framework since 2001.

He is a frequent speaker at several Microsoft events and MSDN talks where he usually presents topics such as .NET Security and other .NET architecture related themes.

He currently spends much of his time working for Microsoft Corporation helping the Patterns & Practices group in building useful stuff such as tools, guidelines, and Application Blocks for the worldwide community of developers. He shares most of this experience with other developers through his weblog.

Acknowledgments

There are many people without whose support and influence writing a book like this would not be possible. First is my wife, Patty. Without Patty's support I would never have been able to see this project through. This time in our lives was met by many more challenges than penning an esoteric technical manual, including her pregnancy with our first child (a source of great joy), a herniated disc in my neck, and three broken bones in her foot (sources of great pain). Luckily, we have each of us to care for the other, and many friends and family who were there to help us through a trying and difficult time; many thanks to all of them.

There are many people who have mentored me and provided opportunities for me through my career. Without the combination of their patience and guidance, as well as their faith in my ability to meet the challenges they've presented me, I would still be waiting tables in Minneapolis. These people include Peter Black, Eric Bowen, Himanshu Palsule, Nancy Carpenter, Ashrom Rofail, Anthony Martin, Tom Salonek, and Yasser Shouhoud. I can only hope that they have received a fraction of the positive influence in their own lives through knowing me that I have through my experiences with each of them.

It takes many people to build a book. Thanks to everyone on the team from Apress, including Beckie Stones, Ewan Buckingham, Lauren Kennedy, Nancy Sixsmith, and the army of technical reviewers it took to render this tome cogent. Being, at heart, nothing more than a prolific code monkey, having a team of accomplished and experienced professionals was indispensable and made the process fun. Many thanks also to my colleagues Dave Zimmerman, David Schueck, and George Politis for the benefits of their insights and experience, and to my veteran coauthors Andrew Troelsen and Tom Barnaby.

And finally, thanks to my father Wayne for bringing home a TRS-80 when I was nine. The machine did next to nothing on its own, and so I took it upon myself to make it do something, unwittingly laying the foundation for a fun, challenging, and entirely unusual career.

Dominic Selly

Introduction

Microsoft has been working on version 2.0 of the.NET Framework and Visual Studio 2005 for a number of years now. Between the bits that were handed out at the PDC in 2003 and the release candidate handed out at the PDC in 2005, there's been an unusually long period of time for curious developers to play around with the new functionality, picking out their favorites, and pining for the day they can be used in a production application. Over that same period of time the features have changed quite a bit. It was also an unusually long period of time for Microsoft's customers to provide feedback about what worked and what didn't, and what should be changed or preserved before putting the bits into production. What has resulted is an impressive set of functionality that should be a boon to any development effort.

Because of the long period of time that some version of "Whidbey" (as it was code-named during the development process) has been available, many folks have been able to play with the features of this new version, and even more have seen demonstrations of these features at conferences, in magazines, and online. At its time of release, the development environment provided by the .NET Framework version 2.0 and Visual Studio .NET 2005 might be the most broadly familiar "new" product ever released.

Many features of the .NET Framework version 2.0 will be very important as we move forward into the new platform provided by Windows Vista and its tangential technologies. These features go much deeper than the wizards and "configurators" that have been added to Visual Studio .NET; they even go deeper than many of the flashy new controls that have been shown to awestruck crowds at conferences and developer events over the last couple of years.

And so in designing this book we decided that we did not want to do the standard "new feature march." This book is not a general introduction to version 2.0 of the ASP.NET Framework. Instead, this book focuses on designing distributed applications using the .NET Framework as your platform. With this as our focus, we treat ASP.NET not as an environment for the generation of HTML, but rather as an application hosting environment, one capable of servicing requests not just for Web Forms, but also for Web Services, for distributed objects via Remoting, even for your own custom application hosting needs. By treating ASP.NET as an application server instead of as a web application development environment, our field of view is dramatically increased. Web Forms become just a single piece of a larger, more complex puzzle, the puzzle of distributed application design. This book does not cover the presentation tier of an application. While there is some discussion of maintaining state and communication between a web browser and a web server, a detailed discussion of the presentation tier is conspicuously absent. Instead, we focus on the middle and data tiers of a layered application, and the communication that occurs between these tiers.

In writing this book, we assume you have used a 1.x version of ASP.NET. We assume you are versed in ADO.NET, at least enough to use data readers, create DataSets, and use a data adapter to update your database data. This book is designed to expand on that base of knowledge, by simultaneously introducing you to the full range of servers and technologies available for you to leverage in distributed application design while showing you the enhancements in version 2.0 of the .NET Framework in each of the different layers and tiers of these applications. This combination is designed to give you a broader understanding of your choices of technologies during application design, while at the same time show you how version 2.0 improves upon the existing technologies in these tiers. By taking this approach, this book might not be your first choice as an introduction to the flashiest of features in ASP.NET 2.0, but the depth of detail and range of technologies covered will make this book continue to be relevant long after you've forgotten a time when you didn't know the subtle nuances of the Smart Tag of the GridView control.

There are many "moving parts" in a distributed application, and many different technologies can come to bear on the different pieces of a solution. We wanted to write a book that addressed this complexity, a book on application design—not a blow-by-blow iteration of Framework features, but a discussion of how you can put the different packages and servers available together across different tiers of a distributed application and how they can meet your real-world requirements. The timing was such that it made no sense to write it on version 1.x of the Framework, as it was soon-to-no-longer-be the latest-greatest. Instead of getting swept up in the rush of feature-enumerating titles that have hit the scene with the fanfare of a parade, we just went ahead and wrote a book on application design. We simply incorporated the features of 2.0 while doing so.

You may have already built a full-blown n-tiered application using ASP.NET. If this is the case, then chances are you can glance through the table of contents and pick out a few technologies that you've used in the past. This book will round that knowledge out, and enable you to make more informed decisions about how to design distributed applications, using the features currently available in .NET 2.0, and anticipating the infrastructure that will be available when Windows Vista arrives. Throughout the entire treatment of the topics that follow, we keep an eye on the coming release of Windows Vista and Windows Communication Foundation. Our guidance and advice on how to build applications today will prepare you for many of the technologies and strategies that will be ubiquitous in these new environments. This way you can expand your application design toolset today, while at the same time get ready to create the applications of tomorrow.

PART 1

■ ■ ■

ASP.NET 2.0 Internals

This is a book about distributed application design. Here ASP.NET pertains not just to Web Forms and the generation of HTML, but also more broadly to its use as an application server.

We start by covering some of the things that you must consider when you design a distributed application, and provide some sample distributed application solutions. Then we delve into the ASP.NET request-processing pipeline. In these chapters you'll come to understand the lifetime of a request, how to extend the request-processing pipeline, and some internals of Web Form processing and communication between the web server and web browser across requests.

Chapter 1

The book starts by examining the forces that come to bear on the design of a distributed application. This chapter is high level, but it sets the stage for the specific technical discussions that follow by taking a look at what influences the decisions you need to make about the technology choices available for a distributed application. There are many resources available to help you with specific technologies, in isolation from the rest of your application. In this chapter, we look at how the specific requirements in your environment get mapped to the selection of specific technical infrastructures. We follow up by examining some sample solutions and discussing how they meet specific requirements.

Chapter 2

Here we step out of the world of ASP.NET Web Form processing and examine the larger infrastructure that this request processing exists within. This is the same pipeline used by Web Services, and it is the same pipeline that will be used by Windows Communication Foundation (WCF). It is also built for extensibility, meaning you can do your own type of request processing by customizing this pipeline.

Understanding this request-processing pipeline is the key to understanding many important aspects of distributed application development, both now and for future applications.

In this chapter, you'll see how requests are moved from IIS to a specific handler, how this pipeline can be extended, and how you can add your own handlers for custom request processing.

Chapter 3

This chapter focuses solely on the `System.Web.UI.Page` class, the fundamental type for Web Form programming. Here we peel the covers back on this type, and examine its internal structure: the control tree, which is fundamental to all ASPX request processing.

We'll also show you some changes that have been made to this model in ASP.NET 2.0, including a new compilation model, new deployment options, and some new events available in the lifetime of the page-request processing.

Chapter 4

This chapter focuses on some of the more subtle communication that occurs between the web server and the web browser in ASP.NET request processing. We'll look specifically at the `ViewState`, enhancements to the scripting model that ease the generation of client-side JavaScript, and an amazing new feature that allows for out-of-band asynchronous callbacks from a web browser to the web server.

This set of features focuses on how to maximize the power and flexibility you have when creating applications within the confines of a web browser. The capabilities afforded by this set of features are seldom fully utilized.

The callback feature is especially important, as it is cross-browser-compatible and has the potential to take web application development to the next level by giving the developer the ability to do a partial page refresh, creating a more responsive and usable interface for the user.

CHAPTER 1

■ ■ ■

Overview of .NET Application Architecture

.**N**ET is complex. Not so much in the same way that COM is complex. Not in the way that makes you want to cry as you realize you're going to have to scrub the registry for references to an old version of a COM server again. Not in the way that gives you nightmares about ghoulish GUIDs taunting you from a misplaced type library. No, .NET's complexity is based more on its sheer size and scale. There are more than 3,000 types in the Framework class library, and these types are designed to do just about anything. The major learning curve to becoming productive in the .NET Framework is not the language, regardless of your language of choice (although moving from VBScript to VB .NET Web Forms has been challenging for more than a few); it's the Framework class library. It calls to question, What's out there? When do I use it? How does it work?

Distributed applications are also complex. A layered architecture results in an application with a lot of moving parts. Simply displaying a data point within a web browser can involve using an object graph with dozens of instances, a call stack that's easily five layers deep, code involving markup, one or more managed languages, Structured Query Language (SQL), and maybe even a proprietary database language such as Transact SQL (TSQL). The path of this stack may span processes, machines within a LAN, platforms and operating systems, and maybe even several LANs. As the architect, you have the task of designing the path of these requests and the rules of interaction for each step of the way.

You'll need to consider more than the business-based, functional requirements. When you're designing the architecture, functional requirements may be relevant, but they're usually secondary to other application requirements, which aren't captured in the "Use Cases." You'll also need to address a multitude of questions:

- What are the scalability requirements for the application?

- How available must the application be, and how will someone know when it's "down"?

- Is it customizable, and if so, when and by whom?

- Is it easy to deploy, upgrade, and maintain over time?

- Are there development cost constraints?

- What connectivity mechanisms will it employ (i.e., will users be fully connected, be partially connected/mobile, use PDAs, etc.)?

These are the questions that keep you awake at night, at your desk, going over your solution one more time.

After you've established the technical requirements of the application, you must map these requirements to the technologies at your disposal, have them drive the adoption of logical tiers in the design, and then decide how to physically deploy these logical tiers. You'll need to address many questions in this process:

- What servers and services will be used at what tiers of the application?

- How will the data be accessed?

- How will requests be marshaled between the logical layers of the application?

- What about when those layers span processes—or span machines?

In this book, we provide a complete traversal of this call stack in the context of a .NET application. Each step of the way, we examine the options and services available to meet different nonfunctional requirements at each tier and between adjoining tiers. This is not to say it's a blueprint for a specific application architecture. You have many choices, and many more possibilities when you consider the number of ways you can combine those choices. The architecture you design depends on the requirements of your application. And believe it or not, all applications are unique.

The answer to any question when it comes to the architecture is, "It depends." This is why you make the big bucks. This is why your job seems so hard. And it is. In this book, we give you the background to make it easier when the .NET Framework is your primary toolset. In the chapters that follow, we offer you a road map that enables you to navigate the application layers, choose what to use with each layer, and move information between layers.

Part 1 starts with this chapter, which provides you with an overview of .NET architectural problems and some examples of solutions. This gives you some concrete endpoints that show what your journey may look like. Then, we'll move the focus to the point where a request comes into a web server. This may be a request for a Web Form (an ASPX page), but it may also be a request for a Web Service, a Remoted component, or some custom processor specific to your application. We take broad view of ASP.NET in this book, looking at its full features rather than focusing just on Web Forms.

Regardless of what's being requested, web server requests travel a common pathway. How do these requests travel from Internet Information Services (IIS) to ASP.NET, and what are the points of extensibility along the way? We'll examine this process in Chapter 2. In Chapter 3 and Chapter 4, we'll focus on ASP.NET as a presentation tier. We'll look at how you can maximize code reuse at the presentation tier, as well as discuss the internals for how an instance of a Page object becomes a stream of HTML. We'll show you how the full features of the browser can be leveraged for the presentation tier, and will cover some of the improvements and new features of version 2.0 of the Framework.

In Part 2, we begin by discussing security in the .NET Framework, as security is the "vertical slice" that passes across all the layers in the stack. We'll then look at Microsoft's options and solutions for the middle tier of a distributed app, examining both those in the present and in the not-so-distant future. In this part of the book, we'll also examine your options for marshaling calls for services and data between layers. Here, we'll consider the options and the technologies in their different permutations. This is the most precarious balancing you'll undertake during application design. Even after you've decided on the technologies to use for the individual tiers and the individual layers, the wrong choices for marshaling can impair your scalability on the one hand, and/or impair your dependability and availability on the other. The perils and importance of these decisions provide a fine segue into Microsoft's next generation messaging stack: Windows Communication Foundation (formerly known as Indigo). Windows Communication Foundation's design goal is to unify the call stack that's used whenever out-of-process communication occurs, be it across application domains, inter-process, across machine boundaries, or across the world.

In Part 3, we move to the final critical tier of our application: the data access layer. This is where all the real action resides, where all the bits people actually want to see are housed, where even the nontechnical business users in your enterprise know the heart of the business lies. This is your critical resource in a distributed application, as it is the transactional nerve center of the enterprise. This is also the layer of a distributed application that tends to get the most reuse. Once you write something down, people tend to want to get to it. The decisions you make in this part of your architecture will make or break your suite of applications.

ADO.NET exposes the data access object model in .NET. We'll examine the ins and outs of using these managed providers of data access, how to pick the right tool for the job, and how to employ best practices when using them. We'll also survey other data access services in .NET, and get a sneak peak at the next generation database server: SQL Server 2005.

Nonfunctional Requirements

Architectural requirements are defined by *nonfunctional requirements*, or *quality attributes*. These are the requirements of the application the business or functional requirements do not describe. It is your job to capture these, and to define a technical infrastructure that meets the captured requirements. A key deliverable you need to provide is a definition of the different atomic pieces of the application that will be used, and justification for using them by explaining how they meet different nonfunctional requirements.

You also need to define how these elements will interact. You need to address how type information will be discovered by a calling processes; how the information will be marshaled to and from the service; the constraints of this interaction; the platforms that must be supported in this communication; as well as which pieces are public knowledge (part of the interface) and which are internal (hidden details of the implementation). You'll need to answer all of these questions in order to design the technical infrastructure.

Many things can fall into the realm of nonfunctional requirements. While these requirements can be considered separately, it's their interactions that become the critical influence on the design: Many of them work against one another, creating a tension between them, and a balance must be struck. Let's look at a few.

Availability

Availability concerns system failure. This brings to question: What are the points of failure in the system? How often do they become unavailable? And how does someone know when a system is unavailable? Further, when there's a failure, how much time passes before the system becomes available again? Also, what percentage of the time does the application need to be available? In an environment where availability is a high priority, this is usually expressed in the "ninety nine and n nines" form. In these environments, it's usually a given that a system has to be available more than 99 percent of the time. A system that's down for three minutes every five hours will likely be problematic. That's almost fifteen minutes per day. This measure doesn't usually include planned downtime, for backups and routine maintenance, for example. On the other hand, some environments don't need to be highly available. In many environments, as long as an application is available during business hours, folks are happy. However, as applications become more connected, more global, and more automated, requirements for availability will increase.

Failure is inevitable. Hardware fails. Disk drives crash. Networks go down. Accepting this is a given; you provide for availability by adding redundancy to the system. You must add redundancy at each point of failure. Having redundancy at every point of failure is frequently called *n+1 reliability*. N is a measure of the amount of resources needed to do the job. The plus one provides the availability when failure occurs. Given n+1 reliability isn't cheap; it's only put in place for mission-critical applications. If a company's entire revenue stream is web based, an unavailable website means zero dollars in the revenue stream. Suddenly the expense of n+1 reliability doesn't seem like so much money, after all. ISPs that host the big websites typically have four T4 lines running to the building, one from each direction on the compass. They may have several diesel generators in case the power fails, and then in case a generator (or two) fails. They may also be fortified, to guard against sabotage, like a bank. The company adds capacity for the servers automatically when a spike in traffic occurs. All of this redundancy allows them to guarantee the sites they host will be available.

Availability of static pieces of the system can be attained by *scaling out*, which is a fancy term for throwing more servers at the problem. Since one web server can go down, another is added to the mix, and a load balancer is put in front of them. A single IP now maps to more than one machine. Failover is provided by the load balancer, which will send all traffic to the live machine when one dies. If these machines are not physically colocated, some type of persistent connection needs to be maintained between them. This can be a factor when a failover strategy also needs to account for a disaster recovery scenario.

These requirements and the decisions made to meet them can affect the design of the software systems that will be hosted on this physical infrastructure. The introduction of a load balancer means anything stored in the memory of the web server can be in the memory of more than one physical machine. This may be fine for read-only information, where more than one copy is acceptable. But for mutable, or user-specific, information, this situation introduces a definite problem. The web server's memory becomes an unsuitable location to store this information. It must be marshaled out-of-process, and stored in a central location. Failure to account for this means failure of the application when a web server blows a gasket. This problem is accounted for with out-of-process session state available in ASP.NET. State information can be stored either in an out-of-process state server (no redundancy), or SQL Server, which can be made redundant with clustering. This introduces a definite performance hit, but architecture is frequently about trade-offs. You must find a balance. Maybe this hit is not acceptable, and the application will be designed not to use session information at all. It depends.

Clustering will actually need to be present in a highly available system, regardless of how session state is being dealt with. Scaling out will not work on the database tier of the application for the same reason it doesn't work with user-specific session information. It changes. There can't be *n* copies of it, because these copies would start to deviate from one another. Clustering maintains a *hot backup* of a single server and a mirrored copy of the information written to disk that the system is dependent upon. Drive crashes? Switch over to the mirror. Server crashes? Switch to the backup. This is also called *scaling up*. "We can scale out at the application tier and scale up at the data tier," says the architect who has done his homework (and has a big budget).

Clustering works great when you're working with a single physical location. In a disaster recovery scenario with multiple geographic locations, it gets a lot harder and may not even be possible depending on the situation and budget. In such instances, you may still be able to consider clustering, but you'll need to explicitly define the following:

- A geographically shared RAID or SAN, using a hardware- or software-centric approach to data synchronization

- The interaction between Windows clustering and SQL Server clustering

- The size of the "pipe" between two or more locations

- Failover vs. failback

There are other exceptions to these points as well. For example, you may be able to have more than one copy of a database if it's a reporting server whose data is updated nightly with data from the previous day's transactions and it doesn't change during the course of the day. *Scaling out* is also possible in the data tier by *horizontally partitioning* your data. Application architecture is all about your enterprise's exceptions to the rules. And exceptions to those exceptions. And repeat.

Scaling out and scaling up are used for more than availability. They'll make another appearance when we discuss (oddly enough) scalability.

Performance

Performance is frequently the most difficult metric to ensure, as it is often ill-defined, and many development shops don't have the skill set, experience, time, and/or motivation to design and run performance tests. Consequently, performance problems often first rear their ugly heads after an application is deployed. Further, these problems tend not to show up right away—only after sufficient data storage thresholds have been met. "Of course the system should respond in less than seven seconds. That's a given," says the consternated manager whose direct reports have been complaining about system performance.

Performance strategies can often work directly against other system design decisions implemented to solve other requirements. You can use the layered software architecture to increase maintainability and reuse, though introducing new layers of abstraction does not necessarily increase performance. An overly deep call stack can actually impede it. However, other driving factors may actually increase performance. It depends.

Performance is closely related to other aspects of the system, like availability, scalability, and robustness. Often a problem in one of these other areas first shows up as a performance problem. A bad memory chip is an availability issue, but it may first be reported as a performance problem. Similarly, for availability or scalability reasons, you may choose to persist data via asynchronous mechanisms. This decision may actually be perceived by the user as a "performance" issue. For example: "I made an update to this widget record, but my changes weren't immediate. I had to wait 4.3422 seconds for my changes to take effect." While maybe it's not ideal for the user, an asynchronous mechanism like Message Queuing (MSMQ) allows for peak load balancing, guaranteed message delivery, and a looser coupling between the presentation tier and service availability. Weighing these against users' experiences and their tendency to crave immediate validation of their work is another architectural trade-off you must sometimes make.

Measurable requirements are necessary in order to test the performance of the system before putting it into production. These measures have to be more concrete than "It has to be as fast as possible," or "There must be no noticeable delay." There are many measures you can use, and you must design a load test that accurately reflects the expected use of the application in the real world. If you're expecting peaks in traffic, you must test a load representing these peaks. You can measure the number of expected concurrent users, the transactions that are processed per second, or the raw throughput of the web server's response stream. Ideally, you should test the system in its less-than-optimum states as well. If you have the website balanced between two web servers, what happens when one of them goes down? Can a single box deal with the entire load? If not, you may need to add a third server to the mix, two to deal with the expected load, and a third for availability (n+1).

There are many tools available from Microsoft that can help you with this process (see Table 1-1).

Table 1-1. *Tools for Measuring Performance*

Tool	Role in Life
ASP.NET Tracing	This tool can be used to measure the amount of time consumed by atomic pieces of the application: It automatically reports on the amount of time spent on each step of the page-rendering process. It can easily be extended to include metrics around different steps in your call stack, such as how long it's taking to execute a stored procedure. You can use it to aggregate reports, which can be sent to custom data stores.
Application Center Test	This is an easy-to-use tool that generates a basic script to send traffic to your application. It watches the requests you make to the web server during a "script recording" session. A Visual Basic script is generated that reproduces the session, and the tool plays back the script, mocking up any number of users and any number of instances of the web browser. The tool then reports on the server's performance. You can modify the script to provide further customization during the test.
Perfmon	This is the standard Windows tool for gathering system metrics. It has dozens of counters added to it when the .NET Framework is installed. You can use these to watch application counts, the number of loaded assemblies, or the average response time of the server, to name a few.
SQL Profiler	This is an invaluable tool for watching what's occurring on SQL Server. It captures all traffic coming into the server, counts connections, and provides execution times of individual queries.
Enterprise Instrumentation Framework	This is a more advanced API for adding instrumentation to your .NET applications. The package leverages several facilities built into the operating system, such as Windows Management Instrumentation (WMI), the event log, and event tracing.
Logging and Instrumentation Application Block	Part of the Enterprise Library, this package standardizes many common tasks required to instrument code. It leverages the Enterprise Instrumentation Framework and an event-based logging infrastructure so the persistent store of the log can be controlled via configuration.

These are but a few of the tools available from Microsoft, and there is, of course, a rich third-party market for more advanced testing in this area.

Remember, if you don't calibrate the performance of your application before putting it into production, you can make no claims about how it will perform once it's deployed. A simple failure to adhere to a best practice, hidden deep in the call stack, could impede the performance of the entire system. This won't show up as developers sit at their workstations and press F5 within IE as fast as they can. It must be put under load. This load should approximate the traffic you expect when the application goes into production.

While performance measures how fast the current system is, *scalability* is a measure of how much performance improves as resources are added to the system.

Scalability

Scalability describes the system's capability to deal with additional load. You may have only a dozen hits a day when your application goes into production, but as it generates a buzz, you may shortly find yourself with hundreds or thousands of concurrent users. Will your application be able to handle this additional load? Have you designed it to scale up and/or scale out, and given it the capability to add capacity?

Scalability is closely related to performance, but they aren't the same thing. *Performance* is a measure of a static deployment of the system. *Scalability* is the measure of how well adding resources to the infrastructure of the system improves its capability to service additional requests. As you add resources, do you get a corresponding bump in the throughput of the application? Or are you losing bang for the bucks that go into these resources?

There are two types of scaling: *scaling up*, which is also called *vertical scaling*, and *scaling out*, also known as *horizontal scaling*.

Vertical Scaling

This is used for the mutable portions of a system, or those that change over time. The database is a tier of the application that must usually be scaled up to deal with additional load, as scaling out at the database tier is difficult and complex. When the database reaches its capacity, you can add more memory, pop another CPU into the box, or purchase a more powerful box. A clustering solution can be introduced for failover, but this won't help with the current load on the system. Scaling up is also used for the middle layer of an application when it hasn't been designed to scale out. This is not a happy situation to find your system in.

Horizontal Scaling

This involves adding servers to the system, and balancing the load of traffic on the system between them. It's sometimes called a *Web Farm* when it's used for web servers, but scaling out can also be used for an application server. When more than one machine is performing work identical to other machines, the IP representing the farm is "virtualized." That is, a load balancer is the first to receive all requests into the system, and that load balancer doles out the request to the servers configured in the Farm. Load balancers can be hardware- or software-based. How the load is distributed depends on the algorithm used by load balancer in use. Some take a "round robin" approach, and just rotate between the servers. Some will "poll" all of the servers in the Farm, and those responding quickly get hit with more traffic (the idea is to approach equilibrium between the servers over time).

Any state information maintained on these servers must be centralized when you're using a Web Farm. Since requests can be sent to any machine in the mix, a change in the memory of one machine won't show up in the memory of another. *Session state*, a feature of both classic ASP and ASP.NET, is an example of this type of user-specific, volatile information that's stored per browser instance. The canonical example of what goes in the Session is the user's shopping cart. This information must be maintained across different requests that the user makes. It must survive for the entire "session" that the user maintains with the application.

While no solution was built into ASP for out-of-process sessions, it's accounted for in ASP.NET. Session information can be stored on a centralized *state server*, or it can be stored in SQL Server. When deciding to use out-of-process session state, keep in mind that only SQL Server provides a solution for n+1 reliability. If you're using the NT State Server and that box goes down, your session information is unavailable, which will, in all likelihood, severely impair (or take down) an application that's dependent on this information. Also be aware that session state in ASP.NET is application specific. ASP.NET provides no solution "out of the box" for sharing session information across IIS applications, which is unfortunate, because this is a common need. If you find yourself needing this type of information sharing, you'll have to code your own solution.

If it's entirely untenable to move session information out of process, there is one other option. Load balancers support an option called *client affinity*, or *sticky sessions*. This means that once a load balancer sends a given user to a specific server, it continues to send that user to that server for the duration of the user's session (it sticks the user to that server). While this allows you to use in-process session information and still have an application that can scale out, it's not the most efficient load balancing algorithm you can employ. It's possible that some servers in the Farm will be under significantly more load than others. It depends on how long users "stuck" to a particular server use the application. If more users stuck to server A stick around, and those stuck to server B leave the application, server A could be under much more load than server B.

This solution also doesn't provide for redundant availability of the application. If a server that a user is "stuck" to goes down, the user's session information goes down with it. While a good load balancer sends those users to a server that's still available, their session information will be lost, and depending on what's being stored there, their experience with the application will likely be somewhat less than ideal. Once again, storing session state in SQL Server is the only way to provide for redundancy when using this feature.

Security

Security attempts to prevent nefarious persons from performing nefarious acts, and simple-minded fools from the tools they shouldn't use. This runs a wide range of activities, from detecting and preventing a denial of service attack on a public web server, to keeping a known user from accessing a function he's not meant to. You'll also need to establish what happens once a security breach does occur. Do you have enough information to detect what happens? Do you have enough to recover? Can you restore your data to a previously known, good state?

There are three main steps to security: *authentication*, *authorization*, and *auditing*. Authentication involves identifying the users of your system, and denying access to functionality to those users who cannot identify themselves. Authorization concerns making sure authenticated users have permissions to run the function or see the data they're attempting to access. Auditing ensures your ability to investigate and recover if something goes wrong with the first two. Can you tell there was unauthorized access or use of the system? Can you undo what was done?

Data must also be secured. You can secure data by encrypting it, or by keeping it in an otherwise secure data store. An opportune time for encryption is when you're moving data around on the network, or sharing data with partners. Typically, when you're done moving it around, you write it down in a source of persistence that keeps it safe for you, like within a relational database that requires credentials for access.

In Table 1-2, we've outlined security concerns and their solutions in .NET.

Table 1-2. *Security Concerns and .NET Solutions*

Concern	Solution	Windows/.NET Solution
Do we know who you are?	Authentication	Windows (Kerberos/ NTLM) ASP.NET Forms-based security Active Directory IIS Passport
Do we know you have permission to do what you're doing?	Authorization	Windows role-based security custom roles in ASP.NET code access security
Can we get the data to you in a secure manner?	Encryption	Secure Sockets Layer (SSL) Certificate Server, Encryption library in the Framework class library
Can we recover from an attack?	Auditing	IIS logs SQL Server logs and backups NT application logs traceability E2E instrumentation (future)
Will this security infrastructure be manageable as we grow?	Integrated security as opposed to a silo-based approach	Security Policy Groups NT application logs Windows integrated security Impersonation Active Directory others.

In Chapter 5, we take a close look at the .NET specific security atoms.

Maintainability

Maintainability is concerned with the evolution of your system over time. It's highly unusual to ship an application and have all business stakeholders and users simultaneously proclaim "Yes! Yes! This is exactly what we needed! It does the job perfectly!" It's more likely that they'll start requesting changes right away. Sometimes they'll wait a day while your team recovers from pulling an all-nighter to get the thing working in production in the first place, but when they do make requests, what type of changes to the system can you expect?

Your initial requirements may be quite a bit more ambitious than what you've committed to ship on the application's first iteration. Office was not built in a day. However, knowing the requirements that will be present in future iterations can be of great benefit during the architectural design phase, as you can take some of these features into account in the solution.

The application may also have a subset of features that are so volatile that it may be worth the investment to create some user interfaces that are entirely polymorphic in their behavior, and create a tool for end users (or power users) to control how this portion of the interface gets rendered. There may even be a vendor-supplied tool that meets these requirements for you. Content management systems and Web portal packages are just a couple of examples of generalized solutions that let qualified users affect the application at a higher level of abstraction than cranking out and compiling code.

Your application may have requirements that can be met by network or application administrators via configuration files or Microsoft Management Console (MMC) snap-ins. These are tasks technical people need to perform, but they don't necessarily require a developer to change code that then needs to be compiled and shipped.

Checking a code file out of source control and having a developer make changes to it is the most expensive kind of change that can be made to a system. It requires a developer (not cheap). It requires the recompilation of binaries. It requires regression testing of all areas of the application that are affected by a change to that binary (testers, automation, and time: aka more money). And then it takes a deployment and all of the requisite worry, heartache, and long hours that can accompany that.

"Customizability" frequently comes up when discussing these types of features. A fully customizable solution is a totally nontrivial undertaking that can doom a project to never even ship a decent V1 (think of how long it took Microsoft to get Access right ... oh wait ... that hasn't happened yet ...). But there may be key features of your application that you can move into configuration, or you can create an administrative applet to tweak, or for which a vendor-supplied solution nicely fits the bill.

The other type of change anticipation involves minimizing how many components of a system will be affected when the inevitable change is requested. Even if the anticipated change does require developer involvement, isolating that change from other functional areas of the system minimizes the number of binaries affected and, therefore, the complexity of the regression testing that must be done. This may be a choice as simple as making some set of functionality interface based, so that a developer can create new implementations of the interface, and the production system can use late-binding and Reflection to pick up and execute an assembly with the new implementation. Intertech Software has an ingenious shell application that can have entirely new applications added to it just by dropping an assembly that implements a predefined set of interfaces into a directory that the shell is "watching." XCopy and you're done; everything else flows from there.

This leads to an important tenet of service design, that of not creating tight couplings between service components in the system. You don't want to be in a situation where a change to a single class causes a cascade effect of changes to other components. This atomic design is the thrust behind "loosely coupled" services. Not only does this increase maintainability, but it also increases the reuse of your services, as the more atomic and independent they are in the work that they do, the more ways they'll be able to be combined with other services.

We discuss the design of loosely coupled components when we look at Web Services in the .NET Framework in Chapter 6.

Connectivity

Connectivity describes the types and speeds of connection mechanisms that will be used to operate the system. It's often assumed that the user will have a persistent connection to your application, and that a broken connection is the explicit result of some action, such as closing the browser. But what if the user is connected via a cell-phone frequency and loses the connection because he traveled through a bad coverage area? What if the user was in the midst of typing a large amount of data and then loses the connection? Have you considered any facilities for retrieving that data (i.e., Auto Save for the Web)?

Your application may need to function effectively through various types of connections, including dial-up, low-speed wireless (cell-phone frequency), high-speed wireless (WiFi, WiMax), broadband, Digital Subscriber Line (DSL), etc. Thus, the system design must explicitly consider how each scenario will be handled technically, and how the user is impacted by loss of connectivity.

Other Nonfunctional Requirements

There are many other requirements that may be relevant to your system. We summarize some of the others that may come up in Table 1-3.

Table 1-3. *Summary of Other Quality Attributes*

Requirement	Meaning In Life
Usability	Often not thought of as an architecture requirement, as it pertains more to the user interface design than to the nonfunctional requirements. However, requirements of usability can definitely affect your system architecture. For example, if the user makes a long running request for data, and there's a usability requirement that any operation taking more than two seconds should be cancelable by the user, you must account for this (asynchrony) in your architecture.
Manageability	This metric has really come into its own over the last couple of years. More and more IT departments are drawing a line in the sand, saying if we can't maintain it, you can't put it into production. Some of the pain of DLL Hell and Distributed Component Object Model (DCOM) account for this metric's meteoric rise. Chances are you'll need to consider this metric for any substantial enterprise development. Products such as Microsoft's MOM and Team System offerings attempt to address this specifically.
Recoverability	This metric is usually considered a subset of availability. It describes the system's capability to recover from fault or failure, which could threaten the system's availability. Tactics include automatic failover (clustering and load balancing), having a spare on hand, and systems that implement the ACID rules of transactions. In addition to deployment issues, this attribute can also pertain to tracing and auditing. When something goes wrong for a user, can the app re-create the data? If there's an attack, can the app recover and restore the data?
Repeatability	This is the attribute that captures whether or not you can repeat processes from one environment to another. Database scripts are a good example of this metric. If the database has been created using a high-level GUI tool, you have no guarantee that the database will look the same in development, testing, staging, and production. Component installation is another process that should be designed for repeatability as well.

Continued

Table 1-3. *Continued*

Requirement	Meaning In Life
Interoperability	This attribute is constantly increasing in importance as Enterprises come to realize the time, money, and churn they spend on integrating existing systems, packages, platforms, and technologies. The new buzzword around these technologies is Service Oriented Architecture (SOA). SOAP, WSDL, and XML Schema have been combined to offer a platform, language, and transport-neutral protocol solution to this problem, called Web Services. This provides a platform for SOA, although it's not the only one. Within .NET, you have interoperability considerations if you need to use legacy COM applications, be it an existing code base, a vendor-supplied package, or leveraging Office or other current COM products. Data access is another example where there's a common need for interop. .NET provides managed providers of ODBC and OLE DB, and the Data Access Application Block can use these providers seamlessly.
Reliability *	This pertains to the system's maturity, fault tolerance, recoverability, and duration of product relevance.
Testability	This important metric pertains to the system's capability to have engineers verify that it's working correctly. To do this, first and foremost, the system must be defined with a requirements document. Without requirements, testers have no way to verify the system is working correctly. When a developer is finished with a component, she hands it off to the tester and tells him what she programmed it to do. Depending on the developer's understanding of the requirements, this may or may not be what it's *supposed* to do. There are strategies you can employ to test the functionality of components in isolation from one another, as well. These include record/playback, separating the interface from the implementation, and creating specialized test harnesses to fully exercise all of the dynamics of a component. Stubs and feeds of domains of data can also be used. These stubs are also sometimes called *Mock Objects*.
Stability	This is a facet of performance, availability, and, also very likely, maintainability. This is a description of the state of an application over time, or how static its state is over time. An example of where stability measurements are important is an application that queries a database table that's poorly indexed. During testing, the row count is low, so load tests perform swimmingly. Over time in production, however, the row count increases, causing the query's performance to degrade, resulting in an unstable system. A *memory leak* is an example of another possible stability problem.
Functionality *	This attribute pertains not just to functional requirements, but also to the intersection of those requirements with the nonfunctional requirements that have been identified as relevant and important to the system.
Portability	This pertains to the system's adaptability, installability, capability to play nicely with others, ease of replacement, and platform independence. This requirement can become important if you're working for an independent software vendor (ISV) who wants to sell their product to run on several platforms. You can see this metric come into play in the application or the database space. Programming to the interfaces of ADO.NET is a way to achieve database portability within .NET. The Java Virtual Machine (JVM) and the Common Language Runtime (CLR) are examples of achieving platform portability for your application code.
Dependability *	This is a superset of other quality attributes, including availability, reliability, maintainability, recoverability, security, and usability. Aspects of all of these attributes can be aggregated to describe the architectural solution for system dependability.

* *These are generally more useful for managers and project stakeholders than for the solution design or technical people.*

■**Note** Table 1-3 captures, perhaps, some of the most common nonfunctional requirements. This list is not exhaustive. Many others may come to bear on your own applications. There's accessibility, adaptability, affordability, compatibility, configurability, controllability, extensibility, flexibility, interoperability, learnability, reusability, versatility, and so on.

Nonfunctional requirements will definitely influence the design of any architecture. Some of these requirements don't affect the software architecture; others do so indirectly; while some have a direct influence. Over the course of the book, as we examine different servers, services, and packages available within and provided for the .NET Framework, we'll revisit these requirements in-as-much as how the features a solution provides are relevant.

Some are far more important than others. Performance is always a critical consideration when you design a system. If it does not perform, it will not be adopted. We'll address this throughout the text in discussions of extensibility, how to know what services to use when, and applied best practices in different areas.

Security is another critically important feature of any system. Not only because it spans all of the tiers of a distributed application, but also because it's the mechanism for protecting critical enterprise data. The reputation or even the continued existence of an enterprise can depend on it. We dedicate Chapter 5 to a discussion of security and how it works in the .NET Framework, and subsequent topics address it specifically as well. You have many different considerations for keeping an application secure as you move across the tiers.

Service Oriented Architecture/Service Orientation

Enterprises have come to realize that integration is expensive, and homogeneity is an ideal that's not practically attainable. A large enterprise with many disparate databases, vendor supplied applications, platforms, operating systems, and languages may come to think that life would actually be better in a totally homogenous environment.

A mission-critical application is purchased from a vendor and rolled out into the enterprise, and soon a business unit decides it would be great to put a web front end on it to expose a subset of the functions to a subset of the users. Much work and coding ensues to integrate the web application with the vendor's back-end database. The web application, of course, adds some of its own requirements to the mix, which drives the creation of another database, hosted on another platform. The web application ships with much fanfare, almost on time, grossly over budget, and is met with accolades from corporate users far and wide.

This success, and the subsequent wide adoption of the processes, fosters a need for another business unit to leverage some of the data and some of the functionality, but again, of course, with some esoteric deviation in the business rules that only an MBA can understand. At this point, it would be nice to leverage the integration work that the original business unit did, extending the functionality and reach of this vendor application. Unfortunately, that group was working with technology flavor of the week "A," and this new groups is using technology flavor of the week "B."

So the new group goes back to the drawing board, designing a new integration strategy with the vendor-supplied application, in addition to integrating with the web application's own data store, and in the process ends up adding its own data store to meet their specific requirements.

This process is iterative. Each subsequent iteration is more difficult, and each iteration becomes more expensive than the last. The applications suffer on account of one business unit's success, and related business units compulsively reinvent the wheel.

But what if this did not need to be the state of affairs? What if IT found the "Holy Grail" of software reuse, and each business unit could leverage the work of the last, reusing the code that accesses data in the disparate systems—the transactional logic that makes updates to those systems—all the while passing the enterprise-wide security tokens along so that all this work could be authenticated, authorized, and audited? Yeah, right, you might say, maybe in a perfect world. Well, this is just what service orientation purports to provide. And with the success of the World Wide Web across all platforms and operating systems, the latest implementation of service orientation, called Web Services, has a real chance of succeeding in this seemingly mythical quest.

In the late nineties, a really smart geek took a look at XML. "This is markup," she said to herself. The Web came to mind. "The Web is a global network for passing markup around. Hmmm … ." The problem with HTML is that it's a specific form of markup, designed for describing how to *display* data. This is great if you're a web browser, and your goal in life is to render an interface that, while somewhat less functional than a Windows Forms interface, is by all accounts, *very pretty.* But what if, instead of looking at a stock price displayed on NASDAQ.com, you want to get a stock price as a double and interact with it programmatically? "But markup could be used to describe the data, instead of describing how to display the data!" this clever geek thought to herself. "And if it can describe data, it can describe a request for data. Actually, it could describe a service request, and could be used like an RPC mechanism … except … it would be a standards-based way to request services! *It could interoperate!*"

This idea started circulating amongst the folks that get excited about these types of things, and since these folks happen to be in positions of power and influence, it generated a definite "buzz." Soon, everyone who worked in IT knew that XML was a marvelous, wonderful thing, that would radically transform the way software works. The problem is, very few folks really understood how it would do this, and a lot of folks couldn't even really see what it was *for.* "What's this do? What's the point of markup that you can't display in a browser?" Alas, most folks are just not visionaries.

Meanwhile, the people that *got it* started writing code. Large enterprises created their own definitions of what this XML should look like and how it was to be used to request services. Any group that knew how to use an implementation of the Document Object Model (DOM) could expose these services, or prepare requests for them and leverage the functionality. In 1999, a sharp young engineer read an obscure specification put out by an XML working group called SOAP. He thought it could be useful in the application he was working on that was using ActiveX controls from IE and requesting services of a business tier written as COM Servers in VB6 and hosted in MTS. He implemented a *messaging stack* that allowed UI developers to use a client-side COM component to prepare requests and submit them. The component would transform them into XML and post them to the server. The server had another process listening for these requests coming into the server, and would turn around and call the corresponding method on the object described by the XML document. The results would be returned to the client as XML. This was a grand boon to the project, as it standardized how information was marshaled between the UI and the business tier. This was a custom implementation of what today is called an XML Protocol Messaging Stack, or a SOAP Stack.

However, this did not solve the problem of interoperability. With everyone writing their own SOAP stacks, interoperability could only be achieved between groups that had direct buy-in to the design. What was needed was an industry-wide specification that could provide a standards-based approach of how to attain platform interoperability.

The standards bodies went to work. And work. And work. And work. It took so long for the W3C to come up with the standard for XML Schemas that Microsoft invented their own, called XML Schema Reduced (XDR). "We'll ditch this when the W3C is done, and we'll support the standard, we swear! Right now, we just need to *ship some product!*" When XML Schema was finally complete, Microsoft did adopt it. They even provided migration tools to move from XDR to XML Schema, but as with all things that get adopted (think ODBC), XDR lingers. Microsoft currently supports them both.

The standards bodies worked on the specs for XML Messaging for so long that the rank-and-file IT masses wrote it off. "Yeah, yeah, yeah. It's another flash-in-the-pan technology. Remember Microsoft Bob? Remember My Services?" Eventually the W3C adopted SOAP (and renamed it the "XML Protocol"). It finalized the spec for the Web Service Description Language (WSDL). The OASIS group created a specification for discovery it dubbed the Universal Description, Discovery, and Integration protocol (read: search engine for services: UDDI).

The funny thing is, in the last couple of years the standards have become ready for prime time. Designs for new things require time and iterations. The first iteration is done and over with. The specs have been adopted and vendors have done a couple of implementations. They've realized what doesn't work and created stacks that do. Folks are adopting parts of the SOAP spec in favor of others because they've *tried them both* and *know from experience what works*. The enterprises that wrote their own stacks years ago now have vendor-supplied tools that provide a standards-based SOAP Stack implementation. *It works*. And it *is* going to transform the way applications are created, deployed, and consumed. It just took awhile.

Today implementing your own SOAP Stack would be like implementing your own database transaction processing. You'd be reinventing the wheel, as there's already a stack available for your platform (regardless of what that is). When you're using .NET, there's a SOAP stack built into the ASP.NET Framework. Remember that engineer who wrote the custom SOAP stack for the product he was working on in the late nineties? Today he's the program manager for XML Web Services at a little company out west, in Redmond, Washington, I believe. Guess that vision thing works out sometimes. It just doesn't always happen right away.

.NET Application Architectures

The following diagram is a fairly complete picture of the common options available to the system architect for .NET applications (see Figure 1-1). This diagram captures some of the technologies you can employ on the individual tiers, as well as some of the different technologies you can use to marshal messages across these tiers. For example, the data access layer (DAL) may be on the client for a Windows application deployed to two physical tiers. At the data access layer of the system, if you're using SQL Server, or some other native relational database management system (RDBMS) communication protocol from other vendors, communication can occur with the RDBMS via Tabular Data Stream (TDS).

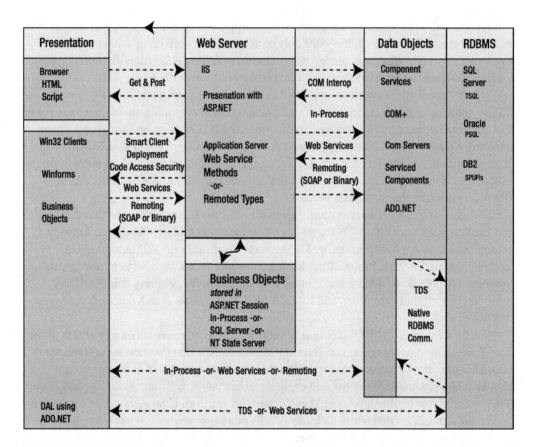

Figure 1-1. *.NET solutions*

While not any .NET application will make use of all of the choices, all of them will make use of some. This book has ASP.NET 2.0 in the title, but we're going to examine ASP.NET in a broader scope than that of its role in the presentation tier. ASP.NET is an application server. IIS listens for incoming HTTP requests and maps them to processes that do all manner of work, and are not limited to generating HTML. To consider ASP.NET as being synonymous with Web Forms is severely limiting. Web Forms (ASPX pages) are but a small part of the functionality that ships with the Framework, and a narrow means of extending the functionality. ASP.NET acts as a host for Web Services, for remoted components, and for Component Services, and when Windows Communication Foundation ships there will be a host of choices there as well. We've dedicated chapters to each of these topics.

Figure 1-1 does not attempt to capture the role of Windows Communication Foundation or SQL Server 2005. For details on how these technologies fit into the picture, see the chapters on these topics specifically (Chapter 9 and the latter part of Chapter 11).

Let's take a look at how a few different architectures might look in production. There are a lot of different services, a lot of different requirements, and lot of ways to put it all together. A few fictitious architectures are created here for discussion, based on solutions that have proven to be effective in production environments.

A Simple Managed Application

Here is a typical simple architecture for a smaller application with a single data store that's not expecting hundreds of concurrent users (see Figure 1-2). All of the components are managed types. The ASP.NET pages use standard controls built into the Framework that generate W3C-compliant HTML. This allows the application to be deployed to any platform or operating system that supports a web browser. The pages use what could be a stateful business object layer, but the application is simple enough that only a few of these stateful types are actually needed. The business object layer, in turn, leverages a data access layer written using the Data Access Application Block and calling SQL Server stored procedures.

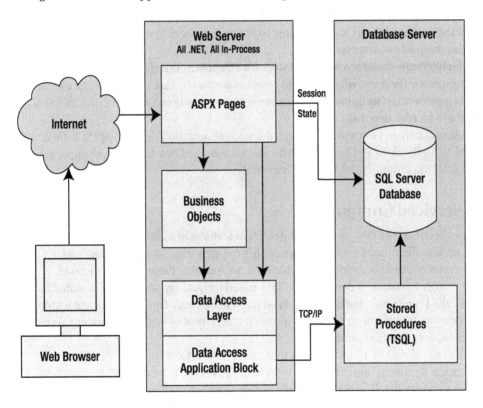

Figure 1-2. *A simple architecture for a managed web application*

In some cases, the UI layer calls the data access layer directly. Although this is a violation of the guidance provided by the layering pattern, in this case, it's acceptable as the business rules aren't that complex and, in many cases, would be nothing more than a "pass-thru" layer, providing nothing but an additional level to the call stack and bloating your code base, assembly sizes, and heap allocations unnecessarily.

Even with this simple design, this application could scale out to handle additional load in the future. The requirements for what needs to be managed in state are minimal enough that they're easily implemented using cookies (good only for small amounts of data), and the database (more coding, but it's persistent, scalable, and available).

Access to the database is synchronous, so any long-running queries would incur a delay in the responsiveness of the application for the user, as there's nothing in this design to address asynchronous operations. The recovery plan, should the server go down, is to drive to the office as fast as possible and repair or replace the machine. This results in a low availability guarantee, which is acceptable because the application isn't mission critical. Any requests in-process during a system crash would be lost.

Deployment of new versions and fixes for this application are worry free. State information is tracked in the database, and correlated to users with a cookie value. Both of these stores survive the reboot of a web server.

This architecture would obviously not work for all applications. There are a number of serious limitations. However, when the requirements are *met* by this solution, it's an excellent choice, because developing applications like these are extremely fast and very easy to learn, compared to a lot of *n*-tiered applications.

We discuss strategies for reuse of code in the web presentation tier in Chapter 3. We cover using ADO.NET effectively in Chapter 10. And we examine the Data Access Layer Application block, a part of the Enterprise Library, in Chapter 11.

Using Serviced Components

Component Services, or COM+, provides a rich set of features in a component-hosting environment, such as distributed transactions, just-in-time activation, object pooling, and asynchronously queued components. In Chapter 7, we examine these features in detail.

Even though Component Services is a COM-based technology, Microsoft has added facilities to the .NET Framework that allow managed types to be easily configured for use within this environment. When you create .NET types that can be hosted under Component Services, they are called Serviced Components.

Here's a logical view of an architecture that uses Serviced Components (see Figure 1-3).

The critical feature of Component Services being leveraged from this architecture is its ability to automatically roll back transactions that span several data sources. Even if the data isn't hosted on the same server or on the same vendor platform, the Distributed Transaction Coordinator will automatically manage and then commit or roll back work that spans different data stores.

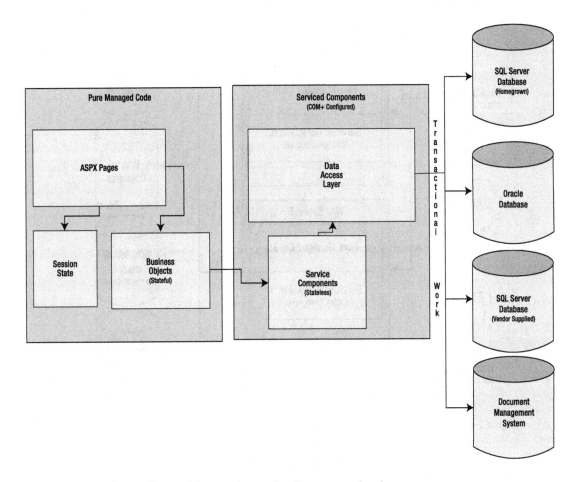

Figure 1-3. *Logical view of an architecture leveraging Component Services*

Since it's a web-based application, it's possible to deploy all of the logical tiers of this system to a single physical tier. Here's a physical view of the deployment of this system into production (see Figure 1-4).

Deployment to a single physical tier means that all layers of the application execute in-process with one another. This is a great boon to performance. An extra hop across a process boundary, or especially a hop across machine boundaries, can make an application perform many times slower than when all components are created in-process.

The other thing to notice about this application is that sticky sessions are in use at the load balancer layer in order to support the use of in-process sessions. The session data is left in-process for the performance benefit gained by avoiding the extra network hop to retrieve and retain the state information.

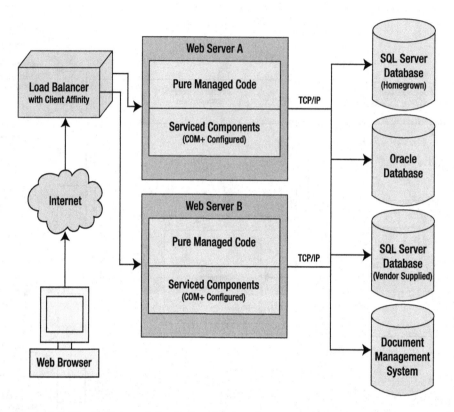

Figure 1-4. *Physical view of the deployed system leveraging Component Services*

One of the trade-offs of this approach is the decreased efficiency of the load balancing algorithm. However, the load of this site is easily handled by the two web servers, and there could be a third in the mix, for failover support, should one of the servers crash. So under normal operations, with three servers handling the traffic, they don't even break a sweat. The loss in efficiency of the load balancing algorithm doesn't sacrifice acceptable application performance.

The other trade-off with this approach is that it makes the user-specific session information prone to being lost when there's a failure. Obviously if a server crashes, the session information from that machine will be lost. It will also be lost when the process hosting the application is recycled. This is done automatically by the ASP.NET Framework when the memory consumed by an application exceeds a predefined threshold. This threshold can be controlled via configuration. Session information will also be lost when a new version of the application is deployed, even if it's just a configuration file change or a hotfix to an ASPX page. The design of the application has to anticipate this, and it must be accounted for in the design of how session information will be used. Managing this without introducing the possibility of your users losing work (even if it's a shopping cart) can be very difficult.

Keep in mind that within the logical layers of the application tiers, it's still a good idea to design as if the layers are going to be deployed to separate physical tiers. This allows the system to be distributed across physical tiers if it becomes desirable to do so at a later date. For example, a Windows Form interface could be added to the application we just described, and leverage the business service layer of the application using Web Services, while the web interface could leverage the same services in-process (see Figure 1-5).

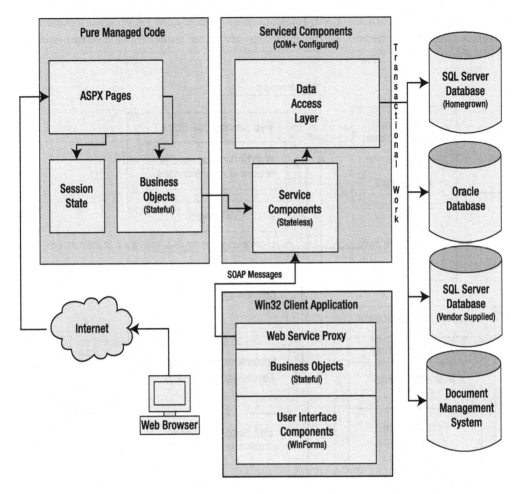

Figure 1-5. *A Win32 interface added to the mix*

Using Component Services does come at a price. While it does not use the same COM Interop layer that's commonly used from .NET to communicate with COM servers, there's still some overhead incurred by hosting managed components in a COM environment. The integration is highly optimized in the design of Serviced Components, but it's still an additional layer of abstraction, and as such, won't make anything faster. The decision to create Serviced Components should be driven by a compelling need for one of the services provided by the hosting environment. In this case, the services of the Distributed Transaction Coordinator clearly fit the bill.

We provide a detailed discussion of the features of COM+ in Chapter 7. In Chapter 8, we look at some of the options for calling services (like SOAP) once they're configured within COM+.

A Widely Distributed Service Application

Web Services can be used to provide a service layer to widely distributed clients. This application deploys a data access layer to the IIS box running Web Services, and uses ASP.NET session state to manage logins and state information (see Figure 1-6). This service layer is then leveraged by Windows Forms and Web applications distributed across several North American locations. Web Service extensions are leveraged to encrypt authentication and sensitive data on the wire.

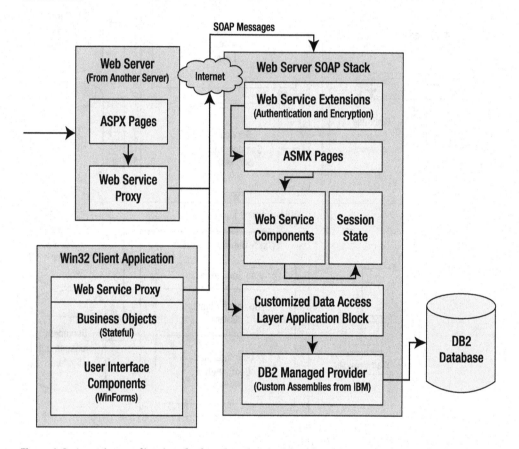

Figure 1-6. *A service application deployed to the World Wide Web*

The data access layer leverages the Data Access Application Block, which is part of a downloadable package called *Enterprise Services*. This set of services ships with all the source code, and so can be customized. The Data Access Application Block ships with support for SQL Server, Oracle, and DB2. DB2 requires the managed provider available from IBM. There is also a stateful business object layer used within the Windows Forms user interfaces and during the processing of a request for an ASP.NET page. It's good to use stateful objects within a process boundary; you need stateless objects when services could possibly be deployed to different machines, processes, or even app domains.

Web Services are designed as a stateless service layer. This is considered to belong to the middle tier of a distributed application, but has a very different design than a typical stateful type designed with the principles described by OOAD.

The funny thing about SOAP, the "Simple Object Access Protocol," is that it is not at all object oriented. Services designed to be exposed using SOAP messages actually look a lot more like traditional procedure function calls might: atomic methods that accept large parameter lists that perform their work based entirely upon the information passed to them, and when finished, are destroyed completely (see Figure 1-7, the class on the right).

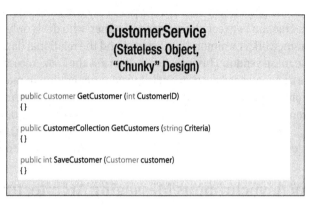

Figure 1-7. *Chunky vs. chatty design in logical application layer designs*

This is what it means to be stateless. There are no "fields" in the object sense. A service class has no variables declared that have class level scope. There'd be no point to it, as instances of a service type don't necessarily survive across requests, even if they're two requests from the same client. If object pooling, or especially if just-in-time activation, is used, then objects must be stateless. If they're not, then state information could be passed from one user to another as instances are grabbed out of the pool. This would yield unpredictable results at best, behavior that could only fairly be described as a bug. This is what it means for an interface to be *chunky*. *Chatty* interfaces are also sometimes called *fine grained*, while *chunky* can also be called *coarse grained* (see Figure 1-7).

SOAP is also not necessarily "simple." This has proven to be such a poor acronym that the W3C has started saying it's not an acronym at all. It's just SOAP. They've renamed it the "XML Protocol" (as if they can *unacronymize* something. That'd be like verbing the word acronym). They should have gone with the "Service Oriented Architecture Protocol." That works, doesn't it?

This service layer sits in front of another generalized stateless layer that acts as the entry point to the data access layer. This layer exposes types, whose methods each map directly to a stored procedure living within DB2. The service layer may aggregate calls to different methods on this data access layer. It may even create several different types from the data access layer, and aggregate the results to prepare an entire result set to send back to the client. This is called *service aggregation*, and it's a common pattern at this public level of a service layer, as it's designed to minimize round trips from the client to the server. The service layer aggregates data that meets the requirements of a specific user interface. Reuse is gained at the data access layer, whose services aren't so tightly coupled to the requirements of a specific application, but instead more generally map to different entities stored in the database.

The data access layer is what accepts a list of method arguments and transforms them into the parameter objects and types defined at the database level. This creates a layer of abstraction between the service consumer, who deals only in types defined in the .NET Framework's Common Type System, and the relational database, whose types depend on the database vendor. This is the layer that calls the Data Access Application Block. This layer may be so generalized as to lend itself to code generation in many cases. Given the definition of a stored procedure, the method to wrap that stored procedure could be generated using types from the CodeDom namespace and schema information from the relational database.

We cover Web Services in Chapter 6, with more on SOAP in Chapter 8. We discuss the Data Access Layer Application Block, part of the Enterprise Library, in Chapter 11.

An Asynchronous Messaging Architecture

Durability and reliability are the main concerns of the architecture presented in Figure 1-8. MSMQ and COM+ Queued Components are used to accomplish this. Clustering was not an option considering the budget on this example project, and so to provide for "availability" of the data access layer, MSMQ and database triggers are leveraged to programmatically synchronize the data in these redundant servers.

This architecture is based entirely on XML. All of the controls in the user interface represent their state as XML documents, and it's XML that gets packed into the body of the MSMQ messages.

Users of this application don't have a very fast connection, so page sizes are kept to a minimum. This means page developers will likely favor caching data on the web server to rebind a control like a grid across postbacks, rather than rely on ViewState to maintain this information on the client (see Chapter 4).

The data access layer on the web server needs to support asynchronous operations. Commands that modify the data are sent to the data access abstraction layer, which doesn't actually execute the command, but packs the XML representing the request into the body of an MSMQ message. This message is then placed in a queue, and execution continues in the call stack on the web server. This means that the web server responses don't wait for the database work to be done before sending a result to the user. Users see a message that their requests were sent and to check back later for results. See Chapter 8 for MSMQ examples.

Of course, sometimes synchronous access to the database is critical. When users want to see data, you cannot tell them that a request for the data they want to see has been submitted, and to come back later to see it. For synchronous requests for data, you use a simple timeout listener loop within the data access abstraction layer. This monitors an incoming MSMQ for a correlated result message, sent back from the queue listener when the work has been completed. This architecture makes it very easy to put in a timeout should the request take too long. This timeout period can (and should) be controlled by a configuration file. With a 10-second timeout specified in the configuration file, users get an error or warning message if they wait any longer for a message to appear in the response queue.

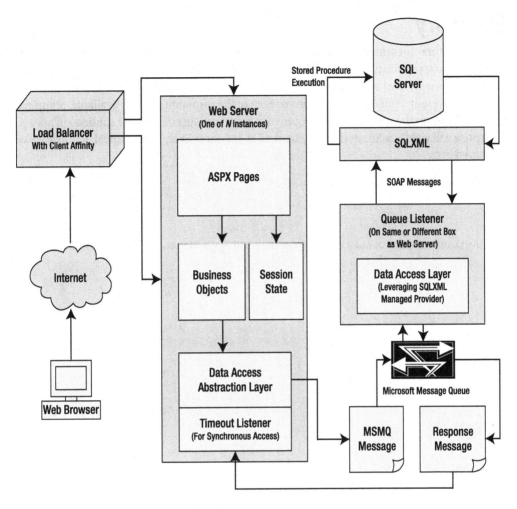

Figure 1-8. *A highly available MSMQ architecture*

Once the message has been placed in the outgoing queue, a listener picks it up and processes it from there. In this architecture, the queue listener extracts the body of the message and posts it to SQLXML as a SOAP request for a Web Service. This facility is built into SQLXML. Any stored procedure can easily be exposed with SQLXML listening for incoming SOAP requests and automatically mapping them to the database stored procedure.

After the database work is complete, a response message may be prepared, depending on whether the request was synchronous or not. For asynchronous requests, a "fire and forget" model is used, and so no response message is necessary.

One major benefit of this architecture is that other non-web applications could leverage the same MSMQ infrastructure (i.e., Windows Services, BizTalk Orchestration). The initiating application need only know how to generate the transaction XML, and then throw it in the queue. The listener takes over from there.

Summary

The architectures presented here are by no means exhaustive of the choices available to you when inventing your own technical infrastructure. We've put forth these to demonstrate some of the various ways the pieces and parts of these services can be put together. The chapters that follow present detailed examinations of each of the disparate services available. Mapping these solutions to the nonfunctional requirements that are specific to your application and enterprise will yield a solution that may be similar, but most likely not identical, to those we've presented here.

CHAPTER 2

■■■

The ASP.NET Request Pipeline

The ASP.NET Framework is the entry point for much of the processing that occurs in the different application architectures we examined in Chapter 1. When many people think of ASP.NET, they think specifically of the Web Forms functionality built into the Framework, which uses an instance of System.Web.UI.Page to generate HTML. This is, of course, the core functionality of web application programming in .NET, and the task that many consider synonymous with ASP.NET development. However, ASP.NET is an entire application hosting framework, of which Web Forms are just a small part. In this chapter, we're going to step into the ASP.NET Worker Process and examine the work that goes on between the time that a request comes in over a named pipe and a response gets marshaled back to Internet Information Services (IIS). The process that occurs during this time is called the *request processing pipeline*. This is because there's a deterministic path that the request flows through, and processing the Page object is just a small part of it. As we move through this pipeline, we'll pay special attention to the points of extensibility along the way, and where you can customize how the request is processed. You'll see that the Page handler, which handles requests for Web Forms (resources with an ASPX extension), is just one of many types of handlers wired into the Framework. We'll also examine how we can create our own handlers to handle specific types of requests.

Application and Context

When a request enters the pipeline, it's handled by an instance of the HttpApplication class. One of the first things HttpApplication does is create an instance of HttpContext and populate it. This context object is available throughout the request processing pipeline, and exposes many familiar types. Table 2-1 provides you with a quick look at some of the members of HttpContext. Keep in mind that while many of these properties will be familiar in the context of HttpContext, they're not properties of the Page object, but properties of HttpContext.

Table 2-1. *A Sample of Members from* System.Web.HttpContext

Member Name	Type	Meaning in Life
Application	HttpApplicationState	An instance of the Application object. This type is a holdover from classic ASP, sticking around for backwards compatibility. There's nothing this object can do that the cache can't do better.
ApplicationInstance	HttpApplication	This property points back to the instance of HttpApplication that's processing the request.
Cache	Cache	The ASP.NET cache object. Another instance that's familiar within Page processing, but is also available outside of handler processing.
PreviousHandler	HttpHandler	An instance of the handler that rendered the previous page. This is used in cross-page postbacks to expose information about the page that rendered the HTML that caused the postback. This is exposed at the page level as the PreviousPage property.
Profile	HttpProfileBase	Used by the personalization infrastructure. It's an instance of the current user's profile object.
Request	HttpRequest	The old familiar request object. Use this to examine the details of the request that has come into the server.
Response	HttpResponse	Another holdover from classic ASP. While Response.Write should not be used anymore, there are actually many useful things that can be done with the type, such as setting the content type of the response, serializing binary data to the client, or creating cookies.
Server	HttpServerUtility	A few useful methods are available on this type that weren't available in classic ASP. For example, there's a Transfer method exposed by this type that moves execution to a different page as Response.Redirect did in classic ASP. Unlike redirection, however, Transfer moves execution to another page without causing another round-trip to the client.
Session	HttpSessionState	Stores user specific session information. This object is actually not available through much of the pipeline, as part of the work done during pipeline processing is the restoration of session state. We'll take a look at the earliest point you can do some pre-processing on the values that may be stored in here.

Most of the process of establishing the HttpContext is just a matter of de-serializing request details as they come in off the wire. The Request object's QueryString collection is nothing more than a convenient way to get to details about the URL of the request. The ServerVariables and Cookies collections are a programmatic convenience that saves you from manually parsing the raw HTTP text of the request. Other parts of the context, such as Session and Cache, are restored from the memory space of the worker process. The ViewState, if present, is restored from the hidden input whose value was posted as part of the request.

All HttpContext properties are available throughout the processing of the request. There's even an Item method that acts as a state bag (like Session, Cache, and Application), so you can pass your own information along through the pipeline. You can use this to pass information from a preprocessor into a Page handler. You'll see an example of this as we move through our examination of HttpApplication.

You can also acquire a reference to the context from any assembly, as long as it has a reference to the System.Web assembly. The IHttpContext type has a static member named Current, which returns a reference to an HttpContext instance. In this code, a property named CurrentWebAppFilter of type WebAppFilter is exposed. This is a custom type created for this sample application that exposes properties any page can use to establish a user context. The instance is stored in the Session, but no pages need be aware of this, as they just use this static property to get to it. Because it's in a shared assembly, the reference to the Context must be programmatically established. This is how the helper class gets to the Session:

```
public static WebAppFilter CurrentWebAppFilter
{
    get
    {
        HttpContext Context = HttpContext.Current;
        if (Context.Session["WebAppFilter"] == null)
            Context.Session["WebAppFilter"] = new WebAppFilter();
        return (WebAppFilter)Context.Session["WebAppFilter"];
    }
    set
    {
        HttpContext Context = HttpContext.Current;
        Context.Session["WebAppFilter"] = value;
    }
}
```

Also keep in mind that this assembly has a reference to the System.Web.dll assembly, and has a using System.Web statement at the top of the code file. You'll need both to resolve the references to the HttpContext type.

HttpApplication is perhaps the most important type in the ASP.NET Framework. It runs the show. It receives the request from IIS, creates the HttpContext, and creates the instance of the handler the request is for. Before it hands the request off to the handler, it authenticates the request, checks the output cache to see if the response has been previously cached, and deals with gathering the response generated by the handler and sending that back to IIS.

The entire pipeline looks something like Figure 2-1.

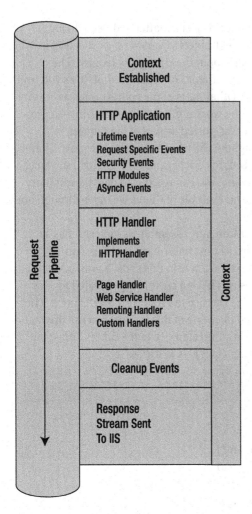

Figure 2-1. *The ASP.NET request processing pipeline*

In the next section we'll take a closer look at the specific events that fire throughout this pipeline. These events are important because extensions to this pipeline are how many ASP.NET features have been implemented. They include Forms-based authentication and HTTP output caching. Many features of the ASP.NET Framework that allow you to use IIS as a host for different types of requests are implemented as HttpHandlers. These include not only Web Form requests, but also requests for Web Services and requests for Remoted or Serviced components.

The HttpApplication Life Cycle

The HttpApplication type raises a number of events as the request moves through the pipeline (see Table 2-2). We'll take a look at a couple of strategies for trapping these events and extending the pipeline a bit later. First, let's examine these events and the order they fire in. Remember that these events fire with every request that's handled by the Framework, so don't do anything really computationally intense, or you'll create a hotspot and impair the application's performance.

Table 2-2. *Summary of Events that Occur in the HTTP Request Processing Pipeline*

Event	Meaning in Life
BeginRequest	First event in pipeline.
PreAuthenticateRequest AuthenticateRequest PostAuthenticateRequest	Leveraged for authentication by Forms-based, Windows-based, and Passport authentication.
PreAuthorizeRequest AuthorizeRequest PostAuthorizeRequest	Used for authorization by the ASP.NET Role Manager. Also taken advantage of by file authorization and URL authorization modules.
PreResolveRequestCache ResolveRequestCache PostResolveRequestCache	Used by the Output Cache module.
PreMapRequestHandler PostMapRequestHandler	New events to exert programmatic influence over the handler to be used for the request.
PreAcquireRequestState AcquireRequestState PostAcquireRequestState	Session state restored for persistence (memory, state server, or SQL Server).
PreRequestHandlerExecute **Page handler Fired** PostRequestHandlerExecute	Last event before and after execution of actual handler for request. After PreRequestHandlerExecute is finished, the ProcessRequest method of the handler is called. This is where the real nuts and bolts of the request processing actually occurs.
PreReleaseRequestState ReleaseRequestState PostReleaseRequestState	Session state returned to persistence.
PreUpdateRequestCache UpdateRequestCache PostUpdateRequestCache	Used by the Output Cache module for moving return value of handler into the web server or client cache.
EndRequest	Last chance to affect the output stream before it's sent back to IIS.
PreSendRequestHeaders PreSendRequestContent	Headers streamed out, and then content streamed out.

After the context of the request is established, the BeginRequest event is fired. Any Session variables that exist are not yet available, but Request and Response, having been established as part of the context, can be examined and exercised. You can check details of the request, such as the protocol the request came in on (Http or Https), details of the URL such as the file type being requested, or incoming cookies.

BeginRequest is the first opportunity you have to extend the processing done in the pipeline. Afterward the security events, AuthenticateRequest and AuthorizeRequest, fire. These are the events that the ASP.NET programmers catch to implement the security models that ship with the Framework. For example, when the AuthenticateRequest fires and Forms-based authorization is set up in the web.config, a check is made to see if the authorization ticket cookie is part of the request. If it's not, the request is redirected to the URL specified in the configuration file for Forms-based authentication. In the authorization event, the users' roles are checked against their allowed roles and the resource they're attempting to access (see Chapter 5 for details of these features).

The number of events in the lifetime of the HttpApplication object has significantly increased for ASP.NET 2.0. This is because for many events, a *Pre* and a *Post* event has been added to the pipeline. At first glance it may seem odd to have an event occur after the original event occurs. For example, AuthenticateRequest fires after the Framework has completed an authentication check. So what do you need PostAuthenticateRequest for? The answer to that lies in environments where many traps may be set up for the AuthenticateRequest event. In these environments, you can ensure your event fires *after all other* processing has occurred by trapping the PostAuthenticateRequest event.

The other consideration is backwards compatibility. The ASP.NET team couldn't just replace all of the events with a *Pre* and *Post* event pair, because that would break all existing global.asax files and HttpModule implementations.

In any case, the flexibility developers have at their disposal has increased dramatically. Most events in the pipeline now have a sister event that occurs before any processing has been done for this step in the pipeline (the *Pre* event), and another that occurs after all processing is complete (the *Post* event).

The built-in Role Manager, a feature new to ASP.NET 2.0, uses the PreAuthorizeRequest event as its entry point for processing. This is where the Role Manager checks to see if role management is on. If it is, the manager checks to see if a user object exists; and if it's not, the manager creates a generic user. This is also where the roles cookie is managed. (We'll examine the Role Manager specifically in Chapter 5.)

Next up after the security events is ResolveRequestCache. *Pre* and *Post* events have been added for this event as well.

In ASP.NET 1.x, this event is the last chance for you to extend the pipeline before an instance of the HttpHandler is created for the request. With the addition of the *Pre* and *Post* MapRequestHandler events (below), this is no longer the case, and this event is now properly the domain of the request cache.

This is the entry point for the Cache module. The Cache module is the extension to the runtime that manages sending and retrieving pages from the cache. You may already be familiar with the OutputCache directive.

```
<%@ OutputCache duration="5"  VaryByParam="*" %>
```

After the first time the page is requested, the actual markup produced during page processing is put into the Output Cache. In this event trap, the ASP.NET runtime examines the details of the request, and sees if there's a corresponding entry in the cache. When it finds a matching entry, the runtime retrieves that pregenerated HTML from the cache, and sends it down the output stream.

An instance of the Page object that would normally handle the request is never even created. This can improve the performance of your application by many orders of magnitude. Output caching can be declared at the UserControl level as well, allowing you to cache static portions of your page, while dynamically generating the parts that are unique across users and requests.

The VaryByParam attribute, when used with the value of *, results in a different entry in the cache for each unique value carried in the URL as a query string, and for each different form value in an HTTP Post. This powerful facility can be used to cache each unique version of a page, even if its content is dynamically generated based on input variables such as these. While output caching is highly recommended, as it can vastly improve the performance of your site, this event is not a common one to trap and extend the pipeline with.

The next events, PreMapRequestHandler and PostMapRequestHandler, are new to ASP.NET 2.0, and follow a different pattern in that there's no MapRequestHandler event. In ASP.NET 1.x, however, MapRequestHandler was a well-known occurrence in the request processing pipeline. For someone trying to dynamically map handlers based on the context of the request (user, path info, and so forth.), it was a problem that no hook existed to intercept this event. Other events further up or down the pipeline had to be leveraged for this purpose, even if they were designed for other types of processing. To address this problem, the ASP.NET team added this new pair of events. You can use them to affect how the pipeline selects a handler, or to override the Framework's choice and select one programmatically yourself. When the Post event fires, an instance of your handler has been created; so by examining the extension of the URL being requested, you can actually cast the generic Handler property of the Context (typed as IHttpHandler) into a concrete class. We'll take a close look at these handy methods later in the chapter in the "HTTP Handlers" section.

The next event is AcquireRequestState. This event exposes your first opportunity to use or create any Session variables. It's also a hook you can use to implement custom session management, but the need for this is rare, since ASP.NET exposes three options (in process, state server, and SQL Server) out of the box, and version 2.0 exposes a provider model for customizing that behavior of the session server. You can check Session variables in this event for user-specific settings, or create a Session variable to use when your handler executes.

For example, let's assume that there's a requirement to log how many Session variables are created on a given request. It's possible that they can be created in a Page Load event, in a control-specific event trap on a page, or in a preprocessor like PreRequestHandlerExecute. To know how many have been created, you'll need to know how many existed at the beginning of the request. You can use AcquireRequestState to count them and squirrel this count away:

```
private void HttpAppBase_AcquireRequestState(object sender, EventArgs e)
{
  HttpContext ctx = HttpContext.Current;
  if (ctx.Handler is ISessionCounter)
    ((ISessionCounter)ctx.Handler).SessionVarCount = ctx.Session.Keys.Count;
}
```

First you acquire a reference to the request context. You'll use this to acquire references to both the Session and the Handler. Next you check to see if the Handler implements the ISessionCounter interface. This is how you can be sure the requested page is one you should track to see how many session variables have been created for it. Let's take a look at the definition of this sample interface.

■ Note All of the code for the Session Counter demo can be found within the Code05 project in Global.asax.cs and CreateSessionVars.aspx.

```
public interface ISessionCounter
{
  int SessionVarCount { get; set; }
}
```

This is a very simple interface, which exposes an integer for you to use to report the count of session variables at the moment session state is restored.

This code allows you to move custom information from a preprocessor into an instance of a request handler. To pass this information to any handler, the implementation needs only to inherit from this interface:

```
public class CreateSessionVars : System.Web.UI.Page, ISessionCounter
{
  private int _SessionVarCount;
  public int SessionVarCount
  {
    get { return _SessionVarCount; }
    set { _SessionVarCount = value; }
  }
  //Snip...
```

This page uses implementation inheritance with System.Web.UI.Page as its base class, as is the usual case for ASPX code-behinds, but then takes the additional step of implementing the ISessionCounter interface. The page will now be instructed by the request preprocessor as to how many session variables existed when the session state was first restored. It can do whatever it needs to with this information. In this case, you'll use it to expose a button to create a user-selected number of session variables, and then track the deltas as postbacks occur.

Leveraging this interface-based approach to polymorphic handler types is a common method to check type information on the handler in a preprocessor, and pass information from the preprocessor pipeline into a handler. You can use custom attributes this way as well, for an aspect-based approach yielding similar polymorphic behavior.

Figure 2-2 shows the page as it appears when it's first rendered.

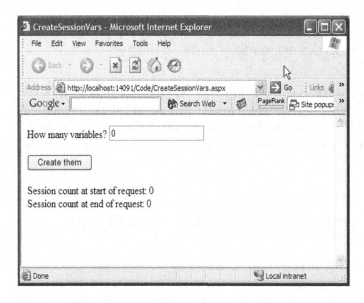

Figure 2-2. *The CreateSessionVars page on its first rendering*

Here is the markup from CreateSessionVars.aspx.

```
<%@ Page language="c#"
        CodeFile="CreateSessionVars.aspx.cs"
        Inherits="CreateSessionVars" %>
<HTML>
  <HEAD>
    <title>CreateSessionVars</title>
  </HEAD>
  <body>
    <form id="Form1" method="post" runat="server">
        How many variables? <asp:TextBox Runat=server id=txtCount text=0 />
        <asp:CompareValidator runat=server ControlToValidate=txtCount
            Operator=DataTypeCheck
            Type=Integer
            ErrorMessage='Must be an integer'
            Display=Dynamic />
        <br><br>
        <asp:Button Runat=server ID=btnSubmit Text='Create them' /><br><br>
        <asp:Label Runat=server ID=lblOutput />
    </form>
  </body>
</HTML>
```

And here are the Button Click and PreRender events from the code-behind of CreateSessionVars.aspx.cs.

```
private void btnSubmit_Click(object sender, System.EventArgs e)
{
    int Count = int.Parse(txtCount.Text) + Session.Keys.Count;

    for (int i = Session.Keys.Count; i < Count; i++)
    {
        Session[string.Format("sessionvar{0}",i)] = i;
    }
}


private void CreateSessionVars_PreRender(object sender, EventArgs e)
{
    lblOutput.Text = string.Format(
        "Session count at start of request: {0}<br>" +
        "Session count at end of request: {1}<br>",
        this.SessionVarCount, Session.Keys.Count);
}
```

Since the preprocessor passes the session variable count into the Page property each time the page is requested, here's how the page renders after a 1 is posted back to the server (see Figure 2-3).

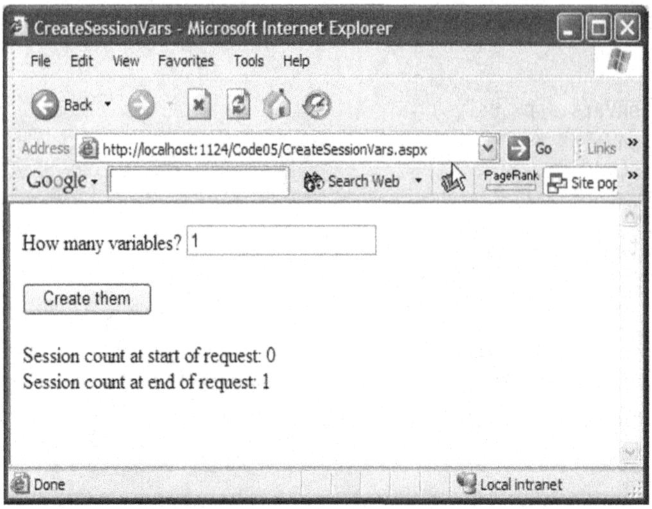

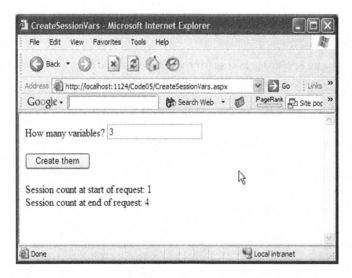

Figure 2-3. *The CreateSessionVars page on its second rendering*

And then, after the first postback, here's the same page after a 3 is posted back (see Figure 2-4).

Figure 2-4. *The CreateSessionVars page on its third rendering*

By trapping the AcquireRequestState while preprocessing the page, you can keep track of how many Session variables are created during the lifetime of the request, regardless of where they're created. In this simple example you're only creating them in the Button Click event trap, but this pattern works even if you're creating or destroying Session variables in other preprocessors.

The next event is PreRequestHandlerExecute. As you'll see in just a bit, any piece of code can process requests that come into the ASP.NET Framework by implementing the IHttpHandler interface. The main task in implementing this interface is to provide code for the ProcessRequest method. This is the last preprocessing event that fires before the ProcessRequest method is called on the handler. It's your last chance to do any pre-processing, before the code from your Page object starts executing.

Almost everything is available to you from this event. The context has been long established, so the Request, Response, Cache, and Cookies are all available. Session state has been restored and is available. Plus, the context handler has been created and the HttpContext.Handler property has exposed an instance of it. In the case of Page processing, the only thing not available at this point are the values ViewState restores, as those don't move from the Post variables to the protected instance variables until the page is initialized. So you couldn't, for example, check the value of a textbox on a well-known Page type that had the textbox declared as public. You could, of course, still retrieve this value from the Post using Request.Form. (We'll examine more of ViewState in Chapter 4.)

You're able to replace the handler at this point with one of your choosing:

```
private void Global_PreRequestHandlerExecute
(object sender, EventArgs e)
{
this.Context.Handler = new Dummy();
}
```

This actually swaps out the handler just before ProcessRequest is called on it. The Dummy type in this example has to use the Page or another type that implements IHttpHandler as its base class, or explicitly provide an implementation of the IHttpHandler interface. In ASP.NET 2.0 you can also do this in the PostMapRequestHandler event. There are a lot of things you can break by doing this, but with careful planning, dynamically choosing a handler at runtime can be a powerful means to provide context- or user-specific handling of requests that are completely in your control.

Another example is to create instances of User Controls depending on user preferences or authorizations, cast the handler into a known page type that exposes those User Controls as properties, and dynamically create instances of the appropriate controls and assign them to the properties. Keep in mind that this all occurs *before any Page specific code is ever executed*. The exception, of course, is the constructor, which has to be fired when the handler is first instantiated. Move initialization code from your constructor to the Page Init method override, and you can avoid issues that might otherwise arise.

At this point the HttpApplication code calls ProcessRequest on the handler. We'll talk about custom handlers shortly. The Page handler has a well-known life cycle. Init is called. The Load event is fired. Control-specific events are fired, the Pre-Render event fires, and then the Unload event fires. (We examine this life cycle very closely in Chapter 3.)

After the Page handler executes and renders, processing returns to the HttpApplication pipeline. The next event in this pipeline is PostRequestHandlerExecute. You can use PreRequestHandlerExecute and PostRequestHandlerExecute in pairs to "box in" the lifetime of a resource over the lifetime of the Page object. When communicating with the Page object, remember to use interfaces to avoid tight couplings between specific instances of Page objects and your more general pre- and post-processing code. As you'll see in the next section, the processors can be used not only across pages in a single application, but also, by implementing HttpModules, they can be reused across applications. Avoiding tight couplings between these processors and Page objects will make it easier to reuse them as your project grows to encompass more than one IIS application.

Built-in Framework Extensions to the Pipeline

One of the best ways to understand how to use the request processing pipeline is to examine the examples that ship with the Framework. Much of the functionality that ships with ASP.NET is implemented by extending this pipeline. We'll examine these extensions in this section.

Each of the events in the pipeline can actually be captured by n different implementations of traps for these methods. Table 2-3 provides a summary of the traps implemented for canned Framework functionality.

Table 2-3. *Summary of Built-in Framework Modules and Events They Trap*

Module	Enters	Leaves	Notes
Windows Authentication	AuthenticateRequest	*None*	If the configuration is set to use Windows security within the ASP.NET Framework (and anonymous access is off at the IIS level), this method loads the user name out of the server variables and creates an instance of the Windows Principal to populate the User property of the context.
Forms Authentication	AuthenticateRequest	EndRequest	If the configuration is set to use Forms-based authentication, this module verifies the existence of the authentication ticket and redirects the user to the login page if it's not present. The EndRequest trap deals with a redirect to the originally requested URL after the user first logs in.
Passport Authentication	AuthenticateRequest	EndRequest	You can leverage Passport authentication using the Passport SDK. (See Chapter 5 for details.)
Role Manager	PreAuthorizeRequest	EndRequest	The Role Manager allows the membership provider to store a role-based resource authorization. PreAuthorizeRequest populates the user object with the roles by loading the roles for the user through the membership API. EndRequest saves this information as a cookie, so it doesn't have to be reloaded with each request.

Module	Enters	Leaves	Notes
URL Authorization	`AuthorizeRequest`	*None*	This trap checks with the configuration file to make sure users have access to the resource. It sets the status code to a security violation if they don't. If this is the case, it terminates the processing of the request with a call to `HttpApplication.`➡`CompleteRequest`.
File Authorization	`AuthorizeRequest`	*None*	Makes sure the requesting users have NT permissions to access the file. Returns a security exception status and terminates processing of the request if they don't.
Anonymous Identification	`PostAuthenticateRequest`	*None*	This module creates the anonymous identification cookie in `PostAuthenticate` request if it doesn't already exist (and anonymous identification is enabled). This module also uses `PostAcquireRequestState` to alter the URL when cookieless anonymous identification is being used.
Profile	`AcquireRequestState`	`EndRequest`	The `Profile` module uses these traps to communicate with the personalization provider to load and store personalization data from persistence.
Output Cache	`ResolveRequestCache`	`UpdateRequestCache`	These events were added specifically to implement output caching. This is where, upon entering, the `Output Cache` module checks incoming requests to see if they match an entry in the cache, and then when it's leaving, it updates the cache with the output if the `OutputCache` directive directs it to do so.

Continued

Table 2-3. *Continued*

Module	Enters	Leaves	Notes
Session	AcqureRequestState	ReleaseRequestState	The Session module uses these events to retrieve and return state variables from persistence, as selected in configuration. EndRequest is also trapped to be sure the ReleaseRequestState was successfully called (relevant when request processing is terminated programmatically). There is also a Session ID module that is used to manage cookieless session IDs.

You can see from Table 2-3 that much of the functionality the Framework provides is implemented as request processing pipeline extensions. This architecture is similar to the "out-of-band" processing in Web Services that so many WS-* specifications describe. Notice how many security-related modules are implemented for the Framework. Security is a natural candidate for out-of-band processing because it's functionality you want applied to every request. It's code you want to keep out of page-specific code files because it applies to all requests and you don't want to have to repeat some logic on a page-by-page basis to enforce it.

There are also many modules for ASP.NET 2.0 that leverage the new, built-in provider pattern. This pattern is a layer of abstraction that allows you to store information in a manner that the consuming code neither knows nor cares about. There are two implementations of the pattern that ship with ASP.NET 2.0: one for Active Directory and one for SQL Server. You can also do your own implementation of the provider pattern if you want to use your own, pre-existing, underlying data stores for persistence. These providers are leveraged by these APIs: membership, personalization, and roles.

■**Note** See the SDK docs for more information on these new functional areas in ASP.NET 2.0.

Extending the Request Pipeline

There are two primary ways to write code to extend the pipeline. The one you choose depends on the scope of the extension you'd like to do, as one way is IIS application specific, while the other can be applied to any number of IIS applications.

The first way is to add a global.asax file to a Web project. The code behind for the global.asax defines a class that inherits from the HttpApplication class. Instances of this class then become the objects that handle all requests for that IIS application. Because of the use of the global.asax, which is deployed to a specific IIS application root, it's not a method that's best suited for reuse across applications and servers. To get reuse out of extensions to the pipeline, you create an `HttpModule`. You can leverage it from any IIS application via a configuration file. We provide a detailed discussion of modules in a bit, but first: a look at the `global.asax`.

Inheriting from HttpApplication

The code template for the code behind the `global.asax` has stubs of traps for a few events in the request pipeline. Also present are `Application_Start` and `Application_End`, as well as `Session_Start` and `Session_End`. These are holdovers from classic ASP. The application start event is fired when the first instance of `HttpApplication` is created within an application domain. Requests are processed within an IIS application from a pool of `HttpApplication` objects.

Session start and end are fired as sessions are created and torn down. You can do your own user-specific allocation and disposal of resources in traps of these events.

The events of the `HttpApplication` pipeline can be trapped by using a method naming convention:

```
Public void Application_OnEventName(Object sender, EventArgs e)
```

The ASP.NET runtime gives `global.asax` special treatment. Even though there's no code creating the delegate and passing it to this event definition, code is generated behind the scenes that sinks the event. This is a very VB-like strategy, telling the developer to "pay no attention to the code generator behind the curtain."

You also cannot override the default constructor and provide your own code to sink these events, as the code generation that occurs at runtime also generates a default constructor for the same class, resulting in a compile error when you provide your own default constructor.

There's also no way to reference any public field defined at the class level with the inline script model. Adding a public static field to this class definition is the recommended alternative to using the `Application` object. Accessing a static field is much quicker than doing a lookup from the `Application` state bag. If any modifications are made to these fields, access must be synchronized, of course. But this is the case with the `Application` object as well (it provides the `Lock` and `Unlock` methods to do this), and it's best to use these fields for read-only information you want to make available to your entire application.

However, with the inline script model, the class doesn't exist until the code generation step at runtime, and unlike most of the dynamically created classes in the ASP.NET 2.0 environment, you cannot reference it within the integrated development environment (IDE) at design time. This is true even when you add the `ClassName` attribute to the `Application` directive.

For these reasons, as well as the other many benefits of the code-behind model, there are benefits you can gain from using the ASP.NET 1.x model for the `global.asax`, instead of relying on the template in ASP.NET 2.0.

When a `global.asax` is added to a Web project, the default template uses on inline script block:

```
<%@ Application Language="C#" %>

<script runat="server">
  ...
</script>
```

To revert to the code-behind model, remove the script block and add the `Inherits` attribute to the Application directive:

```
<%@ Application Language="C#" Inherits='MyImpl' %>
```

Now add a class file to the `App_Code` directory of your project and name it `MyImpl` (or whatever class you named with the `Inherits` attribute). Have this class use `HttpApplication` as its base class:

```
public class MyImpl : HttpApplication
{
...
}
```

This will leverage the ASP.NET 1.x model for the `global.asax`, with the exception that, by default, the class isn't compiled until runtime (as is the case for any class in the code directory). The type will still show up via IntelliSense in the IDE, and you can still code against it in a strongly typed manner.

To trap `HttpApplicaiton` events, you now have two options. The aforementioned naming convention will work. Or you can add delegates to the base class events from the constructor. The following class traps both the `BeginRequest` and `PreRequestHandlerExecute` events: one by explicitly creating the trap; the other by using the naming convention. It also declares a static field that will be available throughout the application:

```
using System;
using System.Web;

public class MyImpl : HttpApplication
{
    public static string SomeStaic = "This is a static variable";

    public MyImpl()
    {
        this.PreRequestHandlerExecute += new
          EventHandler(MyImpl_PreRequestHandlerExecute);
    }

    void Application_OnBeginRequest(object sender, EventArgs e)
    {
        Response.Write("Entering BeginRequest<BR>");
    }

    void MyImpl_PreRequestHandlerExecute(object sender, EventArgs e)
    {
        Response.Write("Entering PreRequestHandlerExecute<BR>");
    }
}
```

There's no runtime difference between these techniques: one relies on a naming convention and "magic" behind the scenes, and the other clearly documents the existence of the
event trap and allows you to use method names of your own choosing.

You can use the following Web Form to exercise your HttpApplication derived class.
Here's the markup for Default.aspx:

```
<%@ Page Language="C#"
        CodeFile="Default.aspx.cs"
        Inherits="_Default" %>
```

And here's the code from Default.aspx.cs:

```
public partial class Default_aspx
{
    protected override void OnInit(EventArgs e)
    {
        this.Load +=new EventHandler(Default_aspx_Load);
        this.PreRender +=new EventHandler(Default_aspx_PreRender);
    }

    void Default_aspx_Load(object sender, EventArgs e)
    {
    Response.Write(MyImpl.SomeStaic + "<BR>");
    }

    void Default_aspx_PreRender(object sender, EventArgs e)
    {
    Response.Write("<b>Page Handler Fired</b><BR>");
    }
}
```

Notice in the ASPX file that all of the markup has been removed. You should do this whenever you use Response.Write, because using this method pre-empts the page-rendering
process. Requesting the page produces the results shown in Figure 2-5.

The first two lines are output during preprocessing, before the Default_aspx type has
executed. The last two lines are output by the page processing, and the first of the two here
accesses and outputs the static field declared on your HttpApplication class. Note that this
value is shared across pages and across users. A change made for one user will be reflected for
all users. Any modifications to it must be synchronized to be thread safe. If the type requires
more complex construction semantics, you can add a static constructor to your derived type,
as in this example:

```
public static DataSet StateList;

static MyImpl()
{
    StateList = new DataSet();
    StateList.ReadXml("http://www.IntertechTraining.com/StateList.xml");
}
```

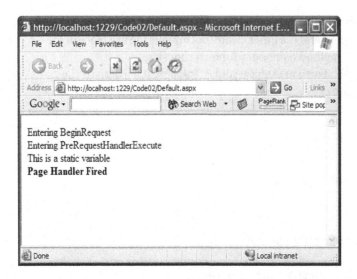

Figure 2-5. *Output of the* Default.aspx *page in an application with our custom* global.asax

One final note about inheriting from HttpApplication: Using the strategies outlined here, the actual global.asax is nothing more than an Application directive. In Visual Studio .NET 2003, the IDE won't actually show the contents of this file; it has to be opened from the file system with another editor to see the directive. Now in Visual Studio .NET 2005, it won't give you a code-behind. Fickle. Figure 2-6 displays your options when you add a new Global Application Class.

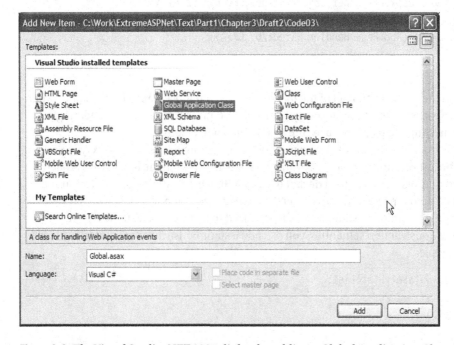

Figure 2-6. *The Visual Studio .NET 2005 dialog for adding a Global Application Class. Notice the option to Place code in separate file is disabled.*

The code file the `global.asax` inherits from doesn't have to be in the `App_Code` directory. In ASP.NET 1.x, it was compiled into the assembly containing all the compiled code behind for the pages. You could place a standalone assembly into the `bin` directory (and add a reference to it to have the IDE copy it in), and reference the fully qualified name of a type in that assembly that inherits from `HttpApplication`.

This is an easy strategy for reusing your `global.asax` implementation across different IIS applications. Just add a reference to the assembly within whatever application you want to use it from. Of course, you'll need to add a reference to the `System.Web` assembly in the project where you create the assembly, as this is where `HttpApplication` is defined. You can even create the class as an abstract base class and have functionality that's customizable from application to application.

Let's take at look reusing a definition of `HttpApplication` across different IIS Applications by creating a new class library project as shown in Figure 2-7.

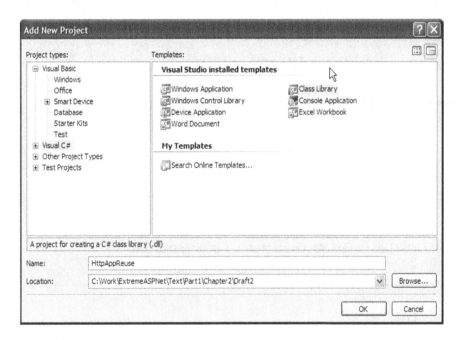

Figure 2-7. *Add the project dialog. Select the Visual C# project type and the Class Library template.*

Add a reference to the `System.Web` assembly by right-clicking the References folder and choosing Add Reference, as shown in Figure 2-8.

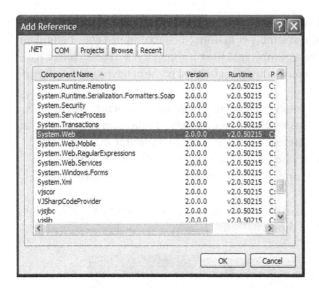

Figure 2-8. *The Add Reference dialog. Select the .NET tab and the* System.Web.dll *assembly.*

Add a class file to the project and name it GenericAbstractHttpApp. Here's the code you can provide for this new abstract base class:

```
using System;
using System.Web;
using System.Web.Mail;

namespace HttpAppReuse
{
    public abstract class GenericAbstractHttpApp : HttpApplication
    {
        public GenericAbstractHttpApp()
        {
            this.Error +=
                new EventHandler(GenericAbstractHttpApp_Error);
            this.BeginRequest +=
                new EventHandler(GenericAbstractHttpApp_BeginRequest);
        }

        public abstract bool RequiresSSL { get; }

        private void GenericAbstractHttpApp_Error(object sender, EventArgs e)
        {
            HttpContext ctx = HttpContext.Current;
            Exception ex = this.Server.GetLastError();
            MailMessage m = new MailMessage();
            string sBody;
```

```
        sBody = ex.Message + "\n";
        sBody += ex.StackTrace;

        Exception ie = ex.InnerException;
        Exception last = ex;
        while (ie != null)
        {
            sBody += "\n\n-------------------------";
            sBody += "\n" + ie.Message;
            sBody += "\n" + ie.StackTrace;
            last = ie;
            ie = ie.InnerException;
        }

        m.To = "YourEmail@YourDomain.com";
        m.Subject = "Intertech Training Exception";
        m.Body = sBody;
        m.From = "Exception@IntertechTraining.com";

        SmtpMail.Send(m);
        Response.Redirect(String.Format
            ("/ErrorOccurred.aspx?Message={0}",
            Server.UrlEncode(last.Message)));

    }


    void GenericAbstractHttpApp_BeginRequest(object sender, EventArgs e)
    {
        HttpContext ctx = HttpContext.Current;

        if (this.RequiresSSL)
            if (!ctx.Request.IsSecureConnection)
                ctx.Response.Redirect(
                    Request.Url.ToString().Replace("http:", "https:"));
    }
  }
}
```

This class provides two pieces of functionality. The first is in the application's Error event. Any IIS application that uses this class as its base class for the global.asax e-mails any error that occurs to the recipient specified in the "To" line of the mail message. This includes the entire call stack of the error and the type and line number where the error occurred. The Error event trap then redirects to a generic error page.

The second piece of functionality enforces that a site must be served over Secure Sockets Layer (SSL). This is where the abstract member becomes relevant. This is functionality you don't want to leverage from any site, only those that need to be served over a secure channel.

E-mailing the error message is functionality that can be used from any application, so the abstract Boolean `RequiresSSL` allows consumers of our type to choose to run this functionality or not.

You can leverage this functionality from your existing website. From the Web project, add a reference to the assembly you've just created, as shown in Figure 2-9.

Figure 2-9. *The Add Reference dialog. Select the Browse tab and the assembly created in the last step.*

Now change the `MyImpl` class to inherit from your new base class instead of directly from `HttpApplication`:

```
public class MyImpl : HttpAppReuse.GenericAbstractHttpApp
```

Since the new base class is abstract, you must also override its abstract member.

```
public override bool RequiresSSL
{
    get { return true; }
}
```

Now all requests to .NET resources in your application will be forced to SLL. You could set the property to false and continue to leverage the error handling mechanism without forcing pages to be served over a secure channel. Notice also that your existing event traps continue to work. You're now extending the functionality of your standalone base class instead of `HttpApplication`.

If you don't need to vary functionality across applications, you can create your class as a concrete base class instead of an abstract one. Then you can reference the class name directly from the `Inherits` attribute of the `Application` directive in your `global.asax`.

Implementing an HttpModule

The second method of extending the pipeline is to implement an HttpModule. Modules are Microsoft's intentional design for reusing pre- and post-processors across IIS applications. The last technique you looked at (that of inheriting from HttpApplication in a standalone assembly and reusing across IIS applications) has a serious limitation that modules don't have: You can only use one class per application (even though you can reuse that same class across several applications).

HttpModules are designed so that several can be plugged into a single IIS application. The extensions that Microsoft adds to the pipeline that you examined previously are implemented as HttpModules. So by default, any IIS application has about a dozen modules plugged in and extending the pipeline.

Modules are designed to be "plugged into" the pipeline using the web.config file. You can add a module to all IIS applications by adding it to the web.config at the root of a web server, or you can add modules to specific applications by adding them to the web.config at the virtual root of an application.

Under the system.web element of the web.config is an HttpModules element. Any number of modules can be added using child Add elements under the HttpModules element. Here's a configuration snippet that adds the module SomeModule.

```
<httpModules>
    <add name="SomeModule" type="ModuleDoc.SomeModule,ModuleDoc"/>
</httpModules>
```

The type attribute is of the format *TypeName, AssemblyName*. The assembly containing this type should be present in the bin directory of the application using the module.

Creating a module is merely a matter of implementing the IHttpModule interface. When you add a type implementing this interface to the request processing pipeline, the Framework calls two methods on this interface: Init and Dispose. These are the hooks to use for setting up and tearing down your module.

Here's the definition of the IHttpModule interface:

```
public interface IHttpModule
{
    public void Init(HttpApplication context);
    public void Dispose();
}
```

Notice the argument passed to the Init method. It's an instance of HttpApplication. With this, the implementation of the module has access to all the details of the current request, and it can act on them in the same way a type derived from HttpApplication can. It's usually a good idea to squirrel away a reference to this context argument in a class level variable so you have access to it from your event traps.

Which events you trap depends on what the module is intended to do. All HttpApplication class events are available. From the Init method, these events can be sunk using the instance passed in as an argument.

In the same project where you created the reusable HttpApplication derived type, add a class file named MyHttpModule, add a using System.Web declaration, and declare it as implementing the IHttpModule interface. In Visual Studio .NET 2005, there's a handy shortcut for implementing the interface. Hover around the name of the interface until you see a bar under the "I." This is called a *Smart Tag*. These are peppered throughout Visual Studio .NET 2005, and can be handy in a number of contexts. Click this and some choices appear, as shown in Figure 2-10.

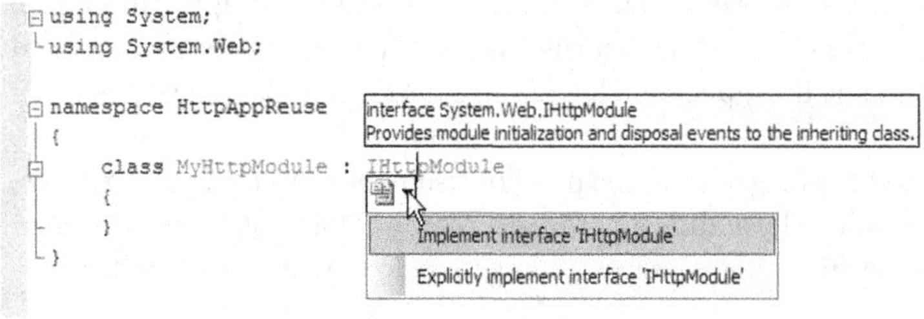

```
using System;
using System.Web;

namespace HttpAppReuse          interface System.Web.IHttpModule
{                               Provides module initialization and disposal events to the inheriting class.
    class MyHttpModule : IHttpModule
    {
                                    Implement interface 'IHttpModule'
    }
                                    Explicitly implement interface 'IHttpModule'
}
```

Figure 2-10. *The interface implementation Smart Tag*

Choose to "Implement interface 'IHttpModule'" and your class will look something like this:

```
public class MyHttpModule : IHttpModule
{
    public MyHttpModule()
    {

    }

    #region IHttpModule Members

    public void Dispose()
    {
        throw new NotImplementedException();
    }

    public void Init(HttpApplication context)
    {
        throw new NotImplementedException();
    }

    #endregion
}
```

Implementation is then pretty simple. Let's implement this module to intercept any request for a page with a CFM extension and rewrite the path to a like-named ASPX page.

First add a private field to the class to squirrel away the reference to the application instance. Then set up a trap for the BeginRequest. That's when the check of the extension is made, and a corresponding rewrite of the path occurs. The finished class looks like this:

```
public class MyHttpModule : IHttpModule
{
    private HttpApplication app;

    public MyHttpModule()
    {  }

    public void Dispose()
    {  }

    public void Init(HttpApplication context)
    {
        app = context;
        app.BeginRequest += new EventHandler(app_BeginRequest);
    }

    void app_BeginRequest(object sender, EventArgs e)
    {
        string s = app.Request.Path;
        if (s.IndexOf(".aspx") == -1)
            if (s.Substring(s.LastIndexOf(".") + 1, 3) == "cfm")
                app.Context.RewritePath(s.Substring(0,s.Length-3) + "aspx");
    }
}
```

To use this module from a web application, add a reference to the assembly where it's defined, and add an add element as a child of the HttpModules element.

```
<httpModules>
    <add name="CFMRedir"
      type="HttpAppReuse.MyHttpModule,HttpAppReuse"/>
</httpModules>
```

The last step is to map the CFM extension to the .NET Framework. You can do this in the Application Configuration section of the IIS properties for the web directory, as shown in Figure 2-11.

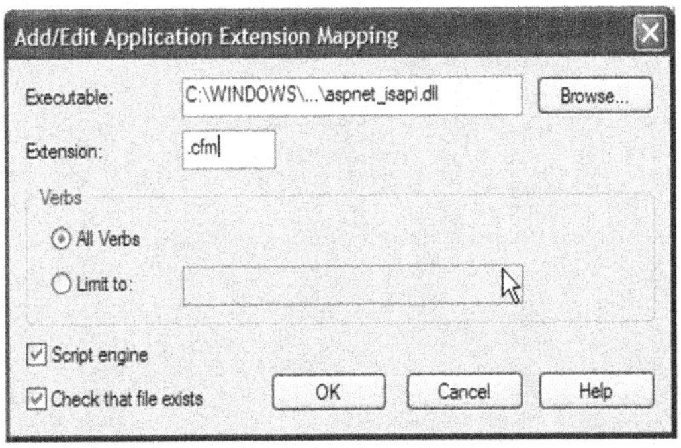

Figure 2-11. *Mapping the CFM extension to the ASP.NET Internet Server Application Program Interface (ISAPI) application*

Now request any page from the site. Change the extension in the address bar of the browser to **.cfm** and resubmit the request. The server redirects to the like-named ASPX page and sends the response down without batting an eye. You can use a similar strategy to ease migration for your users from a website built on an older technology to one built using ASP.NET.

HTTP Handlers

HttpApplication is the type that manages the request as it moves through the pipeline. Up to now we've examined the events along that pipeline and the mechanisms at your disposal for extending its functionality. A critical step of that process is creating and executing the request handler. The Page handler, which is an instance of System.Web.UI.Page (or any type derived from that type), deals with ASPX pages. In this section we're going to take a look at what it takes to be a handler that the Framework recognizes, some of the other handlers that are built into the Framework, and how to create your own handlers to custom process specialized requests.

So what does it take to be a handler? How does the Framework know how deal with an instance of the Page class, a derived type that didn't exist at the time the Framework was compiled? Via polymorphism, of course.

The only thing the pipeline cares about is a simple interface named IHttpHandler. Any type that implements this interface qualifies to receive requests from the ASP.NET Framework and process them however it sees fit. Once a type implements this interface, it's associated with requests via any combination of file name, file extension, or request type.

For example, the extension ASPX is mapped to the Page handler factory. The pipeline hands the request off to this type by calling a method on the IHttpHandler interface. This class looks at the request, creates an instance of the corresponding page object, and hands the request off to it via the same interface method, as shown in Figure 2-12.

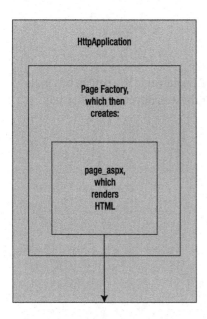

Figure 2-12. HttpApplication *leaves it to the Page Factory to create the correct instance of the page object to process the request.*

Handlers Built into the Framework

A few handlers are built into the ASP.NET 1.x versions of the Framework, and ASP.NET 2.0 adds quite a few more. Handlers can be used for any type of specialized request processing. They can be mapped to a specific URL (as is the case with trace.axd), or the can be mapped to a specific extension (as is the case with *.aspx).

Handlers can also respond to specific HTTP request types (GET, POST, HEAD, and others). There actually is a handler that rejects outright any request type that is not a GET, POST, or HEAD (the HttpMethodNotAllowed handler).

Table 2-4 is a list of the handlers built into the Framework and a brief description of the work that they do. A detailed discussion of some of the more prominent handlers follows.

Table 2-4. *Handlers Built into the ASP.NET Framework*

Http Handler Type	File Name/Extension	Description
System.Web.Handlers. TraceHandler	trace.axd	Responsible for rendering the trace report when tracing is enabled at the application level.
System.Web.Handlers. WebAdminHandler	WebAdmin.axd	Renders an interface for administration of a web application. This handler actually redirects the request to the Web Admin application, passing along the name of the application where the request was made as a query string parameter. (see Chapter 5 for details on this tool). This admin tool then acts as an editor for the web.config of the requesting application.
System.Web.Handlers. AssemblyResourceLoader	WebResource.axd	A handler for extracting resources from assemblies and returning them to clients. The resource is described using query string parameters. This handler can be used from the src attribute of a script or image element, and can also be used from a link element to return a Cascading Style Sheet.
System.Web.Handlers. PrecompHandler	precompile.axd	Used to compile all pages and code in an application after it has been deployed. This handler finds all pages in the site and types in the App_Code directory and proactively compiles them; this way users don't experience any lag when they request a page for the first time.
System.Web.Handlers. WebPartExportHandler	WebPartExport.axd	Support for Web Part layouts for use in portal applications.

Continued

Table 2-4. *Continued*

Http Handler Type	File Name/Extension	Description
System.Web.UI. PageHandlerFactory	*.aspx	The old "tried and true." This handler is responsible for mapping the URL of the request for an ASPX page to the type that services the request.
System.Web.UI. SimpleHandlerFactory	*.ashx	Provides a page directive infrastructure to simplify the mapping of a requested URL to a custom handler (see the "Creating an Http Handler" section that follows).
System.Web. StaticFileHandler	*Any (you choose)*	This handler simply streams the file requested to the client. It's what IIS would do by default. The advantage to this handler is that requests for static content (HTM, JPG, GIF, and so forth) can be mapped to the Framework; therefore, requests for these files go through the entire Http pipeline. This strategy can be used to secure static content when using Forms-based security.
System.Web.Services.Protocols. WebServiceHandlerFactory	*.asmx	The Web Services handler. Depending on the request type and URL, this handler generates the testing interface, generates Web Services Description Language (WSDL) documents, and takes Simple Object Access Protocol (SOAP) messages off the wire and invokes the appropriate method on an instance of the type described in the request.
System.Runtime.Remoting. Channels.Http.HttpRemoting HandlerFactory	*.rem *.soap	The remoting handler. Takes SOAP or binary streams off the wire, invokes the method, and serializes the .NET type back to the caller.
System.Web.HttpForbiddenHandler	*Dozens of extensions, including ASCX, VB, CS, and others*	This handler simply returns an HTTP status of 403, causing a "Forbidden file type" extension to be raised on the client. It's a simple way to secure files of certain types on the server. Do you have an XML architecture where all eXtensible Stylesheet Language Transformation (XSLT) is done on the server? Map *.xml to this handler and no one can pull down the raw XML that lives on your server.

As you can tell from Table 2-4, the Page handler is really just the tip of the iceberg of functionality that ships with the Framework and is implemented as an HTTP handler. Next we'll take a look at how you can further extend the pipeline by creating your own handlers.

Creating an Http Handler

It's possible to create a type that implements the IHttpHandler interface and have it respond to any pattern of URL. The advantage is you have full control over the URL, and the URL of the request doesn't need to correspond to a physical file. The downside is that IIS configuration is required to map the URL into the framework, and ASP.NET configuration is required to map the URL to your specific handler.

The alternative is to use the built-in, simple handler factory. This handler is mapped to files with an ASHX extension. The WebHandler directive is used to point an ASHX page at a type that implements the IHttpHandler interface. Visual Studio adds a file with this directive to your project via the Generic Handler option in the Add New Item dialog window.

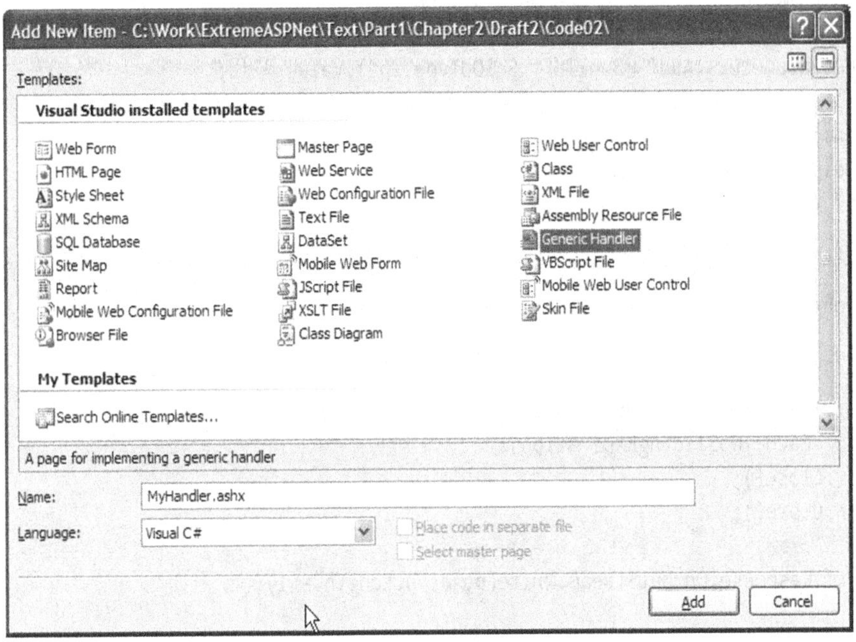

Figure 2-13. *The simple handler project item in the Add New Item dialog window*

The code template included for this file is a complete implementation of a handler, albeit not a very dramatic one. This code gets an image from the database and returns it as a binary stream. It also caches the images for 60 seconds, instead of going to the database for them on each request.

```
<%@ WebHandler Language="C#" Class="MyHandler" %>

using System;
using System.Web;
using System.Web.Caching;
using System.Configuration;
using System.Data;
using System.Data.SqlClient;

public class MyHandler : IHttpHandler {
```

```csharp
    public void ProcessRequest (HttpContext context) {

        byte[] b;
        object id = context.Request.QueryString["BookId"];
        b = (byte[])context.Cache[string.Format("Book{0}",id)];
        if (b == null)
        {
            SqlConnection cn = new SqlConnection(ConfigurationManager.
                ConnectionStrings["Library_local"].ConnectionString);
            string sql = "select CoverImage from BookCoverImage";
            sql += " where bookid = @BookID";
            SqlCommand cm = new SqlCommand(sql, cn);

            cm.Parameters.Add("@BookId", SqlDbType.Int).Value = id;

            cn.Open();
            SqlDataReader dr = cm.ExecuteReader();
            if (!dr.Read())
                context.Response.End();
            b = (byte[])dr[0];
            context.Cache.Insert(string.Format("Book{0}", id),
                b,
                null,
                DateTime.Now.AddSeconds(60),
                Cache.NoSlidingExpiration);
            dr.Close();
            cn.Close();
        }
        context.Response.OutputStream.Write(b, 0, b.Length - 1);
    }


    public bool IsReusable {
        get { return true; }
    }
}
```

The heart of the IHttpHandler interface is the ProcessRequest method. This is where the main work of a handler implementation goes. The only other method on the interface is the IsReusable method, which simply returns a Boolean indicating whether instances of the handler can be pooled or not. Handlers that can be pooled will perform better under load than ones that cannot, as a new instance of a nonpooled handler will need to be created for each request. To make a handler poolable, do not maintain any field level variables that need to be re-initialized with construction semantics, and return true from the IsReusable method.

Notice that the ProcessRequest method gets an instance of HttpContext passed in as an argument. This is where all details of the request are revealed to the handler, where Session and Cache can be used, and where the response is streamed back to IIS.

This handler can now be used from the src attribute of an image element. The advantage here is a much lighter-weight implementation, as none of the overhead of the page's life cycle is incurred. You'll also realize greater performance by using the Cache.

The last option we'll examine is creating a handler from scratch. This can be done by any type that implements the IHttpHandler interface. Without the ASHX factory to decide at run-time what type to create, some configuration entries will be necessary.

For the final example, we'll show you how to handle all requests coming in for resources with the DOM extension. Because you're relying on configuration to map requests to your handler, and not on a physical resource, the filename can actually be used to some other ends. In this example, the filename is used as text that will be painted onto an image. It will be built so the resource can be used as the src attribute of an img element.

```
<p>This handler can be embedded into a page</p>
<img src='This is the handler.dom'>
<img src='The handler is a parrot.dom'>
```

And this static markup dynamically generates the image in Figure 2-14.

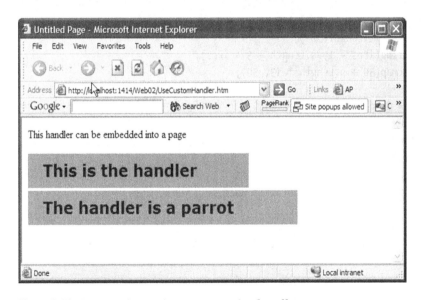

Figure 2-14. *A page using an image-generating handler*

The class that generates the image implements the IHttpHandler interface but it has no WebHandler directive. It's often a class file that lives in the App_Code directory, but it can also be a class in a standalone assembly that a project adds a reference to.

```
using System;
using System.Drawing;
using System.Drawing.Imaging;
using System.Web;

public class DomHandler : IHttpHandler
{
    public DomHandler()
    {}

    public bool IsReusable
    {
        get { return true; }
    }

    public void ProcessRequest(HttpContext context)
    {
        string s;
        Bitmap bm;

        s = context.Request.Url.AbsolutePath;
        int iPos = s.LastIndexOf("/");
        s = s.Substring(iPos + 1, s.Length - 5 - iPos);
        bm = new Bitmap(30 + s.Length * 13, 50);

        Graphics g = Graphics.FromImage(bm);

        g.FillRectangle(Brushes.Goldenrod, 0, 0, bm.Width, bm.Height);
        s = context.Server.UrlDecode(s);
        g.DrawString(s,
            new Font("Verdana", 18, FontStyle.Bold),
            Brushes.Blue, 20, 10);

        bm.Save(context.Response.OutputStream, ImageFormat.Jpeg);
    }
}
```

Notice there are no dependencies within the code that this handler be mapped to *.dom. At this point, it could be mapped to any URL pattern.

To associate the handler with all DOM extensions, you must use the Microsoft Management Console (MMC) snap-in for IIS. Go to the Properties dialog box for the web application. On the Virtual Directory tab, click the Configuration button in the Application Settings section. A list of the mappings for all extensions appears, as shown in Figure 2-15.

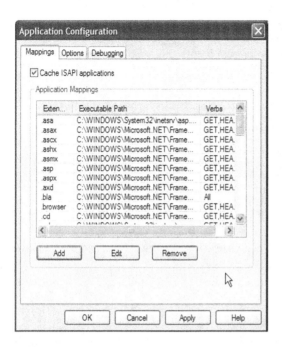

Figure 2-15. *The Application Configuration dialog box from the MMC IIS snap-in*

From here the DOM extension must be mapped to the ISAPI extension for the ASP.NET Framework. It's easiest to copy the entire path to the DLL from an existing entry, then choose Add and paste it into the new entry, as shown in Figure 2-16.

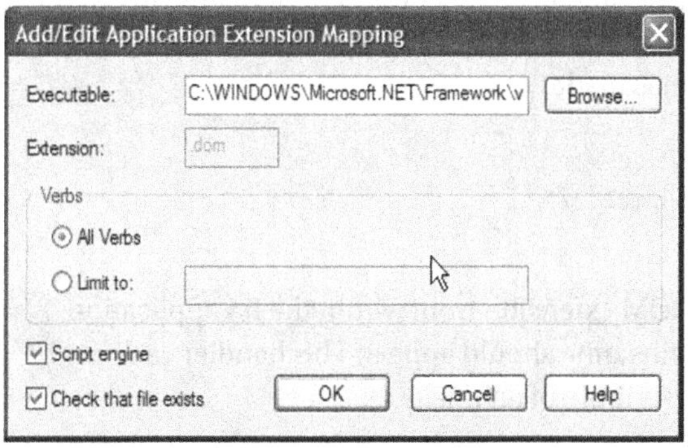

Figure 2-16. *Configuring a new extension for a web application*

Now IIS knows to hand off requests arriving at the Web Server to the ASP.NET Framework. The last step to take is on the ASP.NET tab of the web application properties dialog. From here click the Edit Configuration button, then choose the Advanced tab on the dialog that appears, and the Http Handlers entry from the Section list. Choose the Add button to map *.dom to the DomHandler type, as shown in Figure 2-17.

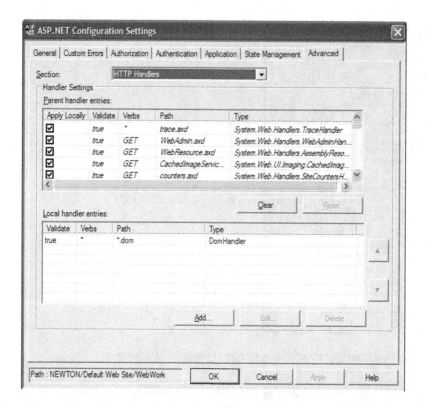

Figure 2-17. *The Http Handlers section of ASP.NET configuration within the MMC IIS snap-in*

This tool, when used in the context of a specific IIS application, generates an entry in the web.config file of that application. From within Visual Studio .NET, open the web.config and you can see the entry the configuration tool has made:

```
<httpHandlers>
  <add path="*.dom" verb="*" type="DomHandler" />
</httpHandlers>
```

Now make a request for any file with a DOM extension from within the IIS application. The dynamically generated image using the filename should appear. This handler can now be used from within any application as the src attribute of an image tag.

Summary

The ASP.NET Framework is a completely extensible application hosting architecture that is hosted by Internet Information Server (IIS). The main points of extensibility are pre- and post-processors in the request pipeline, and the capability to associate HTTP handlers with different URL patterns.

Dozens of hooks are provided to extend the pipeline. These hooks can be trapped using either a type that inherits from HttpApplication or by implementing the IHttpModule interface.

The global.asax is the most common way to inherit from HttpApplication, and this file is given special treatment by the Framework. Namely, its events are automatically "wired."

HTTP modules are set up within a specific application via the web.config file. The advantage with HTTP modules is that any number can be set up to extend the pipeline at the server level or within a specific application. The ASP.NET Framework uses dozens of these to provide a lot of built-in functionality.

Finally, request processing can be customized using HttpHandlers. Again, dozens of these are used within the shipping version of the Framework to process different types of requests. Doing custom request processing is as easy as creating a type that implements the IHttpHandler interface, and there are several options for configuring a handler within an application.

In the next section, we'll shift the focus from the pipeline down to the Page handler. This complex handler processes all requests for ASPX files. We'll also take a look under the hood at how the type that inherits from System.Web.UI.Page is transformed into a stream of HTML.

■ ■ ■

CHAPTER 3

Page Object Internals

You already know from your work with ASP.NET that the Page object is your base class for all ASP.NET pages. You're probably familiar with the event life cycle of the Page object, at least the Load event and control-specific events that execute when a postback occurs. In this chapter we're going to pull back the covers on System.Web.UI.Page. We'll examine the pieces and parts of its infrastructure that allow you to interact programmatically with control objects, while still sending a stream of HTML back to the client.

Sometimes the layer of abstraction between you and the stream of HTML going to the client can be frustrating. There are times you'll want to have specific control over the HTML that you're generating, and the Web Control just won't be generating the HTML quite the way you'd like it to.

The good news is there's nothing stopping you from exercising exactly as much control over the generated HTML as you need. With a thorough understanding of the work that the Page object does, the structure and touch-points of its control tree, and how the rendering process accomplishes its work, you have a toolset to help you greatly increase your control over the generated HTML.

The Page object orchestrates the entire construction of the web page. It houses the process life cycle, the event infrastructure, and the hierarchical control tree that generates the page's HTML. In this chapter, we'll drill into these internal components of the page-processing infrastructure.

Structure of a Web Form

The Page object's fully qualified name is System.Web.UI.Page. In the last chapter you saw how this type is an implementation of the IHttpHandler interface, and it simply plugs into the ASP.NET request processing pipeline. Now take a closer look at the object graph of this particular handler, which is shown in Figure 3-1.

This object graph applies to Web Forms, as long as you leverage the code-behind model. When no code-behind is used, the "code-behind page" object is removed from the graph; in this case, the markup contains the code in server-side script blocks.

In version 2.0 of the .NET Framework, a new Web Form model that supports a *partial classes* feature is baked into both C# and VB .NET. Partial classes introduce a number of subtleties into the structure of a Web Form that warrant a closer examination.

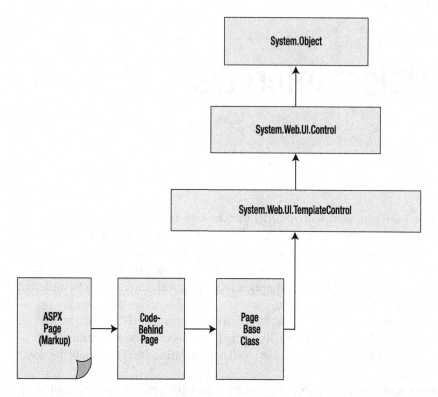

Figure 3-1. *The* Page *object's ancestors and descendants (when you're using the code-behind model)*

Options for Building Web Forms

With partial classes, you have a new approach to building Web Forms that involves a partial class inheriting from the Page base class. One file for the partial class is the code you'd normally add to the code-behind. The other file for the partial class isn't created until a run-time compilation step occurs. This is where all of the code that the designer would normally generate during development gets added to the mix.

Let's take a look at an example of a page in version 1.x and the changes required to use it in version 2.0. Consider the following markup:

```
<%@ Page language="c#"
    Codebehind="WebForm1.aspx.cs"
    Inherits="WebDemo.WebForm1" %>
<HTML>
    <HEAD>
        <title>WebForm1</title>
    </HEAD>
    <body>
        <form id="Form1" method="post" runat="server">
            <asp:Label id="Label3" runat="server">User Name</asp:Label><br>
            <asp:TextBox id="TextBox1" runat="server" /><br>
            <asp:Label id="Label2" runat="server">Password</asp:Label><br>
```

```
            <asp:TextBox id="TextBox3" runat="server" /><br><br>
            <asp:Button id="Button1" runat="server" Text="Login" /><br>
            <asp:Label id="lblOutput" runat="server" />
        </form>
    </body>
</HTML>
```

In version 2.0, Microsoft has dropped support for the CodeBehind attribute, and, instead, substitutes the new CodeFile attribute. Here's functionally equivalent markup in 2.0. The only difference is CodeFile replaces CodeBehind.

```
<%@ Page language="c#"
        CodeFile="WebForm1.aspx.cs"
        Inherits="WebDemo.WebForm1" %>

<HTML><HEAD><title>WebForm1</title></HEAD>
  <body>
    <form id="Form1" method="post" runat="server">
            <asp:Label id="Label3" runat="server">User Name</asp:Label>
            <asp:TextBox id="TextBox1" runat="server" />
            <asp:Label id="Label2" runat="server">Password</asp:Label>
            <asp:TextBox id="TextBox3" runat="server" />
            <asp:Button id="Button1" runat="server" Text="Login" />
            <asp:Label id="lblOutput" runat="server" />
    </form>
  </body>
</HTML>
```

Realize that version 2.0 does not support the CodeBehind attribute. This is a code breaking change that requires a conversion to move Web Forms from 1.x to 2.0. Considering that most of the changes for 2.0 are backwards compatible and require no changes to work in 2.0, this is worth noting.

The code-behind file contains much more significant differences. Here is the 1.x version of the code-behind for the markup we just examined.

```
public class WebForm1 : System.Web.UI.Page
{
    protected System.Web.UI.WebControls.Label Label3;
    protected System.Web.UI.WebControls.Label Label2;
    protected System.Web.UI.WebControls.TextBox TextBox3;
    protected System.Web.UI.WebControls.Button Button1;
    protected System.Web.UI.WebControls.Label lblOutput;
    protected System.Web.UI.WebControls.TextBox TextBox1;

    private void Page_Load(object sender, System.EventArgs e)
    {
        // Put user code to initialize the page here
    }
```

```
#region Web Form Designer generated code
override protected void OnInit(EventArgs e)
{
    //
    // CODEGEN: This call is required by the ASP.NET Web Form Designer.
    //
    InitializeComponent();
    base.OnInit(e);
}

/// <summary>
/// Required method for Designer support - do not modify
/// the contents of this method with the code editor.
/// </summary>
private void InitializeComponent()
{
    this.Load +=new EventHandler(Page_Load);
}
#endregion
}
```

Not only is there an entire region of generated code for this very simple Web Form but also the designer generates all of the control declarations that immediately follow the class declaration. This region of generated code, along with the requisite control declarations (as determined by your markup), are what is left out of the version 2.0 code-behind and then added with the second partial class file at runtime (see Figure 3-2). Here's the same code "converted" to work in 2.0:

```
public partial class WebForm1 : System.Web.UI.Page
{
    protected void Page_Load(object sender, EventArgs e)
    {

    }
}
```

That's it. Really. "Well, this code does nothing!" you might say. True, it does nothing. But if you look closely at the version 1.x block of code above, you'll realize that it also does nothing. That's a lot of code to do nothing, isn't it? This is the main benefit of using partial classes. It removes a lot of the internal "goo code" that adds no value to your development experience.

Note This model changed from Beta 1 to Beta 2. If you've played around with, or have read up on, the Framework changes with the PDC Bits, or Beta 1, you'll have a different story for the changes to the page model than the one we present here. People hated the PDC Bits model, so Microsoft changed it with the release of Beta 2. It reverted the model to look much more like the one in version 1.x.

You may have already heard about *partial classes*. This feature gives you the capability to split a single class file across more than one physical file. Version 1.x provided support for including more than one class in a single file, but there was no way to tell the compiler that a single class spans several files. Partial classes do just this.

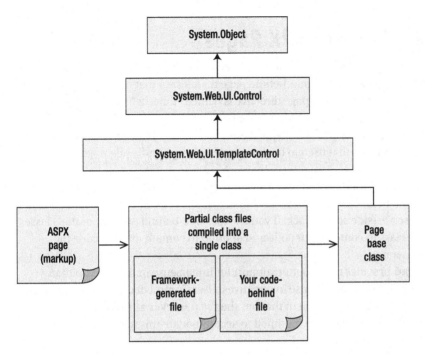

Figure 3-2. *The* Page *object's ancestors and descendants (with version 2.0 partial classes)*

While some folks talk about partial classes supporting "really big classes," this is not the real driving force behind adding the feature. It's true that a large class could be split among several physical files, but the true benefits come into the picture when you start to consider code generators. The .NET Framework is constantly generating code: code for COM Interop, code for proxies, code based on markup. The Framework team realized during version 1.0 development that they were going to be doing so much code generation that they decided to create a set of types to help them do this programmatically: System.CodeDom.

The problem with generated code has always been that it can step on your toes. If you've spent any amount of time coding traditional ASP, you've likely experienced an HTML-generating tool squashing your server-side script blocks. Or maybe you've added some code to the InitializeComponent method of the Page class, only to have the VS .NET Designer strip it out later.

With partial classes, code generation can occur in the code generator's own file. This file is declared as being a partial definition of the class the code is being generated for, and when it comes time to compile, the compiler simply merges the files to create a single class definition in the resulting Intermediate Language (IL) that's generated. This removes any possibility of having your own code squashed. The Page object orchestrates the entire construction of the web page. It houses the process life cycle, the event infrastructure, and the hierarchical control tree that results in the generation of the web page's HTML.

When an ASP.NET page is created using the code-behind model, two derived classes are actually created. The first is the code-behind, which uses the Page class as its base class. The second is the ASPX file itself, which is actually a type that inherits from the class that's defined in the code-behind (as shown in Figure 3-1).

Code Generation of ASPX Pages

How does the markup in your ASPX file become an instance of a binary executable at runtime? How does the work that's done in the code-behind page manifest in that markup? What does it really mean when an attribute of the page directive is named "Inherits" and its value is the fully qualified name of the class in your code-behind?

The code generator answers all of these questions The ASP.NET Framework actually puts off a lot of the code generation that used to be done at design time until code is generated for the ASPX file's markup.

You have a few options for the structure of a Web Form. You can choose to use inline coding or the code-behind model. If you choose code inline, your code will be encapsulated in the ASPX page within a server-side script block. If you choose code-behind, you use partial classes (the 2.0 model); one class to contain your code and another to contain markup code the Framework auto-generates.

Visual Studio 2005 provides much better support for IntelliSense in the markup than Visual Studio 2003 did. You get IntelliSense in directives, User Control declarations, and yes, in inline code (code within a script element that has the runat=server attribute).

The Add Web Form dialog has been modified to accommodate this new structure, as shown in Figure 3-3.

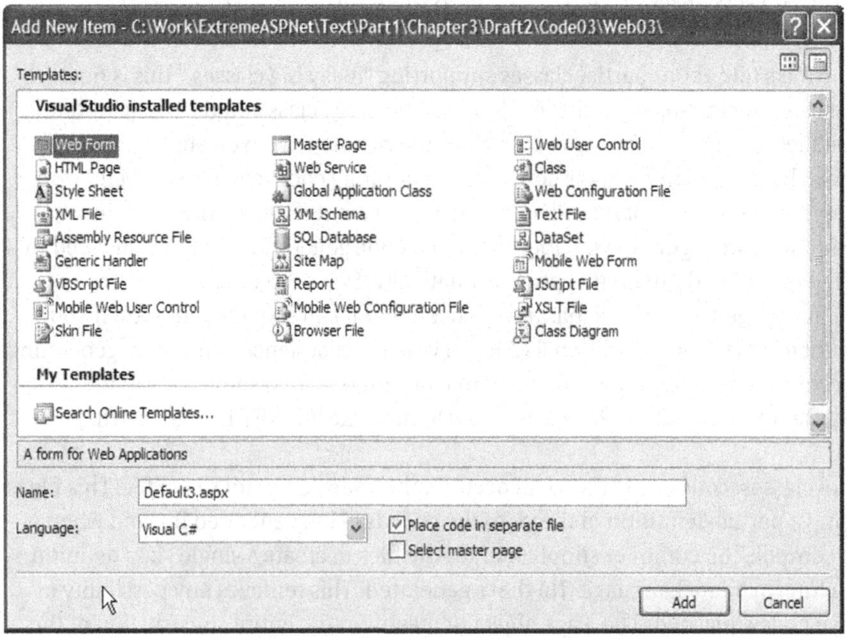

Figure 3-3. *The Add Web Form dialog in Visual Studio .NET 2005*

The Place code in separate file check box lets you choose between the code-behind model and putting code inline with your markup within server-side script elements.

Probably the single biggest improvement in this whole arena is the addition of IntelliSense support to script blocks within the integrated development environment (IDE), shown in Figure 3-4.

```
<%@ Page Language="C#" %>

<script runat="server">
    void Page_Load(object sender, EventArgs e)
    {
        this.FindControl("form1").Controls.Add(new liter|
    }
</script>
```

void ControlCollection.Add(Control child)
Adds the specified System.Web.UI.Control object to the collection.

Exceptions:
    System.ArgumentNullException
    System.Web.HttpException

- ListItemControlBuilder
- ListItemType
- ListSelectionMode
- ListSourceHelper
- Literal
- LiteralControl
- LiteralControlBuilder
- LiteralMode
- LoaderOptimization
- LoaderOptimizationAttribute

```
<html xm
<head ru
```
ontrol
ext, and any other strings in an ASP.NET page that do not require processing on the
```
        <form id="form1" runat="server">

        </form>
</body>
</html>
```

Figure 3-4. *IntelliSense using inline code with Visual Studio .NET 2005*

The inline coding model (and Web Matrix) is severely limiting with its lack of support for IntelliSense, especially once you become used to this feature. In Visual Studio .NET 2005, using inline code is now a viable option. There still are some real benefits to separating code from content, especially in a team development environment where there are web designers and a source control system present. But the inline code model is certainly easier to use in VS .NET 2K5.

So how does the markup in the ASPX file become a class at runtime? And how does the work that is done in the code-behind the page manifest in that markup?

Code Generation of ASPX Files

In ASP.NET, the aspx file containing your markup is transformed into a class definition at runtime. This happens the first time a request is made for the page after it's deployed. The generated class is defined as inheriting from the class defined in your page's code-behind file. This class is then compiled, and the compiled class is used to respond to requests for your aspx page from there on. This happens once: the first time a request is made for a page. Subsequent requests reuse the compiled class. A change to the aspx file or an assembly it depends on causes this process to repeat.

This means that the markup in an aspx file is actually just an abstraction created for you as a programming convenience! Web developers are familiar with the model of adding server-side tags to markup. It's the model in several web development environments, and since that's what web developers are accustomed to, it's one Microsoft provides with the ASP.NET Framework. However, at runtime, no markup is involved; it's pure binary executable code.

Consider the following, now familiar, markup:

```
<HTML>
<HEAD><title>WebForm1</title></HEAD>
<body>
<form id="Form1" method="post" runat="server">
  <asp:Label id="Label3" runat="server">User Name</asp:Label>
  <asp:TextBox id="TextBox1" runat="server" />
  <asp:Label id="Label2" runat="server">Password</asp:Label>
  <asp:TextBox id="TextBox3" runat="server" />
  <asp:Button id="Button1" runat="server" Text="Login" />
  <asp:Label id="lblOutput" runat="server" />
/form>
</body>
</HTML>
```

The first time the page is requested at runtime, several things occur.

- The markup is transformed into a class file. This class file is named after the aspx file. For example, markup in WebForm.aspx becomes a class named WebForm_aspx under the namespace ASP. If you're using code-behind, a partial class is also generated to accompany it. This generated class is declared as being a partial definition of the class defined in the page's code-behind.

- The class file is compiled with the rest of the class definition from the code-behind file. References are dynamically added to any other assemblies the Web Project depends on. This results in an assembly, but it's a Dynamic Link Library (DLL) and not an EXE. Remember that the Page class is an implementation of the IHttpHandler interface, and, therefore, it plugs into the request processing pipeline of the ASP.NET infrastructure (see Chapter 2). Another generated type, named FastObjectFactory (under a namespace called __ASP), creates and serves instances of this type to the Framework as requests come in.

- This DLL is just-in-time (JIT) compiled (meaning the IL is transformed to binary executable code) and written to disk. This is called a *shadow copy* DLL (oooh). This *shadow copying* is the reason you can XCopy a new version of your application to a server while your application is under a production load. Dependencies are set up (using file system events) between the shadow DLL, the ASPX containing the markup used to generate the class file, the Web Project Assembly, and any other dependant assemblies. If any of these dependencies change, the shadow DLL is deleted, and the next time your ASPX page is requested, the whole process starts from scratch to account for the new version.

- In the meantime, as long as no dependencies are changed, this precompiled, shadow DLL services subsequent requests. No file parsing, no interpretation, no code generation—not even a JIT compilation needs to occur. This shadow copy survives reboots of the web server. If any dependencies change, the compilation will be redone using the previously generated class file. The only time the generated code for the class needs to be created again is when the aspx file or code-behind files change. This is why there's a noticeable delay for the first request of a Web Form after you deploy a new version. There's a lot going on out there!

The runtime keeps the shadow assemblies in a directory where you can examine them. For the markup we've listed above, let's put it in a project named Web03 and a file named WebForm1.aspx that uses a code-behind class named WebForm1. When we compile the project and request the page, we can navigate out to the following directory.

```
C:\WINDOWS\Microsoft.NET\Framework\v2.0.50215\Temporary ASP.NET
Files\web03\EightRandomDigits\AnotherEightRandomDigits
```

In there you'll find any number of randomly named files with variously odd extensions. One of them is your generated shadow DLL from WebForm1.aspx. You can open this DLL using ILDASM. A snippet of what it will look like is displayed in Figure 3-5.

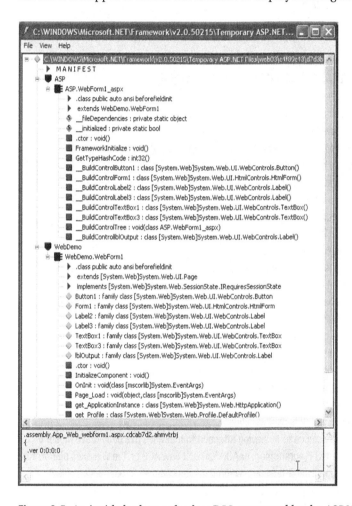

Figure 3-5. *An inside look at a shadow DLL generated by the ASP.NET Framework*

A quick glance through the structure of this assembly reveals how the markup is transformed into a code file. In the ASP namespace lives the class that's generated when the Framework transforms your markup into a class. Notice that it extends the class named WebForm1, which you partially defined in your code-behind, and partially provided by code generation of the Framework. That class exists in the WebDemo namespace (a namespace of our choosing from the code-behind) and it extends System.Web.UI.Page. Refer to Figure 3-2 for a picture of this inheritance chain. What you're looking at in ILDASM (Figure 3-5) is the mani-festation of that object graph within the Framework at runtime (where the proverbial rubber meets the road).

■**Note** There's actually a set of services in the Framework Class Library specifically designed to write code that generates code. Microsoft is doing this all over the place in the .NET Framework. Obviously it's doing it for ASP.NET; it's generating code for Web Service proxies and for COM Interop assemblies, just to name a few. This functionality lives in the System.CodeDom namespace. Check it out if you find yourself in a situation where you need to dynamically generate code!

DECLARATIVE VS. IMPERATIVE CODING

The markup in an ASP.NET page is an example of what's called *declarative coding*. It's a different coding model from the one most developers have become used to over the years, which is called *imperative coding*. Declarative coding is a technology that Microsoft is totally gung-ho about. In the 2.0 version of ASP.NET, the declarative model has been dramatically extended, so that it's now possible to create applications with very rich features, without writing a single line of code. It can all be done in the markup. One of the design goals of ASP.NET 2.0 was to dramatically reduce the amount of code you need to write for common tasks. Microsoft has accomplished this using declarative coding in the markup. By also adding high-powered graphical tools that generate this markup into the IDE, it's added some real productivity enhancement. Markup is very easy to generate programmatically, whereas source code is not.

As we look forward to the next generation of the Windows operating system (named Windows Vista), Microsoft plans on creating a new model for Windows development as well, called XAML, or XML Application Markup Language. This subsystem, named Windows Presentation Foundation, will be available for Windows 2003 and Window XP, and is a declarative model for Windows-based application development.

The real power in XAML lies in the fact that code is relatively static. It's like taking all of the declarations and initializations of variables out of your imperative code and moving them into a document of their own. In XAML, there will be a code-behind model as well, so the more complex, dynamic code will still be written there. Microsoft plans to couple a page-based development model with the richness in functionality of the Windows development model. Go to http://msdn.microsoft.com/Longhorn to see some concept videos of the type of application that will be produced with this new paradigm.

If there are any trends in computer science to be paying attention to today, it's this declarative model of programming coupled with Aspect Oriented Programming, or AOP. You first saw AOP on the Windows platform in Microsoft Transaction Server. In this application-hosting environment you could set properties on objects specifying, for example, their transactional requirements and behavior. This would affect the run-time charac-teristics of the type without requiring any modification to the imperative source code.

.NET attributes extend this model by promoting attributes to first-class citizens within the Common Language Runtime (CLR) and .NET languages themselves. Anytime you add the [Serialization] or [WebMethod] attributes to a class definition, you're using AOP. And again, *you're affecting the runtime behavior of your type without touching the imperative code.*

Declarative coding and AOP are worth knowing about. Realize what they are and pay attention to the tools (.NET 2.0, Windows Communication Foundation, Windows Presentation Foundation, Windows Vista) coming out over the next few years, because these models are really going to come to the fore.

Another new piece of the ASP.NET 2.0 infrastructure is when and how this code genera-tion and compilation happens. There are important differences between the compilation model in version 1.x that give you more choices for building and deploying projects.

Compilation and Deployment

There are a lot of complaints with version 1.x about the lack of support for deployment activi-ties. You can copy files to a remote web server via FrontPage extensions, or deploy to a network share. However, this rudimentary support is generally not sufficient for most real-world deployment scenarios. Once deployed, the one-time performance hit that occurs for the first request for a Web Form (while it performs the code generation and compilation steps we just examined) is also unacceptable in sites with thousands of pages. A single change to the Assembly containing the compiled images of the site's code-behind classes causes every Web Form to be delayed by several seconds on its next request.

Microsoft has listened and responded to their customers' cries of despair. Let's look first at the improvements it made to deployment. Then we'll examine the new compilation model.

When you select a Web Project and choose the Copy Web Site button from the Solution Explorer within Visual Studio, an entirely new interface appears, as shown in Figure 3-6.

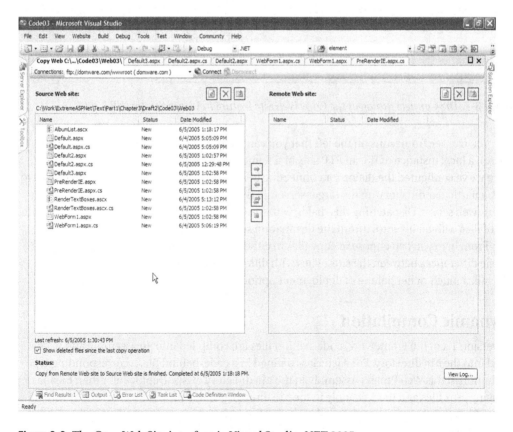

Figure 3-6. *The Copy Web Site interface in Visual Studio .NET 2005*

All your project files appear in the list on the left. This interface clearly allows you to deploy whatever set of files you need to at a given time. The list on the right is the really exciting piece. You can click the Connect button to see the rich array of deployment target choices (see Figure 3-7).

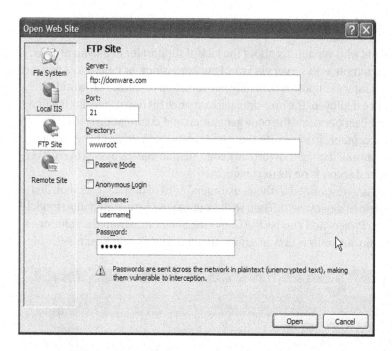

Figure 3-7. *The Connect dialog of the Copy Web Site feature in Visual Studio .NET 2005*

You can see from icons on the left that you can choose from the File System (a network share), a local instance of IIS, an FTP site, or a Remote Site running FrontPage Extensions. Here we've configured the dialog for connecting to a server via FTP. You even have an option to pick a particular directory on the target server; in this case, we're using it to drill into the root of this web server. Dispatching this dialog with the Open button populates the right-hand side list of files with an inventory from the destination server (see Figure 3-8).

From here you can choose to copy files in either direction, overwrite existing files, or reconcile differences between the sites. Files with differences are also flagged with the ? icon. Overall, a much richer palette of deployment options is available in the new IDE.

Dynamic Compilation

In version 1.x of the Framework, code-behind files are compiled into an assembly and packaged into the `bin` directory. For each class defined in a code-behind file, a corresponding type definition in this Web Project Assembly in the `bin` directory exists. Deployment then means copying `aspx` files and the Assembly in the `bin` directory onto a production server. Any other assemblies the project depends on—images, CSS, script files, etc.—need, of course, to be copied out as well.

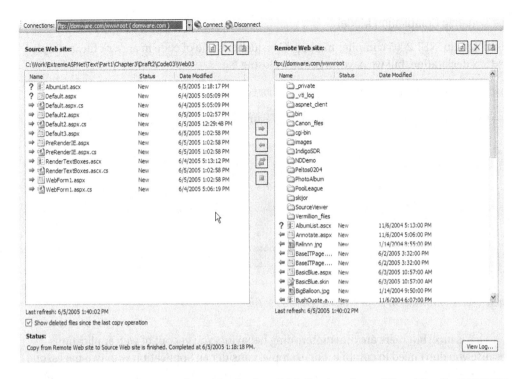

Figure 3-8. *A source and target selected in the Copy Web Site interface of Visual Studio .NET 2005*

The problem with this model came into the picture during the maintenance stage that always follows a deployment. Any change to any code behind the page has to be recompiled into the Assembly in the `bin` directory. When a new version of that Assembly gets copied to the production server, each and every Web Form in the site regens and recompiles upon its next request. Considering the extensive overhead involved in this process, multiplied by the number of pages in the application, you're looking at a serious cost to incur for what often is just a minor change to a class.

Well, no more. Because the code-behind is now a partial class, and because that class isn't generated until runtime, there is no "Web Project Assembly" that needs to be deployed anymore. This means that you can create and deploy a Web Project without a compilation step. You can leave it until runtime. Just code it, copy it out, and you're done.

Sounds great, no? No? No you say? You like to compile your application before deploying it? What kind of nonsense is that? You never had to compile classic ASP!

Of course you like to compile. Compiling is a beautiful thing. Compiling finds typos, enforces type safety, validates references, and generally makes our lives much easier. The good news is Visual Studio .NET allows you to compile before deploying, even though it's not technically *required* to compile before deploying. Compilation is actually more powerful in Visual Studio .NET 2005 than it is in Visual Studio .NET 2003. In 2003, for example, there is no compilation for markup (aka your `aspx` files). An error in an `aspx` page is not caught until the page is actually requested, when the runtime code-gen and compilation occurs. VS .NET 2K5 compiles `aspx` files, which means you catch more problems earlier in the process—a good thing, to be sure. This is just one of a handful of features that fall under an umbrella called *Dynamic Compilation*.

The Dynamic Compilation Model

Visual Studio .NET 2005 compiles markup. Consider this line of code in an aspx file, a simple TextBox declaration, but we have forgotten a closing tag:

```
<asp:TextBox ID=txtFirstName Text='Bob' runat=server>
```

Compiling produces the errors shown in Figure 3-9, pulled from the Error List window.

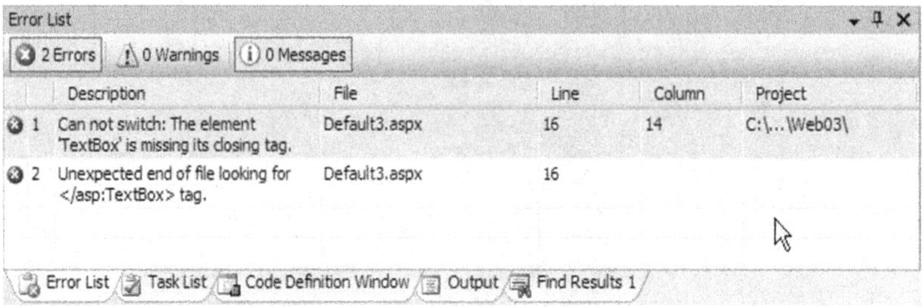

Figure 3-9. *A compilation error caused by an* aspx *file*

This is nice, but there are other interesting behaviors you get out of web applications because you don't need to compile. For example, consider an application with two pages, one that works great (Default.aspx) and one that won't compile (Default3.aspx). Before you fix Default3.aspx, you want to make a change to Default.aspx and test it. For example, you may add the following code to the page load of the Default page:

```
protected void Page_Load(object sender, EventArgs e)
{
    FindControl("form1").Controls.Add(new LiteralControl("Hello"));
}
```

This code works fine. When you compile, however, you still get the error previously listed (see Figure 3-9) because of the error in Default3.aspx. In VS .NET 2K3, this means the Web Project Assembly failed to get created when compiling, and the completely unrelated change you made to your code-behind in Default.aspx is not baked into a new version of the Assembly.

In this environment, though, compilation is optional. The fact that the compile failed is irrelevant. You can right-click on Default.aspx in Solution Explorer and tell the IDE to display it in the browser. The IDE fires up a browser instance and, voila! the page appears just fine, as demonstrated in Figure 3-10.

This demonstrates a couple of interesting things. First, when you make a change to a code-behind file, you don't have to recompile. If you just request the page anew, your change shows up. In VS .NET 2K3 this is true if you make a change to an aspx file. Without recompiling, the change shows up on the next request to the page. Now, since all compilation is put off until runtime, the same is true of code-behind changes.

The other interesting thing this demonstrates is that not everything in the site has to be working in order to request pages in the site. With version 1.x of the Framework, this is not true, because if there are any problems in the code-behind you cannot successfully build the Web Project Assembly.

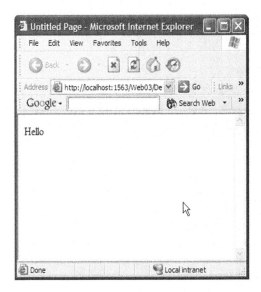

Figure 3-10. *A page displayed from a project that works even with a compilation error in another page*

Now none of this is relevant for production systems, you realize. These are subtleties that are, however, very nice changes while doing development. You can make and exercise changes with much less overhead.

In addition to the features we've looked at so far, the Dynamic Compilation model also provides some very handy functionality via the App_Code directory. Adding the App_Code folder is a special choice from within Solution Explorer, as shown in Figure 3-11.

You can place any source file into this directory, and it's immediately available to the rest of the code in your application. For example, here's a simple helper function for loading and caching XML documents.

```
public class WebStatic
{
    public static DataSet GetXmlDoc(string fileName)
    {
        HttpContext ctx = HttpContext.Current;
        DataSet ds;

        ds = ctx.Cache[fileName];
        if (ds == null)
        {
            ds = new DataSet();
            ds.ReadXml(fileName);
            ctx.Cache.Insert(fileName, ds, new CacheDependency(fileName));
        }
        return ds;
    }
}
```

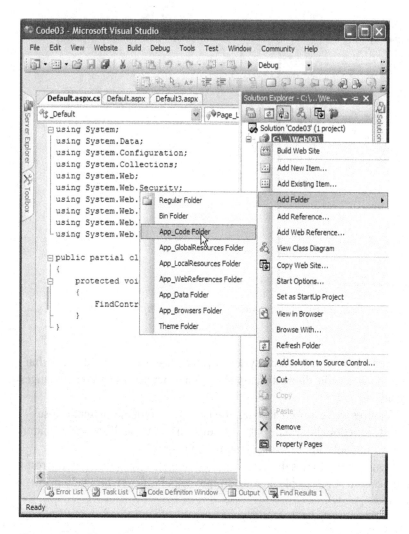

Figure 3-11. *Adding the* App_Code *directory*

By placing this cs file into the App_Code directory, it's instantly available from all the pages in your site. It even shows up via IntelliSense (see Figure 3-12), again without even compiling.

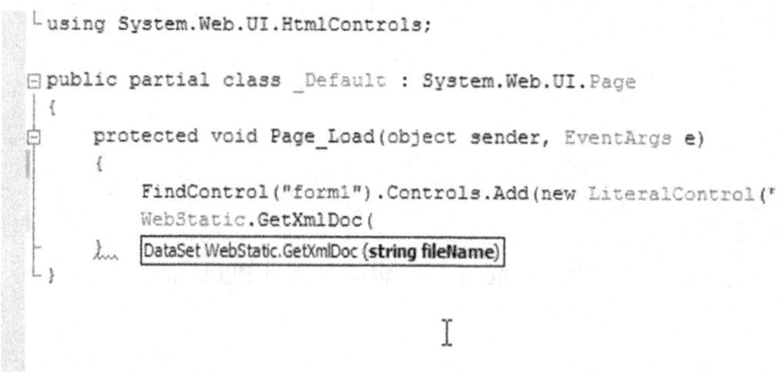

```
using System.Web.UI.HtmlControls;

public partial class _Default : System.Web.UI.Page
{
    protected void Page_Load(object sender, EventArgs e)
    {
        FindControl("form1").Controls.Add(new LiteralControl("
        WebStatic.GetXmlDoc(
        DataSet WebStatic.GetXmlDoc (string fileName)
}
```

Figure 3-12. *IntelliSense for type in the* App_Code *directory*

Similar facilities exist for WSDL documents, which are made available as Web Service proxies; XML Schema Definition (XSD) documents, which become exposed as strongly-typed datasets; and resources.

Of course, this whole dynamic compilation model requires you to deploy your code to your production server, which not everyone is going to be thrilled about. It also does nothing to address the problem of run-time compilation causing a huge performance hit for the first request of every page in the site. These problems have not gone unchecked, though. They're addressed by *precompilation* (a feature so cool they made up a new word for it).

Precompilation

There are a couple of different ways to precompile your site. One does an in-place compilation, which basically has the effect of making the first request for each page and leaves the application ready for live requests. This is done on the production server after deployment. The other option precompiles before deployment, which creates a copy of your website suitable for deployment. This copy compiles all code-behind and classes in the App_Code folder into assemblies that it places in the bin directory. Only files needed at runtime are copied into this folder. Using this option reduces the flexibility you have in deploying changes, but it keeps your source code off the production servers and improves the performance of the first request of the pages.

For both options, you use the aspnet_compiler command line tool. To precompile in place, simply pass the tool the -v switch and the virtual directory of the application you want compiled:

```
aspnet_compiler -v /Web03
```

Precompilation for deployment works the same way: You simply need to further specify a target location where the precompiler will place the compiled image ready for deployment:

```
aspnet_compiler -v /Web03 c:\ProductionImage
```

This site is all packed up and ready to go now (see Figure 3-13). You can open the directory with VS .NET 2K5 to use the deployment tool, XCopy the files, or FTP them to the production box.

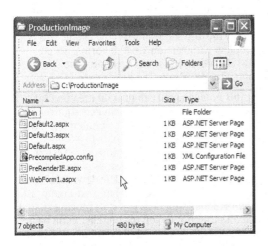

Figure 3-13. *The production ready, precompiled image of the* Web03 *application*

Basics of the Control Type

In examining the ASPX markup, the class that gets generated from it, and the code-behind that it compiles with, we've looked at all of the types that have the Page object in their inheritance trees. This is where code for the least general functionality goes. The code of the Page object itself is then the first class in the object graph that contains general functionality. This is familiar territory, as it's leveraged to create every ASP.NET page. We're talking about the Init and Load events of the Page type, the various server-side event traps, like Button.Click or TextBox.TextChanged, you can set up to trap events as they occur on the client.

The Page level events, however, aren't specific to the Page type. If you follow the inheritance chain of the Page class up, you'll find the old familiar Control type. System.Web.UI.Control is the base type for every element you put on a web page. It's a base type for HTML Controls, for Web Controls, for User Controls, and for Custom Controls. It's very interesting to note that it's also a base type for the Page class itself.

This means that the properties and methods of this type are exposed on practically everything you interact with programmatically on your page and on your Page object as well. Thus, understanding what's housed within this type is learning you can leverage everywhere in your development of Web Forms.

Table 3-1. *A Sample of Members from* System.Web.UI.Control

Member Name	Type	Meaning in Life
Controls	ControlCollection	This is a strong-typed collection of Control objects. The Page type's Control collection is what stores the base elements of your web page. Elements that are children of other elements then become instances of the Control type in their parent element's control collection. Together these aggregated ControlCollections create an in-memory tree of Control objects that models the hierarchy of the resulting web page. We'll be examining the ControlCollection in greater detail as we move forward.
ControlState	ControlState	This new feature of ASP.NET 2.0 separates information critical to the functionality of the control from content-based ViewState information. This allows you to turn off ViewState without losing the ability to store some state on the client. This is a big problem with version 1.x Web Forms, which ControlState fixes in the new version. (See Chapter 4 for details on ControlState.)
EnableViewState	Boolean	Using this Boolean, you can turn off the ViewState of any control. This is the data that gets squirreled away by individual controls in the hidden input that goes to the client. By persisting data to a hidden input on the client, the information gets POSTed back to the server, and so it becomes possible to restore that state on postbacks. The downside is this hidden input can get extremely large extremely fast, and performance suffers as you start moving all that data across the connection to your client and back to the server with a post. (We'll examine some best practices for minimizing the ViewState size in Chapter 4.)

Member Name	Type	Meaning in Life
ID	String	This is the unique ID that identifies any element on the page with the runat=server attribute on it. This should also be the same as the name of the variable you plan to use in your code-behind. The code-generation step automatically declares a variable with this name that overrides the declaration from your code-behind base class. This means that at runtime, the element in your markup and the variable declared in your code-behind *are the same instance of the same class.* This is why everything you do to a Web Control from code-behind shows up in the resulting page. This dual-declaration infrastructure is eliminated in version 2.0 via partial classes.
Page	System.Web.UI.Page	This is an instance of the Page object. For controls, this value will point to the instance of the Page that the control is living on. For a Page object, this value will point to itself. So (this.Page == this) is necessarily true in a type that inherits from the Page object.
Parent	System.Web.UI.Control	This is the instance of the Control that has this Control in its control collection. For a Page object, this value is null, as the Page is the root of the tree. For a Form object living on a Page, this value will point to the Page. So for a Form, it's true that (this.Page == this.Parent). However, for a Control living on the Form, the Parent is the Form object.
Visible	Boolean	Every control can have its visibility set to false. This is a nice feature, because while the control will squirrel away its state in the ViewState hidden input, it won't render any HTML to represent itself at all. This is very different than using Cascading Style Sheets (CSS) or script to make an element hidden once it gets to the client. This makes it possible to code a Wizard-style interface using Panel controls, where only one Panel is visible at a time. All of the children of the panel will store their state in the ViewState, but their markup will be generated only when the Panel is visible, keeping the response stream as short as possible. Of course, this also means you can set the visibility of the Page itself to false, but we've yet to find any usefulness in a page you can't see.
HasControls()	Boolean	This will return true if there are any controls in the ControlCollection of the Control you've called the method on. It's useful for quickly checking if a Control has any children of its own.
Init	Event	This event occurs when the server control is initialized, which is the first step in its life cycle.

Continued

Table 3-1. *Continued*

Member Name	Type	Meaning in Life
Load	Event	This is the first event to fire after the control tree and ViewState of the page have been created and restored. Generally you use this event for page initialization, wrapping your code in a clause that causes it not to fire on postbacks, as postback logic usually lives in an event handler of a specific control.
PreRender	Event	This event occurs just before the page does a recursive descent of its control tree and calls the render method to assemble to output stream. More on this event later.
Unload	Event	This event fires after the output stream has been rendered and sent back to IIS. You cannot modify the output stream from this event. The only thing to be done from this event is to "clean up" any resources you've held onto over the lifetime of the Page object instance.

■**Note** The Page object has some new events in version 2.0 that we'll look at a bit later. Table 3-1 displays properties and events specific to the Control class, which the Page object (and all Web Controls) inherits.

Control Tree Essentials

Since all controls expose their own control collection, it follows that any control can contain its own child controls. This correlates to what you'd expect in HTML, where many of the elements on a page contain child elements.

Since the Page object also inherits from the Control collection, it acts as the root of this whole coil. While there is not a one-to-one correlation between the in-memory structure of the control tree and the hierarchy of the elements in the generated HTML, there is a definite relationship. Later, we'll examine the places where the hierarchy of the HTML gets flattened in the control tree and why.

After the PreRender event fires, the Page enters its rendering behavior. If you've ever written a Custom Control, you know that the critical piece of work that needs to be done is to override the Render method of the Control base class. The Page starts by calling the Render method of the first control in its control tree. That control *renders* (which is just a fancy way to say it generates some HTML based on its current state), and checks to see if it has any controls in its own ControlCollection. If it does, it calls Render on the first of those, which is where you meet the recursion of your algorithm. This is done for every control in every control collection in the entire tree. The Page object happily aggregates all the rendered HTML as this recursive descent of the control tree transpires, and when all of the controls have made their contributions, the Page returns the rendered HTML to IIS as the response stream.

Along the way, any state information that controls might need when a postback occurs is squirreled away in the ViewState (unless, of course, ViewState is turned off for that control).

The rendered size and contribution to the ViewState can be seen on the Trace output report. You can see this report simply by adding trace=true to the Page directive at the top of your ASPX file, as shown in Figure 3-14.

Control Tree				
Control UniqueID	Type	Render Size Bytes (including children)	ViewState Size Bytes (excluding children)	ControlState Size Bytes (excluding children)
__Page	ASP.WebForm1_aspx	603	0	0
ctl00	System.Web.UI.LiteralControl	71	0	0
Form1	System.Web.UI.HtmlControls.HtmlForm	510	0	0
ctl01	System.Web.UI.LiteralControl	6	0	0
Label3	System.Web.UI.WebControls.Label	34	0	0
ctl02	System.Web.UI.LiteralControl	6	0	0
TextBox1	System.Web.UI.WebControls.TextBox	51	0	0
ctl03	System.Web.UI.LiteralControl	6	0	0
Label2	System.Web.UI.WebControls.Label	33	0	0
ctl04	System.Web.UI.LiteralControl	10	0	0
TextBox3	System.Web.UI.WebControls.TextBox	51	0	0
ctl05	System.Web.UI.LiteralControl	6	0	0
Button1	System.Web.UI.WebControls.Button	65	0	0
ctl06	System.Web.UI.LiteralControl	6	0	0
lblOutput	System.Web.UI.WebControls.Label	28	0	0
ctl07	System.Web.UI.LiteralControl	8	0	0
ctl08	System.Web.UI.LiteralControl	22	0	0

Figure 3-14. *An excerpt from the Trace output report showing the relative rendered and view state sizes of the controls on the page*

Any element in the markup that doesn't have the runat=server attribute added to its declaration will be flattened in the control tree. That is to say, not all elements in the markup become objects in the control tree. To create an object for each element would be horribly wasteful and inefficient. The whole point of having an element represented as an object in the control tree is to interact with it programmatically. If there's no need to deal with it programmatically, then there's no need to incur the overhead of allocating on object to the managed heap to represent the element. Consider the previous example of our markup (see WebForm1.aspx in the Web03 project):

```
<HTML>
<HEAD><title>WebForm1</title></HEAD>
<body>
<form id="Form1" method="post" runat="server">
  <asp:Label id="Label3" runat="server">User Name</asp:Label>
  <asp:TextBox id="TextBox1" runat="server" />
  <asp:Label id="Label2" runat="server">Password</asp:Label>
  <asp:TextBox id="TextBox3" runat="server" />
  <asp:Button id="Button1" runat="server" Text="Login" />
  <asp:Label id="lblOutput" runat="server" />j
</form>
</body>
</HTML>
```

For this markup, how many objects would be in the Page's collection of controls? The answer, which may surprise you, is three, as shown in Figure 3-15.

To see why, let's scan the markup for the first element that has the runat=server attribute. We find that it's the form element. So this element is definitely represented in the Page object's control tree. All of the other elements with the runat=server attribute are children of the form element. This means that the instance of the Control object representing the Form element has six children in its control collection, as shown in Figure 3-15.

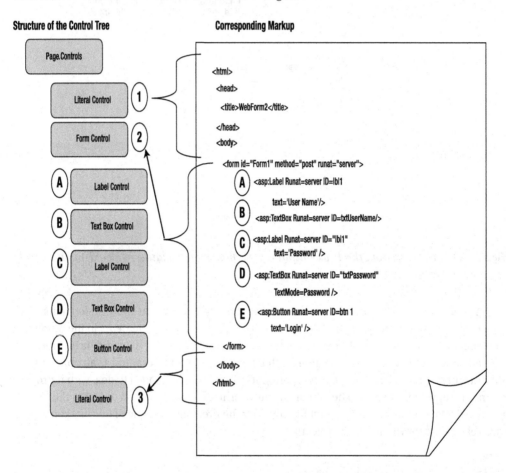

Figure 3-15. *The control tree of our simple markup, where the controls in the* Page's *control collection are numbered, and the controls in the Forms collection are lettered.*

That leaves the other two objects in the Page's control collection to identify. If you look at everything preceding the Form declaration, you can see that it's all static markup. These are hierarchical elements as far as the web browser is concerned, but to the ASP.NET engine on the server, it's a meaningless arbitrary string. Since there are no runat=server attributes, there will be no code interacting with this markup; and so the text is all *flattened* and represented in the control tree as a *single* LiteralControl.

A `LiteralControl`, in case you're not familiar with it, is just that. Whatever you set to its `Text` property is literally what it will render. The `LiteralControl`'s constructor accepts a string to use as its `Text`, so using the `LiteralControl` is very easy.

```
this.Page.Controls.Add(
new LiteralControl("<p>Here is some static markup I want on my page</p>");
```

So in the case of our markup above, the first control in the control collection is a literal control, whose text contains all of the static markup preceding the form declaration. The third literal control just carries the end `body` and end `html` elements as its text.

Because the other controls appear between the `form`'s begin tag and the `form`'s end tag, they are all children of the `form`, and are, therefore, housed in its control collection.

Web Form Event Model

In ASP.NET 1.x, the `Page` type inherits its event model from `System.Web.UI.Control`. This is nice, because it means all controls placed on a Web Form share an event model with the `Page` object. This simplifies responding to events on User Controls, and is especially nice while you're developing custom Web Controls, because there's only one event model you need to become familiar with.

Ironically, this event model is lacking when it comes to developing User Controls and custom controls. Sometimes there's an action that needs to be taken at the page level *after all* instances of a specific event have fired on controls, or *before any* instances fire on controls, and there's no hook to do this. This is one of the driving forces behind some new events on the `Page` type in version 2.0 of the Framework.

The other driver is some of the new functionality exposed in 2.0. Some of this functionality is wired before the `Init` event fires at the `Page` level (that is, Master Pages and Themes). To facilitate making changes to these features from code, an event has been added that fires before the `Init` event does.

Keep in mind that the purpose of a lot of these events may not be obvious when thinking about a single ASPX page using canned Web Controls. A lot of these events become relevant when you're coding User Controls, when custom control development is part of the project, when you're using Master Pages, or when an application is using generic types derived from the `Page` type as base classes for ASPX pages, instead of just inheriting directly from `System.Web.UI.Page`. Then, rather than a single `Init` event firing, for example, there are `Init` events that fire for controls up and down the control tree—for User Controls, for Master Page classes, and for any classes extending the inheritance chain between the ASPX and the `Page` class. If there's some code that you need to run *after everything is initialized,* this can be tricky to accomplish in version 1.x. The *PreXXX* and *XXXComplete* events have been added to the page to reduce the complexity of timing the code in applications with all of these moving parts. Let's examine these events in the order that they occur.

PreInit

This is a new page-level event. This event gives the developer a chance to run some code before control and page initialization occurs. This is a good place to programmatically set the Master Page that a `Page` object is going to consume. It's also a good spot to programmatically determine the Theme that a page is going to use. Since both of these features are implemented in page initialization, this is your last chance in the pipeline to exert programmatic influence on them.

This is also a good place to put any code that needs to be executed before controls get initialized. If a page is programmatically adding controls to the control collection, this is the ideal place for that code to execute, as it precedes control initialization.

Init

This is a control-level event that also exists in version 1.x. An important detail to be aware of is that control initialization fires before page initialization. This means that when the `Init` event fires at the `Page` level, all of the controls for the page are already initialized. This is why if, for example, you need to set the Theme for the page, you must do this from the `PreInit` event trap, as it fires before the controls of the page are initialized.

InitComplete

This is a new page-level event. It fires after everything has been initialized. This includes all controls in the control trees (recursively), any Master Page code (even when you're using nested Master Pages), and all types in the inheritance chain of the `Page` object. Because all controls should be initialized at this point in the page-processing life cycle, any dynamic control generation should be done prior to this event firing, either during preinitialization or initialization. While this won't always be possible, it should be done whenever at all possible, to avoid bugs and improve to predictability of the `Page`'s behavior.

PreLoad

This is a new page-level event. It fires before any `Load` event fires anywhere in the control tree or `Page` object graph. It provides a place from the page to do any setup needed in loading of controls on the page. It's also guaranteed to fire *after* everything in the control tree is initialized.

Load

This is a control-level event that also exists in version 1.x. This is the classic entry point into page processing. At this moment in the request processing cycle, control state is initialized, View State has been restored on a postback, and any editing that a user has done has been moved from the HTTP headers into the corresponding property values. Types in the `Page` object graph have their `Load` events fire, and then the controls in the control tree have their `Load` events fire.

Control-Level Postback Events

Any number of events can fire during this time during a postback. If there are seven textboxes on a page, and each of them has a TextChanged event trap set up, and there's also a submit button on the page to cause a postback, then you could have up to eight events fire during this part of the page's life cycle. For controls created dynamically, their event traps will be properly sunk and fired, as long as you create the controls somewhere in the tree before the end of the Page Load event.

LoadComplete

This is a new page-level event. It fires just after all Load events from the entire control tree and object graph finish. It's an ideal time to respond to work done during loading of the page and controls, and work done during any event traps that occurred at any level of the control tree hierarchy. It's also guaranteed to fire before any PreRender events fire, ensuring that the processing here gets done before, for example, any prerendering work gets done in a page's base classes.

PreRender

This is a control-level event that also exists in version 1.x. It fires on the types in the page's object graph, and then does a recursive descent of the controls in the tree, firing for each of those.

PreRenderComplete

This is a new page-level event. This is your last chance to make changes to the output stream that gets sent back to IIS. See the following section for a detailed discussion of this event.

SaveStateComplete

This is a new page-level event. After PreRenderComplete is fired, state information for all controls is committed to view state. This event fires after that work is complete. (See Chapter 4 for an example of how to make use of this event during control state persistence.)

Control Events vs. Page Events

Some of these events are part of the definition of System.Web.UI.Control. Some are defined by System.Web.UI.Page. Since the Page type inherits from the Control type, they're all exposed at the Page level. Whether these events are defined at the Control or Page level only starts to make a difference in the context of custom control development. Events defined by Control are available during control development. Events defined by the Page are only available during Web Form development.

Even if you're not doing custom control development, this distinction can be important when you're using User Controls during Web Form development. Only events defined by the Control base class are available from the code-behind of your User Controls.

These differences can be seen in the SDK docs on MSDN, the Visual Studio .NET object browser, or other reflection-based documentation systems. They're shown here in Figure 3-16.

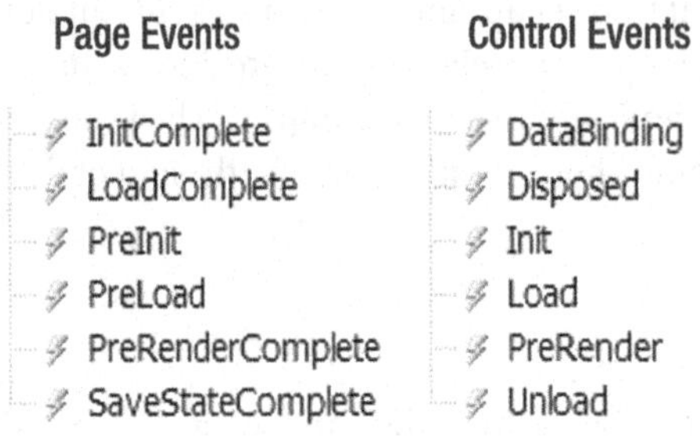

Page Events	Control Events
⚡ InitComplete	⚡ DataBinding
⚡ LoadComplete	⚡ Disposed
⚡ PreInit	⚡ Init
⚡ PreLoad	⚡ Load
⚡ PreRenderComplete	⚡ PreRender
⚡ SaveStateComplete	⚡ Unload

Figure 3-16. Page *class events are distinct from* Control *class events*

The Special Role of the PreRender Event

The PreRender event is fired just before the Render method is called on the Page object. It is, therefore, your last chance to make changes to the Page's output stream.

This is frequently a very useful event to trap. When you're using User Controls on your page, the event model is sequenced such that the Load event of the Page fires, the Load event of the User Control fires, control specific events of the Page object fire, and then control specific events of the User Control fire.

So what do you do if you want to respond at the Page level to the work that the User Control has done? A common pattern is to raise an event from the User Control back to the Page. This is a very good model and you should use it whenever appropriate. Sometimes, however, that just won't do the trick. For instance, you may want to be sure that the User Control has done all of its work before your processing fires at the Page level. When this is the requirement you face, the PreRender method is the place to be. Consider the following code, which is markup from PreRenderIE.aspx:

```
<%@ Page Language="C#"
        AutoEventWireup="true"
        CodeFile="PreRenderIE.aspx.cs"
        Inherits="PreRenderIE" %>

<%@ Register TagPrefix="uc1"
            TagName="RenderTextboxes"
            Src="RenderTextboxes.ascx" %>

<HTML>
    <HEAD>
        <title>PreRenderIE</title>
    </HEAD>
    <body>
        <form id="Form1" method="post" runat="server">
            <asp:Label Runat=server ID=lblOutput>
```

```
            Change some fields and press the button
            </asp:Label>
            <br>
            <uc1:RenderTextboxes id="RenderTextboxes1" runat="server" />
            <br>
            <asp:Button Runat=server ID=btn Text='Postback' />
        </form>
    </body>
</HTML>
```

And here's the code from the corresponding code-behind, PreRenderIE.aspx.cs:

```
public partial class PreRenderIE : System.Web.UI.Page
{
    private int ChangeCount = 0;

    override protected void OnInit(EventArgs e)
    {
        RenderTextboxes1.FieldChanged +=
            new EventHandler(RenderTextboxes1_FieldChanged);

        base.OnInit(e);
        this.PreRender += new EventHandler(PreRenderIE_PreRender);
    }

    private void RenderTextboxes1_FieldChanged(object sender, EventArgs e)
    {
        ChangeCount++;
    }

    private void PreRenderIE_PreRender(object sender, EventArgs e)
    {
        if (this.IsPostBack)
        {
            lblOutput.Text = string.Format(
                "You changed {0} fields on the User Control",
                ChangeCount);

            this.Controls.Remove(this.Controls[0]);
            this.Controls.AddAt(0, new LiteralControl(string.Format(
                "<html><head><title>{0} Changes</title></head><body>",
                ChangeCount)));
        }
    }
}
```

Here you're using a User Control event to count the number of controls whose values have changed. All of the TextBoxes on the User Control raise this event when their TextChanged event fires. Here is the code from the User Control:

```
public partial class RenderTextBoxes : System.Web.UI.UserControl
{
    public event System.EventHandler FieldChanged;

    override protected void OnInit(EventArgs e)
    {
        for (int i = 0; i < 10; i++)
        {
            TextBox t = new TextBox();
            this.Controls.Add(t);
            t.TextChanged += new EventHandler(t_TextChanged);
        }                    }
        base.OnInit(e);
    }
}

    private void t_TextChanged(object sender, EventArgs e)
    {
        if (FieldChanged != null)
        {
            FieldChanged(this, new EventArgs());
        }
    }
}
```

In any given execution of the event trap at the Page level, you can't be sure that it's the last time the event will fire. So you wait until the PreRender event fires to act on the data you're creating as you trap events from the User Control. You could do this work from the FieldChanged event trap of the User Control (relying on the fact that it would be correct the last time it fired), but this is less efficient and won't work for all types of processing. Imagine if you were updating the database or doing a redirect as a result of the work being done on the User Control. Clearly the PreRender event is a better option.

As an improvement over version 1.x, even if the Page code needs to respond to work done in the User Control's PreRender event trap, you have the page-level PreRenderComplete event that fires after all PreRender events fire for all controls in the tree.

Also in the PreRender event trap, you're replacing the first control in the page's control collection with an instance of a new User Control (see Figure 3-17). This example (setting the title of the page) is pretty trivial, but it's there to illustrate that you still have full random access to the entire control tree when this event fires. You can do anything to any part of the Page because nothing has been committed to the output stream (see Figure 3-18). Later on we'll show you how you can capture the rendered output and send it somewhere else (like to a file or a database, or as the body of an e-mail) from this trap.

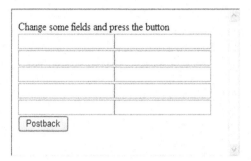

Figure 3-17. *The initial rendering of the User Control that raises an event*

You changed 6 fields on the User Control

abc	123
def	456
Dominic	Selly

Postback

Figure 3-18. *The same page after making modifications to textboxes and posting back*

Resource Consumption when Data Binding

We've examined how all of the work you do while an ASP.NET page is processing is stored as state of control objects in the control tree. We've also examined how no markup is committed to the output stream until *after* all of your code has executed, most specifically, after the PreRenderComplete event fires.

But what about data binding? Surely when the DataBind method is called, the bound control generates HTML that's committed to the output stream right away, doesn't it? The answer is most definitely no. Data binding is no exception to the rule.

When DataBind is called, the control doing the binding generates any number of instances of objects that it stores in its own collection. List controls generate ListItem objects. The DataGrid generates DataGridItem objects. Each data bound control has its own type that it uses to represent an individual row in what eventually will become the HTML output stream. Because these collections of items are a contained collection of the bound control, the binding operation is really state information stored in the control tree.

When Render is called on the bound control, the control iterates over the objects in its particular item collection, transforming each into HTML. The DropDownList generates option tags. The DataGrid generates table rows, and so on.

If this comes as a surprise to you, it's going to come as an absolute shock what happens with memory consumption during this process (see Figure 3-19). Carefully consider the resources you're consuming when you're binding a DataGrid to a DataSet with the following code:

```
private void Page_Load (object sender, System.EventArgs e)
{
    SqlConnection cn = new SqlConnection("server=.;database=pubs;uid=sa;pwd=");
    SqlCommand cm = new SqlCommand("select * from authors", cn);
    SqlDataAdapter da = new SqlDataAdapter(cm);

    DataSet ds = new DataSet();

    da.Fill(ds);
    DataGrid1.DataSource = ds.Tables[0];
    DataGrid1.DataBind();
}
//Page Rendering…
```

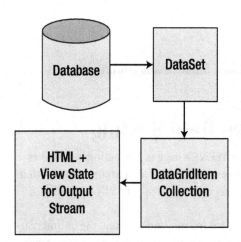

Figure 3-19. *Consumption of resources while data binding*

The first hit you take on the web server's memory is when you call Fill on the DataAdpater. This marshals your entire result set from the database into the process space of the web server. The DataSet carries not only the current values as read from the database, but also the original values as the data was read out of the database, as well as metadata about the structure of the DataTable objects contained in its TablesCollection. The DataSet is a very powerful object, but it's also a very fat object. You take a hit whenever you load one into memory. If you're doing this on your home page, you're taking this hit not once, but once for each user that comes to your site. But wait, it gets worse.

The next thing you do is set the DataSource of the DataGrid and call DataBind. As we just went over, this creates an in-memory collection of DataGridItems. This collection is probably just as large as your DataSet. If you're only outputting a couple of columns, maybe it won't be as large. If you're using a complex column template with a lot of markup, the size of this collection could exceed the size of the `DataSet`. So at this point you've got about a 2X hit on the web server memory (X being the size of your result set).

After that, your code is done executing. Your `DataSet` goes out of scope, but the `DataGrid` won't go out of scope until you're done rendering. Furthermore, the `DataSet` hangs around on the managed heap until the garbage collector does a couple of sweeps, which probably won't happen until after your rendering is complete. So as you enter the rendering stage of your `Page` object, we're still holding onto memory resources of the web server equal to approximately twice the size of the result set.

When the `DataGrid` renders, it does a couple of things. First, it transforms its `DataGridItem` collection into HTML. This is, again, probably as big as your initial result set, so you're at 3X memory consumption. Then the grid squirrels away all of the `DataGridItem`s into the `ViewState` of the page. After all, it will need these to restore its state when a postback occurs. If it didn't hold onto these, the grid would need to be rebound on every postback. 4X the size of your result set in web server memory resources is consumed. Swap out X for a 250K result set and multiply that by your number of concurrent users. You can see this rather innocuous operation gets very expensive very quickly.

So what do you do? You have a number of options. Which one you employ depends upon your requirements.

The first option is to use a `DataReader` instead of a `DataSet`. A `DataSet` is an in-memory representation of your result set. Having this in memory is very nice for a number of things, such as sorting, filtering, caching, modifying, and marshaling. However, in this case, you're doing none of those things. In fact, a `DataReader` is ideal for binding operations when you're generating markup. You don't need all that data in memory at once! A `DataReader` reads a row at a time from the database, and then discards it. So as you move through the result set, you maintain a nice low memory footprint, equal to the size of one row of your result set.

The `DataReader` is not suited for all purposes. You can only read forward through the `DataReader` once. You cannot modify data. You cannot cache a pointer to the `DataReader` or marshal it across processes. When you have the need to do these things, by all means use a `DataSet`. Just don't go to the `DataSet` unless you have a specific requirement that drives you there.

The next thing you can do is disable the `ViewState` on the `DataGrid`. `ViewState` is nice, but for a `DataGrid` it's generally too expensive, especially if you have dial-up users. Not only does it bloat the size of the response stream, but also the whole thing gets sent back to the server when a postback occurs, so it bloats the size of any subsequent HTTP request on a postback as well. Your page is generally going to get better performance by rebinding the grid when the page posts back. This won't work for editable grids, but for most of the rest of the functionality, this pattern should serve you fine. Of course, if you're writing an Intranet application and it's only ever going to run on a 100-mbps connection, `ViewState` bloat might not be a big deal, and you may get better performance using it than re-binding on every postback. These options should be put under a load that approximates the conditions in your production environment as closely as possible, and then you can see which one is faster. (See Chapter 4 for further discussion of `ViewState`, and the new 2.0 feature, `ControlState`, which helps to manage this problem in many circumstances.)

You can also mitigate the impact of both the `DataSet` size and the resources the `DataGrid` consumes by binding to smaller result sets. If this isn't an option because you have large result sets, then use the custom paging feature of the `DataGrid`, and implement paging at the database level. The automatic paging feature of the `DataGrid` is *not* a good solution to the problems we're speaking of, as it requires binding to the entire result set on every postback, and then just whittles down the visible rows to the selected page. (However, default paging can work alright with a cached DataSet, as we show in a bit). With custom paging, you can have the database return a single page of data at a time, and display only that page to the user. This saves on the network traffic between the database server and the web server, minimizes the size of the DataSet, and reduces the DataGrid's consumption of resources for its DataGridItem collection, the rendered HTML, and the ViewState. (In Chapter 11 we'll take a look at the new Data Source Controls and the Web Controls that bind to them [like the GridView], and examine their behavior and interaction with ViewState across postbacks.)

And finally, if there's high contention for a single resource, get it out of the database at once and programmatically put it into the Cache. This significantly reduces the footprint, because all users will now share a single copy of the DataSet. The DataSet can still be filtered in-memory if different users require seeing different subsets of the data. Put the superset into the memory, and then filter it down on a per-user or per- page basis.

You should also test this strategy by putting it under load, given in-memory filtering of the DataSet doesn't perform as well as querying the database, *even when you factor in the network round-trip*. This is especially true for large result sets (DataTables with more than 50,000 rows). (See Chapter 11 for details on the new Cache dependency types, which allow the Cache to automatically purge entries as changes are made to the database data.)

Capturing the Rendered Output Stream

The Page object renders and sends the generated HTML down the IIS output stream. However, the rendering behavior is publicly exposed, and that stream can be captured and sent to other output formats.

This may be useful if you're pregenerating a website: You can render all permutations and combinations of the output of the site and write them to disk or send them to the database. You can have specialized pages that dynamically generate output once, and then store it in a static ASCX file for use as a User Control on another page.

■ **Tip** The author of this chapter originally discovered the capturing of the rendered output stream capability when he had a *digital signature* requirement. When users selected a check box and filled in their names, their digital signatures were to be treated legally as their real signatures. In order to audit the "signing" of the page, the HTML needed to be captured "exactly as the user was seeing it" and put it into the database. He scratched his head on this for a while, but then realized that because of the ViewState maintenance, he could call Render on the page when the postback occurred and the output *would look just as it had to the users when they submitted it*. He created a file with this markup, sent it into the document management system, and redirected the users to a page thanking them for signing away their first born.

But perhaps the most useful thing to do with the captured rendered output is to pack the HTML into the body of an e-mail message and send the web page to somebody via Simple Mail Transfer Protocol (SMTP). This is what we're doing on Intertech Training's website. Figure 3-20 shows a page displaying a course outline.

Figure 3-20. *Course outline from* www.IntertechTraining.com

Users can click the E-mail button, type their e-mail addresses into a text box on a pop-up dialog, and get the same course outline delivered to their inboxes, shown in Figure 3-21.

This is amazingly easy to do. The same User Control generates the outline whether the output is going to the Web or getting packed into the body of a mail message. Here's the code that captures the Page rendering and sends it off via SMTP.

```
StringBuilder sb = new StringBuilder();
HtmlTextWriter t = new HtmlTextWriter(new StringWriter(sb));
this.Render(t);

string s = sb.ToString();
MailMessage m =new MailMessage();

m.BodyFormat = MailFormat.Html;
m.From = "Enrollment@IntertechTraining.com";
m.To = txtEmail.Text;
m.Subject = "Course Description";
m.Body = s;
SmtpMail.SendEmail(m);

Response.Write("<body onload='window.close();'>");
Response.End();
```

Figure 3-21. *Course outline as delivered via e-mail*

If you've ever created a Custom Control, you know that the Render method expects an instance of an HtmlTextWriter. This type is handy for easing the programmatic generation of HTML. In this case, it's the key to capturing the output stream. The first couple of lines of code create an instance of the HtmlTextWriter, but instead of using the IIS output stream, it uses a StringBuilder and a StringWriter. This effectively has all of the controls send their output into the character buffer of the string builder instead of down the output stream.

The next line simply calls Render and passes the HtmlTextWriter. The next few lines create and configure the mail message that will contain the rendered output. Notice the BodyFormat property is being set to MailFormat.Html. Failure to do this will send raw markup as the body of your mail message (although your users will see this anyway if their mail clients do not support HTML e-mail, but that's *sooo* 20th century). The body of the message is created by converting the StringBuilder's buffer into a string.

The last very important point to notice is that the processing is then terminated by calling Response.End, but not before a little JavaScript gets sent down the pipe instructing the dialog to close itself. You can also terminate the process by redirecting the user to another page. You cannot allow the Page to enter its rendering process again, as the Page has already rendered and will throw an exception if asked to do so a second time.

Summary

You've seen in this chapter how the core structure of the Page object is the control tree. The control tree is exposed by the System.Web.UI.Control type, so all controls you use expose their own control collection. This is how the control tree models the hierarchy of your HTML document. Markup without the runat=server attribute gets flattened into a LiteralControl in this control tree. So the Page object is nothing but a big state machine, and the code you write alters the state of this control tree, so that when the page finally renders, you get the HTML you need.

Deployment and compilation are problematic in version 1.x. Microsoft has added several features to the environment to address these issues, including a new deployment tool, dynamic compilation, and the ability to precompile an application in place or before deployment.

When you're working with all of the Web Controls, User Controls, and custom controls that may be in the control tree, on top of base types sitting between your pages and the Page type, the timing of processing can become very complex. Several PreEventName and EventNameComplete events have been added to the Framework to help you manage this complexity.

Nothing is committed to the output stream until the page renders, so you can make any changes to the control tree that you need until the page does render. The PreRenderComplete event is your last chance to affect the output stream. Because of this control tree infrastructure, data binding can be a memory intensive operation. You have a number a ways to control this rampant consumption, including turning off the ViewState of the bound control.

Finally, instead of sending the output stream back to IIS, you saw how you can capture it, and compel it to do your bidding.

CHAPTER 4

■■■

ViewState and Scripting

ASP.NET is intrinsically a server-side technology. All of the code that goes into creating a Web Form executes on the web server. The entire .NET Framework is geared toward generating markup compliant with the HTML 4.0 specification (www.w3.org). There's no facility for spawning a .NET process on the client. With ASP and COM there are ActiveX controls. With Java there are applets. With .NET—*nada*.

While this may strike some as an omission, it's actually by design. ASP.NET is designed for creating web applications that cast the widest possible net for supporting the browsing public. The presupposition is that the .NET Framework *is not installed on the client*. If the Framework is installed on your entire client base, and you want to leverage the power of .NET in that process space, then smart clients—a hybrid model that combines the advantages of a web-based deployment model with the richness of a Win32 application interface—is the development model you need to be looking at.

This does not leave you, however, without options for dynamic behavior on the client. The HTTP 4.0 specification defines many advanced features of the protocol (think of the richness of HTML Forms), and JavaScript (an Ecma standard with broad cross-browser support) is at your disposal, as well as the rich feature set that's exposed via Cascading Style Sheets (CSS).

The ASP.NET Framework leverages and supports these features extensively. All page postbacks actually occur via a JavaScript function that the page-rendering process generates whenever there's a form element with the runat=server element present on a Web Form. And the state maintenance done across postbacks that cannot be accomplished with standard HTTP Post elements uses an HTML hidden input named ViewState.

So while there's no support for executing .NET code within the browser, nothing from your browser bag of tricks is taken away from you when you're using the Framework. Additionally, there's generally some .NET code you can leverage server side that supports using standard browser features.

In this chapter we'll first examine ViewState closely. Most Web Form developers are familiar with this hidden input, and almost all love and take advantage of the state maintenance features it affords them. Here, we'll take a closer look at exactly how ViewState works, some performance impacts to be aware of, enhancements that have been added in version 2.0, and advanced strategies for leveraging and managing it.

In the latter half of the chapter, we'll take a look at using JavaScript in your ASP.NET application. Whether you're shipping static script files to the browser or dynamically generating script code from your Web Forms, we'll show you how the Framework supports and aids these efforts. We'll also take a look at the new capability of ASP.NET 2.0 to do asynchronous "out-of-band" callbacks to the server via script, making the highly coveted "partial page refresh" easily attainable in a variety of contexts.

The Role of ViewState in ASP.NET

Creating rich functionality using ASP.NET requires much less code than it does using ASP and other web development environments. You realize a large portion of this savings through the "state maintenance" the Framework provides. This accounts for, among other things, a drop-down list's capability to maintain the entries in the list across postbacks, all HTML input controls being able to maintain their values across postbacks, and, in more advanced cases, the capability of the DataGrid to maintain its entire HTML table when one of its events causes a postback.

The magic of ViewState is accomplished with the aid of a hidden input named __VIEWSTATE.

```
<input type="hidden" name="__VIEWSTATE" id="__VIEWSTATE"
 value="/wEPDwUJNzgzNDMwNTMzZGTpOBWhvZM7mmZGfhpcnI4aNOFFbw==" />
```

All controls on a page can put whatever values they want into this hidden input. The Framework manages these values, basically as a collection of named value pairs. The Framework also manages delimiting values put into ViewState through different controls on the page. It also manages encrypting and decrypting the values before they go to the client and when they're posted back to the server. This means that the Framework provides a complete layer of abstraction between the consumer of ViewState and the details of its actual implementation. This makes using ViewState very easy from custom controls or from the code for a Web Form.

Let's start by examining how one of the built-in Web Controls uses ViewState. We'll take a look at the DropDownList control. It maintains the entries in its list across postbacks using ViewState. For each list item that's in the collection of list item objects, the display name, its underlying value, and whether or not it's visible is added to ViewState. ViewState is nothing more than a simple state bag, or collection of tuples. So the DropDownList has an entry in ViewState for its ListItemCollection value, and that value is a collection of tuples, one for each ListItem in the collection. Each of those values, in turn, is a triplet, containing the name, value, and whether or not the field is visible.

This organization scheme results in a hierarchical tree of tuple collections, where each control gets its own node of the tree to squirrel away its own values. When the state of the control tree is being saved, each control in the page's control tree has its SaveViewState method called. This is a virtual method of the Control class, and so any control developer can write an override for it.

Understand that the Microsoft engineer who wrote the code for the DropDownList did so exactly the same way someone creating a custom Web Control for her own application would, by interacting with the property bag interface.

You can see the impact the DropDownList has on the resulting HTML in a couple of different ways. First, there's the trace output report that shows you a control-by-control report of the size each control adds to ViewState (see Figure 4-1).

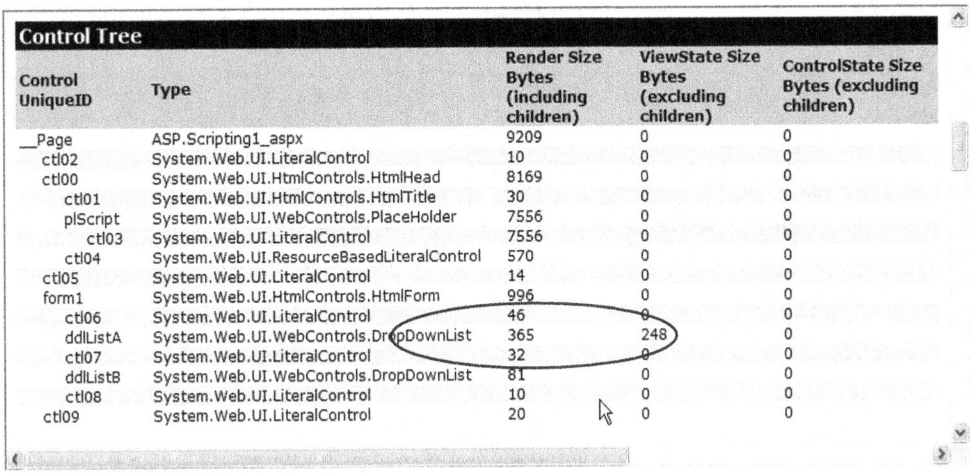

Control Tree

Control UniqueID	Type	Render Size Bytes (including children)	ViewState Size Bytes (excluding children)	ControlState Size Bytes (excluding children)
__Page	ASP.Scripting1_aspx	9209	0	0
ctl02	System.Web.UI.LiteralControl	10	0	0
ctl00	System.Web.UI.HtmlControls.HtmlHead	8169	0	0
ctl01	System.Web.UI.HtmlControls.HtmlTitle	30	0	0
plScript	System.Web.UI.WebControls.PlaceHolder	7556	0	0
ctl03	System.Web.UI.LiteralControl	7556	0	0
ctl04	System.Web.UI.ResourceBasedLiteralControl	570	0	0
ctl05	System.Web.UI.LiteralControl	14	0	0
form1	System.Web.UI.HtmlControls.HtmlForm	996	0	0
ctl06	System.Web.UI.LiteralControl	46	0	0
ddlListA	System.Web.UI.WebControls.DropDownList	365	248	0
ctl07	System.Web.UI.LiteralControl	32	0	0
ddlListB	System.Web.UI.WebControls.DropDownList	81	0	0
ctl08	System.Web.UI.LiteralControl	10	0	0
ctl09	System.Web.UI.LiteralControl	20	0	0

Figure 4-1. `ViewState` *on the trace output report*

This provides a good breakdown of the relative sizes, but unfortunately there's no total for the `ViewState` value. The easiest way to measure this is to use the built-in functionality of your web browser. While viewing any ASP.NET page from the browser, choose View ➤ Source. From the instance of Notepad displaying the markup, choose File ➤ Save As… and write the file out anywhere on your file system (i.e., **c:\tmp.htm**). Now add `EnableViewState=false` to the page directive:

```
<%@ Page language="c#"
              CodeFile="ViewStateIE.aspx.cs"
              Inherits="APressWebWork.ViewStateIE"
              EnableViewState=false %>
```

Go back to the browser, refresh the page, view the source again, and write the markup out to another file. The difference in the sizes of these files lets you know the total size of `ViewState` for the page.

Let's look a little more closely at exactly what's stored in `ViewState`. You'll start by adding a `textbox` control to a Web Form, and setting its `EnableViewState` property to `false`. You'll also add some simple code to the `Load` event trap, to show whether the request is a postback or a first request.

```
<%@ Page Language="C#"
        CompileWith="ViewStateIE.aspx.cs"
        ClassName="ViewStateIE_aspx"
        Trace="true" %>
<html>
<head runat="server">
    <title>ViewStateIE</title>
</head>
<body>
    <form id="form1" runat="server">
```

```
        <asp:TextBox Runat=server ID=txtDemo EnableViewState=false />
    </form>
</body>
</html>
```

And here are the contents of the code-behind:

```
public partial class ViewStateIE_aspx : System.Web.UI.Page
{
    void Page_Load(object sender, EventArgs e)
    {
        if (this.IsPostBack)
        {
            lblOutput.Text = "Postback";
        }
        else
        {
            lblOutput.Text = "First Request";
        }
    }
}
```

When you request the page, type something into the input and hit return. A postback occurs and you can see that the TextBox has maintained its value (see Figure 4-2).

Figure 4-2. *The test page after a postback*

This is what comes to mind for a lot of folks when state maintenance is mentioned. But for this control, you've disabled ViewState (by setting EnableViewState=false). You can verify this on the trace report, where it's reported that the textbox has contributed zero bytes to ViewState. So how was the value maintained across postbacks? An input of type text sends its value to the server whenever an HTML Form is submitted. This is, of course, the underlying architecture of a Web Form postback. The ASP.NET Framework will leverage this whenever it can in the service of state maintenance. Aside from input values, text area input, and select elements, not much more state information is naturally included in a post. You can easily modify the demo code to demonstrate this. In this code, you'll set a CSS attribute only on the first rendering of the page:

```
void Page_Load(object sender, EventArgs e)
{
    if (this.IsPostBack)
    {
```

```
        lblOutput.Text = "Postback";
    }
    else
    {
        txtDemo.BackColor = System.Drawing.Color.LightSkyBlue;
        lblOutput.Text = "First Request";
    }
}
```

So on the first rendering of the page, the back color of the TextBox is set to light blue (see Figure 4-3).

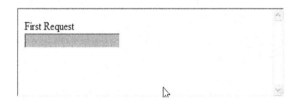

Figure 4-3. *First rendering of the page setting a CSS attribute programmatically*

On postbacks, the back color will not be set. The line of code setting the back color will not execute, and the TextBox will render with its default background color (see Figure 4-4).

Figure 4-4. *The test page after a postback*

Now let's turn ViewState on and rerun the tests. The page looks the same on the first request. Notice now that some bytes are being consumed by the control in ViewState (see Figure 4-5).

Now when you enter a value and do a postback, the back color of the TextBox is maintained, in addition to the field value. The field value is still maintained using information in the HTTP Post, whereas you've used ViewState to maintain the CSS value.

Web Control properties that render as an inline CSS Style attribute in the resulting HTML are but one example of control state information that must be tracked in ViewState. The collection of list items for a list control is another good example, as you saw earlier. Since the only piece of information about a list that automatically gets sent to the server when a post occurs is the value of the control; anything else that needs to be tracked across postbacks must be put into ViewState.

Control Tree

Control UniqueID	Type	Render Size Bytes (including children)	ViewState Size Bytes (excluding children)	ControlState Size Bytes (excluding children)
__Page	ASP.ViewStateIE_aspx	548	0	0
ctl02	System.Web.UI.LiteralControl	10	0	0
ctl00	System.Web.UI.HtmlControls.HtmlHead	44	0	0
ctl01	System.Web.UI.HtmlControls.HtmlTitle	31	0	0
ctl03	System.Web.UI.LiteralControl	14	0	0
form1	System.Web.UI.HtmlControls.HtmlForm	460	0	0
ctl04	System.Web.UI.LiteralControl	10	0	0
lblOutput	System.Web.UI.WebControls.Label	41	36	0
ctl05	System.Web.UI.LiteralControl	16	0	0
txtDemo	System.Web.UI.WebControls.TextBox	88	36	0
ctl06	System.Web.UI.LiteralControl	14	0	0
ctl07	System.Web.UI.LiteralControl	20	0	0

Figure 4-5. *Our test page with* `ViewState` *enabled for the textbox*

It doesn't follow, however, that in order to use Web Controls properties you must leave `ViewState` enabled. Properties that are set from markup (that is, attributes set on the Web Control in the actual ASPX page) don't need `ViewState` to maintain these values across postbacks. As you saw in Chapter 3, the markup actually becomes a piece of code that gets executed at runtime. Each attribute set from control declarations in the markup becomes a line of code calling a property `set` method in the generated code. This code gets executed with each page request, postback or not.

So you need `ViewState` when you interact with controls programmatically from a branch of code that executes only on the first request for a page, but you want those changes to persist across postbacks. It follows, then, that your choices are to leverage `ViewState` or to place code in a branch of logic that executes with every request of the page. In the example of setting the back color of the textbox, it doesn't make much difference if you send an additional 36 bytes to the client or execute one additional line of code with each postback. Where it does start to matter more is with operations that are more computationally intense or (perhaps more commonly) when an extra network hop is involved, such as when you go to the database to get a set of values to use in a data-binding operation.

Once you peel back the layers of abstraction that exist between the developer and the actual implementation of `ViewState` functionality, how and when to use `ViewState` becomes a question of resource consumption and bandwidth that's familiar whenever state must be maintained in a web application. When maintaining state in a web application, you basically have three choices: the client, the web server, or (to accommodate a Web Farm) a server-side location out-of-process to the web server. We list the pros and cons for each location in Table 4-1.

A lot of these choices are driven by the type of state information being maintained and the requirements of your specific application. You must make different choices for state information shared across all users vs. state information that's user specific. Some choices are eliminated when a single point of failure isn't an option. If you must accommodate users with cookies disabled, your choices become seriously constrained. In Table 4-1, you can see where `ViewState` firmly lands in the scheme of things. It's a page-specific, user-specific, client-side state maintenance mechanism.

Table 4-1. *Pros and Cons of State Maintenance Locations in a Web-Based Application*

State Location	Pros	Cons	Examples
Client	Not consuming any server-side resources State information "pinned" to client that the information is about	Increases request and response sizes Page specific (hidden inputs only)	Cookie Hidden inputs ASP.NET ViewState (layer of abstraction on top of a hidden input)
Web server	Lives closest to process servicing request Does not increase request or response sizes	Consumes web server resources Can be problematic in a Web Farm Must still have client-side mechanism to tie state to requestor	ASP session ASP.NET session (with mode set to InProc)
Server side, out-of-process	Does not consume web server resources Does not increase request or response size Can be configured to work in a Web Farm	Process hop can cause a performance hit Network hop can cause a performance hit Must still have client-side mechanism to tie state to requestor	Database ASP.NET session (with mode set to StateServer or SQLServer)

When evaluating your use of ViewState and the resources it's consuming, be sure to take a balanced approach. There are many people who view the source for a page with a significant amount of ViewState, and based on the number of rows it takes Notepad to display it, become shocked and immediately assume it's totally unacceptable. However, you may want to consider that 4K, for example, isn't that much data. This increases the payload of data being sent in a connection that's already established to the web server for a request it's already processing. Contrast that with an image. An image frequently is greater than 4K in size. How many images are included on your home page? Amazon.com has more than 50. Each of these images is *an additional round trip to the server*, not just a few K more for a request that's already being serviced.

So the point is that ViewState isn't that expensive in regard to resource consumption when you consider the typical way web sites are built today. The big difference is that ViewState increases not just the response payload, but the request payload as well (when a postback occurs). This makes it more like a cookie than an image. However, cookies are sent to the server with every request (including image requests), whereas ViewState is sent only as part of the HTTP Post that makes up the submission of a form (aka a postback). As a matter of fact, Amazon.com hosts their images on a different domain than the one the server markup comes from, in part to lose cookie transmission on image requests.

As a final corollary, don't misconstrue this point as an argument that you should ignore all of the warnings about ViewState. When it's 40K instead of 4K, you have much more cause for concern. When a control isn't using or doesn't need the feature, then it should, of course, be turned off. Just be sure to take a balanced approach with your evaluation of the feature as a resource consumer. As you'll see in the sections that follow, version 2.0 of the Framework addresses some large drawbacks that came to light in 1.1 applications, making the feature useful in even more contexts.

The ViewState Value

The actual value of the __VIEWSTATE hidden input is hashed and then encrypted by the Framework before it is sent to the browser. The Framework does the encryption for you to secure the value and to prevent a malicious user from posting a spoofed value to the server, possibly tricking an application into performing work it would not normally do.

The algorithm for hashing the value has changed from version 1.1 to version 2.0 of the Framework. We'll take a look at that in the next section. The new algorithm produces a smaller string for encryption, resulting in a smaller ViewState size overall.

There are a few different types of encryption you can use. You can choose from SHA1, MD5, or Triple-DES.

The key used for the encryption and decryption of the data exists on the web server. The Framework does the encryption not only for ViewState data, but also for the value of an authentication ticket cookie when using Forms-based authentication—as well as to protect session data when it's out of process. Since there's no facility to change or add items to ViewState from the client, there's no need for the client to ever be able to read the value. The key's sole purpose is to restore state when it's posted back to the server. So the server uses a key to encrypt the value, it's sent to the client (where it's truly meaningless) and then it's posted back to the server, where it's unencrypted and used to restore the state of any controls that put values into ViewState when first rendering.

The default behavior is for the Framework to automatically generate the 128-character key value used for encryption. This can become a problem in a Web Farm. Consider a request that server A services that uses its own generated key to encrypt ViewState data. The user posts the page back to the server, and the load-balancing algorithm routes the request to server B. This server uses its own auto-generated key to try and decrypt ViewState, it fails, and a run-time error is thrown.

To avoid this, when you're using a Web Farm, the load balancer must use *sticky sessions* (so each user is routed back to the same server once he or she has made an initial request), or you must manually specify the key value to use for encryption and decryption within the Machine.config file for each server in the Farm. You do this using the <machineKey> element. This configuration element is also where the encryption type is specified. Here we see a sample machine key element, with the key values truncated for brevity.

```
<machineKey
    validationKey="F1213F81D...AD2D58F8FB0D9096F"
    decryptionKey="E177A93C...0A608553FA73FDD99"
    validation="SHA1"
/>
```

This element is then added to the <system.web> section of the Machine.config or the Web.config file at the root of the web server. While you can add it to the configuration file of an individual IIS application, this would only make sense in an environment where different encryption is being used for different applications in the same Web Farm.

■**Note** See the SDK article http://support.microsoft.com/default.aspx?scid=kb;en-us;313091 for a detailed explanation and nifty piece of code that randomly generates this entire declaration for you.

2.0 ViewState Enhancements

As developers write applications and put them into production, many things about ViewState that were not known or realized during the original design of ASP.NET come to light. Real-world applications always do this. By talking with and listening to developers, Microsoft has been able to identify some of these biggest problems in version 1.x, and then address them in version 2.0 of the Framework.

1.x Problem: Action Attribute Constraints

The HTML specification states that when an HTML Form is submitted, the browser automatically navigates to the URL the Action attribute specifies on the form declaration. The values for any inputs contained on the form are sent along as part of the request. If the method attribute is set to GET, the values will be appended to the URL as query string values. If the method attribute is set to POST, the values will be packed into the header of the request (as *named-value pairs*).

In ASP.NET version 1.x, the architecture is designed so that the action attribute is always set to the rendering page, causing the web browser to navigate *back to the page that originally generated the response*. This is the ASP.NET definition of a postback. A form is submitted to the page that originally rendered the output stream. Many of the best features of ASP.NET (like state maintenance and server-side event traps) depend upon this one presupposition.

This is a big change from traditional ASP, where the coding model made such a mess of things so quickly that you frequently had to dedicate a page to each stage of processing a transaction with the user. The first page might render the interface for a user to provide information for the transaction. That page would post to another page that would validate and process the transaction. Depending on how things went, that page might redirect to a success page or render an error message when something went wrong. In some application patterns, an ASP page was nearly analogous to a function call in a procedural program.

In ASP.NET it's much easier to put a lot of functionality into a single page. The separation of code from content is a large part of this reason. This leaves the page with the markup containing only markup, and isolates the code in another physical file. Server-side event traps also greatly increase the readability and maintainability of a page, making it very easy to find where particular events are processed and easy to read much of the code and understand what may invoke it. Add to this the fact that you can actually use *types* (as opposed to VBScript Variants), that the page can be compiled before it's executed (as opposed to interpreted at runtime), better reuse mechanisms, and the fact that you have to declare variables (what a radical notion!), it's easy to see why many developers quickly made the adjustment to having to post to the same page that rendered the content in the first place.

But sometimes it's nice to use a form's action to navigate to another page. Having HTML inputs on a page is a great way to maintain state, and the layer of abstraction created for the ViewState mechanism makes this a great programming convenience. But because of this particular architectural constraint, it's impossible to put a value into ViewState on one page and retrieve it from another. If you specify the action attribute on a Form element (or programmatically alter it using script on the client before submitting the form), the new target page cannot read the ViewState value that gets posted to it.

2.0 Solution: Cross-Page Postbacks

In ASP.NET 2.0, the ability to post to a different Web Form has been added. However, rather than having ViewState restored by the new target page, there's a new property of the Page type named PreviousPage. This property is also an instance of the Page class, and is an instance of the Page that did the cross-page postback (see Figure 4-6).

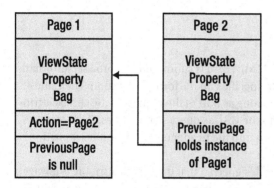

Figure 4-6. *Cross-page postback object reference*

Typically, you can set the action attribute of a Form element in your markup. In ASP.NET, however, the action attribute is always set to the page that's rendering the form. You accomplish cross-page postbacks with a bit of client-side script that's rendered by the Framework. To generate this script you need to set the PostBackUrl attribute of a Button Web Control. Here's a simple example of a page with a Button that posts to a different Web Form:

```
<%@ Page Language="VB"
        CodeFile="CrossPage.aspx.vb"
        Inherits="CrossPage" %>
<html>
<head id="Head1" runat="server">
    <title>Cross Poster</title>
</head>
<body>
    <form id="form1" runat="server">
        Make a page that has:<br />
        Background: <asp:TextBox Runat=server ID=txtBgcolor />
        <br />
        And displays: <asp:TextBox Runat=server ID=txtText />
        <br />
        In the color of:<asp:TextBox Runat=server ID=txtTextColor />
        <br />
        <asp:Button Runat=server ID=btn1
                        Text=Submit
                        PostBackUrl="~/CrossPage2.aspx" />
    </form>
</body>
</html>
```

You must give types careful consideration when one page does a postback to another. The biggest reason for this is that the page that does the posting is exposed on the target page via the PreviousPage attribute. This is an instance of a Page object, which is all well and good, but when it comes time to do something with the information on the Page that did the posting, you must make some assumptions about the that page. You may even find yourself casting the PreviousPage property into the type of the posting page. In doing so, you're creating a tight coupling between these pages, which may minimize reuse of the page that gets posted to, something you should be aware of during design.

Let's take a look at a few ways you can get to the information from the posted page. Perhaps the easiest is to use the FindControl method of the Page type. Here's some code you can use from the page that gets posted to (CrossPage2.aspx):

```
string bodyColor = ((TextBox)this.PreviousPage.FindControl("txtBgcolor")).Text;
```

Here a string is declared and set equal to the Text property of a TextBox. To obtain the reference to the TextBox, you pass its ID (as declared on CrossPage.aspx) to the FindControl method. Since FindControl returns a reference to a System.Web.UI.Control object (the base class of TextBox), you must explicitly cast it to the TextBox type in order to drill into the Text property.

This coupling doesn't mean that only CrossPage.aspx can use CrossPage2.aspx. The coupling it creates is this: Any page posting to CrossPage2 must contain a TextBox named txtBgcolor. This isn't necessarily a problem, and it doesn't mean CrossPage2 cannot be reused; it's just something you need to take into account during design.

This method of accessing the previous page is very "late bound." If txtBgcolor doesn't exist, this will not show up as a problem until runtime. To create a much looser coupling, you could check the return value of FindControl for nulls (the value returned when the control isn't found) and deal with this case is a separate branch of code:

```
TextBox txt = (TextBox)this.PreviousPage.FindControl("txtBgcolor");
string bodyColor;
if (txt == null)
    bodyColor = "Lime";
else
    bodyColor = txt.Text;
```

FindControl does a recursive descent of the page's control tree, which can be expensive if there are a lot of controls to search through and/or you're seeking references to many different controls. You're also doing a run-time type coercion, which could also fail if someone gives a control (like an input of type text) an ID of txtBgcolor.

When a stronger-typed reference to the previous page is required, you can use the PreviousPageType directive. Let's take a look at the markup for CrossPage2.aspx:

```
<%@ Page Language="C#"
        CompileWith="CrossPage2.aspx.cs"
        ClassName="CrossPage2_aspx" %>

<%@ PreviousPageType VirtualPath="~/CrossPage.aspx" %>
```

```
<html>
<head runat="server">
    <title> Cross-Posted To (CrossPage2) </title>
</head>
<body runat=server id=body>
    <form id="form1" runat="server">
        <asp:Label Runat=server id=lblOutput />
    </form>
</body>
</html>
```

In this markup, after the page directive, you're declaring that `CrossPage.aspx` is going to post to you. This doesn't just cause run-time coercion on the type of the `PreviousPage` attribute; it actually changes the type of the property. It even shows up during design time, giving you IntelliSense on the property while coding, and the Watch window and other coding conveniences while debugging.

Let's add a public property to `CrossPage`, which will return the color the user wants the text displayed as.

```
public System.Drawing.Color outputColor
{ get { return System.Drawing.Color.FromName(txtTextColor.Text); } }
```

This is a read-only property named `outputColor`. It's strongly typed as a `Color`. From `CrossPage2`, it's now possible to use a line of code to reference it.

```
lblOutput.ForeColor = PreviousPage.outputColor;
```

This is really interesting because you're not casting to an instance of `CrossPage` at run-time. *The `PreviousPage` property is now of type* `CrossPage_aspx`. There are many advantages to this over the `FindControl` strategy we looked at first. The property is strongly typed, giving you compile time checking and more run-time safety. The property provides better encapsulation of this value. The consuming page is concerned with neither the name of the control this property is gathered from, nor even that it gets gathered from a control at all. You could change `CrossPage` to use a `DrowDownList` of colors and the code on the consuming side wouldn't have to change at all. And obviously, you could add some safety code to the `get` method of the property, returning a default color when nothing is in the textbox or the value entered is not a valid color.

This polymorphism of the `PreviousPage` property is wired by the run-time engine during code generation. Visual Studio .NET is smart enough to pick it up in the IDE and give you some design-time productivity gains to boot.

You may also want access to values in `ViewState` of the posting page from the page you're posting to. With a reference to the `PreviousPage`, this may seem relatively straightforward at first. A line of code like this on `CrossPage2.aspx` may seem to be just the thing you need.

```
//This reference does not work because ViewState is a protected property
string s = PreviousPage.ViewState["SomeValue"].ToString();
```

This, however, will not compile. `ViewState` is a *protected* member of the `Page` class. This means it's only accessible from types using the `Page` type as a base class. When you're writing code in a code-behind file, you're creating a type that inherits from the `Page` class, and so the protected ViewState is in scope and is inherited for free from the base class. From a cross-page postback, however, you need to expose this ViewState value explicitly. Here's another property you'll add to the CrossPage code:

```
public string SomeValue
{ get
    {
    if (ViewState["SomeValue"] == null)
        return "SomeValue not set. ";
    else
        return ViewState["SomeValue"].ToString();
    }
}
```

This allows CrossPage2 to obtain a strongly typed reference to this value, again with better encapsulation, as CrossPage2 doesn't need to be concerned with where this value comes from.

If the ViewState entries are dynamic, and, therefore, cannot be known in advance, the entire state bag could be explicitly exposed to the consuming page.

```
public object GetViewStateValue(string ViewStateEntryName)
{ return ViewState[ViewStateEntryName]; }
```

Let's continue with the example, which demonstrates pulling information from the posting page using each of these techniques. You've seen the markup and most of the code for the posting page, which is named CrossPage.aspx. You'll add this code, which populates the SomeValue property you've exposed by pulling in a value from the query string:

```
//This is the page load of CrossPage, not CrossPage2
void Page_Load(object sender, EventArgs e)
{
    if (!this.IsCrossPagePostBack
        && Request.QueryString["SomeValue"] != null)
        this.ViewState["SomeValue"] =
            Request.QueryString["SomeValue"].ToString();
}
```

This code brings up some very interesting things to note about the lifetime of a Page object used in a cross-page postback. The first thing that this code checks is a new Boolean property of the page named IsCrossPagePostBack. This value is false when CrossPage is first created and true when CrossPage2 is first created after CrossPage posts to it.

Using this Boolean on the page being posted to (like CrossPage2) is very straightforward. You can design a page to accept cross-page postbacks, but have a default rendering behavior if it's requested with a fresh "get." The property can be used to calibrate which way to render. On a cross-page postback, realize also that IsCrossPagePostBack is true, while IsPostBack is false, so you can also design a page to accept a cross-page postback, as well as process postbacks of its own.

The page originating the post warrants a closer examination (CrossPage in this example). You can also design this page to postback to itself, and then, after completing a process, or some other precipitating event, do a post to a different page (a game could do a cross-page postback when the game is over to the high-score board and pass along the score, for example).

This makes the need for possibly checking the IsPostback property in the page load obviously enough, but when will the other Boolean, IsCrossPagePostback, ever be true? In order to see the answer, you have to think about what happens on CrossPage2 when CrossPage posts to it. Under the hood, a new instance of CrossPage is created. Even though there has not been a request for this page, and even though the page won't be expected to render any output, the page's life cycle is still kicked off; and so the page Load event still fires.

You can clearly see this behavior by putting a break point in the page Load trap of CrossPage. The debugger stops there the first time the page is requested, and stops there again when the user clicks the button, even though you're requesting a different page.

This is important to realize for a couple of reasons. Here you're short-circuiting logic that you would rather not see get executed on the postback. In this case, there would be no harm in letting the code execute, but if you were doing a read from the database, this would be a much bigger deal. You could also take some specific action to prepare for CrossPage2's processing.

Here's the complete code-behind for CrossPage2.aspx, which references CrossPage using the different techniques we've discussed:

```
protected void Page_Load(object sender, EventArgs e)
{
    //Straight reference to textbox that would break if
    //posting page does not have a textbox named txtText
    string output =
    string.Format("<h1>{0}</h1>",
    ((TextBox)this.PreviousPage.FindControl
    ("txtText")).Text);

    //This is safer code, that accounts for txtBgcolor
    //not being present and sets a default value
    TextBox txt = (TextBox)this.PreviousPage.FindControl("txtBgcolor");
    string bodyColor;
    if (txt == null)
        bodyColor = "Lime";
    else
        bodyColor = txt.Text;
    body.Attributes.Add("bgcolor", bodyColor);

    //Strong typed reference to previous page type
    //can leverage a public property
    lblOutput.ForeColor = PreviousPage.outputColor;
    lblOutput.Text = output;

    //ViewState is exposed via strong type property as well
    lblOutput.Text +=
        "<BR>Value from ViewState: "
        + this.PreviousPage.SomeValue;
}
```

In summary, this code is using the late-bound `FindControl` method to access a couple of field values, and then using the early-bound, property-based method to access a couple of others. The late-bound method creates a looser coupling between the page types, but could lead to more run-time errors and will perform more slowly. The early-bound method creates a tight coupling between the pages, but provides compile-time type checking, better encapsulation (and so a better object-oriented design), and improved performance.

1.x Problem: Fat Serialization

The Framework `Machine.config` file encodes and encrypts the `ViewState` value before packing it away as the value of the hidden input and sending it to the client. This is nice because it keeps the value secure, but the Base64 encoding can really cause the size of the field to bloat.

Let's examine a simple example of binding the `authors` table to a `DataGrid` using version 1.1 of ASP.NET. The `authors` table contains about 4K of data. You can see this opening a connection to the `pubs` database with Query Analyzer, selecting star from the `authors` table, and viewing the results as text (see Figure 4-7). When you write the results out to disk, the resulting file is 4K in size. In order to avoid any overhead of metadata for the report file, copy the data from the Query Analyzer window and paste it into Notepad. Write this out to disk as a file named `au_data.txt`.

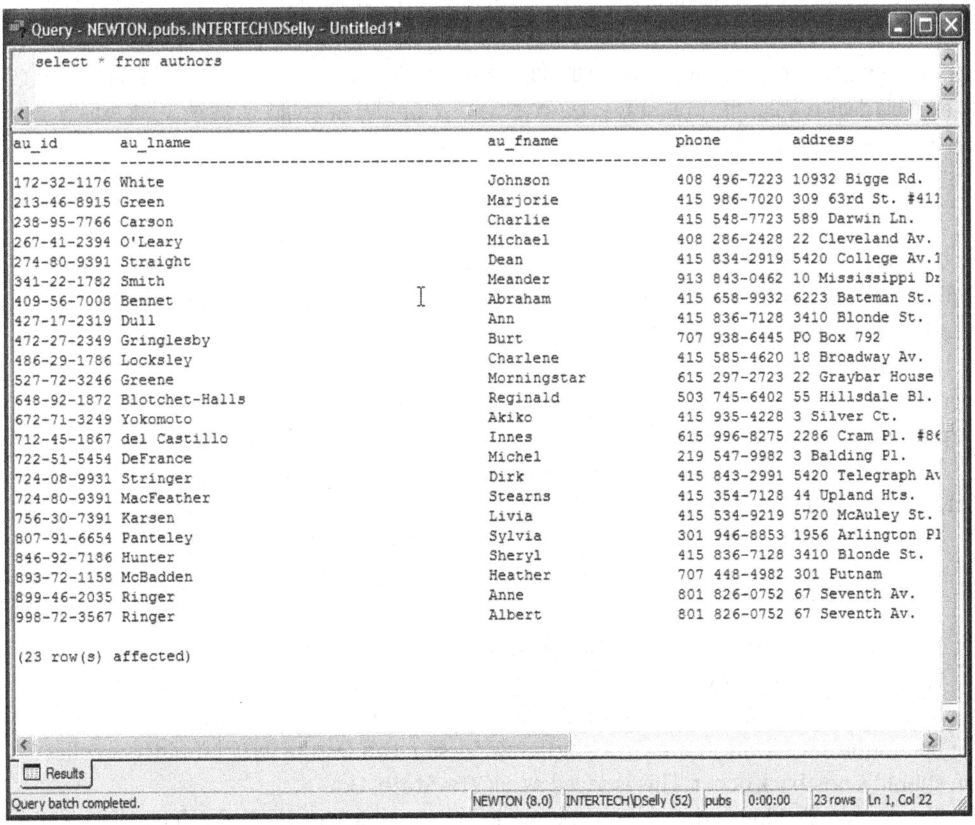

au_id	au_lname	au_fname	phone	address
172-32-1176	White	Johnson	408 496-7223	10932 Bigge Rd.
213-46-8915	Green	Marjorie	415 986-7020	309 63rd St. #411
238-95-7766	Carson	Charlie	415 548-7723	589 Darwin Ln.
267-41-2394	O'Leary	Michael	408 286-2428	22 Cleveland Av.
274-80-9391	Straight	Dean	415 834-2919	5420 College Av.
341-22-1782	Smith	Meander	913 843-0462	10 Mississippi Dr
409-56-7008	Bennet	Abraham	415 658-9932	6223 Bateman St.
427-17-2319	Dull	Ann	415 836-7128	3410 Blonde St.
472-27-2349	Gringlesby	Burt	707 938-6445	PO Box 792
486-29-1786	Locksley	Charlene	415 585-4620	18 Broadway Av.
527-72-3246	Greene	Morningstar	615 297-2723	22 Graybar House
648-92-1872	Blotchet-Halls	Reginald	503 745-6402	55 Hillsdale Bl.
672-71-3249	Yokomoto	Akiko	415 935-4228	3 Silver Ct.
712-45-1867	del Castillo	Innes	615 996-8275	2286 Cram Pl. #86
722-51-5454	DeFrance	Michel	219 547-9982	3 Balding Pl.
724-08-9931	Stringer	Dirk	415 843-2991	5420 Telegraph Av
724-80-9391	MacFeather	Stearns	415 354-7128	44 Upland Hts.
756-30-7391	Karsen	Livia	415 534-9219	5720 McAuley St.
807-91-6654	Panteley	Sylvia	301 946-8853	1956 Arlington Pl
846-92-7186	Hunter	Sheryl	415 836-7128	3410 Blonde St.
893-72-1158	McBadden	Heather	707 448-4982	301 Putnam
899-46-2035	Ringer	Anne	801 826-0752	67 Seventh Av.
998-72-3567	Ringer	Albert	801 826-0752	67 Seventh Av.

Figure 4-7. *The data from the* `authors` *table in Query Analyzer*

You'll marshal all of this data to the web server and transform it into HTML using the following code from the Page_Load of a Web Form:

```
private void Page_Load(object sender, System.EventArgs e)
{
    SqlConnection cn = new
    SqlCnnection("server=.;database=pubs;uid=sa;pwd=");
    SqlCommand cm = new SqlCommand("select * from authors", cn);

    DataGrid DataGrid1 = new DataGrid();
    this.FindControl("form1").Controls.Add(DataGrid1);
    cn.Open();
    DataGrid1.DataSource = cm.ExecuteReader();
    DataGrid1.DataBind();
    cn.Close();
}
```

Note In Version 2.0 of the Framework, Microsoft has shipped the GridView control. This Web Control is the replacement for and enhancement of the existing DataGrid. Because GridView has non-backwards compatible changes, and because Microsoft is making an effort to maintain backwards compatibility, it created a new control rather than enhancing the functionality of DataGrid. We use DataGrid here, since this example demonstrates the ViewState size in version 1.x. GridView would, however, work exactly the same for this example in 2.0.

You'll now compare the relative sizes of the pieces and parts of the output you've generated. Choose View ➤ Source from the browser. Choose File ➤ Save As from Notepad and write the entire page out to disk as a file named au_page.

Highlight all of the markup for the authors table, starting with <table> and ending with </table>. Open a new text document and copy and paste the table markup into it. Write this out to disk as a file named au_markup.txt.

Repeat the process, this time copying the value of the hidden input named __VIEWSTATE. Write this out to disk as a file named au_viewstate.txt.

Then, just for fun, add this line of code to the method above:

```
DataGrid1.EnableViewState = false;
```

Refresh the browser, view the source again, and save this one as au_page_noviewstate.txt.

What should the relative sizes of these files be? You have a result set from the database saved as au_data.txt. You've transformed it into markup, saved as au_markup.txt. This has also been squirreled away in ViewState by DataGrid, so it can restore its DataGridItem collection should a postback occur. This is saved as au_ViewState.txt.

Since you're dealing with three representations (data, markup, hashed values) of the same basic data, they should be about the same size, right? Not quite (see Figure 4-8).

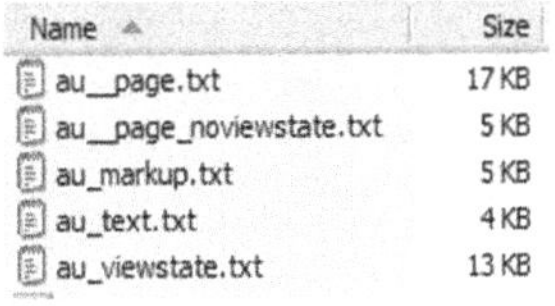

Name ▲	Size
au__page.txt	17 KB
au__page_noviewstate.txt	5 KB
au_markup.txt	5 KB
au_text.txt	4 KB
au_viewstate.txt	13 KB

Figure 4-8. *Sizes of different parts of your output, side-by-side for comparison*

Actually, they're not even close. While the data and the markup are about the same size, the ViewState data is more than twice as large. It's three times the size as the raw data! You can really see the effects of this on the resulting page size when you compare the total size of the output streams with ViewState on and off. ViewState more than triples the entire size of the output stream.

Now this example must be taken in context. This is a small page, with no other content. It isn't normally true that ViewState triples the size of the entire page, as, normally, there is markup on the page not related to DataGrid. Also, ViewState is data that's sent down with an existing connection (the connection for the markup of the page request). Many designers and web developers think nothing of adding a 12K image to a page, which is just as much data being sent *and* an additional network round trip.

No, the intended take-away from this is a concrete demonstration is how hashing and encoding the ViewState value causes its size to bloat.

2.0 Solution: Optimized Serialization

This is obviously a problem you'll need to address. In the previous example, ViewState would-n't be so bad if it would constrain itself to 4K or 5K. But an additional 13K? What would be worth it? In 1.x implementations, it's frequently a better option to rebind the grid on each and every postback instead of incurring the hit of sending the ViewState value down the pipe with each response and lugging it back with every postback.

So in 2.0, Microsoft fixed it. By optimizing the hashing and using less verbose encoding, the size of ViewState is dramatically reduced. You can repeat your experiment in 2.0 using the following page:

```
<%@ Page language="c#" %>
<%@ Import Namespace='System.Data.SqlClient' %>
    <script runat=server>
        private void Page_Load(object sender, System.EventArgs e)
        {
            SqlConnection cn = new SqlConnection
    ("server=.;database=pubs;uid=sa;pwd=");
            SqlCommand cm = new SqlCommand("select * from authors", cn);

            //DataGrid DataGrid1 = new DataGrid();
            GridView DataGrid1 = new GridView();
            //DataGrid1.EnableViewState = false;
            this.FindControl("form1").Controls.Add(DataGrid1);
            cn.Open();
            DataGrid1.DataSource = cm.ExecuteReader();
```

```
            DataGrid1.DataBind();
            cn.Close();
        }
    </script>
<HTML>
    <HEAD>
        <title>ViewStateSize</title>
    </HEAD>
    <body>
        <form id="Form1" method="post" runat="server">
        </form>
    </body>
</HTML>
```

■**Note** This optimization is dependant on the use of the new GridView instead of the old DataGrid, an important difference in functionality to be aware of!

Repeat the process of viewing the source and copying ViewState to a new instance of Notepad, and save a new file named au_ViewState_20.txt. You can see now that ViewState for exactly the same process has been reduced from 13K to 7K, almost a 50-percent reduction. The size is still larger than the raw data, because some metadata has to be present to map the raw data back to DataGrid and its internal structures.

1.x Problem: Losing All Properties When ViewState Is Off

During custom control development, to have your control correctly do its work, you may have a critical property that you need to put into ViewState that you pull out when a postback occurs. Problem is, ViewState can be turned off for any control. When this happens, your critical information doesn't get serialized into the ViewState and isn't present for you to process when the postback occurs.

2.0 Solution: Control State

Version 2.0 of the .NET Framework fixes this by separating state information for a control into two categories. ViewState still exists, and for GridView, the collection of items stored in the grid is still squirreled away here. There's a new "state bag" called ControlState. This is a place to put properties that are critical to the functioning of your custom control. The information is all put into the same hidden input. The big difference is when ViewState is turned off, ControlState is still tracked, and so the critical property you need to be present in order to correctly process a postback works just as you intended.

So ViewState is now just that, state information used to maintain what the user is viewing. ControlState is a separate dedicated state bag designed for information critical to the behavior of the control.

Although a few properties of existing controls are now stored in `ControlState` instead of `ViewState`, this feature will be most useful when you're doing custom control development. Some examples of existing properties moved into `ControlState` are the selected index of the list controls, and the edit, selected, and page index of `GridView`. `DataGrid` has not been upgraded to utilize `ControlState`.

Replacing ViewState Persistence

Sometimes the functionality of `ViewState` is sorely needed, though the performance hit from increasing the request and response size causes unacceptable performance degradation. When you find yourself needing the functionality, you have another option. You can replace the persistent location of the `ViewState` data.

In the shipping implementation of the Framework, an HTML hidden input is used as the persistent location for state information, as you've seen. This causes the information to be marshaled to the client, and when a postback occurs, it gets marshaled back.

To replace the `ViewState` persistence location, you'll use an abstract base class that inherits from the `Page` class. Any page where you need an alternate persistence location will then inherit from this class instead of directly from the `Page` class. In this new base class, you have then only to override two virtual members of the `Page` class:

```
protected override void SavePageStateToPersistenceMedium(object state)
protected override object LoadPageStateFromPersistenceMedium()
```

The first method is called toward the end of a page request. At this point in time, view state data has been gathered from all of the controls on the page. The default implementation of this method transforms the `object` passed in as an argument named `state` into a Base64 encoded `string`, encrypts it, and populates the value of the `__VIEWSTATE` hidden input in the output stream.

The second method is then called early in the processing of a postback. The default implementation of this method pulls the value from the hidden input, decrypts it, and deserializes it back into the `object` instance.

You'll replace this functionality by serializing the object into SQL Server instead of into the hidden input. The database you'll use will have a single table to store the object instance. You need to identify the user and the page where the data came from. To do this you'll use the full name of the page requested and create a hidden input of your own to store a key for the page. You'll use two values as a composite primary key for your state table. The definition of the table is shown in Figure 4-9.

Column Name	Data Type	Length	Allow Nulls
PageName	varchar	400	
SessionID	varchar	50	
StateData	image	16	✓

Figure 4-9. *The definition of the table to store* `ViewState` *information*

The database also has two stored procedures, one to save the state and one to retrieve it. These procedures do some management of these rows, but the table in Figure 4-9 would steadily grow over time and require a periodic task to purge rows that are no longer relevant. You could add a data column to record the last update and to delete older rows.

Note Find `PersistDB.sql` in the `Web04` project directory and execute it in Query Analyzer to create these database objects.

With your persistence medium in place, you only need to provide overrides of the base class methods. Here's the complete class (from `DB_ViewState.cs`):

```
using System;
using System.Web.UI.HtmlControls;
using System.IO;
using System.Web.UI;
using System.Data.SqlClient;
using System.Data;

public abstract class DB_ViewState : System.Web.UI.Page
{
    //Replace this with a connection string to your database
    private string connStr = "server=.;database=VS_Persist;uid=sa;pwd=";

    protected override void SavePageStateToPersistenceMedium(object state)
    {
        HtmlInputHidden vsk =
            (HtmlInputHidden)this.FindControl
            ("__VIEWSTATE_KEY");

        if (vsk == null)
        {
            vsk = new HtmlInputHidden();
            vsk.ID = "__VIEWSTATE_KEY";
            vsk.Value = Guid.NewGuid().ToString();
            this.Page.FindControl("Form1").Controls.AddAt(0, vsk);
        }
        //Use the limited object formatter to serialize
        //the instance into the memory stream
        LosFormatter bf = new LosFormatter();
        MemoryStream ms = new MemoryStream();
        bf.Serialize(ms, state);

        SqlConnection cn = new SqlConnection(connStr);
        SqlCommand cm = new SqlCommand("usp_SaveState", cn);
```

```csharp
    cm.CommandType = CommandType.StoredProcedure;

    cm.Parameters.Add(
        "@PageName",
        SqlDbType.VarChar, 400).Value =
        Request.Url.AbsoluteUri;

    cm.Parameters.Add(
        "@SessionID",
        SqlDbType.VarChar, 50).Value = vsk.Value;

    cm.Parameters.Add(
        "@StateData",
        SqlDbType.Image).Value = ms.ToArray();

    cn.Open();
    cm.ExecuteNonQuery();
    cn.Close();
}

protected override object LoadPageStateFromPersistenceMedium()
{
    if (Request.Params["__VIEWSTATE_KEY"] == null)
        return null;

    string viewstatekey =
        Request.Params["__VIEWSTATE_KEY"].ToString();

    SqlConnection cn = new SqlConnection(connStr);
    SqlCommand cm = new SqlCommand("usp_LoadState", cn);
    SqlDataReader dr = null;

    cm.CommandType = CommandType.StoredProcedure;

    cm.Parameters.Add(
        "@PageName",
        SqlDbType.VarChar, 400).Value =
        Request.Url.AbsoluteUri;

    cm.Parameters.Add(
        "@SessionID",
        SqlDbType.VarChar, 50).Value = viewstatekey;

    try
    {
        cn.Open();
        dr = cm.ExecuteReader();
```

```
        if (dr.Read())
        {
            LosFormatter bf = new LosFormatter();
            object data = bf.Deserialize
                (new MemoryStream((byte[])dr[0]));
            return data;
        }
        else
            return null;
    }
    finally
    {
        if (dr != null) dr.Close();
        cn.Close();
    }
}
}
```

Note Notice that you're using the `LosFormatter` to serialize your data into the database. This is the "limited object serializer" formatter. It's like the `BinaryFormatter`, but is highly optimized for strings, arrays, and hashtables.

Realize that there are only specific circumstances where this type of solution benefits your application. The first is, obviously, a thin client pipe. If you're writing an intranet application on a 100mbps LAN, you really don't need to worry about the size of ViewState. It's just not going to make that big of a difference.

Even with a thin client pipe, the extra round trip to the database must be taken into account. If you're not using a Web Farm, you can put a dedicated instance of SQL Server on the web server to act as an exclusive ViewState server. This saves you a network round trip, but still introduces a process hop.

If you're binding a grid, it may be just as expensive to marshal this state data to the database and back as it would be to rebind the grid with the original data. As with all things in application architecture, the solution that makes the most sense depends on your specific requirements and circumstance.

The class above will work in both 1.x and 2.0. It will be useful more often in 1.x implementations, as the introduction of ControlState in 2.0 provides a solution for many situations where ViewState was previously imperative but can now be disabled.

Post-Cache Substitution

Post-cache substitution is a handy feature that is designed for performance optimization. It dovetails with output caching. The functionality is exposed via a web control named Substitution, but you can think of this feature as a modification to the output caching infrastructure present in version 1.x of ASP.NET.

Output caching allows you to take the markup generated by a page object or user control and squirrel it away in the memory of the web server. You do this very simply by adding a directive to the top of the markup file.

```
<%@ OutputCache Duration=15 VaryByParam=None %>
```

The `Duration` attribute expresses the number of seconds the output should be cached. The `VaryByParam` attribute allows you to make different cache entries for different requests, creating a unique entry per query string value, for example.

When a page is output cached, the next time a request comes in for the page, the pregenerated markup is pulled from the cache and sent as the response to the request. This saves the time and expense of creating an instance of the page object and executing all of the code it contains, and can even save network hops to the database.

Output caching is screaming fast, as the results are in memory and the Framework doesn't even have to read a file from the disk (as it would for a static HTML document). The results are returned right from memory.

■**Note** Output caching has been a feature of the ASP.NET Framework since version 1.0. If you're not familiar with it, please see the SDK documentation on it. We don't give it full coverage in this section, as this is about the new feature of ASP.NET 2.0, post-cache substitution.

So let's suppose you have a page that is mostly static, with just a small bit of markup that needs to be dynamically generated with each request. That is, all of the markup for this page could be cached using the output caching feature, but a little remaining bit of the page needs to be dynamically generated with each incoming request.

Post-cache substitution accommodates this situation by allowing you to cache the entire page, but leave a certain part left out for regeneration with each incoming request.

The part of the page that shouldn't be cached is marked with a `Substitution` element. The content for this element is returned as a string from a static method you add to the code-behind of your page.

Let's take a look at a simple example. The page shown in Figure 4-10 displays the time that the code for the page was last executed on the left and the last time it was requested on the right.

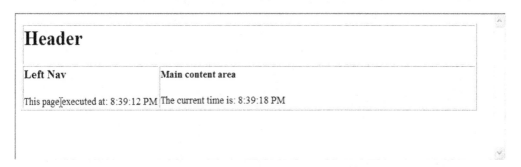

Figure 4-10. *Using post-cache substitution with output caching*

Here's the markup that generates this page:

```
<%@ Page CodeFile="SimpleSub.aspx.cs" Inherits="SimpleSub" %>
<%@ outputcache duration="15" varybyparam="none" %>
<html>
<head runat="server">
    <title>Simple Substitution</title>
</head>
<body>
    <form id="form1" runat="server">
        <table border=1>
            <tr>
                <td colspan=2><h1>Header</h1></td>
            </tr>
            <tr>
                <td width=30%>
                <h3>Left Nav</h3>
                This page executed at:
                <asp:Label runat=server ID=lblRendered />
                </td>
                <td>
                <h4>Main content area</h4>
                The current time is:
                <asp:Substitution runat=server ID=subTimestamp
                            MethodName='GetStamp' />
                </td>
            </tr>
        </table>
    </form>
</body>
</html>
```

Because of the OutputCache directive at the top of the page, the markup generated by this page will be cached for 15 seconds at a time. This means when a request comes in for this page, the code will run only once, and thereafter the same markup will be cached and returned for 15 seconds, during which time the page will not be executed again.

For the markup where the Substitution element is declared, however, the Framework will call the static method named by the MethodName attribute in the control declaration. The name of this method is up to you. There must be a method with this name in your code-behind, it must be declared as accepting an instance of HttpContext as an argument, and it must return a string. Here's the code behind for this sample page:

```
public partial class SimpleSub : System.Web.UI.Page
{
    public static string GetStamp(HttpContext context)
    {
        return DateTime.Now.ToLongTimeString();
    }
    protected void Page_Load(object sender, EventArgs e)
```

```
    {
        lblRendered.Text = DateTime.Now.ToLongTimeString();
    }
}
```

This means that even though most of the markup for this page is pregenerated and cached in the memory of the web server, each request will have the most current date and time inserted where the Substitution element is declared.

The extension to the output caching functionality provided by the post-cache substitution feature is a powerful facility that allows you to take a very fine grain of control over the performance of your pages. There's no reason you need to limit yourself to small pieces of markup when using this feature. Larger blocks of markup could be generated by the static method doing this work. Here's a sample method that's programmatically binding GridView and returning its rendered markup as a string.

```
public static string GetData(HttpContext context)
{
    GridView gv = new GridView();
    DataTable dt = getAuthorsDataTable();
    gv.DataSource = dt;
    gv.DataBind();
    cn.Close();
    StringBuilder sb = new StringBuilder();
    HtmlTextWriter t = new HtmlTextWriter(new StringWriter(sb));
    gv.RenderControl(t);
    return sb.ToString();
}
```

Creatively combining output caching a post-cache substitution will be a technique you can leverage to super-charge the performance of your ASP.NET 2.0 web applications.

Scripting

With ASP.NET, you don't generally write code that executes in the process space of the client. More often when you're using script, what you create using a managed language runs on the web server and dynamically generates client-side script. Oftentimes you'll use a control that generates client-side script based on how you've declared it; and as a developer you may not even be aware that it's leveraging client-side script to do its work.

Client-side script is very good at a number of things. It executes in the process space of the client, without requiring a trip across the network to talk to the server. This means it's fast. The work it does can happen instantly, with no delay for the user whatsoever. Combined with the object model exposed by DHTML and the power of CSS, you can create very rich functionality using script. Some common tasks you do with script are early validation of data entry; expanding, hovering, or moving ads and dialogs; pull-down menus; rollover highlights; and swapping out images.

Even if you've never learned how to code JavaScript, you can still leverage its power from your Web Forms. Every time you lay down a validation control on a page, it generates script on your behalf. There is a rich and broad set of canned, publicly available script that you can use (just choose View ➤ Source from your browser to see what we mean!). Many times we've written managed code to dynamically generate client-side script using an existing set of script libraries as a base, and added custom data as we generate the code. As an example, you can have interdependent drop-down lists, where the entries in list B depend on the choice users make in list A. Using JavaScript, you can dynamically populate list B when a choice is made in list A, without doing a round trip back to the server. The server-side code can dynamically generate the arrays that are used by the script, driven by a back-end data store.

This type of work is very easy to do in a postback, but for users with slow connections, a postback for this type of event (based on focus leaving a control) is very unnatural and interrupts the flow of their work. It's borderline unusable.

Generating Client-Side Script

Let's start with an interdependent drop-down list example. This page displays two drop-down lists. The first is a list of cities. When the user makes a selection from the list of cities, the second list is populated with a list of pool halls in that city. This is an example of something you can easily do with a postback. For the sake of performance and usability, we'll show you how do it with client-side script instead, eliminating the need for a round trip to the server.

This shows how, starting with some static script code that embodies the functionality you want, underlying data can be dynamically generated on the server. You'll start with this simple script, which represents an example of what you want to produce. You'll write code to write this code. You'll use this as a starting point, the same way you'd use a "wire frame" screen shot as a starting point for presentation tier development. You may also want to review the finished product, scripting1.aspx, in the Web04 project, to get an idea of where you're headed.

```
<html>
<head>
<SCRIPT LANGUAGE="JavaScript">
listsB = new Array;
valuesB = new Array;

listsB[0] = new Array;
listsB[0][0] = "A J Billiard Parlor";
listsB[0][1] = "Campus Room";
listsB[0][2] = "Champion Billiards";

valuesB[0] = new Array;
valuesB[0][0] = "33";
valuesB[0][1] = "34";
valuesB[0][2] = "35";

listsB[1] = new Array;
listsB[1][0] = "Amsterdam Billiard Club";
listsB[1][1] = "Bernardos Billar and Cafeteria";
listsB[1][2] = "Billiard Club";
listsB[1][3] = "Broadway Billiard Cafe";
```

```
valuesB[1] = new Array;
valuesB[1][0] = "0";
valuesB[1][1] = "1";
valuesB[1][2] = "2";
valuesB[1][3] = "3";
valuesB[1][3] = "4";

listsB[2] = new Array;
listsB[2][0] = "Ballbusters";
listsB[2][1] = "Broad Street Billiards";
listsB[2][2] = "Country Club Billiards";
listsB[2][3] = "Pablo's Billiards";
listsB[2][4] = "River City Billiards";

valuesB[2] = new Array;
valuesB[2][0] = "106";
valuesB[2][1] = "107";
valuesB[2][2] = "108";
valuesB[2][3] = "109";
valuesB[2][4] = "110";

function populateListB()
{
  ctlListB =
    document.Form1.ddlListB;
  itemarray =
    listsB[document.Form1.ddlListA.selectedIndex];
  valuearray =
    valuesB[document.Form1.ddlListA.selectedIndex];

  for (i=ctlListB.options.length; i>0; i--)
  {ctlListB.options[i] = null;}

  for (i=0; i<itemarray.length; i++)
  {ctlListB.options[i] = new Option(itemarray[i],valuearray[i]);}

}
</SCRIPT>
</head>
<body onload='populateListB()'>
<FORM name="Form1">
<h4>Pool Halls</h4>
<SELECT NAME="ddlListA" onChange="populateListB()">
    <OPTION>Chicago</OPTION>
    <OPTION>New York</OPTION>
    <option>Philadelphia</OPTION>
</SELECT>
```

```
<BR><BR>
<SELECT NAME="ddlListB"
    onchange='alert(document.Form1.ddlListB.value);'>
</body>
</html>
```

This presents two drop-down lists. The choices in the second list are determined by what's selected in the first list. You do this with simple JavaScript arrays. For now, the second list simply displays the underlying value of the option tag when it's selected. You're going to transform this static piece of code into a dynamically generated script function. It may not seem static, but it is to the server. As far as the server is concerned, this is *flat text*. It has no life until it gets to the client.

Starting with a working set of client code makes it easier to add the abstractions necessary to dynamically generate it on the server. For each step, you'll take a piece of the previous HTML document and transform it into server-side code that generates it. Let's start with the markup. Here's the markup you want to generate:

```
<SELECT NAME="ddlListA" onChange="populateListB()">
    <OPTION>Chicago</OPTION>
    <OPTION>New York</OPTION>
    <option>Philadelphia</OPTION>
</SELECT>
<BR><BR>
<SELECT NAME="ddlListB"
    onchange='alert(document.Form1.ddlListB.value);'>
```

And here's the server-side code that generates it:

```
<asp:DropDownList
    Runat=server
    ID=ddlListA
    onchange='populateListB();' />
<br /><br />
<asp:DropDownList
    Runat=server
    ID=ddlListB
    onchange='alert(this.value);' />
```

Each of the HTML Select elements become DropDownList controls. Since the whole point of this exercise is to use data to drive the list entries, you'll strip out the static option elements. Later you'll add page load code to bind these lists. You usually set property values of server controls with attributes in the markup. That is, there is usually a one-to-one correspondence between an attribute in the markup and a property on the Control type. However, there is no onchange property of the DropDownList. This is a client-side event trap (for a server-side event you'd use OnSelectedIndexChanged, which fires during a postback). Since there is no mapping of the attribute back to a property of the class, the rendering engine is smart enough just to pass the attribute into the output stream. You could also do this from the code-behind with a line like the following:

```
ddlListA.Attributes.Add("onchange", "populateListB();");
```

The other part of the static page you need to modify is the script code in the head of the page. The JavaScript function can stay as is. You'll need to generate the data structures that precede this function in the HTML. You'll dynamically generate this in the code-behind, and then use a PlaceHolder to inject it into the output stream. Here's the entire server-side block of markup for the head element:

```
<head runat="server">
    <title>Pool Halls</title>
    <asp:PlaceHolder Runat=server ID=plScript />
    <script language=javascript>

        function populateListB()
        {

        itemarray =
            listsB[document.all.ddlListA.selectedIndex];
        valuearray =
            valuesB[document.all.ddlListA.selectedIndex];
        ctlListB =
            document.all.ddlListB;
        for (i=ctlListB.options.length; i>0; i--)
        {ctlListB.options[i] = null;}

        for (i=0; i<itemarray.length; i++)
        {ctlListB.options[i] = new Option(itemarray[i],valuearray[i]);}

        }
    </script>
</head>
```

Notice that your PlaceHolder is declared outside of the client-side script block. An element declared with the runat=server attribute within a client-side script block will not be recognized during server-side page processing. Not only is it unavailable during server-side processing, but it also will get left in the script block, causing a JavaScript error on the client.

For this reason, when you generate JavaScript on the server, you'll wrap it in your own script element and inject the entire block into the output using your PlaceHolder.

You'll bind your lists to XML. The cities will be bound to a simple list:

```
<Cities>
    <City>New York</City>
    <City>Los Angeles</City>
    <City>Chicago</City>
    <City>Houston</City>
    <City>Philadelphia</City>
    <City>Minneapolis</City>
</Cities>
```

The second list will be "bound" by client-side script. The XML structure you'll use to generate this client-side script code contains simple pool hall name and address information:

```
<PoolHall>
    <Name>Amsterdam Billiard Club</Name>
    <Address>210 E 86th St</Address>
    <City>New York</City>
    <State>NY</State>
    <Phone>212-570-4545</Phone>
    <id>1</id>
</PoolHall>
```

You'll bind the list and generate the code by trapping the page's Load event. First you pop open the XML doc and bind the list of cities:

```
DataSet ds = new DataSet();
ds.ReadXml(Server.MapPath("PoolHalls.xml"));

ddlListA.DataTextField = "City_text";
ddlListA.DataSource = ds.Tables[1];
ddlListA.DataBind();
```

Next comes the dynamic generation of the client script code. Specifically, you're generating the arrays that are used from within the populateListB method. The client-side script needs to look like this:

```
listsB = new Array;
valuesB = new Array;

listsB[0] = new Array;
listsB[0][0] = "A J Billiard Parlor";
listsB[0][1] = "Campus Room";
listsB[0][2] = "Champion Billiards";

valuesB[0] = new Array;
valuesB[0][0] = "33";
valuesB[0][1] = "34";
valuesB[0][2] = "35";

listsB[1] = new Array;
listsB[1][0] = "Amsterdam Billiard Club";
listsB[1][1] = "Bernardos Billar and Cafeteria";
listsB[1][2] = "Billiard Club";
listsB[1][3] = "Broadway Billiard Cafe";

valuesB[1] = new Array;
valuesB[1][0] = "0";
valuesB[1][1] = "1";
```

```
valuesB[1][2] = "2";
valuesB[1][3] = "3";
valuesB[1][3] = "4";
//etc...
```

The two initial arrays are both arrays of arrays. There will be an array containing a list of display items and an array of values for each item in the first list.

You'll get going with the initial first few lines of code, which are static. Remember that you need to wrap your array declarations in their own script block.

```
StringBuilder sb = new StringBuilder();
sb.Append("<SCRIPT LANGUAGE='JavaScript'>\n");
sb.Append("listsB = new Array;\n");
sb.Append("valuesB = new Array;\n");
```

Then, for each row in the table the first list is bound to, you'll add an array of display items and an array of item values. You'll use a DataView to find all of the pool halls in that city.

```
int i = 0;
foreach (DataRow dr in ds.Tables[1].Rows)
{
    sb.Append(
        string.Format(
        "listsB[{0}] = new Array;\n",i));

    sb.Append(
        string.Format(
        "valuesB[{0}] = new Array;\n", i));

    DataView dv = new DataView(
        ds.Tables[2],
        string.Format("City = '{0}'", dr[0]),
        "", DataViewRowState.CurrentRows);
```

Then, for each matching pool hall, you'll generate an entry in each of the two nested arrays:

```
int j = 0;
foreach (DataRowView drv in dv)
{
    sb.Append(
        string.Format(
        "listsB[{0}][{1}] = \"{2}\";",
        i, j, drv["Name"]));

    sb.Append(
        string.Format(
        "valuesB[{0}][{1}] = \"{2}\";",
        i, j, drv["id"]));
```

```
    j++;
}
i++;
```

Finally, you'll close the script tag and inject the JavaScript into the control tree by adding it as a child of the `PlaceHolder` in the `head`.

```
sb.Append("</script>");
plScript.Controls.Add(new LiteralControl(sb.ToString()));
```

The output for both the static example and the dynamically generated version is the same, as shown in Figure 4-11. The page behaves exactly the same way as the static example, except now the lists are data driven (the complete code for this demo is in `Scripting1.aspx` of the `Web04` project).

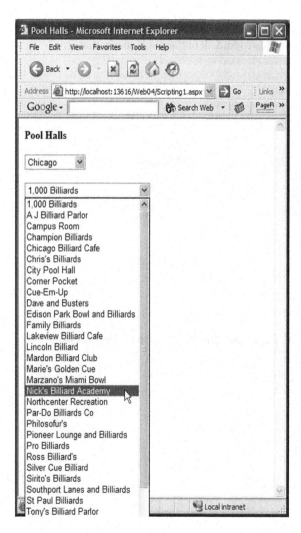

Figure 4-11. *The interdependent drop-down lists*

The last thing you need is to populate the list upon first arriving at the client. We'll save this for the next section, where we discuss some built-in support the Page type has for scripting.

There are a number of improvements you can make to the sample. This code looks nothing like the script code you started with. Maintenance may be difficult. It's good to keep the original static script around; you can use it to troubleshoot and change the behavior of the page, and then you can map those changes into the script-generating code.

The biggest downside shows up when your page does a postback. ddlListB won't behave as you'd expect it to. On a postback, you'd probably write some code to access ddlListB.SelectedValue to do some processing. This would not be populated. The DropDownList relies on a collection of list items and view state. You never populated the list server side, and so no ViewState exists for it. To retrieve this value, you have to resort to the old-fashioned ASP-style syntax of Request.Form["ddlListB"].

For this reason you'll probably want to pull the code for these lists out into their own control. Even a User Control would suffice (if you did not plan to use it in more than a single application). This way you could add a public property to the control to expose the second list's value, and not have to burden consumers of your control with details of its implementation. While you're at it, you may as well generalize its functionality to create two lists against any data source, instead of just the XML file in this example.

Page Support for Scripting

As you descend into the details of moving your interdependent lists into a control of their own, more issues will arise. What if someone uses two instances of your control on a page of her own? You'd have duplicate populateListB methods injected into the page, which would not make the browser happy. What if you wanted the static parts of your code in their own file (.js)? How can you be sure to inject this only once?

The Page object has a number of types and methods designed to help with just such problems.

Client Script Manager

Version 1.x of the Framework has a handful of methods hanging off of the Page object to help with client-side scripting. One of these, for example, is RegisterClientScriptBlock. This handy method accepts two strings. The first one names the script block; the second is the actual script you want to inject into the page.

You use this from controls to inject script into the page while avoiding duplicate script blocks. If more than one instance of a control attempts to inject the same script block, the runtime is smart enough to inject it only once. From the previous example, you could pull the populateListB method out into a file named Interdepends.js. From the implementation of the interdependent lists control, you could add a line of code to include it:

```
this.RegisterClientScriptBlock(
    "Interdepends",
    "<script language='JavaScript1.2' src='/Interdepends.js'>");
```

This is a two-fold improvement over the previous example. It gets the script out into its own file (for easier maintenance and versioning), and it guarantees that the block will be included in the page only once.

All of the `RegisterXYZ` methods (see Table 4-2) have been deprecated in version 2.0 of the Framework. Instead, the page object now carries an instance of the new `ClientScriptManager` type, named `ClientScript`. This centralizes the functionality for managing scripts; you no longer have a handful of random methods hanging off the page object.

Table 4-2. *Methods of the Page Object That Are Officially Depreacted in Version 2.0*

Deprecated Script Methods
RegisterArrayDeclaration
RegisterClientScriptBlock
RegisterHiddenField
RegisterOnSubmitStatement
RegisterStartupScript

Of course, you must realize that 2.0 attempts to be backwards compatible, so just because these are deprecated doesn't mean they go away. They will survive in-perpetuity in the name of backwards compatibility (or until Microsoft ships a non-backwards compatible version of ASP.NET), so your existing code will continue to work.

With new development, however, you should use the methods of the client script manager. Let's take a look at these. The point of a lot of these register methods is first and foremost to avoid duplicating the code that's being sent to your page, which can happen easily when a control is generating code and more than one instance of the control is placed on a single Web Form. Some of these methods also do a bit of code generation for you, but it's nothing substantial.

Table 4-3. *Methods of the* `ClientScript` *Object That Help Manage JavaScript*

Method	Role in Life
RegisterArrayDeclaration	Helper method to declare a page-level array. Accepts two strings, the array name, and the array declaration. When the page renders, these strings do a little bit of code generation to wrap the array in a script block and initialize it.
RegisterCallbackEventReference	Generates a client-side script function call to do an out-of-band asynchronous callback to the server on a background thread of the browser. See the "Out-of-Band Callbacks" section that follows for details.
RegisterClientScriptBlock	Accepts two strings, the first being a name for the script block, and the second being a string containing the script you want added to the page. Dynamically generate this string, load it from the database, or load it from some other source of persistence.
RegisterClientScriptInclude	Accepts two strings, a name for the registration, and the name of the JavaScript file to include. Script includes give you a clean separation of the script from your markup, and allows the browser to cache a script file used from several pages, reducing total page size.

Method	Role in Life
RegisterClientScriptResource	Used by the resource manager to retrieve resources from assemblies with a dedicated handler (see the MSDN SDK docs for details).
RegisterHiddenField	Allows you to add a hidden input to your form simply by providing a name and a value. Rendering generates the input element for you.
RegisterOnSubmitStatement	An easy way to interject some client-side code that will execute before a postback occurs. A very common example of this is when you have a delete button on a page, and want to verify with the user that he's serious before doing a round trip to the server.
RegisterStartupScript	Places code inline within a script block—yet outside of a function—so it executes as soon as the browser loads the page. Similiar to adding code to the onload event of the body element.
IsClientScriptBlockRegistered	Checks to see if a named script block has already been registered using RegisterClientScriptBlock.
IsClientScriptIncludeRegistered	Checks to see if a named script include has already been registered using RegisterClientScriptInclude.
IsOnSubmitStatementRegistered	Checks to see if a named script block has already been registered using RegisterOnSubmitStatement
IsStartupScriptRegistered	Checks to see if a named script block has already been registered using RegisterStartupScript.

Let's refactor the interdependent lists example to leverage some of the features of the client script manager. First you'll get the second list populated with the correct entries for the default selection in the first list by calling RegisterStartupScript (see ClientManagerIE.aspx in Web04 for the complete sample).

```
this.ClientScript.RegisterStartupScript
    (this.GetType(),
    "PopList",
    "populateListB();",
    true);
```

The first argument associates the registration with a specific type. This is designed to be used from custom controls, so each type can do its own registrations. Since you're writing page code, you'll pass an instance of the Type object associated with the Page type. The second argument is the name of the registration, which keeps it unique. The third argument is the code you want to execute, which matches the call you make from the onchange of list A. The fourth argument is a Boolean telling the rendering engine to wrap your function call in a script tag for you.

Next let's break the static script (the part not being generated) out into a file named Interdepends.js. This includes nothing more than the populateListB method, and it allows the client to cache this script, reducing your page size. To include it on the page, you have only to call the new RegisterScriptInclude method:

```
this.ClientScript.RegisterClientScriptInclude
    ("Interdepends",
    "Interdepends.js");
```

The first parameter is a name, or a key really, that prevents the same include from being added to a single page multiple times. The second is the URL of the script file. This simplified call automatically generates the script include element for us.

The last change you'll make is to use the `RegisterClientScriptBlock` method of the script manager to inject the dynamically generated array declarations onto the page, instead of using the `PlaceHolder`. You'll replace this line of code:

```
plScript.Controls.Add(new LiteralControl(sb.ToString()));
```

with this one:

```
this.ClientScript.RegisterClientScriptBlock
    (this.GetType(),
    "InterArrays",
    sb.ToString());
```

This simple change prevents the same block of script from being loaded more than once. If you broke these lists out into their own control (`UserControl` or custom control), you'd actually want more than one of these sets of array declarations, as you would need a unique set for each instance of the control on the page. This would require you to incorporate the `ClientID` attribute of the control into the array names, in order to avoid naming conflicts on the client.

The client script manager is a nice improvement over the disjointed state of affairs for scripting in 1.x. While existing code will continue to work, the new features and methods of the script manager will be nice to leverage as you move forward into 2.0 development.

Focus

Another common problem has been resolved in 2.0 using client-side script. This is the problem of *control focus*. It's very common to need to programmatically determine the focus of a control. When using custom validation on the server, it's nice to set the focus to the first control that's found to be in an invalid state. This way the user is ready to correct the problem as soon as the postback completes and the browser refreshes. Doing this in 1.x was possible, but it required awkward, and sometimes arbitrary, code generation.

In 2.0, the `Control` type exposes the `Focus` method. This can be called on any control on the page. The control automatically generates the appropriate client-side script to ensure the focus is placed there when the page is displayed in the browser.

Out-of-Band Callbacks

One of the biggest complaints about ASP.NET is the postback infrastructure, which is ironic, because it's also one of things people like the most. But there are some situations where a postback is just overkill. The previous example of interdependent drop-down lists is a good one. You need to affect the second list programmatically, but it just doesn't seem to warrant an entire round trip back to the server. In that example, you do the processing on the client instead, but you do so by shipping *all values* for *all choices from list one*. This increases your page size with the array script you generate, and chances are you won't use most of that data each time the page is sent to a user.

For some operations, shipping data for all possible user selections is just not an option. A TreeView control is a good example. There may be hundreds or thousands of nodes in a large TreeView. You definitely don't want to ship all of the data for all of those nodes to the client when the client first requests the page. This would cause a huge up-front performance hit, and negatively impact the usability of the application. A postback for each click on the node is annoying too. The page renders quickly but its performance thereafter is kludgey and slow (and probably just plain unusable).

So it would be nice, in many circumstances, if another option existed. Can you go back to the server and get just a little more data without having to rerender and resend all of the markup for the entire page? This facility has been built into ASP.NET 2.0, and it's the last scripting feature we'll examine.

The feature is called *out-of-band* callbacks, because it executes asynchronously on a worker thread of the web browser. This is good, because the user interface stays responsive while the browser makes a request to the server in the background.

The callback is kicked off by an event on the client. A user action can cause it—button clicks, change events, mouse events, whatever. The client-side script to launch the call to the server is automatically generated by a call to a method of the ClientScript object. Values from the web page can be gathered and passed back to the server as a string. Two values are passed, an argument and a context (more values could easily be passed using a delimited string). The argument can be used from the server-side processing, but the context cannot. It is actually passed to the callback method to establish, client-side, how the event originated. Another critical parameter that you specify is the name of the JavaScript function that should be called when the work is done and a response is sent back. You can also, optionally, specify the name of a client-side function to call if an error occurs.

The server-side processing can do any work, but can only return a string. Again, if you desire a more complex structure, you can build a delimited string on the server and split it when it gets to the client. You can also have the server return HTML, which can be displayed on the client from the callback method using DHTML.

Let's modify the interdependent drop-down list example to display the pool hall's address when the user makes a selection out of the second list. This is a good example of not wanting to make a full round trip back to the server, but also not wanting to totally bloat your page size by returning all of these addresses proactively when your user is only seeking a single address.

The process of establishing a callback is fairly complex compared to the ease with which you can accomplish most tasks in ASP.NET. The steps are as follows:

1. You must create a page that not only inherits from the Page base class, but also implements the ICallBackEventHandler interface.

2. This interface exposes one method, RaiseCallbackEvent. This is the method that will fire when the callback occurs. It's a lot like any other server-side event trap, except the browser makes the request on a background thread instead of doing a full page refresh. The other big difference is that instead of generating an HTML document (as a normal postback would), this method simply returns a string, which is received by script code on the client.

3. The callback is fired by client-side code. The script code that causes the callback is generated server-side by a call to GetCallbackEventReference. You must write server-side code to generate this callback invocation, and also to generate client-side script that will trap some event that causes the callback.

4. Once the callback invocation is wired, the server-side RaiseCallbackEvent method is executed and generates a string. This string is returned to another function in client-side script. You must write this function, and this function must process the string returned from the server (by setting the InnerHtml property of a div element, for example).

The big picture involves the process and code displayed in Figure 4-12. You may also want to examine the code from the Callback.aspx Web Form in the Web04 project before reading through this section. You're dealing with code-generating code, server-side code, and client-side code, so as you come to understand this infrastructure, "There's a lot of threads in old dooder's head," as Jeffrey Lebowski would say.

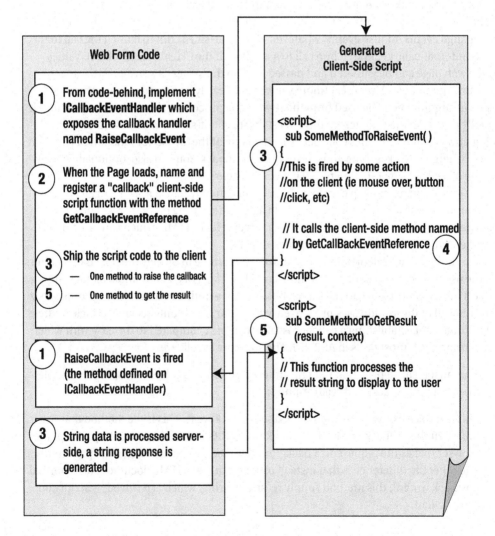

Figure 4-12. *Process and code for establishing a callback*

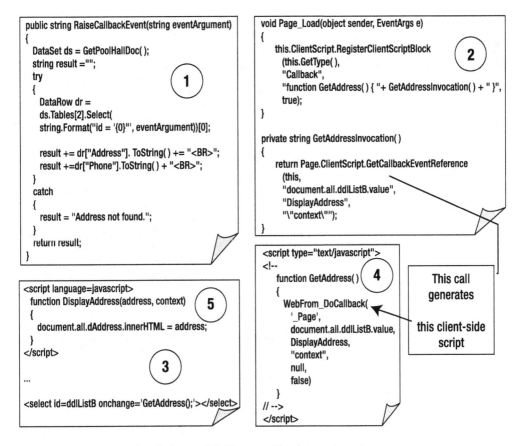

Figure 4-12. *Process and code for establishing a callback (continued)*

Let's start by adding the client-side pieces of functionality. First you'll need to alter the onChange event of the second list to call a helper method instead of just popping its value in a message box:

```
<select  id=ddlListB onchange='GetAddress();'></select>
```

The GetAddress method will be dynamically generated from your code-behind. This is generated by a call to GetCallbackEventReference, and the behavior of the callback is determined entirely by the parameters that are passed to this method (see Table 4-4).

Table 4-4. *Arguments of the* GetCallbackEventReference *Method*

Argument	Type	Meaning
control	Control	The control that implements ICallbackEventHandler. This interface defines a single method that will be invoked when the callback occurs. It accepts a string as a parameter. This is the only information that can be passed from the client to the server. You can implement this interface at the Page level, or a user control or custom control can implement and accept the callback event.

Continued

Table 4-4. *Continued*

Argument	Type	Meaning
argument	String	This is the data that gets passed from the client to the server. Any client-side script can be executed to generate this value before the callback is executed. If an atomic value will not provide for your functionality, pass a delimited string and split it when it gets to the server. You can pass a string expression as a value (i.e., a client-side variable or *ControlName.value*), and it will be evaluated on the client, as it's baked into the output stream as client-side script.
clientCallback	String	This is the name of the function that gets executed when the callback completes. This argument is typed as a string, but acts more like a function pointer, pointing to the callback function. The callback function accepts two arguments. The first is the return value from the server-side processing, and the second is the context string that was passed as second argument with the original call.
context	String	This can be used to establish where the event occurred. For example, you could bind a GridView, and have each row provide a link that would fire a callback. In order to establish which row the click originated on, you could pass the ID of the row as the context. When the call returned to the client, this information is passed back as the second argument of your callback function.
clientErrorCallback	String	The name of the client-side function that should be executed if an error occurs. This argument is optional. (There is another argument list that accepts only four values.)

Let's take a look at the code you'll use from the page's Load event to generate the code for the callback. Remember that earlier you programmed list B to call a function named GetAddress when the list entry changes. Here's the server-side code to programmatically generate that client-side function:

```
this.ClientScript.RegisterClientScriptBlock
    (this.GetType(),
    "Callback",
    "function GetAddress() { " + GetAddressInvocation() + " }",
    true);
```

And here's the code for GetAddressInvocation, called from the fourth argument in the preceding line of code:

```
private string GetAddressInvocation()
{
    return Page.GetCallbackEventReference
        (this,
        "document.all.ddlListB.value",
        "DisplayAddress",
        "\"context\"");
}
```

This code yields a client-side function that acts as a simple wrapper method for the invocation of the callback. Here's the code that gets generated and registered in the output stream:

```
<script type="text/javascript">
<!--
    function GetAddress()
    {
        WebForm_DoCallback
            ('__Page',
            document.all.ddlListB.value,
            DisplayAddress,
            "context",
            null)
    }
// -->
</script>
```

You're wrapping it in the GetAddress function so that you can fire the callback at will from a number of places on your form. Let's examine the call to WebForm_DoCallback for a moment, and see how your call to GetCallbackEventReference created it. The first parameter you passed, this, resulted in the reference to __Page as the first parameter. If you were using a control, this parameter would be the ID of that control. Next, your string expression resulted in a line of code that pulls the current value of list B from the interface via DHTML. This is the value you're passing back to the server. DisplayAddress is the name of the client-side function to be called when the server is done with its work. It's passed as a function pointer. And finally, your literal "context" is passed as the literal string "context." A null value is passed for your error callback, since you specified none.

In the same way that __doPostback causes a postback to occur, WebForm_DoCallback fires the out-of-band callback to the server in the background. When the server returns, the DisplayAddress function pointer is invoked, and the value from the server is passed to it.

Let's hop over to the server-side callback event trap. This is determined by the reference to the type you passed as argument one to GetCallbackEventReference. It must be an instance of a type that implements ICallbackEventHandler. Let's examine your implementation of this interface.

First, of course, you must modify the page object to declare its intent to provide an implementation of this interface:

```
public partial class Callback : System.Web.UI.Page, ICallbackEventHandler
```

There's a single method on the contract of this interface, RaiseCallbackEvent.

```
public string RaiseCallbackEvent(string eventArgument)
{
    DataSet ds = GetPoolHallDoc();
    string result = "";
    try
    {
        DataRow dr =
```

```
        ds.Tables[2].Select(
        string.Format("id = '{0}'", eventArgument))[0];

    result += dr["Address"].ToString() + "<BR>";
    result += dr["Phone"].ToString() + "<BR>";
    }
    catch
    {
        result = "Address not found.";
    }
    return result;
}
```

The argument is what your client-side function that launched the callback passed. Because of how you built your expression, this is the ID of the current selection in list B. You will use this ID to look up the address information for the corresponding pool hall, build that into an HTML string, and send it back to the client.

When this string is returned to the client, the DisplayAddress function will be invoked. Here's the code for that function. Note that this is client-side JavaScript.

```
function DisplayAddress(address, context) {
    document.all.dAddress.innerHTML = address;
}
```

Address is the string you built on the server, and context is the literal string "context" that gets passed to the callback method, but not to the server. Again, it's designed to be used to track where the callback originated on the client. dAddress is a div element at the bottom of the page:

```
<div id=dAddress style="font-family:Verdana;color:Navy;"></div>
```

Now you only have to tie up loose ends. The address will be displayed when the user makes a selection out of list B, but this list has a default selection when the page first renders. You'll modify the page load script to populate it then:

```
this.ClientScript.RegisterStartupScript
    (this.GetType(),
    "PopList",
    "populateListB();GetAddress();",
    true);
```

List B also gets a default selection when a choice is made from list A. You'll make a similar change there:

```
<asp:DropDownList
    Runat=server
    ID=ddlListA
    onchange='populateListB();GetAddress();' />
```

This page is now ready to go. The results are quite different from similar functionality provided by postbacks. The lists populate quickly, the UI remains responsive while the address is looked up in the background, and the browser is not "clicking" and running its status bar for refreshes. Even on a LAN, this interface is more responsive and usable than it would be using postbacks.

One of the greatest things about this feature is that it's cross-browser compatible. In Figure 4-13 you see the Pool Hall Address Lookup page running in the Firefox browser.

Figure 4-13. *A page leveraging out-of-band callbacks running in Firefox*

Even though all of the features you've looked at in this chapter are cross-browser compatible, this feature is worthy of note: In the past, it would have been safe to assume it was IE only. The new TreeView Web Form control also makes use of this callback infrastructure, meaning that this new control is also cross-browser compatible.

Summary

The ASP.NET Framework provides a rich set of features for leveraging client-side functionality, including JavaScript. The ViewState and ControlState features use HTML hidden input to store state information on the client, which saves you from writing a lot of redundant boilerplate code. However, you must carefully monitor ViewState because it can quickly bloat your requests and responses. Version 2.0 increases the efficiency of the hashing algorithms in use to generate the ViewState value, decreasing the size of the value stored in the hidden input. In some situations, the ViewState size will still cause an unacceptable performance hit; in these cases, you have the option of replacing the location where the ViewState value is stored with one of your choosing (like Session, Cache, or a database).

ASP.NET script-generation features have been aggregated and extended via the services the new `ClientScript` object provides. This object, a property of the `Page` object, exposes many methods you can use to generate JavaScript, and to avoid sending duplicate blocks of JavaScript to the client.

There is a powerful new facility for doing out-of-band callbacks from the client to the server, which allows you to do partial page refreshes and avoid the overhead of a full postback to the server.

PART 2

■■■

.NET Middle Tier Solutions

The middle tier is frequently the heart of a distributed application. All the information moves through this layer: data on its way from the database to the user interface and user information posted from a form that kicks off a transaction. This is where the brains and the rules of the application reside.

More than the concept of "business objects," the functionality of this tier of the application can fall within many categories. As service orientation continues to gain momentum, it becomes more important to understand and leverage messaging infrastructures. For Web-based applications, the application is intrinsically stateless, so frequently the work you need to do does not involve stateful business objects, but rather stateless services processing and preparing messages.

There are also many permutations and combinations of layers and tiers in a distributed application. How the layers of an application are deployed across physical tiers will affect the options you have for communicating across these layers. Making the correct choices among these options is critical for the success of any distributed application, as they make up the "plumbing" of your application.

Chapter 5

This chapter focuses on security, the "vertical slice" of any distributed application. Here you'll see how to keep assemblies secure and how you can leverage encryption in the .NET Framework, as well as some new security features in ASP.NET 2.0.

Chapter 6

This chapter is on Web Services in the .NET Framework. We'll take a look at why you would want to use Web Services, we'll examine them from a vendor-neutral perspective to see how they provide for excellent cross-platform interoperability, and then we'll delve into some of the new features for Web Services that are built into version 2.0 of the .NET Framework.

We'll wrap this chapter up with a quick look at Web Service Enhancements, an add-on package of functionality available from Microsoft.

Chapter 7

This chapter is about COM+. We enumerate its features and look specifically at what steps you must take with .NET types for them to function in the COM+ environment.

Chapter 8

This chapter focuses on processes, hosts, and marshaling. These topics are seldom discussed under a single banner, and the decisions you make regarding them affect every distributed application.

We'll examine some of the options available for hosting applications and also some of the options for communicating across the different processes. Through the course of this discussion, we'll examine Message Queuing in some detail, as well.

Chapter 9

This chapter provides a brief introduction of Windows Communication Foundation, Microsoft's next-generation messaging stack that sets out to unify (or at least unite) MSMQ, COM+, Remoting, and Web Services.

■ ■ ■

CHAPTER 5

.NET 2.0 Security

The goal of this chapter is twofold. The first order of business is to provide you with a high-level overview of various security technologies the .NET base class libraries offer. You'll learn the role of strongly named assemblies, hash codes and role-based security (RBS) systems. Do understand, however, that we will not be diving into each and every detail regarding these topics. Rather, this information will give you a context for the major mission of this chapter, which we outline under the second order of business.

Our second (major) task with this chapter is to address the details of securing ASP.NET web applications using Windows-based and Forms-based authentication. Once you understand the basics behind each model, you will learn how to implement Forms-based authentication under ASP.NET 2.0. As you will see, developers can use numerous new techniques (including the Membership and Roles classes, server-side security controls, and cookieless authentication) that simplify the process. We'll then wrap up the chapter by examining a (much welcomed) Web-based UI editor for web.config files.

A Survey of Core Security Services

Historically speaking, security is often perceived by many in the Windows programming community as *someone else's problem*. Because security programming using the raw Win32 APIs is so complex and tedious, few developers relish the idea of diving into the gory details. Rather, these same (often well-intentioned) individuals attempted to pass the buck to "the security guy/gal."

To make matters worse, many (again, well-intentioned) software companies often view security as an afterthought that is bolted onto an almost-completed product. Unless you happen to be a security-savvy individual who works at a security-savvy company, it is too often the case that the security is not factored into the initial design of a system. As you would guess, this approach seldom results in truly secure or extendable software.

Thankfully, the .NET platform has greatly simplified the process of building secure applications. Not only can .NET developers utilize a well-designed set of namespaces, they can also leverage design time support provided by the Visual Studio 2005 integrated development environment (IDE).

Since the initial release of the .NET platform, Microsoft has made it quite clear that security is a critical topic that must be addressed during an application's initial design. Not only has Microsoft designed a whole set of security best practices, it has also integrated security into the very fabric of the base class libraries. To better understand the reach of .NET security, consider the .NET 2.0 security-centric namespaces shown in Table 5-1.

Table 5-1. *The .NET 2.0 Security Namespaces*

Security-centric Namespace	Meaning in Life
System.Security	This is the core security-centric namespace that defines common types used by the run-time security model.
System.Security.AccessControl	This new .NET 2.0 namespace provides types that enable you to interact with access control lists (ACLs) and other related security descriptors programmatically.
System.Security.Authentication	This new .NET 2.0 namespace provides types that enable you to determine the state of secure connections (such as SSL).
System.Security.Cryptography	The .NET platform provides numerous cryptographic namespaces that cover hash code, symmetric, and asymmetric cryptography.
System.Security.Permissions	Defines core types used when programming with the role-based and code access security models.
System.Security.Policy	Defines numerous types that are used specifically with code access security.
System.Security.Principal	Defines numerous types that are used specifically with role-based security.
System.Web.Security	Defines numerous types that are used to secure ASP.NET web applications.

In addition to these specific namespaces, security atoms can be found lurking within XML configuration files, assembly metadata, and various development and configuration tools. While space doesn't permit a complete discussion of these aspects, we'll begin this chapter by briefly examining the following topics:

- The role of strongly named assemblies

- Encryption services

- Role-based security

After we provide an initial overview of common .NET security technologies, in the remaining bulk of the chapter we address the details of securing ASP.NET 2.0 web applications using the types within the System.Web.Security namespace.

■**Note** Again, the initial part of this chapter is only intended to provide an overview of select core .NET security technologies. If you require a full treatment of the topics we've just outlined (including Code Access Security), consult *.NET Security* by Bock et al (Apress, 2002).

The Role of Strongly Named Assemblies

Many .NET developers assume that the only reason to assign a strong name to a .NET assembly is to deploy it to the Global Assembly Cache (GAC) as a shared assembly. While this is one important aspect of strong names, it is, in fact, considered a .NET best practice to provide *every* assembly with a strong name given the intrinsic security boundary it provides.

To understand how a strong name can provide a level of security, you must understand the concept of *round trip engineering*. Simply put, this term explains the process of disassembling a compiled .NET assembly into Common Intermediate Language (CIL), modifying the contents, and compiling the modified CIL into a new (identically named) binary. This process is not as esoteric as you may think. In fact, the .NET Framework 2.0 SDK ships with the very tools you need to perform a round trip: ildasm.exe (the CIL disassembler) and ilasm.exe (the CIL assembler).

An Example of Round Tripping

Assume you have authored the following type using C# contained in a file named MyCriticalClass.cs:

```
using System;

public class MyCriticalClass
{
  public string GetSensitiveInformation()
  {
    return "The magic value is 9";
  }
}
```

If you were to compile this code file into a .NET code library at the command line using the following command:

```
csc /t:library *.cs
```

you could now view the generated CIL code, type metadata, and manifest information by issuing the following command to the ildasm.exe utility (see Figure 5-1):

```
ildasm MyCriticalClass.dll
```

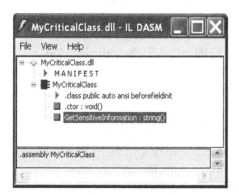

Figure 5-1. *Viewing the internal composition of a .NET assembly using ildasm.exe*

Given that ildasm.exe is a free tool that ships with the .NET Platform 2.0 SDK, this, obviously, means any individual is able to view the internal composition of your code libraries. Worse, using the File ➤ Dump menu option of ildasm.exe, it is possible to dump an assembly's CIL code to a local file. If you were to do so, you could open the resulting *.il file using any text editor.

If an evildoer has some basic knowledge of the syntax of CIL, he or she could now alter any member to perform any evil task (scan the local hard drive for sensitive information, inject viruses, etc). Just for illustrative purposes, assume that you have updated the CIL code to change the string literal within GetSensitiveInformation to return "The magic value is FOO!" rather than the intended "The magic value is 9" (see Figure 5-2):

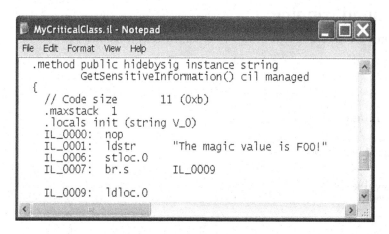

Figure 5-2. *Modifying CIL code using notepad.exe*

Once an *.il file has been edited, the evildoer can recompile the CIL code into an identically named *.dll using the CIL assembler, ilasm.exe:

```
ilasm /dll /out:MyCriticalClass.dll MyCriticalClass.il
```

Clearly the potential of round trip engineering is unnerving if you ship your *.dll or *.exe files to an end user's machine. If an evildoer alters, recompiles, and redeploys your code base, you're the one to blame as far as the end user is concerned. Do understand that not all round trips are dangerous. This same technique can be very helpful when you need to modify an assembly you no longer have source code for, or happen to be building a sophisticated assembly for the purposes of communicating between COM and .NET. Nevertheless, the chances are good that you would like to prevent others from tampering with your compiled binaries.

Preventing Roundtrip Engineering via Strong Naming

As you may know, a strong name is based in part on two mathematically related keys (the public key and the private key), which are generated using a command line utility named sn.exe (strong name). Like most command line tools, sn.exe has a great number of options; however, if you're simply interested in generating a new key pair, the -k flag is all you require:

```
sn -k mykeypair.snk
```

Once you have generated a *.snk file, you should regard its contents as *extremely sensitive*. Given that the whole point of a strong name is to establish your identity in the .NET universe, if another (possibly evil) individual were to gain access to your key information, they could pretend to "be you." Assuming this is not the case, you are now able to inform the C# compiler where to find your *.snk file via the /keyfile option.

```
csc /keyfile:mykeypair.snk /t:library *.cs
```

By doing so, your assembly will now be assigned a *strong name*. Formally speaking, the C# compiler will use data within the supplied *.snk file as so:

- The full public key is recorded in the assembly's manifest.

- A digital signature is created based on the private key and a hash code generated using the assembly contents (CIL code / metadata).

- This digital signature is encrypted into the assembly.

Figure 5-3 illustrates the process. (Do recall that a single *snk file contains both the public key and private key data.)

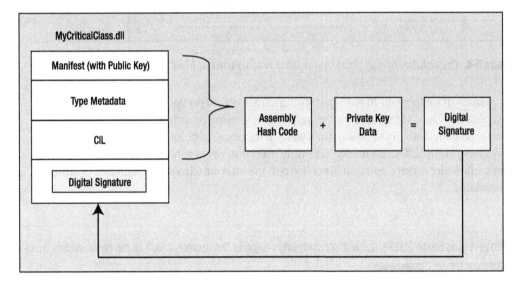

Figure 5-3. *Key pairs are used to generate a* digitial signature *for a given assembly*

Now, assume you have deployed your strongly named assembly to an end user's machine. If an evildoer were to attempt a round trip, she would not have access to your key pair data. Even if this individual specified a new *.snk during compilation process, an entirely new digital signature is produced. In fact, the .NET runtime automatically verifies an assembly's digital signature (provided it has been strongly named) using the following sequence of events:

1. The embedded digital signature is decrypted using the public key.

2. The current assembly's hash is recomputed.

3. If the hash values match, the CLR knows the assembly has not been tampered with after deployment.

4. If the hash codes *do not* match, the CLR refuses to load the binary and throws a File-LoadException.

Figure 5-4 illustrates the process.

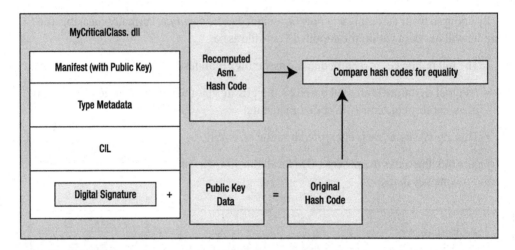

Figure 5-4. *The validity of a digitial signature is recomputed at load time*

Finally, it's important to note that strong names do *not* prevent evildoers from loading your assembly into ildasm.exe for the purposes of viewing proprietary code. If you wish to limit an evildoer's ability to do so, you'll want to make use of obfuscation software. As you may know, obfuscators essentially "scramble" the contents of a .NET assembly in such a way that while its intended operation is persevered, the internal CIL code is rendered essentially unreadable.

■**Note** Visual Studio 2005 ships with a community edition of Dotfuscator, which as the name implies, is an obfuscator for .NET assemblies.

Encryption Services

The next security topic we'll discuss is *encryption*. Simply put, encryption is the process of keeping sensitive information safe and sound. More formally, encryption is used to ensure that message data (such as a social security number, bank account ID, or user password) cannot be altered and/or understood by evildoers. From a high level, encryption addresses the following security issues:

- *Integrity*: If the message has been intercepted and modified during transport, the receiver should detect it. You ensure this using a cryptographic *hash code*.

- *Confidentiality*: The message data shouldn't be directly readable if it's intercepted by prying eyes. You accomplish this using *encryption* and *decryption* techniques.

- *Authentication*: The receiver of the message should be able to ensure the message came from the anticipated sender. You achieve this using *digital signatures*.

Although each flavor of encryption addresses a specific need (integrity, confidentially, and authentication), the programming model used to work with hash codes, encryption services, and digital signatures is more or less identical. Given this fact, we'll limit this part of our security overview to the role of hash codes.

Understanding Hash Codes

To address the issue of integrity, it is common to make use of *hash codes*. In a nutshell, a hash code is a numerical value that is tied to a fixed input. One interesting aspect of hash code values is the fact that they provide a form of *one-way encryption*, given that the generated numeric value contains no trace of the original message data.

For example, in the previous section, we examined how a strongly named assembly is assigned a digital signature based (in part) on a hash code value obtained from the assembly contents. Clearly a numerical value such as 79BB0DA9D45C6AE29F8 has no trace of the original assembly contents (types, methods, etc).

To further illustrate the nature of hash codes, consider the method System.Object.GetHashCode. This virtual method may be overridden by derived types to generate a hash value based on its internal state data. The System.String class has overridden this method to return a unique hash value for the current character data. Thus, if you have two identical strings (in the same case), System.String.GetHashCode will return the same value. If even one character differs by case or content, you receive a unique numerical value. Ponder the following class definition:

```
class Program
{
    static void Main(string[] args)
    {
        Console.WriteLine("***** Fun with Hash Codes *****");
        Console.WriteLine("Hash of 'Hello': {0}", "Hello".GetHashCode());
        Console.WriteLine("Hash of 'Hello': {0}", "Hello".GetHashCode());
        Console.WriteLine("Hash of 'HellO': {0}", "HellO".GetHashCode());
        Console.ReadLine();
    }
}
```

Notice that the first two string objects have identical content and case, while the final string has a capitalized letter O. Now ponder the output (see Figure 5-5).

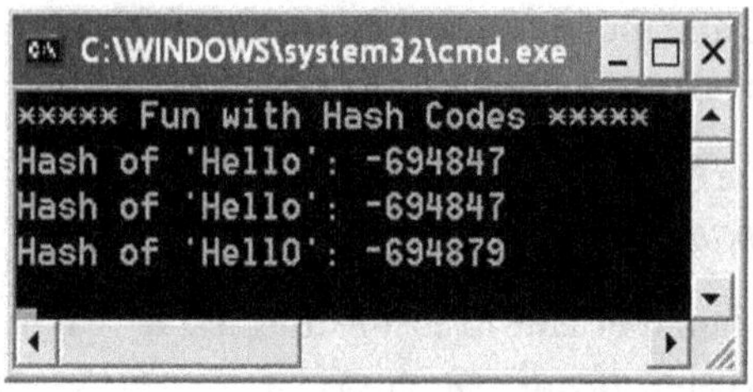

Figure 5-5. *Hash codes are unique based on their input.*

Of course, when you're interested in generating hash codes for large blocks of data or sensitive user information, you won't leverage GetHashCode. Truth be told, overriding this virtual method is only useful when you're designing types that may be placed in a Hashtable collection.

Luckily, the .NET platform ships with types that provide implementations of many well-known hash code algorithms. Each type is capable of operating on different input blocks and may differ based on the size of the message data and/or the size of the generated hash code. Table 5-2 documents your choices.

Table 5-2. *The .NET Hashing Algorithms*

.NET Hash Algorithm	Input Block Size	Message Limit (In Bits)	Hash Code Size (In Bits)
MD5 (MD = Message Digest)	512	2^{64}	128
SHA1 (SHA = Secure Hash Algorithm)	512	2^{64}	160
SHA256	512	2^{64}	256
SHA384	1024	2^{128}	384
SHA512	1024	2^{128}	512

Hashing a File

Once you've determined the hash code algorithm you wish to use, you can create an instance of the algorithm using the static HashAlgorithm.Create method. Simply pass in a string name of the algorithm you require (MD5, SHA1, SHA256, SHA384, or SHA512). Assume you wish to generate a hash code for a file on your local machine:

```
static void Main(string[] args)
{
    // Open a local file on the C drive.
    FileStream fs = new FileStream(@"C:\MyData.txt", FileMode.Open);

    // Now generate a hash code for this file using MD5.
    HashAlgorithm alg = HashAlgorithm.Create("MD5");
    byte[] fileHashValue = alg.ComputeHash(fs);
```

```
// Print out the generated hash code.
Console.WriteLine("Hash code of MyData.txt");
foreach (byte x in fileHashValue)
    Console.Write("{0:X2} ", x);
fs.Close();
Console.ReadLine();
}
```

Notice how hash values are represented using a simple array of bytes. Therefore, if MyData.txt contained thousands of lines of text, the entire contents might be represented as:

79 DC DA F4 5B F6 5C 0B B0 DA 9D 45 C6 AE 29 F8

If you were to change even a single character within MyData.txt, the new hash code will be entirely unique:

B3 E3 DD 14 96 2D D2 EB 0E C3 68 BF 08 04 D5 80

Again, using hash codes you're able to represent sensitive data as a unique byte array that contains no trace of the original message data. In a distributed system, one of the most common uses of this technology is for the purposes of storing password information. By storing a user's password in a hash code format, you increase the security of your system given that this numerical value has no trace of the original password. When the end user attempts to log into your system again, you simply rehash the message and perform a comparison against the persisted value.

Note Many hash code algorithms also enable you to specify a "salt" value. Simply put, *salting* is the process of incorporating a random value to the input of the hash algorithm, in order to further ensure a strong hash.

Role-Based Security (RBS)

Many applications, especially intranet or other such localized applications, require the capability to restrict access to resources based on the "role" of the currently logged-on user. For example, assume you have a set of known users (such as members on an NT domain) who have been placed into specific groups named "Sales People," "Managers," and "Developers". Using role-based security (or simply *RBS*), it is possible to programmatically determine the role of the current user interacting with a given type or type member.

Note The process of creating users and assigning them to their respective roles, which we won't cover here, is typically the job of your friendly network administrator.

When you wish to programmatically obtain the identity of the current user via the role-based security model, you must obtain a *principal object* from the current thread of execution via `Thread.CurrentPrincipal`. Simply put, a principal object represents the identity of the current user and each role to which he belongs. Technically speaking, a principal object is some type implementing the `System.Security.Principal.IPrincipal` interface:

```
public interface IPrincipal
{
    IIdentity Identity { get; }
    bool IsInRole(string role);
}
```

As you can see, the read-only `IPrincipal.Identity` property returns an object implementing `System.Security.Principal.IIdentity`, which is defined as so:

```
public interface IIdentity
{
    string AuthenticationType { get; }
    bool IsAuthenticated { get; }
    string Name { get; }
}
```

Before obtaining a principal object via `Thread.CurrentPrincipal`, the calling assembly needs to inform the CLR of the *principal policy* it's interested in leveraging. As of .NET 2.0, there are four possible principal policies:

- *Forms*: A RBS implementation for ASP.NET.

- *Generic*: Enables you to define your own custom RBS system.

- *Passport*: A RBS implementation for MS .NET Passport.

- *Windows*: A RBS implementation for Win32 user account systems.

As you'll see in just a bit, the Forms-based principal policy is used extensively when securing ASP.NET web applications. Until then, you'll assume a Windows-based principal policy that is fitting for known users on an internal NT network. Establishing a principal policy requires a call to `SetPrincipalPolicy` on the current application domain. These things being said, the following code illustrates how to obtain various statistics regarding the current caller via the members defined by the `IPrincipal` and `IIdentiy` interfaces:

```
private DisplayUserInformation()
{
    // Set the default principal policy for threads in this AppDomain.
    AppDomain myDomain = AppDomain.CurrentDomain;
    myDomain.SetPrincipalPolicy(PrincipalPolicy.WindowsPrincipal);

    // Get the current principal.
    WindowsPrincipal wp = (WindowsPrincipal)Thread.CurrentPrincipal;

    // Print out some stats.
```

```
string wpInfo = string.Format("Name is: {0}", wp.Identity.Name);
wpInfo += string.Format("\nIs authenticated?: {0}",
  wp.Identity.IsAuthenticated);
wpInfo += string.Format("\nAuth type: {0}",
  wp.Identity.AuthenticationType);
wpInfo += string.Format("\nIs user a guest?: {0}",
  wp.IsInRole(@"Developers"));

MessageBox.Show(wpInfo, "Current Principal Info");
}
```

Restricting Access Based On User Identity

Now that you have seen how to obtain details regarding the current caller, the next logical step is to understand how to constrain what the current caller may do based on her identity. The .NET role-based security model enables to you restrict access to type allocation and type member invocation using one or two approaches:

- *Imperative RBS*: Use RBS types directly in your code, making run-time demands and decisions where needed.

- *Declarative RBS*: Use .NET attributes to require demands.

When you use declarative RBS, you are able to apply numerous attributes that inform the .NET runtime to ensure the current caller is within a specified role before creating a given type or invoking a given member. This approach results in hard-coded assembly metadata, and, therefore, you have fewer ways to customize the process of handling run-time exceptions.

For example, assume you have authored a class method that should never be successfully invoked by any user who is not within the built-in NT Administrators role. Using a declarative approach, you would apply the PrincipalPermission attribute to the method as so:

```
[PrincipalPermission(SecurityAction.Demand,
 Role = @"BUILTIN\Administrators")]
private void SomeMethod()
{
    // If we got this far, the user is in the correct role.
    DoAdminStuff();
}
```

If you would rather take an imperative approach, you gain the capability to monitor access violations gracefully in code via try/catch constructs or simply deny a given course of action. Ponder the following related code example:

```
private void SomeMethod()
{
    // Set the default principal for threads in this appdomain.
    AppDomain myDomain = AppDomain.CurrentDomain;
    myDomain.SetPrincipalPolicy(PrincipalPolicy.WindowsPrincipal);
```

```
// Get the current principal.
WindowsPrincipal wp = (WindowsPrincipal)Thread.CurrentPrincipal;

// Do 'admin stuff' if caller is in role.
if(wp.IsInRole(WindowsBuiltInRole.Administrator))
  DoAdminStuff();
}
```

Now, be very aware that ASP.NET web applications also provide an RBS implementation, which is similar (but not identical to) the RBS model you just examined.

Note It should be mentioned that the .NET platform also provides a manner to assign a run-time identity to the assembly itself. Once this identity has been established, the Code Access security (CAS) model enables a system administrator to restrict what the assembly may (or may not) do via a set of configurable (and very flexible) rules.

Securing ASP.NET Web Applications

Now that you have seen the role of various .NET security atoms, you can turn your attention to the specifics of securing ASP.NET web applications. Do recall, however, that an ASP.NET web application is ultimately just another valid .NET assembly. Like any assembly, your ASP.NET web applications contain CIL code, type metadata, and manifest information. Given this point, many of the previous security-centric topics apply directly to Web development under the .NET platform (storing passwords as hash codes, strongly naming external assemblies, and so forth).

In addition to the general .NET security options, ASP.NET does provide Web-specific services that address the issues of *authentication* and *authorization*. Under ASP.NET, these two security needs are addressed in part by tweaking various settings within a server side web.config file. Like other XML-based files, web.config files can contain any number of subelements under the root <configuration> node, each of which can contain various attributes and possibly further subelements. At a very high level, a web.config file can be broken into the following skeleton:

```
<configuration>
    <system.web>
        <authentication/>
        <authorization/>
        <browserCaps/>
        <clientTarget/>
        <compilation/>
        <customErrors/>
        <globalization/>
        <httpHandlers/>
        <httpModules/>
        <httpRuntime/>
```

```
        <identity/>
        <machineKey/>
        <pages/>
        <processModel/>
        <securityPolicy/>
        <serviceDescriptionFormatExtensionTypes/>
        <sessionState/>
        <trace/>
        <trust/>
        <webServices/>
    </system.web>
</configuration>
```

■Note The purpose of this chapter is *not* to detail each and every option within a `web.config` file (that would require a small book on its own). Rather we focus on select security-specific elements. If you wish to see each and every option, look up the "ASP.NET Settings Schema" topic using the .NET 2.0 Framework SDK Documentation.

While it's not mandatory to include a `web.config` file as far as the ASP.NET runtime is concerned, they are downright mandatory when securing an ASP.NET web application. So much so that it's not uncommon for a single ASP.NET web application to make use of multiple `web.config` files. By doing so, you're able to leverage *configuration inheritance*.

Understanding Configuration Inheritance

Most ASP.NET web applications contain, at the very least, a single `web.config` file that sits in the root directory. When you insert a new `web.config` file using Visual Studio 2005 (via the Website ➤ Add New Item... menu option), the default XML looks something like the following (comments have been removed for clarity):

```
<?xml version="1.0"?>
<configuration xmlns="http://schemas.microsoft.com/.NetConfiguration/v2.0">
    <appSettings/>
    <connectionStrings/>
    <system.web>
        <compilation debug="false"/>
        <authentication mode="Windows"/>
    </system.web>
</configuration>
```

Note that the scope defined by `<system.web>` is where all of your ASP.NET security settings end up. The optional `<appSettings>` and `<connectionStrings>` elements provide a handy location to enter application-specific data and ADO.NET connections string values that may be obtained programmatically (see Chapter 10 for a close look at using and encrypting the new `connectionStrings` element).

In any case, when you have a `web.config` file located within the root directory, each subdirectory "inherits" the settings it defines. However, if you require, you may include specific `web.config` files that can effectively "override" the settings found in the parent `web.config` files higher up in the directory structure. Figure 5-6 illustrates one possible use of configuration inheritance.

Figure 5-6. *Configuration inheritance under ASP.NET*

Notice that this site has a subdirectory named `SiteAdmin` that contains its own unique configuration file, while the site as a whole is configured using the settings found within the root level `web.config` file. The idea (as you may suspect) is that access to `SiteAdmin` is more restrictive than the than of the root directory's content, and is, therefore, constrained using custom configuration settings.

■**Note** If your websites do not contain a specific `web.config` file, they will inherit all of the default settings found within the machine-wide `machine.config` file. Given this, understand that a root level `web.config` file is actually overriding various settings in `machine.config`.

Understanding ASP.NET Authentication Options

As we briefly mentioned in Chapter 1, *authentication* is often the first step in securing a system (Web-based or otherwise). Simply put, authentication services provide a way to validate the identity of the current user. Assume you're building an ASP.NET website that demands any and all unauthenticated users supply login credentials before proceeding. Using ASP.NET, you may choose between three possible flavors of authentication (which happen to map to the various principal policies examined during our discussion of role-based security):

- *Windows Authentication*: Supplied credentials are validated against the WinNT Security Accounts Manager (SAM) or alternatively by using Active Directory.

- *Passport*: Supplied credentials are validated against a Microsoft centralized authentication service.

- *Forms-Based Authentication*: Supplied credentials are validated against an application-specific data store (such as a server-side database or an XML file).

Note You may also specify an authentication setting of "None" to build a website that requires no authentication (e.g., you only expect unauthenticated users) or to build a website that is providing custom authentication techniques.

While you may be familiar with these options, here's a brief walkthrough for the uninitiated.

Windows-Based Authentication

Windows-based authentication services (which is the default behavior for new ASP.NET web applications) is perhaps the simplest approach from a programmer's point of view, given that there is no need to design a UI that prompts the user for his username/password and no need to author extensive boilerplate code. Using Windows authentication, the operating system provides the necessary infrastructure. To enable this behavior, simply define the following <authentication> element within your project's web.config file:

```
<configuration>
    <system.web>
        <authentication mode="Windows"/>
    </system.web>
</configuration>
```

One obvious downfall to Windows-based authentication services is the fact that all users must be "known individuals" on the SAM or an established Active Directory. Given this restriction, Windows-based authentication only works when anonymous access is turned off within IIS.

Passport-Based Authentication

As an alternative, developers may choose to use a specific Microsoft API termed *Passport*. Passport services enable developers to design their websites in such a way that Microsoft persists and validates user-supplied credentials. The major benefit of Microsoft Passport services (as far as the end user is concerned) is the fact that the same username/password can be used for any website participating in the Passport initiative (this approach is termed *single sign-in* or SSI). This is the security model sites such as Hotmail and MSN.com use. The downside (as far as the developer is concerned) is she must now learn a new object model.

Assuming your web application has been injected with the necessary Passport API calls, your web.config file will now be designed using a nested <passport> element that specifies the name of the page to redirect to if the current user has not supplied valid passport credentials:

```
<configuration>
    <system.web>
        <authentication mode="Passport"/>
            <passport redirectUrl="Login.aspx"/>
        </authentication>
    </system.web>
</configuration>
```

■Note We don't examine the details of the Microsoft Passport API in this chapter. If you require further details, consult the official Passport home page at www.passport.com.

Forms-Based Authentication

The fact of the matter is that Windows-based and Passport-based authentication is typically not a valid solution for large-scale public websites. For applications of this type, the most common authentication option will be Forms-based, which splits the workload between the .NET framework itself and the web developer. The developer is required to build a logon page and author the necessary code to compare the values of the supplied credentials and the persisted credentials. The framework responds by automatically redirecting the user to the requested page upon successful validation. If the validation is successful, the framework attaches an authentication ticket (issued by default as a cookie) to the current request. Figure 5-7 illustrates the Forms-based authentication model.

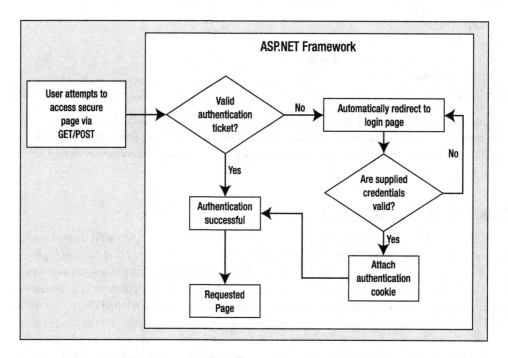

Figure 5-7. *The ASP.NET Forms authentication model*

■Note The authentication ticket is automatically encrypted (using Triple-DES) and protected via data validation to prevent any across the wire tampering.

Leveraging the Forms Authentication Model

If you have previous experience working with Forms authentication under .NET 1.x, you will be happy to know that your existing code is 100 percent backwards compatible (as are most other aspects of ASP.NET 2.0). As you would suspect, ASP.NET 2.0 provides a number of new types to simplify Forms-based authentication. However, before examining these new items, let's review the core model.

To leverage Forms-based authentication under ASP.NET, the first step is to author a custom aspx file that will provide the necessary UI to prompt for user credentials, such as a username and password. Figure 5-8 illustrates a typical logon.aspx page consisting of two TextBoxes, a handful of Labels and RequiredFieldValidators, and a Button type used to post back to the web server.

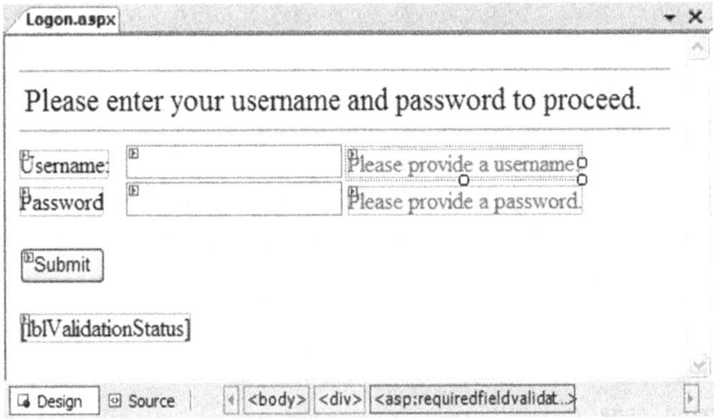

Figure 5-8. *Building a Logon.aspx page*

The Button's server-side Click event handler is responsible for extracting the supplied username and password values and validating them against the previously persisted values, which again may be located in a server-side XML file or, more commonly, in a table in a given database. Once you determine that the credentials are valid, the final step is to call the static FormsAuthentication.RedirectFromLoginPage method to attach the authentication cookie and redirect the user to the requested page. Consider the following logic:

```
public class Logon : System.Web.UI.Page
{
    protected void btnSubmit_Click(object sender, EventArgs e)
    {
        // Scrape out uid and pwd.
        string uid = txtUserName.Text;
        string pwd = txtPassword.Text;

        // Call a helper function to determine valid user.
        if (UserIsValid(uid, pwd))
            // Success! Redirect user to requested page.
            FormsAuthentication.RedirectFromLoginPage(uid, false);
        else
            // Oops!  User not found.  Display error message.
```

```
                lblValidationStatus.Text =
                    "Invalid login.  Please try again.";
    }

    private bool UserIsValid(string uid, string pwd)
    {
        // TODO: Generate hashcode of
        // incoming password if necessary.

        // TODO: Add ADO.NET logic to validate user.

        // Assume successful validation.
        return true;
    }
}
```

The final step is to update the project's web.config file to make use of Forms-based authentication. Notice that the <authentication> element now defines a nested <forms> subelement, which specifies the aspx file in the project that should be displayed by the framework.

```
<configuration>
    <system.web>
        <authentication mode="Forms">
            <forms loginUrl ="Logon.aspx"/>
        </authentication>
        <authorization>
            <deny users = "?"/>
        </authorization>
    </system.web>
</configuration>
```

Also note that this web.config file also defines an <authorization> subelement. This element is used in conjunction with <authentication> to inform the runtime when the automatic redirection should take place. By specifying <deny users = "?"/>, you are blocking all anonymous users (via the "?" token).

With this, your Forms-based authentication model is complete. As a simple test, run the web application. Because you haven't yet supplied valid credentials, your request doesn't have an attached authentication ticket and, therefore, you're automatically redirected to Logon.aspx (see Figure 5-9)

For this example, the IsUserValid helper method has been hard-coded to always return true; therefore, you're able to enter any sequence of characters into the TextBox controls. However, when IsUserValid returns false, the user is presented with your custom error message (see Figure 5-10).

Figure 5-9. *Automatic redirection to Logon.aspx*

Figure 5-10. *Invalid credentials do not result in redirection from the logon page.*

Details behind the <authentication> Element

As you've already seen, the opening tag of the <authentication> element supports a mode attribute that is used to establish the level of authentication for your web application. This element may include an optional <forms> or <passport> subelement based on your authentication choice. Given this, the basic skeleton of the <authentication> section of a web.config file is as so (where the pipe notation (|) represents selecting a single member of the set):

```
<authentication mode="Windows | Forms | Passport | None">
    <forms/>
    <passport/>
</authentication>
```

Details behind the <forms> Element

The <forms> element is where a majority of the authentication action can be found. The previous example was quite simple, as you only specified the loginUrl attribute on the opening element. As you might be suspecting, the <forms> element may be adorned with various attributes and subelements. As of .NET 2.0, the skeleton of the <forms> element is realized as so:

```
<forms name="name"
    cookieless=UseCookie | UseUri | AutoDetect | UseDeviceProfile
    defaultUrl=[Url]
    domain=domain name
    loginUrl="url"
    protection="All | None | Encryption | Validation"
    timeout="30"
    path="/"
    requireSSL="true | false"
    slidingExpiration="true | false">
        <credentials passwordFormat="Clear | SHA1 | MD5">
            <user name="username" password="password"/>
        </credentials>
</forms>
```

While full details for each value can be found using the .NET 2.0 Framework SDK Documentation, Table 5-3 describes some (but not all) of the optional attributes of interest.

Table 5-3. *Attributes of the* <forms> *Section*

<forms> Attribute	Meaning in Life
name	This attribute specifies the name of the authorization cookie. If you do not specify a name value, .ASPXAUTH will be used as the default.
cookieless	Under .NET 2.0, it is now possible to make use of "cookieless authentication tokens." See the next section for full details.
protection	Specifies the type of encryption, if any, to use for cookies.
timeout	Specifies the amount in minutes before an authentication cookie expires. If unspecified, the default is set to 30.
requireSSL	Specifies whether an SSL connection is required to transmit the authentication cookie.

The first point of interest is the name attribute. When you're running multiple ASP.NET web applications on a single Web server that each require their own login, you should specify a unique name for the authentication cookie. Conversely, if several applications need to share logins, you can set this name the same across those applications and the authentication ticket will only need to be created once, giving you single sign-in for Forms-based authentication. This value can be any sequence of characters; however, you'll obviously want to provide a meaningful value for the task at hand. For example:

```
<authentication mode="Forms">
    <forms loginUrl ="Logon.aspx" name ="WebEntryPoint"/>
</authentication>
```

Cookieless Authentication Support under ASP.NET 2.0

The next attribute of interest is `cookieless`. To understand the impact of this attribute, realize that ASP.NET 1.x's implementation of forms authentication was dependant upon cookies (in fact, the second parameter supplied to `FormsAuthentication.RedirectFromLoginPage` is a Boolean used to enable or disable a persistent cookie). The obvious limitation is that you cannot guarantee that the target browser will support cookies.

To address this issue, ASP.NET 2.0 now supports a cookieless manner to handle the authentication ticket, which is consistent with the frameworks support for cookieless sessions. Specifically, the `cookieless` attribute may be assigned to any of the following values (see Table 5-4).

Table 5-4. *Settings of the* `cookieless` *Attribute*

Cookieless Attribute Setting	Meaning in Life
UseCookies	Specifies that your Web program will always use cookies to represent the authentication ticket (e.g., you are emulating ASP.NET 1.1).
UseUri	Specifies that your Web program will *never* use cookies to represent the authentication ticket.
AutoDetect	Enables or disables cookie support based on dynamically discovering the settings of the client browser.
UseProfileDevice	This is the default setting. If the browser has the capability to support cookies (regardless of if the user has disabled cookies) a cookie will be used. Unlike AutoDetect, no dynamic discover step is taken.

For most ASP.NET web applications, the default value of `UseProfileDevice` will be sufficient. If you're required to support users who disable their cookies, `AutoDetect` is a nice option because it will use cookies for those that have them enabled, and only those users with support disabled will have their URLs modified. This feature is also cross browser-compatible. Also realize that the difference between `UseProfileDevice` and `AutoDetect` is this: `UseProfile` device determines if the browser supports cookies, which browsers mostly have for the last eight years or so. However, a user can have a browser that *supports* cookies, but the user still chooses to turn off *support* for cookies. `AutoDetect` must be used to detect this user specific setting within the browser.

For the sake of illustration, here is a `web.config` file that explicitly prevents the use of cookies to represent the authentication ticket:

```
<authentication mode="Forms">
    <forms loginUrl ="Logon.aspx" name ="WebEntryPoint"
        cookieless ="UseUri"/>
</authentication>
```

Now that you know how to disable (or enable) cookies for purposes of user authentication, you may be wondering how ASP.NET 2.0 will maintain the authentication ticket when cookies are not used. Again, given that cookieless authentication mimics the model used for cookieless sessions, the answer is that the encrypted ticket is packed into the URL. Thus, if you updated your web.config file as shown previously, you would find a URL something like the following upon successful validation (the embedded ticket is shown in bold):

```
http://localhost:1096/Asp_Authentication/(F(xWbfAoTTWrBjxrBTqlZdIxO45S-
ikcm2AFdU3mOa5N76bpAkpDxNVsb5vspUzUzkd-
tOe3xrw5Q4up5FOVpHUA2))/default.aspx
```

Details behind the <authorization> Element

As you see in the current web.config file, the <authorization> element may contain an <allow> subelement to control who can access a particular resource. Additionally, the <authorization> element can contain a <deny> subelement to explicitly *deny* access to a particular resource. The <allow> and <deny> subelements each support a users attribute that can be assigned to the "?" token (to specify anonymous users) as well as "*" (to specify all users). In its simplest form, the <authorization> element has the following skeleton:

```
<authorization>
    <allow users="? | *"/>
    <deny users="? | *"/>
</authorization>
```

If you so choose, the users attribute can contain a comma-delimited set of known users and/or roles recognized by the Win32 SAM or Active Directory. While specifying a set of individual users or groups for a publicly accessible site may seem odd, we are sure you can imagine a subset of your website that should only be accessed by a known set of users. For example, assume you have a subdirectory of your site that contains a number of configuration utilities for your site. If you were to include a new web.config file for that directory, you could enable Windows authentication and specify that *nobody* outside the role of "Admins" should be able to access the contained content. (Notice that the <allow> element is now making use of the roles attribute rather than the more specific users attribute.)

```
<configuration>
    <system.web>
        <authorization>
            <allow roles="Admins"/>
            <deny users="*"/>
        </authorization>
    </system.web>
</configuration>
```

In addition to supporting roles and users, the <allow> and <deny> elements can be further qualified using a set of *verbs*. Simply put, the optional verbs attribute enables you to specify which form(s) of HTTP transmission are allowed to access the specified resource. ASP.NET 2.0 honors the following verb values:

- GET

- HEAD

- POST

- DEBUG

This being said, the complete set of options supported by the <authorization> element can be understood as so:

```
<authorization>
    <allow users="comma-separated list of users"
        roles="comma-separated list of roles"
        verbs="comma-separated list of verbs"/>

    <deny users="comma-separated list of users"
        roles="comma-separated list of roles"
        verbs="comma-separated list of verbs"/>
</authorization>
```

Details behind the FormsAuthentication Type

Regardless of how you author your web.config file, the values assigned to the <authentication> and <authorization> elements will typically be consumed programmatically via the static members of FormsAuthentication. You have already seen one member from this type in use: RedirectFromLoginPage. FormsAuthentication defines other members of interest. First up, this type defines a number of read-only properties, which extract the values assigned to various attributes in the open tag of the <forms> element:

```
public sealed class FormsAuthentication
{
    public static string CookieDomain { get; }
    public static HttpCookieMode CookieMode { get; }
    public static bool CookiesSupported { get; }
    public static string DefaultUrl { get; }
    public static bool EnableCrossAppRedirects { get; }
    public static string FormsCookieName { get; }
    public static string FormsCookiePath { get; }
    public static string LoginUrl { get; }
    public static bool RequireSSL { get; }
    public static bool SlidingExpiration { get; }
    ...
}
```

Further, FormsAuthentication defines additional static members beyond RedirectFrom-LoginPage, a subset of which are shown in Table 5-5.

Table 5-5. *Select Members of* FormsAuthentication

FormsAuthentication **Member**	**Meaning in Life**
Authenticate()	Validates a username and password against credentials stored in application's *.config file.
GetRedirectUrl()	Returns the redirect URL for the original request that caused the redirect to the logon page.
HashPasswordForStoringInConfigFile()	Produces a hash password which can be stored in a *.config file.
RedirectFromLoginPage() RedirectToLoginPage()	Redirects the user to or from the specified login page.
SignOut()	Removes the Forms authentication ticket from the browser.

Working with the <credentials> Element

Recall that when you're making use of Forms authentication, you have some flexibility as to where you wish to store persisted user credentials. In our first example, the assumption was made that the username and password values were stored within a given table in a specific database. However, in some cases you may wish to define valid users directly within a *.config file. Again, it's not likely you'd use this approach in a large-scale public web application; however, if you had a region of your site that was to be accessed by a small group of known individuals, you might mark them using a <credentials> segment.

The opening element of the <credentials> section enables you to specify how passwords are represented within the *.config file (plaintext, or via MD5/SHA1 hash algorithms). Within a <credentials> scope can then be any number of <user> elements, each of which defines a name and password element. Consider the following update to our web.config file:

```
<configuration>
  <system.web>
    <authentication mode="Forms">
      <forms loginUrl ="Logon.aspx" name ="WebEntryPoint"
        cookieless ="UseUri">
      <credentials passwordFormat="SHA1">
        <user name="atroelsen"
          password="27CE4CA7FBF00685AF2F617E3F5BBCAFF7B7403C" />
        <user name="dselly"
          password="D108F80936F78DFDD333141EBC985B0233A30C7A" />
        <user name="tbarnaby"
          password="7BDB09781A3F23885CD43177C0508B375CB1B7E9"/>
      </credentials>
    </forms>
    </authentication>
    <authorization>
      <deny users = "?"/>
    </authorization>
  </system.web>
</configuration>
```

With this, the `Button Click` event handler now makes a call to `FormsAuthentication.Authenticate`, rather than performing custom ADO.NET database retrieval logic. For example

```
protected void btnSubmit_Click(object sender, EventArgs e)
{
    // Scrape out uid and pwd.
    string uid = txtUserName.Text;
    string pwd = txtPassword.Text;

    // Rehash password via helper function.
    string hashedPwd = GetHash(pwd);

    // See if we have a match in the web.config file.
    if (FormsAuthentication.Authenticate(uid, hashedPwd))
        FormsAuthentication.RedirectFromLoginPage(uid, false);
    else
        lblValidationStatus.Text = "Invalid login.  Please try again.";
}
```

So, at this point you have either (a) become enlightened as to how the ASP.NET runtime performs Forms-based authentication or (b) skipped over this entire section given that you have been doing Forms authentication since the early betas of .NET 1.0. In either case, we hope the core model is solid in your mind. With this, let's now examine how ASP.NET 2.0 extends and simplifies the core architecture.

Forms Authentication Improvements under ASP.NET 2.0

While establishing Forms authentication under ASP.NET 1.1 was certainly not rocket science, you may agree that there is room for improvement. First and foremost, the Web-based UI that defines a typical `logon.aspx` page is more or less identical across web applications (add Labels, TextBoxes, Buttons, etc). As well, the validation code found within the code-behind files of an ASP.NET 1.1 `logon.aspx` page is also more or less identical (open a database connection, format the SQL, submit the SQL, and so forth).

While you could encapsulate these details using a custom `UserControl`, this approach to UI reuse presents a new set of snags. ASP.NET 2.0 simplifies authentication/authorization tasks with the following new security-centric techniques:

- The Membership class

- The Role Manager class

- Authentication-centric ASP.NET Web Controls

As an added bonus, ASP.NET 2.0 also offers a Web-based UI editor for `web.config` files. Not only does this help prevent the developer from indirectly introducing malformed XML, this Web-based editor also facilitates remote website administration. You'll come to know the ASP.NET Web Site Administration Tool at the conclusion of this chapter.

Understanding the Membership Type

Recall that the first example of Forms authentication that we showed you in this chapter required the developer to author ADO.NET code in order to retrieve previously stored credentials. While this approach is still perfectly valid under ASP.NET 2.0, you can now leverage a new type within the System.Web.Security namespace that will do so *automatically*.

The Membership class can be configured to perform user validation with various *membership providers*. To date, ASP.NET provides membership provider implementations for Microsoft SQL Server or Active Directory. The providers that ship with the Framework provide a "canned" implementation of data storage for user information. If you have your own data store of user information, then you will need to implement your own provider to talk to your own database. One very nice benefit of the membership programming model is that your presentation layer code will not need to be altered regardless of the underlying membership provider.

For example, assuming your web application has been configured correctly, the following Button Click event handler validates the supplied user credentials against "some" membership provider. As before, if the supplied and stored credentials match, the user is redirected via FormsAuthentication.RedirectFromLoginPage to the requested page:

```
protected void btnSubmit_Click(object sender, EventArgs e)
{
    // Scrape out uid and pwd.
    string uid = txtUserName.Text;
    string pwd = txtPassword.Text;

    // Let the Membership type do the dirty work.
    if (Membership.ValidateUser(uid, pwd))
        FormsAuthentication.RedirectFromLoginPage(uid, false);
    else
        lblValidationStatus.Text =
            "Invalid login.  Please try again.";
}
```

Note Like most aspects of the .NET platform, you are able to extend the Membership framework to fit your liking. If you wish to develop a custom membership provider, you are able to extend the abstract MembershipProvider base class. Interested readers are invited to lookup the topic "Implementing a Membership Provider" using the .NET 2.0 Framework SDK Documentation.

Despite the usefulness of this type, the Membership class exposes only a small number of static members. Using these members you are able to programmatically

- Create new users

- Store and update membership data

- Authenticate users

- Manage passwords

Table 5-6 documents some (but not all) of the members of the Membership type.

Table 5-6. *Select methods of the* Membership *Type*

Membership Member	Meaning in Life
CreateUser	Adds a new user to the membership store.
DeleteUser	Removes a specific user from the membership store.
FindUsersByEmail FileUsersByName	These members return a strongly typed MembershipUserCollection object, which represents a set of users based on specific search criteria.
GetUser	Obtains a specific user from the membership store.
UpdateUser	Updates the underlying membership store with new user information.

Another interesting aspect of the Membership type is that if you choose to make use of any of the new ASP.NET 2.0 Login controls (Login, LoginView, LoginStatus, LoginName, and PasswordRecovery), authentication can be achieved "code-free," as these new server-side controls manipulate the Membership type behind the scenes. You'll get to know the role of these new controls in just a bit. However for now let's see how to make use of the Membership type directly.

Specifying a Membership Provider for your Website

ASP.NET membership is enabled for all new ASP.NET applications automatically. The default membership provider is the local instance of Microsoft SQL Server. This out-of-the-box behavior is catalogued within the <membership> element in the machine.config file. If you were to locate and open this file (located by default under C:\WINDOWS\Microsoft.NET\ Framework\v2.0.50215\CONFIG), you would find the following:

```
<membership>
    <providers>
        <add name="AspNetSqlMembershipProvider"
          type="System.Web.Security.SqlMembershipProvider,
          System.Web, Version=2.0.0.0, Culture=neutral,
          PublicKeyToken=b03f5f7f11d50a3a"
          connectionStringName="LocalSqlServer"
          enablePasswordRetrieval="false"
          enablePasswordReset="true"
          requiresQuestionAndAnswer="true"
          applicationName="/"
          requiresUniqueEmail="false"
          passwordFormat="Hashed"
          maxInvalidPasswordAttempts="5"
          passwordAttemptWindow="10"
          passwordStrengthRegularExpression="" />
    </providers>
</membership>
```

Notice that the `<provider>` element documents the known providers using the `<add>` subelement, each of which are qualified by numerous attributes. Given the intended purpose of XML, many of these attributes are thankfully self-describing. However, do note that the `requiresQuestionAndAnswer` attribute has been set to `true`. Keeping these default settings in your mind will demystify the process of adding new users.

Once your web application has specified which membership provider it wishes to make use of (including the act of doing nothing and accepting the default settings), you are able to interact with the `System.Web.Security.Membership` type programmatically. In fact, there is one interesting behavior that might surprise you. If you author code that interacts with the `Membership` type and then run the web application, the ASP.NET runtime automatically creates a new `mdf` data file under the `App_Data` folder of your project if one does not currently exist (see Figure 5-11).

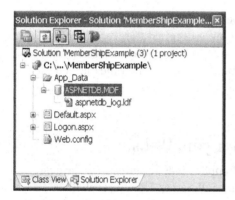

Figure 5-11. *The generated* `mdf` *file used by the* `Membership` *type*

If you examine the Solution Explorer perspective in Visual Studio 2005, you will also find that a data connection has been added to your project. Here you can view the database objects that are being manipulated in the background by the `Membership` type (see Figure 5-12).

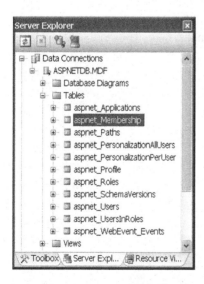

Figure 5-12. *The generated data connection*

Adding New Members

The first aspect of the Membership type we'll examine is the ability to add members to the data store maintained by the membership provider via Membership.CreateUser. This method has been overloaded a number of times; however, do note that each version returns an instance of the MembershipUser class type, which of course, represents the currently created user. (If the call to CreateUser fails, the return value is null.)

```
public static class Membership
{
...
    public static MembershipUser CreateUser
        (string username, string password);

    public static MembershipUser CreateUser
        (string username, string password, string email);

    public static MembershipUser CreateUser
        (string username, string password,
         string email, string passwordQuestion,
         string passwordAnswer, bool isApproved,
         out MembershipCreateStatus status);

    public static MembershipUser CreateUser
        (string username, string password,
         string email, string passwordQuestion,
         string passwordAnswer, bool isApproved,
         object providerUserKey,
         out MembershipCreateStatus status);
...
}
```

To illustrate the process of adding new users via code, assume you have authored a page named NewUser.aspx, which provides a series of TextBox widgets to account for the following points of data:

- Username

- Password

- E-mail

- Password retrieval question

- Answer to password retrieval question

Why so many input fields you ask? Recall that the machine.config file sets the requiresQuestionAndAnswer attribute to true. Furthermore, to provide this information, you must use of an overloaded version of CreateUser, which requires a string parameter representing the user's e-mail. This being said, ponder the following Button Click event handler:

```
protected void btnSubmit_Click(object sender, EventArgs e)
{
    // Initialize variable…
    MembershipCreateStatus status =
        MembershipCreateStatus.UserRejected;
    try
    {
        Membership.CreateUser(txtUserName.Text,
            txtPassword.Text, txtEmail.Text,
            txtPassword.Text, txtAnswer.Text,
            true, out status);
    }
    catch (Exception ex)
    {
        lblValidationStatus.Text = ex.Message;
    }
    lblValidationStatus.Text = status.ToString();
}
```

Once you scrape out the required data from the TextBox input fields, the call to CreateUser automatically updates the aspnet_Membership table within your project's mdf file. Again notice that you have authored no ADO.NET logic to do so. Also note that you pass in an output parameter of type MembershipCreateStatus. This enumeration describes the possible error conditions that may occur. Assuming all is well, this argument is set to MembershipCreateStatus.Success.

The MembershipUser Type

When a call to CreateUser completes successfully, you are returned an instance of the MembershipUser type:

```
MembershipUser newUser = Membership.CreateUser(…);
```

As you would guess, this type represents a single user stored in the membership system. Using this type, you are able to call various user-specific operations, including obtaining the same pieces of data that were submitted at the time of creation using properties such as Email, PasswordQuestion, UserName, and so on. As well, MembershipUser provides additional points of interest, some (but not all) of which are documented in Table 5-7.

Table 5-7. *Select Members of* MembershipUser

MembershipUser **Member**	**Meaning in Life**
CreationTime	Returns a DateTime representing when this user was added to the membership data store.
IsOnLine	Returns a Boolean that represents if the current user is in session.
ChangePassword	Enables you to change the stored password for the current user.

`MembershipUser` **Member**	**Meaning in Life**
`ChangePasswordQuestionAndAnswer`	Enables you to change the stored password question/answer for the current user.
`GetPassword`	Retrieves the currently stored password for the current user.

`LastActivityDate`
`LastLoginDate`
`LastPasswordChangeDate`
	Several methods of `MembershipUser` return `DateTime` objects that represent various timestamps regarding their activity.

Updating a User's Properties

Now assume you've designed a specific segment of your Web UI to allow the user to change his stored credentials (password, password question/answer and so on). The first task is to obtain a `MembershipUser` object that maps to the currently logged-on user via a call to `Membership.GetUser`. Next, simply feed in the new data using any of the members of `MembershipUser` and call `Membership.UpdateUser` to complete the update:

```
protected void btnChangeUserPasswordQandA_Click(object sender, EventArgs e)
{
    // Get currently logged on user.
    MembershipUser currUser = Membership.GetUser();

    // Change select aspects of MembershipUser object.
    currUser.ChangePasswordQuestionAndAnswer(txtPassword.Text,
        txtQuestion.Text, txtAnswer.Text);

    // Update membership.
    Membership.UpdateUser(currUser);
}
```

Deleting a User

Removing a user from the underlying membership data store is as simple as creating or updating one. Simply obtain the stored username for the current user and call `Membership.DeleteUser`:

```
protected void btnDeleteCurrentUser(object sender, EventArgs e)
{
    // Get currently logged on user.
    MembershipUser currUser = Membership.GetUser();

    // Delete based on username.
    Membership.DeleteUser(currUser.UserName);
}
```

At this point you have seen how the `Membership` and `MembershipUser` types can be used to automatically maintain the underlying data store used by a specific membership provider.

Remember that the core purpose of these types is to encapsulate the required SQL goo on your behalf. As you might agree, this is a large improvement from ASP.NET 1.1; however, at this point the examples still demand that you author the necessary Web UI to add users, update user accounts, validate credentials, and whatnot. Using ASP.NET 2.0, you can rectify this issue as well.

Working with the Security Server Controls

To alleviate the pain of building repeatable and redundant security-related Web UIs, ASP.NET 2.0 provides the server controls we describe in Table 5-8.

Table 5-8. *The .NET 2.0 Security-centric Server Controls*

Security-centric Server Control	Meaning in Life
Login	Provides a standard UI to enable the user to supply credentials.
LoginStatus	Toggles between two messages based on the login status of the current user.
LoginName	Provides simplified access to the name of the currently logged-on user.
PasswordRecovery	Provides a Web-based Wizard that allows the user to obtain her password based on a stored password question and answer.
ChangePassword	Provides a consistent UI that allows the end user to change her stored password.
CreateUserWizard	Provides a Wizard-based model to add new users to your site.

As you read over the next several pages, do be very aware that each of these new security-centric controls leverages the membership architecture you previously examined. Given this fact, you may find that by using these controls, you are able to provide full and complete authentication services without authoring a single line of code.

Note Like any ASP.NET Web Control, the new security controls define numerous properties, methods, and events. Given that full details of each member can be found within the .NET Framework 2.0 SDK Documentation, we'll stay focused on the core behavior of each type.

The Login Control

The Login control provides an out-of-the-box Web UI for the purposes of credential validation. Beyond offering the traditional UI, the Login control makes use of the specified membership provider to perform validation. Given all of this intrinsic functionality, you are able to build a Login.aspx file with *no* code whatsoever. Figure 5-13 illustrates an unmodified Login control:

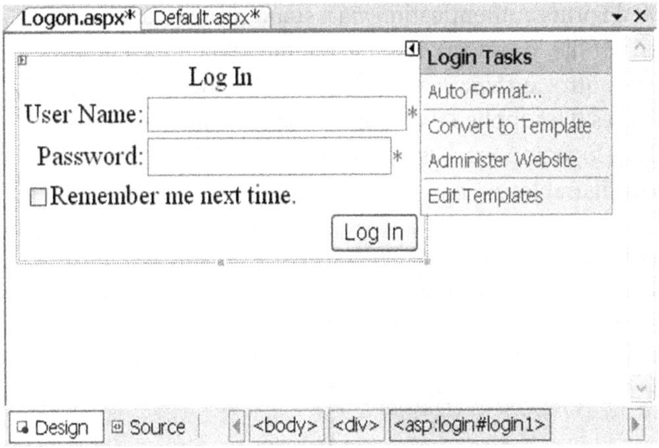

Figure 5-13. *The default* Login *control UI in the Visual Studio .NET Designer*

If the default look and feel does not suit your needs, you are most certainly able to alter the UI using the Visual Studio 2005 Properties window or manually update the opening `<asp:Login>` tag and the nested subelements that map to the contained controls. By way of example, the following `<asp:Login>` definition results in the UI shown in Figure 5-14.

```
<asp:Login ID="Login1" runat="server"
  BackColor="#EFF3FB" BorderColor="#B5C7DE" BorderPadding="4"
  BorderStyle="Solid" BorderWidth="1px" Font-Names="Verdana" Font-Size="0.8em"
  ForeColor="#333333" TitleText="Please Log in to the Site">
    <LoginButtonStyle BackColor="White" BorderColor="#507CD1"
      BorderStyle="Solid" BorderWidth="1px"
      Font-Names="Verdana" Font-Size="0.8em" ForeColor="#284E98" />
    <TextBoxStyle Font-Size="0.8em" />
    <TitleTextStyle BackColor="#507CD1" Font-Bold="True"
        Font-Size="0.9em" ForeColor="White" />
    <InstructionTextStyle Font-Italic="True" ForeColor="Black" />
</asp:Login>
```

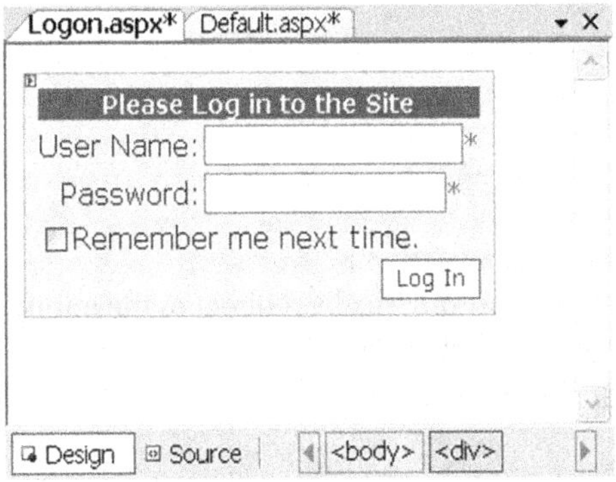

Figure 5-14. *A modified* Login *control*

Now, assuming you have enabled Forms authentication via a standard web.config and added some users to your generated mdf file, your work is done. Literally. When the end user clicks on the LogIn button, the Login control automatically tests each field for content (via RequiredFieldValidators) and validates the supplied username and password against the registered membership provider. If the login is unsuccessful, the result is an expected error message (which, of course, is also configurable) as seen in Figure 5-15.

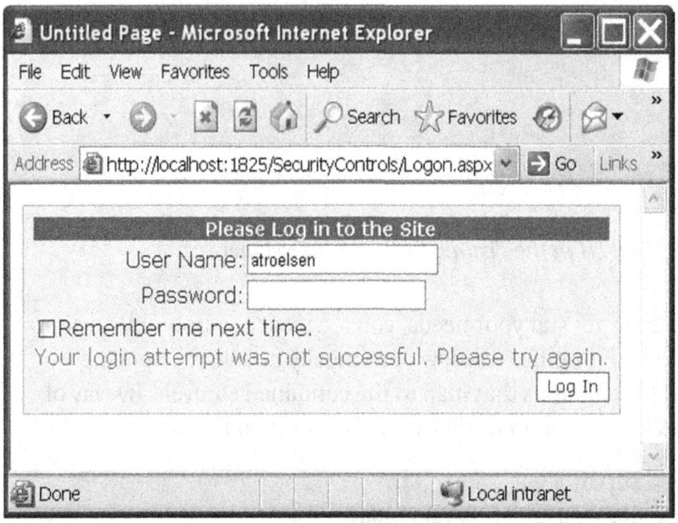

Figure 5-15. *An unsuccessful login attempt*

On the other hand, if the supplied and stored credentials match up, the user is automatically redirected from the login page to the requested resource.

The LoginStatus Control

LoginStatus is a simple security-centric control that (as the name suggests) displays the current logon status for the current user. When the user is logged on to the site, the UI takes the form of a hyperlink whose caption is controlled by the LogoutText property. Conversely, if the user is currently logged out, the hyperlink caption is controlled by the LoginText property. Consider the following LoginStatus declaration:

```
<asp:LoginStatus ID="LoginStatus1" runat="server"
  LoginText="Please Log in"
  LogoutText="Please Log out when finished!" />
```

Figure 5-16 illustrates the UI when the user is currently logged on:

Now assume you wish to have the LoginStatus control automatically redirect to the applications' logon.aspx page (e.g., the *.aspx file specified within the <forms> element of the web.config file). To do so, you can set the LogoutAction property as so:

```
<asp:LoginStatus ID="LoginStatus1" runat="server"
LoginText="Please Log in"
LogoutText="Please Log out when finished!"
LogoutAction="RedirectToLoginPage" />
```

Figure 5-16. *If you are currently logged in, you are asked to log out.*

With this, when the user clicks on the logout link, he is, indeed, returned to your logon page. In fact, if you were to update the logon.aspx file with its own LoginStatus as so:

```
<asp:LoginStatus ID="LoginStatus1" runat="server"
  LoginText="Please Log in"
  LogoutText="Please Log out when finished!" />
```

you would find the control automatically displays the LoginText value (see Figure 5-17).

Figure 5-17. *If you are currently logged out, you are asked to log in.*

The LoginName Control

The LoginName control enables you to quickly obtain the name of the currently logged-on user and is perfect for presenting a friendly salutation. Of course, you are always able to obtain this same information using the following ASP.NET logic:

```
string currUser = HttpContext.Current.User.Identity.Name;
lblGreetingsMsg.Text = currUser;
```

If you were to instead make use of the LoginName control, you can save yourself a few lines of code. This is perhaps the simplest of all security-centric controls, given the small number of configurable properties. In fact, beyond the expected UI properties (BackColor, CssClass, etc) the only property of interest is FormatString. By default, the value is nothing more than a curly-bracket placeholder used with .NET string formatting ({0}). However, this can be updated with additional textual content:

```
<asp:LoginName ID="LoginName1" runat="server"
FormatString="Hello, {0}! Welcome!" />
```

Of course, the placeholder value is updated on the fly based on the username of the currently logged-on user.

The PasswordRecovery Control

When you establish a membership provider to work in conjunction with your ASP.NET 2.0 web application, one option you have is to enable password recovery (which is the case if you are using the default membership provider). Assuming this is the case, you can use the PasswordRecovery control to allow the user to obtain her stored password based on her username, password question, and password answer. To illustrate assume you have a user stored in the project's mdf file that matches the credentials in Table 5-9:

Table 5-9. *Properties of the* PasswordRecovery *control*

Control Property	Assigned Value
Username	Chucky
Password	chu@k123!!
Email	chucky@myprovider.com
Password Question	What is your favorite NBA team?
Password Answer	Timberwolves

Now assume your default.aspx file has been updated with a PasswordRecovery control. Beyond updating the initial UI with a desired look and feel, the only additional requirement is to set the details of the MailDefinition element. This segment of the <asp:PasswordRecovery> scope enables you to configure the properties of the e-mail that will be sent upon successful recovery.

This brings up a very important point: By default the PasswordRecovery control will use the SMTP mail server on the local Web server (using the default SMTP port of 25). This information is recorded within the <smtpMail> element of the machine.config file. If these default settings do not fit the bill, you are free to add a custom <smtpMail> element within a web.config file; for example:

```
<system.web>
    <smtpMail
      serverName="MySmtpServer"
      serverPort="15"
      from="me@here.com">
        <fields>
              <add name="smtpauthenticate" value="2">
        </fields>
    </smtpMail>
</system.web>
```

All this being said, here is one possible PasswordRecovery declaration:

```
<asp:PasswordRecovery ID="PasswordRecovery1" runat="server"
    BackColor="#F7F6F3" BorderColor="#E6E2D8"
    BorderPadding="4" BorderStyle="Solid" BorderWidth="1px"
    Font-Names="Verdana" Font-Size="0.8em">
        <MailDefinition From="admin@mySite.com" Subject="Here is your e-mail">
        </MailDefinition>
        <InstructionTextStyle Font-Italic="True" ForeColor="Black" />
        <SuccessTextStyle Font-Bold="True" ForeColor="#5D7B9D" />
        <TextBoxStyle Font-Size="0.8em" />
        <TitleTextStyle BackColor="#5D7B9D" Font-Bold="True"
            Font-Size="0.9em" ForeColor="White" />
        <SubmitButtonStyle BackColor="#FFFBFF" BorderColor="#CCCCCC"
          BorderStyle="Solid" BorderWidth="1px"
          Font-Names="Verdana" Font-Size="0.8em"
          ForeColor="#284775" />
</asp:PasswordRecovery>
```

Now, when the user first encounters the PasswordRecovery control, he is prompted for his current username (see Figure 5-18).

Figure 5-18. *Providing the username to the* PasswordRecovery *control*

Once the user clicks on the Submit button, the membership provider retrieves the stored password question, which is rendered back into the HTTP response stream (see Figure 5-19).

Figure 5-19. *Requesting an answer . . .*

If you supply the correct answer (which is to say, the supplied answer matches what is currently maintained in the mdf file), the current user will be e-mailed his current password. If not, an expected error message is displayed within the PasswordRecovery control.

The ChangePassword Control

Changing a password is also extremely simple to do via the ChangePassword control. As you might guess by this point, this widget will perform all of the heavy lifting of updating the underlying data store maintained by the membership provider. Assume the following <asp:ChangePassword> declaration using the default UI:

```
<asp:ChangePassword ID="ChangePassword1" runat="server">
</asp:ChangePassword>
```

With this, the end user would find the following page (see Figure 5-20).

Of course, if the supplied and stored passwords match, the underlying data source is updated with the new password value.

The CreateUserWizard Control

Earlier in this chapter you learned how to programmatically create a new user via the CreateUser method of the Membership type. As you have seen, a MembershipUser instance consists of numerous possible points of data beyond a simple username/password (e-mail, password retrieval question/answer, etc). If you were to add a new CreateUserWizard control onto a page designer, you would find that the initial UI addresses each of these core issues. As expected, this out-of-the-box implementation will automatically insert a new user into the data store maintained by the designated membership provider.

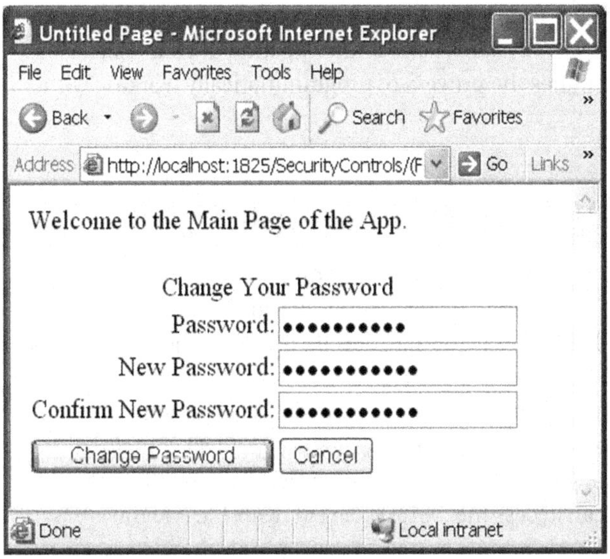

Figure 5-20. *The* ChangePassword *control*

Like other Web-centric Wizards provided by ASP.NET 2.0, the CreateUserWizard control can be updated with additional steps that address any application-specific user data. We'll allow the interested reader to dig into the details if you so choose; however, as you can see in Figure 5-21, the page designer provides hyperlinks that launch the process of adding additional pages (via Add/Remove WizardSteps…).

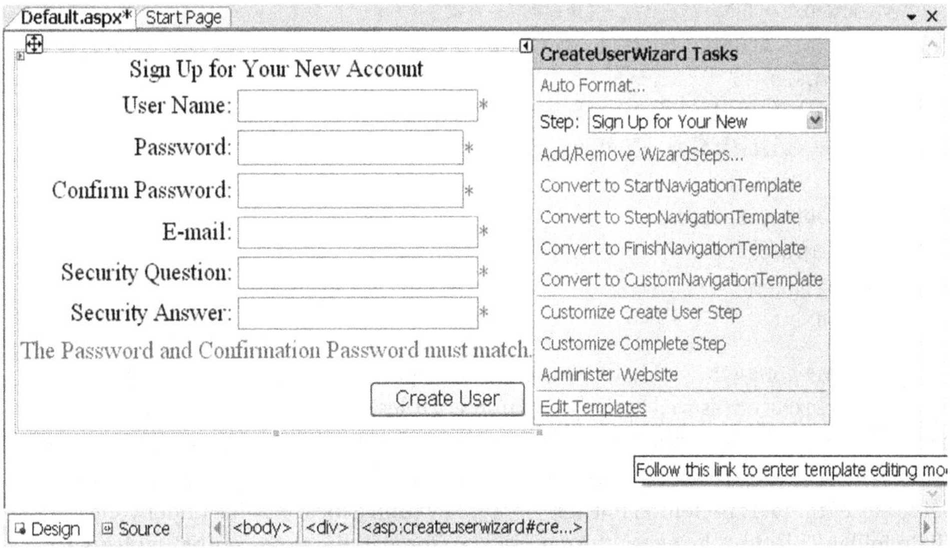

Figure 5-21. *The* CreateUserWizard *control*

Sweet! As you have just seen, the new security-centric server controls encapsulate virtually every detail regarding the creation, maintenance, and authentication of your users. Next up, let's examine how ASP.NET 2.0 simplifies the process of programmatically working with user roles.

Understanding ASP.NET 2.0 Role Membership

Once users have been authenticated, the ASP.NET runtime may optionally attempt to assign users to a known *role*. Recall from earlier in the chapter that role-based security models enable you to restrict what a given individual may (or may not) do based on the role to which they belong.

Under ASP.NET 1.x, roles were configured using the <authorization> segment of a web.config file. For example, the following web.config file denies access to all contained resources for unauthenticated users and ensures that only authenticated users that are assigned to a role named DeluxeUser can access the DeluxeContent.aspx file (via the <location> element):

```
<configuration>
    <system.web>
        <authentication mode="Forms">
            <forms loginUrl ="Logon.aspx"/>
        </authentication>
        <authorization>
            <deny users = "?"/>
        </authorization>
    </system.web>
    <location path ="DeluxeContent.aspx">
        <system.web>
            <authorization>
                <allow roles ="DeluxeUser"/>
                <deny users ="*"/>
            </authorization>
        </system.web>
    </location>
</configuration>
```

While the previous web.config file would function perfectly under ASP.NET 2.0, creating roles such as DeluxeUser (as well as assigning users to roles) can be automated using the Role Manager. Much like the membership provider examined earlier in the chapter, the role management system relies on a specific provider to store the role-based data, which by default is AspNetSqlRoleProvider; therefore, role data is stored within a local mdf file under your App_Data folder. This time, however, the data will be stored in the "role-centric" tables, such as aspnet_Roles (see Figure 5-22).

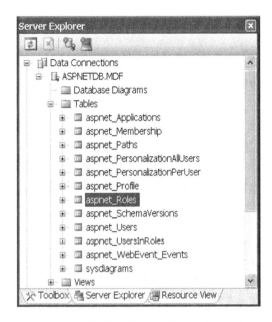

Figure 5-22. *Role data is stored in various role-centric tables of the* ASPNETDB.mdf *file.*

Enabling Role Membership Services

Unlike the membership provider, the Role Manager is not automatically enabled in the machine.config file. To enable role services for your web application, simply update your web.config file with the following <roleManager> element:

```
<configuration>
    <system.web>
        <roleManager enabled="true" />
        <authentication mode="Forms" />
    </system.web>
</configuration>
```

As you would guess, the <roleManager> element can be decorated with additional attributes that fine-tune how the Role Manager operates. The .NET Framework 2.0 SDK Documentation provides all the gory details; however, the possible attributes are as follows:

```
<roleManager
  enabled="true | false"
  defaultProvider="provider name"
  cacheRolesInCookie="true | false"
  maxCachedResults="maximum number of role names cached"
  cookieName="name"
  cookiePath="/"
  cookieProtection="All | Encryption | Validation | None"
  cookieRequireSSL="true | false "
  cookieSlidingExpiration="true | false "
```

```
cookieTimeout="number of minutes"
createPersistentCookie="true | false"
domain="cookie domain"/>
```

At this point, you are able to add and configure user roles using the Roles type.

Understanding the Roles Type

When you wish to create, delete, or manage roles in code, you'll make use of the Roles class. Beyond a number of read-only properties that allow you to obtain the values assigned to the attributes within the <roleManger> element, Roles provides a number of interesting methods:

```
public static class Roles
{
...

    // Methods to add new users to existing roles.
    public static void AddUsersToRole(string[] usernames, string roleName);
    public static void AddUsersToRoles(string[] usernames,
                                       string[] roleNames);
    public static void AddUserToRole(string username, string roleName);
    public static void AddUserToRoles(string username, string[] roleNames);

    // Create / validate roles.
    public static void CreateRole(string roleName);
    public static bool RoleExists(string roleName);

    // Methods to delete existing roles.
    public static bool DeleteRole(string roleName);
    public static bool DeleteRole(string roleName, bool throwOnPopulatedRole);

    // Various methods to determine role membership.
    public static string[] FindUsersInRole(string roleName,
                                           string usernameToMatch);
    public static string[] GetAllRoles();
    public static string[] GetRolesForUser();
    public static string[] GetRolesForUser(string username);
    public static string[] GetUsersInRole(string roleName);
    public static bool IsUserInRole(string roleName);
    public static bool IsUserInRole(string username, string roleName);

    // Methods to remove users from roles.
    public static void RemoveUserFromRole(string username, string roleName);
    public static void RemoveUserFromRoles(string username,
                                           string[] roleNames);
    public static void RemoveUsersFromRole(string[] usernames,
                                           string roleName);
    public static void RemoveUsersFromRoles(string[] usernames,
                                            string[] roleNames);
}
```

While these members are quite self-explanatory, here's a brief walkthrough of working with the Roles type in code.

Note Although the Roles type does enable you to manage roles and their users programmatically, most ASP.NET web applications will do so using the ASP.NET Web Application Administration Tool.

Creating, Obtaining, and Deleting Roles

If you wish to programmatically add a set of roles to your web application's mdf database, simply call the static Roles.CreateRole method. On a related note, if you wish to obtain the names of each role stored in the aspnet_Roles table, Roles.GetRoles will do so by returning an array of strings. Consider the following Button Click event hander:

```
protected void btnCreateAndDisplayRoles_Click(object sender, EventArgs e)
{
    try
    {
        Roles.CreateRole("DeluxeUser");
        Roles.CreateRole("Managers");
    }
    catch { }
    gridCurrentRoles.DataSource = Roles.GetAllRoles();
    gridCurrentRoles.DataBind();
}
```

Figure 5-23 shows the expected output.

Figure 5-23. *Programmatically creating and obtaining roles*

If you should need to programmatically remove a role from the underlying data store, simply call Roles.DeleteRole by passing in the name of the role to be removed:

```
Roles.DeleteRole("Managers");
```

Assigning Users to Roles

Once you have established the roles to be used by your web application, the next logical step is to assign users to their respective role (or set of roles). Again, this can be automated via the ASP.NET Web Application Administration Tool; however, you may also do so in code using the AddUserToRole, AddUsersToRole, AddUserToRoles, or AddUsersToRoles methods:

```
protected void btnAddUsersToRoles_Click(object sender, EventArgs e)
{
    string[] theUsers = {"Fred", "Mary"};
    string[] theRoles = {"DeluxeUser", "Managers"};

    // Add a single user (or set of users) to a role
    // (or set of roles).
    Roles.AddUsersToRole(theUsers, "Managers");
    Roles.AddUsersToRoles(theUsers, theRoles);
    Roles.AddUserToRole("Joe", "DeluxeUser");
    Roles.AddUserToRoles("Mitch", theRoles);
}
```

On a related note, if you wish to determine the set of roles to which a user has been assigned, simply call Roles.GetRolesForUser:

```
string[] userRoles = Roles.GetRolesForUser("Fred");
```

Determining Role Membership

Once you have established roles and role membership, the Roles.IsUserInRole method enables you to make run-time decisions based the role membership of the current user. For example, assume you have a method that can be called by any user on your system; however, within the scope of said method, you wish to ensure a specific set of statements will only execute if the current caller is a member of the Managers role:

```
private void InsertRecord(DataSet ds)
{
    // Insert any updated rows
    // to general database…

    if(Roles.IsUserInRole("Managers"))
    {
        // Update manager-centric database
        // with rows marked for deletion…
    }
}
```

Here, the assumption is that the "manager-centric" database should only be updated if the current user is indeed in the Managers role. If this is not the case, the entire set of statements within the if scope will be skipped.

ASP.NET Web Application Administration Tool

As we've shown during much of this chapter, establishing security settings for your ASP.NET web applications involves considerable updates to your web.config file. While the end result is quite spectacular (major changes in behavior with minimal fuss and bother), few of us enjoy manually authoring the necessary XML data. Not only is the process error prone and tedious, but also remotely updating these files requires modifying and uploading a local file.

As of ASP.NET 2.0, you now have a GUI-based Web front end to edit the web.config files for a given website. You're able to load the ASP.NET admin tool directly by specifying the WebAdmin.axd suffix to your site's URL:

```
http://MyWebSite/WebAdmin.axd
```

While this approach is ideal for remote administration, you are also able to leverage the ASP.NET admin tool at the time you are developing your web applications by activating the Website ➤ ASP.NET Configuration menu option of Visual Studio 2005. Either way, you are greeted with the following web page (see Figure 5-24).

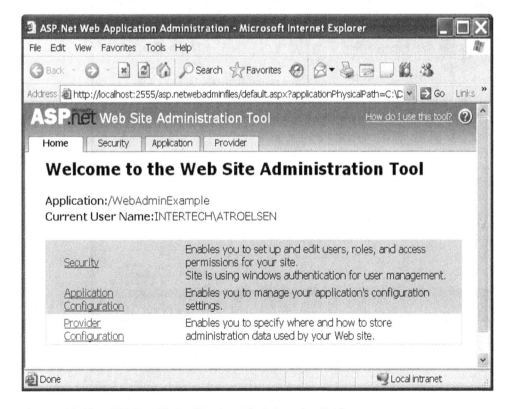

Figure 5-24. *The ASP.NET Web Application Administration Tool*

As you can see, you are able to configure core security settings, user data (including the roles of known users), as well as application-specific settings (such as SMTP settings and default error pages) using the provided tabs and/or hyperlinks found on the home page. As you explore the tool, you'll find that the UI is quite easy to understand (especially if you understand the coding concepts we've presented over the course of this chapter).

To take this new tool out for a spin however, assume you have created a brand new ASP.NET web application using the File ➤ New ➤ WebSite… menu option in Visual Studio 2005. Once you have done so, load the ASP.NET admin tool and select the Provider link. Here you can verify that your web application is indeed making use of the default membership provider found in your machine.config file.

Now, select the Application tab. Here you are able to create and manage various application-specific settings—the most notable, the name/value pairs contained within an <appSettings> element. As you may know, these elements can be programmatically obtained using the System.Diagnostics.AppSettingsReader type. You can now also get to these settings by using the new System.Configuration.ConfigurationManager.AppSettings method. By way of a simple test, click on the Create Application Settings link on the Application page and enter a sample name/value pair (see Figure 5-25).

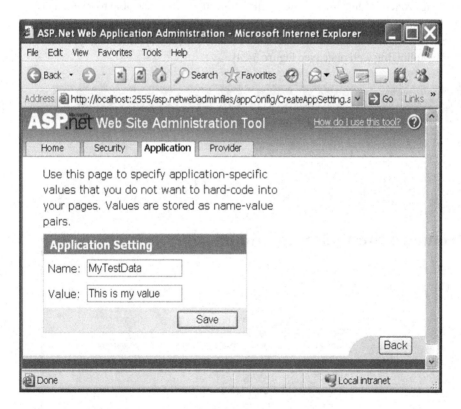

Figure 5-25. *Establishing an* AppSettings *segment*

Now, save your application settings and navigate to the Security tab. Here is where you are (obviously) able to edit the various security settings you've seen in the chapter. You should be able to verify that that default authentication level (Windows) is enabled, as this is the value found established within machine.config. To set your site's authentication level to Forms, simply click on the Select authentication type link on the leftmost Users column. From the resulting page, select the From the Internet radio button and click the Done button.

You should now be back at the main Security page, and at this point, you can specify the initial set of users who can access your site by clicking on the Create User link. Once you do, you are presented with a page that enables you to enter the expected new user credentials. For testing purposes, enter yourself as a new user (see Figure 5-26).

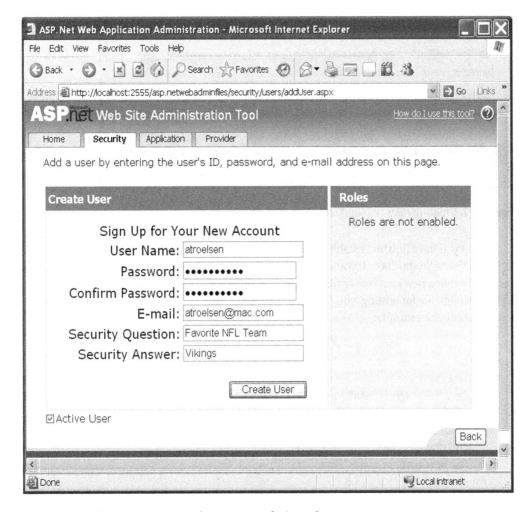

Figure 5-26. *Adding new users via the ASP.NET admin tool*

Finally, you are able to enable role support from the Security tab via the Enable Roles link. Once you do, you are able to create new roles via the same Security page via the Create or Manage roles link (see Figure 5-27).

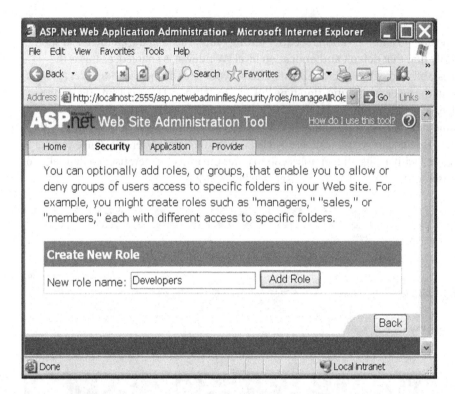

Figure 5-27. *Creating roles via the ASP.NET admin tool*

When you have finished establishing your site's configuration options, close the tool and return to Visual Studio 2005. If you now look within the Solution Explorer perspective, you should see that a new web.config file has been automatically added to your current project. If you open the file for editing, you'll find your configuration choices are represented by the required XML; for example:

```
<?xml version="1.0" encoding="utf-8"?>
<configuration xmlns="http://schemas.microsoft.com/.NetConfiguration/v2.0">
    <appSettings>
        <add key="MyTestData" value="This is my value" />
    </appSettings>
    <system.web>
        <roleManager enabled="true" />
        <authentication mode="Forms" />
    </system.web>
</configuration>
```

Summary

The first goal of this chapter was to introduce you to the various security components supplied by the .NET 2.0 base class libraries. As you have seen, there are numerous security-centric namespaces, most of which have a direct impact on ASP.NET web applications. Recall that the framework provides numerous types to work with standard encryption atoms (hash codes, asymmetric/symmetric encryption) and traditional role-based security.

The remainder of this chapter focused exclusively upon the ASP.NET security framework. We began by reviewing the core Forms authentication model, which has been present since the inception of the .NET platform. Once we established the basics, we examined how the Membership type and various server controls can be used to simplify the authentication process. Next, we revisited the notion of role-based security within the context of the Roles API.

Last but not least, this chapter introduced you to a new Web-based interface, which you can use to edit web.config files: the ASP.NET Web Application Administration Tool. While a single chapter cannot cover all possible aspects of the .NET security model, we believe this puts you are in a very good position for further exploration.

CHAPTER 6

■■■

SOA in .NET: Web Services

In this chapter, we'll examine Service Oriented Architecture (SOA) and Web Services. You'll see what SOA is, or at least what a lot of people in the industry are saying it is. Then we'll examine Web Services as an implementation of SOA. Web Services in version 2.0 of the .NET Framework has many new features, so we'll take a look at them, including how to use them and exactly how they're improvements over Web Services version 1.x. We'll wrap it up with a brief look at Web Services Enhancements (WSE), which is an add-on package of functionality from Microsoft that extends Web Services with many industry-standard areas of functionality based on specifications.

SO What?

What exactly is service orientation (SO)? Any time there's so much hype and buzz about a term, it invariably starts to mean different things to different people. Let's start by dissecting some of the definitions being kicked around out there.

> *A set of components which can be invoked, and whose interface descriptions can be published and discovered.*

> World Wide Web Consortium
> Standards body for the World Wide Web

The statement a "set of components" is rather vague, as a service may be a set with only a single operation. This definition is very general, almost too general to really capture what service orientation is. Distributed Component Object Model (DCOM) and .NET remoting both seem to meet this definition, even though they're not generally considered implementations of SOA. The final part, stating that the components' "descriptions can be published and discovered" is an important element, one which is common to all of the definitions we'll look at.

> *SOA is an architectural style whose goal is to achieve loose coupling among interacting software agents.*

> Hao He
> Architect, Thomson Corporation

Here, Hao He introduces the second thread, that of "loose coupling." However, his definition doesn't speak to discovery at all. Discovery and loose coupling are two elements that are very important in service orientation. They both facilitate reuse.

This is called out more sharply by the next definition, which likens the level of interoperability to the Holy Grail.

> *SOA is kind of an IT manager's Holy Grail, in which software components can be exposed as services on the network, and, so, can be reused time and time again for different applications and purposes.*
>
> Preston Gralla
> Technology Journalist

In some larger enterprises, reuse is the "Holy Grail" of IT, as system integration can be costly and cause a lot of churn. Integration strategies have to be reinvented time and again as a system is integrated with others that may be on disparate platforms. Service orientation allows you to write integration code once and reuse it over and over again, regardless of platform, operating system, or language. Another definition of service orientation is

> *The policies, practices, frameworks that enable application functionality to be provided and consumed as sets of services published at a granularity relevant to the service consumer. Services can be invoked, published and discovered, and are abstracted away from the implementation using a single, standards-based form of interface.*
>
> David Sprott and Lawrence Wilkes
> Principal Analysts, Computers by Design, Inc.

This definition takes on the W3C (World Wide Web Consortium) definition specifically in the fact that it calls out a "set" of components. The "granularity" of the service is independent of the fact that it's a service-oriented implementation. While we can still speak of "coarse-grained" or "fine-grained" services, what's important is that the design is relevant to the service consumer. Separating the implementation from interface is first called out here, but it's really just a more concrete invocation of "loose coupling." Consumers of a service need a description of that service; they do not need the libraries containing the implementation. In fact, consumers don't even need to be aware of how the implementation is done. It may be .NET; it may be Java; it may be a hundred hamsters on exercise wheels. Consumers care not, just so long as they get SOAP formatted messages back as a response. Finally, the "single, standards-based from of interface" is a more concrete way of saying "interoperable."

> *Rather than explicitly declaring how systems will interact through low-level protocols and object-oriented architectures, SOA provides an abstract interface through which a service can interact with other services or applications through a loosely coupled (often asynchronous), message-based communication model. It can be imagined as an interconnected process-based enterprise that exposes a set of loosely coupled, coarse-grained services.*
>
> Soumen Chatterjee
> Senior Consultant, Cap Gemini Ernst & Young

This definition goes on to call out a little about how SOA is different from Remote Procedure Call (RPC). It's an important distinction, and one that's easy to miss when you're first coming to an understanding of service orientation. This is a message-passing infrastructure, and not an RPC mechanism. In this definition, we see our invocation of a "message-based" approach, a distinction that's more metaphorical than anything else, and one we'll carry through our entire discussion. It changes how you think about services, changes that should influence how they're designed. This distinction is lost on many, however, because it doesn't change how services are consumed. At the end of the day, you create an instance of a type, call a method, and get a value returned. It looks like RPC. It acts like RPC. But it is not RPC.

The message is the medium.

Don Box
Architect, Microsoft Corporation

These definitions seemingly land all over the board. SOA really seems to mean a lot of different things to different people. There are some common themes here, though, and pulling out these threads should give you a more vivid idea of what the SOA tapestry reveals.

SO What Are the Themes?

The first theme is that a service provider needs a way to publish its service. Since the infrastructure is intended to facilitate reuse, publishing the service is a critical step to "get the word out," so others can make use of the service. A company may have a central repository for all of the services available within the enterprise. When a team has a new set of requirements they're planning to meet, they can query the repository and see if any piece of their functionality is already available from another department. When that team, in the process of meeting these requirements, creates new services, they publish them in the repository as well, so that others can find and use them moving forward.

With Web Services, this publishing is done using a Universal Description Discovery Integration (UDDI) repository. We'll examine UDDI in a bit.

The second theme is that the providers and consumers are *loosely coupled*. What does it mean to be loosely coupled? Let's contrast it to *tight coupling*. DCOM is tightly coupled. The server and the client both need to be using COM. An instance of a Customer object on the server is represented as an instance of the same COM type on the client. The client and server have COM-type fidelity. This is about more than the definition of that type; it's about how that type is actually allocated and represented in the memory of the process consuming the type. Both parties understand Interface Definition Language (IDL); both parties leverage the COM infrastructure; and both parties must have the same version of the binaries installed, creating administrative havoc at times, especially during updates. If a party shows up without COM, then there's no party at all, as the system is coupled to COM.

With the .NET Framework, you can get tight coupling of .NET types on both tiers of a distributed system by using remoting. This is the RPC mechanism built into .NET, and it creates a system that's tightly coupled to the .NET Framework. .NET must be on the server, and it must be on the client.

A loosely coupled system exposes no such constraint. In a loosely coupled system, the parties agree on the interface, but not on physical details for how a type is represented in memory. Types in Web Services are actually described using XML Schema. So with Web Services, the client and server have fidelity with XML Schema types. Since XML Schema is an open, public standard, schema types can be consumed from any platform that has an implementation of these standards. Today, there are SOAP Stacks implemented for many different platforms.

This combination of loose coupling and XML Schema type affinity is a subtle, yet important, point. It's somewhat obfuscated in .NET Web Services (and typically on other platforms as well) because a service is consumed via a proxy, which exposes types that may look just like the types on the server. When a Web Service client and server are both .NET, these proxies can create the *illusion* of type fidelity.

For example, a GetCustomer method is defined as returning an instance of a Customer object. The client creates an instance of this service and calls GetCustomer. They obtain a reference to a Customer type. These types, however, are not the same physical type on the client and the server. They don't live in the same assembly, and they don't have the same underlying Intermediate Language (IL) and metadata defining them. They're both consistent with the XML Schema type that's used to describe what's actually on the wire, which is XML packed into a SOAP message. The structure of this message is defined using XML Schema; thus, the only fidelity to type that you have in this system is to XML Schema (see Figure 6-1).

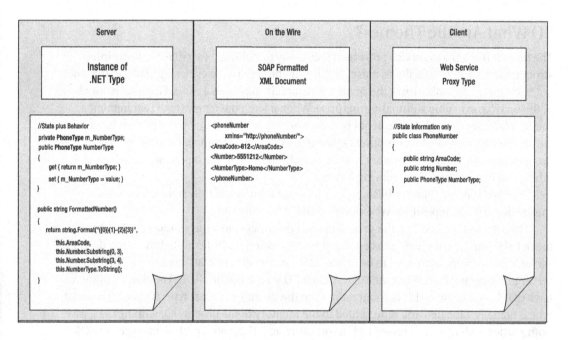

Figure 6-1. *Schema type fidelity displaying a real .NET Business Object on the server, XML for SOAP message on the wire, and a proxy type generated by Visual Studio .NET 2003 on the client.*

It's easy for confusion to ensue because there's a complete layer of abstraction between you (the developer) and the message-based communication that's actually occurring on the wire. That's why we're going to examine these details over the course of the chapter. We'll peel back some of the abstraction between you and the messages on the wire, and you'll gain a better understanding of the primacy of XML Schema in this messaging infrastructure.

The next theme that emerges from these definitions is the importance of the *interface*. An interface is a contract between software components. It's what enables you to write a library of functionality and use it from a different program after the library has been compiled. The interface is separated from the implementation. This means that the interface is all a service consumer needs to use the service. No details of how the work behind the interface is done should be exposed to the consumer. None at all. In this highly interoperable environment, this abstraction goes so far as to hide the operating system, platform, and language that's being used to implement the service from the consumer. This is possible because the interface is standards based. It's described using Web Service Description Language, or WSDL. We'll take a closer look at WSDL in a bit.

The last theme is that services are coarse-grained (compared to objects designed using traditional OOAD and that they are aggregated in a way that makes sense to the consumer. These facets are not so different from other RPC environments, where interfaces are always chunky, as opposed to chatty, and methods are logically grouped within types.

So why adopt this type of architecture? The first three biggest reasons are reuse, reuse, and reuse. If you have several platforms and languages within your Enterprise, this infrastructure is definitely the way to go. You can start the move to service orientation by simply wrapping entry points to different systems of records (usually databases) with Web Services. This creates independence and reuse across different data access technologies, and it makes the data in the Enterprise available to all. You can also wrap the functionality of packaged applications with Web Services. You may have a document management system that exposes its functionality programmatically as a COM library. Wrap it with Web Services, and the folks writing Java on Linux will be able to get documents out of it. Then, as adoption increases, business logic can start to be designed in a manner that facilities exposing that business logic as services. The more buy-in you can get across the groups involved, the more effective this strategy becomes. The goal is to eventually have software assets discovered, bound to, and executed in a technology-neutral, standards-based way across the Enterprise.

Throw up a UDDI registry and you also have a technology-neutral, standards-based approach to service publishing and discovery.

Now we're really illuminating some of the major differences of service orientation from traditional RPC infrastructures. Loose coupling between components facilitates platform-neutral reuse of software assets. Standards-based publishing simplifies discovery and binding. The fact is, traditional RPC mechanisms are not a good solution for reuse in an environment with heterogeneous technologies.

RPC does provide type fidelity between systems. With services, your type fidelity is to XML Schema, and this can be a big sacrifice. We'll examine some ways to design around and manage this as we move through the chapter.

The other major difference between service orientation and RPC is method invocation versus message passing. Again, this difference is more important when you're doing design than it is when you're writing code that uses services. In RPC you invoke a method and receive a return value. The types passed as arguments and the return values are all native to your platform and language of choice. With services, you pass messages. The messages are formatted as XML within SOAP envelopes. The XML is described with XML Schema. The server receives the message and may respond with a message of its own creation, although this is not required (it is possible to have one-way, fire and forget service operation). What happens on the server to service the request is completely abstracted away from and independent from the consumer of the service. The fact that what *does* actually *happen* is that a method is invoked on a type is irrelevant. What should be considered when the service is designed (and sometimes when the service is consumed) are the messages on the wire; how they are formed, what they contain, and how the information is described using XML Schema.

Web Services as an SO Implementation

Web Services are not the only way of providing an implementation of service orientation. They're just all the rage at the moment. The academics of service orientation actually predate Web Services by a long shot. The resurgence of service orientation as a viable architectural option has occurred on account of Web Services, and Web Services have surged in relevance on account of the World Wide Web. Everything is finally in place to do a proper implementation of SOA that's truly interoperable. This has been attempted before, but these attempts have been met with limited success. By piggybacking on the success of the Web, Web Services have a real chance of success. There's a lot of support for this technology from standards bodies and industry heavies, including Microsoft, Sun Microsystems, BEA, IBM, and Oracle. There's also a lot of effort going into solving the thorny problems of really making this solution interoperable. These efforts can be described under the umbrella of "the WS-* initiatives." We'll take a look at some of these standards (see Table 6-1), and the .NET implementations of them.

Many technologies provide the underpinnings of the infrastructure for Web Services.

Table 6-1. *Specifications and How They Play a Role in Web Services*

Specification	Role in Web Services
XML	This specification for the flexible creation of markup is the underpinning of all the structures in use in Web Services.
XML Schema	This is used for message format definitions, providing the common type system used by service provider and consumer. Different platforms will then employ their own methods of translating the information described by the schema into native types to work with programmatically.
WSDL	The XML document used for service description. This description defines the interface of the service. Given this description, service consumers have all of the information they need to call operations on the service.
SOAP	The XML Protocol specification defines the SOAP envelope as the fundamental structure used for passing messages at runtime.
UDDI	The specification describes the repository of XML used for publishing and discovery.
SOAP Stacks	This is an actual platform-specific implementation of a Web Service infrastructure. .NET has a SOAP Stack implemented within the ASP.NET Framework, based on ASMX pages (commonly called the "As-Em-Ex" stack).

Many of the WS-* initiatives are owned by the WS-I (www.ws-i.org; the Web Services Interoperability Organization). The WS-I works to develop guidelines that facilitate interoperability between Web Services. Even if they adopt all of the standards listed in the Table 6-1, different organizations might adopt different versions of the different specifications, and this can introduce problems in interoperability. To further standardize the adoption of these standards, the WS-I has created the *Basic Profile*. By adhering to the Basic Profile, different parties (be they companies or different departments within an Enterprise) vastly increase their chances of successfully using one another's services. The Basic Profile employs the *Web Service stack* (see Figure 6-2), which determines the version of each specification in use at every level of the Web Service infrastructure, from discovery down to the format of the message on the wire at runtime.

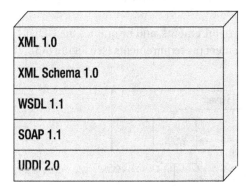

XML 1.0

XML Schema 1.0

WSDL 1.1

SOAP 1.1

UDDI 2.0

Figure 6-2. *The WS-I Basic Profile service stack*

You can see this profile just adds a version qualifier to each level of the stack. This "service stack" is different from a SOAP Stack because it provides another layer of specification, whereas a SOAP Stack is an actual implementation of the specifications, and generally involves tools and processes that are used during design and at runtime.

Because more developers are more familiar with traditional OOAD concepts than with service orientation, it can help to liken the two, albeit analogously, as we do in Table 6-2.

Table 6-2. *Service Orientation Analogies to Traditional OOAD*

Service Orientation	OOAD	Meaning in Life
Message	Method Invocation	Instead of calling a method, a service consumer passes a message to the server. Instead of getting a return value from a method call, the service consumer receives another message from the server. A method that would be called "void" in object oriented (OO) is simply a "one-way message" in SO.
Operation	Method	In OO, a method defines a typed argument list and a return type. In SO, a message describes the schema of a snippet of XML that's used to describe a service request. The return value of an operation is described by a second message, also conforming to a structure defined by an XML Schema.
Port Type	Interface	A Port Type is a logical aggregation of operations, and specifies a protocol that will be used to communicate with the service, usually HTTP.
Service	Class	The Service is a logical aggregation of Port Types, like a class implementing interfaces. A Service can have only one Port Type, like a class with a single interface (as is common in COM).

Different parts of the service stack are used at different stages during service design, during development, and at runtime. When someone has defined and created a service, she will deploy it to a server running a SOAP Stack, deploy a WSDL document to describe the service, and create an entry in the Enterprise UDDI registry describing the service (and pointing to the WSDL document).

Along comes a developer looking to meet some requirements, and he queries the UDDI registry to see if there are services that can help him meet his requirements (see Figure 6-3).

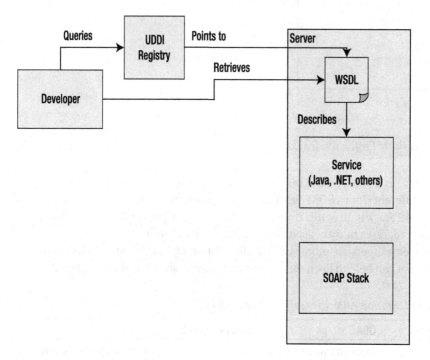

Figure 6-3. *A developer uses a UDDI registry to find a service and retrieve the WSDL describing the service.*

Typically the UDDI registry contains the URL of a WSDL document describing the service. With the WSDL document in hand, the developer has all of the information he needs to prepare SOAP messages and post them to the service, and knows what SOAP messages to expect back. WSDL uses XML Schema and the XML Protocol specification (SOAP) to create this description.

Instead of manually writing code to prepare these messages and post them to the server, SOAP Stacks include tools that generate client-side proxies. The proxies expose types and members that mirror the schema the WSDL describes. To consume the service, the developer then has only to add a reference to the proxy type, create an instance of it, and call a method on it (see Figure 6-4). The proxy translates the values from the native type system into SOAP messages, puts them on the wire, receives the messages off the wire, and translates that back into a native type. This largely explains why Web Service programming looks so much like (and so often gets confused with) RPC programming.

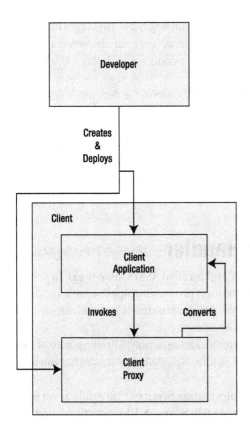

Figure 6-4. *The developer uses a tool to create a proxy based on the WSDL document and creates a process that invokes the generated client-side proxy.*

So far you've seen how UDDI and WSDL are used in concert during development to discover the service and generate a client-side proxy for calling the service. At runtime, SOAP messages are prepared, put on the wire, and taken off the wire by the proxy. XML and XML Schema are used throughout the process, as are different pieces of the SOAP Stack (see Figure 6-5).

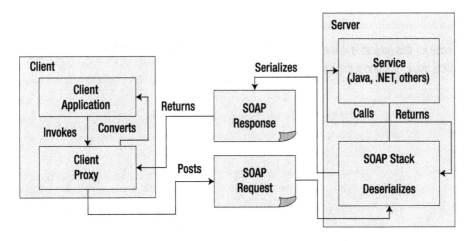

Figure 6-5. *At runtime, the proxy and the SOAP Stack process on the server collaborate to create and move the SOAP messages across the wire.*

You can see here that at runtime you're just creating and passing SOAP messages on the wire. This isn't entirely dissimilar from the request/response paradigm in use between a browser and web server. This process actually has *a lot* more in common with this model than with a traditional RPC model.

The SOAP Stack provides a complete layer of abstraction between the developer and the messaging on both the client and the server. The server-side process and the client proxy make the entire infrastructure look like RPC. This is merely a convenience mechanism for you to keep you in your comfort zone by making things look like traditional OO. You can see here that your type system and your messages are all based not on types from your platform of choice, but rather on XML Schema. Let's see how simple it can be to use Web Services in the .NET Framework 2.0.

ASMX and the Web Service Handler

The .NET Framework SOAP Stack is a part of ASP.NET and is called ASMX (as-em-ex). In Chapter 2 you saw how you can extend the ASP.NET request processing pipeline with an implementation of the IHttpHandler interface. The Web Service handler is just such an extension, and is mapped to requests with an extension of asmx.

An ASMX page is a very simple file. It points to a type in an assembly. The simplicity of this is obfuscated by Visual Studio .NET 2003. With Visual Studio .NET 2005, the model has been simplified quite a bit.

First of all, just as with Web Forms, an Internet Information Services (IIS) Application is not required for a Web Service project. When you choose File ➤ New ➤ Web Site, the dialog displayed in Figure 6-6 appears.

Notice you have a choice of location type. You can choose from the file system, HTTP, or File Transfer Protocol (FTP). While HTTP gives you the old tried and true IIS Virtual Directory to do development in, file system and FTP are new. With the file system, you can point to any directory on the system, and the IDE uses a development Web Server instead of an IIS Virtual Directory. An IIS application isn't required. In fact, IIS isn't required on the development machine at all. FTP allows you to connect to a project via FTP instead of using IIS and Front-Page Server Extensions.

■**Note** The code for this project is in the Web06 directory, a subdirectory of Code06. The Code06 solution opens all projects used throughout the chapter.

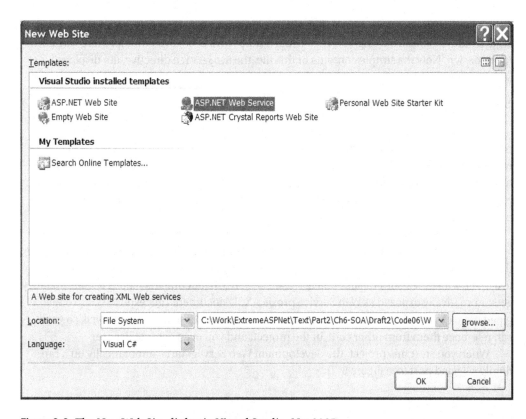

Figure 6-6. *The New Web Site dialog in Visual Studio .Net 2005*

After you create your file system-based project, you can see that the ASMX development model is different by default, as well. The ASMX template is much simpler. There's no hidden region of code, just a class with a single Web Method in it:

```
using System;
using System.Web;
using System.Web.Services;
using System.Web.Services.Protocols;

[WebService(Namespace = "http://tempuri.org/")]
[WebServiceBinding(ConformsTo = WsiProfiles.BasicProfile1_1)]
public class Service : System.Web.Services.WebService
{
    public Service () {

    }

    [WebMethod]
    public string HelloWorld() {
        return "Hello World";
    }
}
```

The IDE also now shows you the ASMX document itself. This was something that was always hidden behind a Design View in Visual Studio .NET 2003, even though there was nothing to design. Now the simple contents of this file, the WebService directive, are displayed (see Service.asmx in Web06).

```
<%@ WebService CodeBehind="~/App_Code/Service.cs" Class="Service" %>
```

The only thing about this directive that's relevant at runtime is the Class attribute. It names the class where the service implementation lives. Any methods of this named class with the WebMethod attribute applied will be exposed as operations on the service. Even this has been simplified. In Visual Studio .NET 2K3, it needed to be a fully qualified class name. Now even though there's just a local class name carried as the value, it will still be found and invoked at runtime.

The CodeBehind attribute is especially interesting. This points to a file contained in the App_Code directory. This directory gets special treatment from ASP.NET 2.0. Any files placed in this directory get compiled automatically and are available to use from within the project they live in. This includes both C# and VB.NET code files. WSDL documents placed in this directory get automatically exposed as Web Service proxies. XSD documents get exposed as strongly typed DataSets. The IDE does a design-time compilation of these resources as well, so you can reference them from other code in the project, and you even get Intellisense.

When you start this project, the development Web Server starts automatically on a randomly selected port (see Figure 6-7).

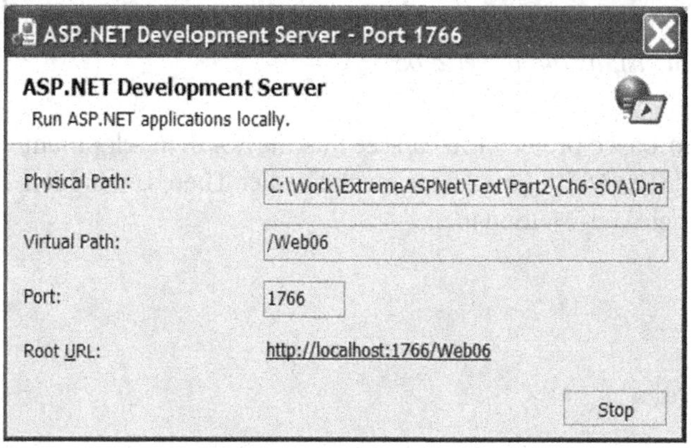

Figure 6-7. *The ASP.NET Development Server information window*

The ASMX handler then renders the old familiar Web Service testing interface, shown in Figure 6-8.

Figure 6-8. *The test harness rendered when an ASMX page is requested via an HTTP GET*

Notice that the test harness is unhappy about the namespace. This is something you should always change from the template code. In Visual Studio .NET 2003, the WebService attribute isn't added to the class declaration by default. In the 2005 template, it's there with the tempuri namespace as the default:

```
[WebService(Namespace = "http://tempuri.org/")]
```

You need only to change it to something more meaningful within your own organization; for example:

```
[WebService(Namespace = "http://www.IntertechTraining.com/Hello")]
```

You can now refresh your view in the browser, and the test harness is much happier (see Figure 6-9).

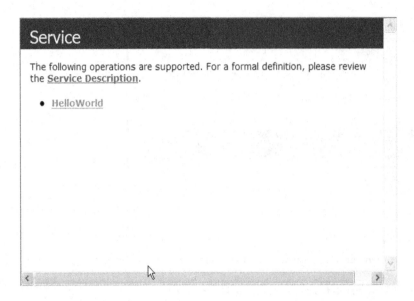

Figure 6-9. *The happy test harness does not complain about the namespace.*

2.0 ASMX Enhancements

The changes to the project model and the default template within Visual Studio .NET are just scratching the surface of the changes made to the ASMX call stack for version 2.0 of the Framework. Many more modifications have been made to the ASMX infrastructure. Since Web Services intrinsically lack a user interface, they don't lend themselves well to flashy demos of new code-generating wizards. For this reason, these significant enhancements have been slipped in with little fanfare (while all the accolades go to the architecturally questionable data source controls; see Chapter 11).

However, these enhancements are worth noting in some detail, as they address real issues people encounter using 1.1 of ASMX in production systems and pave the road to the Windows Messaging Framework for those considering adopting Web Services today.

■Note Windows Messaging Framework is Microsoft's next generation out-of-process call stack. It's a unified way to use Web Services, COM+, remoting, and Message Queuing (MSMQ). This technology is not part of .NET 2.0, but will be available for Windows XP and Windows 2003; and in the future, it will be built right into the operating system. See Chapter 9 for a preview of this exciting new technology.

1.x Problem: No Type Sharing Across Proxies

Given when you're using Web Services, types are determined by schema and not managed classes, whenever a method returns a class type, the client-side proxy generates code to represent it. This can be a problem when two services return the same type: they can become represented on the client as different types in different proxies. Consider this simple type (which you'll find in the SchemaImp project in the Code06 solution):

```csharp
public class PhoneNumber
{
    public PhoneNumber() { }

    public PhoneNumber(
        string AreaCode,
        string Number,
        PhoneType NumberType)
    {
        this.AreaCode = AreaCode;
        this.Number = Number;
        this.NumberType = NumberType;
    }

    private string m_AreaCode;
    public string AreaCode
    {
        get { return m_AreaCode; }
        set { m_AreaCode = value; }
    }

    private string m_Number;
    public string Number
    {
        get { return m_Number; }
        set
        {
            value = value.Replace("-", "");
            value = value.Replace(" ", "");
            if (value.Length != 7)
                throw new System.Exception
                        ("Number must be seven digits");

            m_Number = value;
        }
    }

    private PhoneType m_NumberType;
    public PhoneType NumberType
    {
        get { return m_NumberType; }
        set { m_NumberType = value; }
    }

    public string FormattedNumber()
    {
        return string.Format("({0}){1}-{2}({3})",
```

```
                this.AreaCode,
                this.Number.Substring(0, 3),
                this.Number.Substring(3, 4),
                this.NumberType.ToString().Substring(0, 1));
    }
}


public enum PhoneType
{
    Home,
    Work,
    Office,
    Fax,
    Cell
}
```

Now we'll mock up two services that use the PhoneNumber type. The first one will return an instance. (This code is in PhoneNumberLib.cs in the App_Code directory of the Web06 project.)

```
public class PhoneNumberLib
{
    [WebMethod]
    public PhoneNumber GetNumber()
    {
        return new PhoneNumber("612", "555-3434", PhoneType.Home);
    }
}
```

And the other will accept an instance as an argument:

```
public class Dialer
{
    [WebMethod]
    public bool SendSMS(PhoneNumber Number, string Message)
    {
        //Code to use Number and send message
        return true;
    }
}
```

These are exposed with a couple of asmx files named NumberLib.asmx and Dialer.asmx (also found in the Web06 project). These files are nothing more than WebService directives pointing at these types.

As you'd expect, a usage pattern of these services is likely to involve retrieving a number from the NumberLib service, and sending a Short Message Service (SMS) message to it using the SendSMS operation of the Dialer service.

Note The following client project can be found in the Code06 folder under Web06_2K3. All demonstrations using 1.x of the Framework for this chapter use this project. You'll need to set up the Web06_2K3 directory as an IIS application using the Microsoft Management Console (MMC) configuration snap-in for IIS.

To understand the enhancement in the .NET Framework 2.0, you have to understand the behavior in 1.x. To demonstrate the problematic behavior, you'll need to add a Web Reference to both services from a Visual Studio .NET 2003 client project, using the respective ASMX documents (see Figure 6-10).

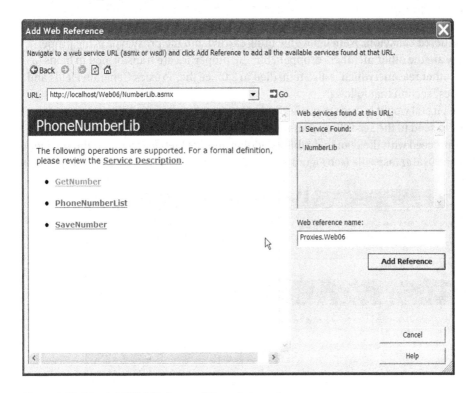

Figure 6-10. *The Add Web Reference Wizard at work*

Notice we've changed the Web Reference name from the default (localhost, in this case) to something more meaningful. This becomes the namespace that the proxy gets created within. After the wizard runs and generates the proxy, you have some types available in the Proxies.Web06 namespace; NumberLib (your service class) and PhoneNumber (the proxy type the GetNumber operation returns).

Remember that PhoneNumber is the same type across the services on the server side of the equation. Its fully qualified name is WSDemo.PhoneNumber. On the proxy side, the PhoneNumber class is *not the same type as on the server* (see Figure 6-11). This is what it means to lose .NET type affinity and have schema type affinity instead. Only data is represented in schema (aka state information). The PhoneNumber types reflect this in their structure.

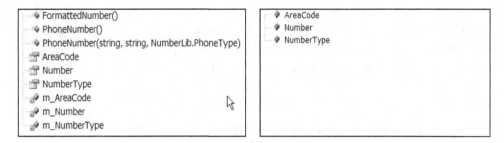

Figure 6-11. *The PhoneNumber server and proxy types compared*

The server type has the custom constructor and the FormattedNumber method, which are behaviors. It also has three properties, which are special case methods, and can, therefore, also be considered behaviors. Notice the only thing carried into the proxy type is the properties. Not only are the other members dropped, but the properties are transformed to fields (a problem for other reasons, which is also remedied in 2.0; see the "Proxies Generate Fields and Not Properties" section that follows).

However, it still would be nice to use GetNumber on one service to get an instance of PhoneNumber to send to the SendSMS operation on the other service (even if they're only proxy types). Let's proceed with the plan to do this by adding another Web Reference to the service exposed by the Dialer.asmx file (see Figure 6-12).

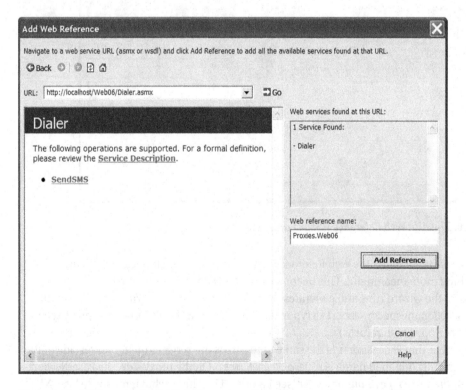

Figure 6-12. *Adding another Web Reference to the same namespace from within Visual Studio .NET 2003*

Again, we've changed the Web reference name from the default to `Proxies.WSDemo`. This creates the proxy types needed for the second service in the same namespace, where you can hopefully share the definition of the `PhoneNumber` proxy type.

However, as you've probably anticipated (due to our subtle literary foreshadowing), your expectations will be met only with agony. Let's take a peek at the Web References in Solution Explorer (see Figure 6-13).

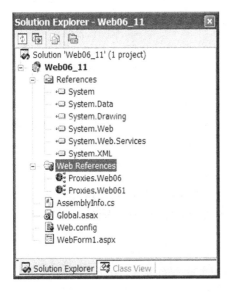

Figure 6-13. *The namespaces that actually get created in the project*

At this point your hopes are dashed. Each of these namespaces has a definition of the `PhoneNumber` proxy type. They're basically identical, as they're based on the same type information on the server, but they're completely different types as far as the CLR is concerned. One is named `Proxies.Web06.PhoneNumber`, the other `Proxies.Web061.PhoneNumber`. This means that no matter how hard you try, code like this won't work.

```
Proxies.Web06.NumberLib l = new Proxies.Web06.NumberLib();
Proxies.Web061.Dialer d= new Proxies.Web061.Dialer();
Proxies.Web06.PhoneNumber p = l.GetNumber();
d.SendSMS(p,"wuzgoinon?");
```

To fix this you could modify the generated proxy code. This is a valid technique, but the downside is that if you ever have to regenerate your proxy (should the service definition ever change), you'd then have to reapply your proxy modifications. This can be a pain, especially during development, when the service might still be evolving via iterative design.

The .NET Framework 2.0 addresses this problem. In the next example, doing everything the same, you'll only get a single proxy type on the client. The proxy generator is smart enough to see that the `PhoneNumber` type comes from the same namespace in both instances and only generate the type once.

Figure 6-14. *The namespaces that get created in VS .NET 2K5 when you create proxies for the same service*

The code using the PhoneNumber proxy type works in a 2.0 client, because the type has been defined only once in the generated proxy code. (This sample client can be found in the Web06Client project.)

```
Proxies.Web06.PhoneNumber number;
Proxies.Web06.PhoneNumberLib proxy1 = new Proxies.Web06.PhoneNumberLib();
Proxies.Web06.Dialer proxy2 = new Proxies.Web06.Dialer();

number = proxy1.GetNumber();
proxy2.SendSMS(number,"wuzgoinon?");
```

1.x Problem: Program to a Class, not an Interface

One of the major tenets of service orientation is to separate the implementation from the interface, but in version 1.x of the .NET Framework, the only way to create a Web Service is to decorate a class (a piece of implementation code) with attributes.

It would be nice to formalize this separation by defining the service contract with an interface, and then having any type come along and implement the interface. This is not only a cleaner model conceptually but it is also cleaner at the code level, since the attributes determining the structure of the contract are on the interface, and are not cluttering up the code for the implementing class. At the physical level, this allows you to literally separate the interface from the implementation, enabling you to move the contract definition (and the metadata of the interface in the compiled assembly) around independently from the implementation (the CIL in the implementing type's assembly).

Let's consider the following interface, which you'll use as the starting point for your service contract. (This interface definition can be found in App_Code\IPhoneLib.cs of the Web06 project).

```
[WebServiceBinding(Namespace =
    "http://www.IntertechTraining.com/WSDemo/PhoneNumberLib")]
public interface IPhoneNumberLib
{
    [WebMethod()]
    PhoneNumber GetNumber();
    [WebMethod()]
    bool SaveNumber(PhoneNumber number);
    [WebMethod()]
    [XmlInclude(typeof(PhoneNumber))]
    ArrayList PhoneNumberList(string criteria);
}
```

Notice that this interface definition contains all of the Web Service specific information. When a type implements the interface, it automatically gets its methods exposed as Web Services via the attributes applied to the underlying interface. This completely separates the definition of the WSDL interface from the implementation of the service. (You'll find this code in App_Code\NumberService.cs of the Web06 project.)

```
public class NumberService : System.Web.Services.WebService , IPhoneNumberLib
{
    public PhoneNumber GetNumber()
    {
        return new PhoneNumber("612", "555-3434", PhoneType.Home);
    }

    public bool SaveNumber(PhoneNumber number)
    {
        return true;
    }

    public System.Collections.ArrayList PhoneNumberList(string criteria)
    {
        ArrayList al = new ArrayList();
        al.Add(new PhoneNumber("612","5551212",PhoneType.Cell));
        al.Add(new PhoneNumber("612","5551213",PhoneType.Fax));
        al.Add(new PhoneNumber("612","5551214",PhoneType.Home));
        al.Add(new PhoneNumber("612", "5551215", PhoneType.Office));
        return al;
    }
}
```

Wsdl.exe has also been updated with the ability to generate the server-side stub of an interface to describe the WSDL document. You accomplish this with the /serverInterface switch.

```
wsdl.exe /serverInterface SomeWsdlDoc.wsdl
```

This generates a C# source file containing a definition of the interface described by the WSDL document. For example, a WSDL document containing a single operation (SomeMethod) that accepted a string element (SomeArgument) and returned a string element generates the following interface:

```
[System.Web.Services.WebServiceBindingAttribute(
    Name="sampleBinding",
    Namespace="SoapInterop")]
public partial interface ISampleBinding {

    /// <remarks/>
    [System.Web.Services.WebMethodAttribute()]
    [System.Web.Services.Protocols.SoapRpcMethodAttribute("#Sample",
        RequestNamespace="SoapInterop",
        ResponseNamespace="SoapInterop")]
    [return: System.Xml.Serialization.SoapElementAttribute("Sample")]
    string SomeMethod(string SomeArgument);
}
```

The only thing left for you to do at this point is to define a type that implements this interface and write the implementation. Pointing an ASMX document at this implementing type automatically uses the attributes defined at the interface level to appropriately expose your type as a Web Service. This is also a great way to get reuse out of your XML Schema files by taking a WSDL first approach. In this scenario, you start with your WSDL and XML Schema, and use this tool to generate the interface as a starting point, as opposed to starting with your implementation and generating the schema and WSDL.

The other important thing about using an interface to describe a service contract is that it provides a cleaner migration path into WCF, where this will be the default approach (see Chapter 9 for more on Windows Communication Foundation).

1.x Problem: Proxies Generate Fields and Not Properties

The proxy types generated to represent the state information of complex elements coming in off the wire use fields to expose this information. For example, let's take a look at the proxy type generated for the PhoneNumber class in Visual Studio .NET 2003:

```
[System.Xml.Serialization.XmlTypeAttribute(Namespace="http://phoneNumber/")]
public class PhoneNumber {

    /// <remarks/>
    public string AreaCode;

    /// <remarks/>
    public string Number;

    /// <remarks/>
    public PhoneType NumberType;
}
```

This class definition isn't suitable for a data binding operation. Consider the following simple code that should result in a list of numbers (see TryToBind.aspx in Web06_11):

```
private void btn1_Click(object sender, System.EventArgs e)
{
        Proxy.PhoneNumberLib p = new Proxy.PhoneNumberLib();

        ddl.DataSource =  p.PhoneNumberList("");
        ddl.DataTextField = "Number";
        ddl.DataBind();
}
```

Instead of a fine drop-down list, this code produces the following travesty (see Figure 6-15).

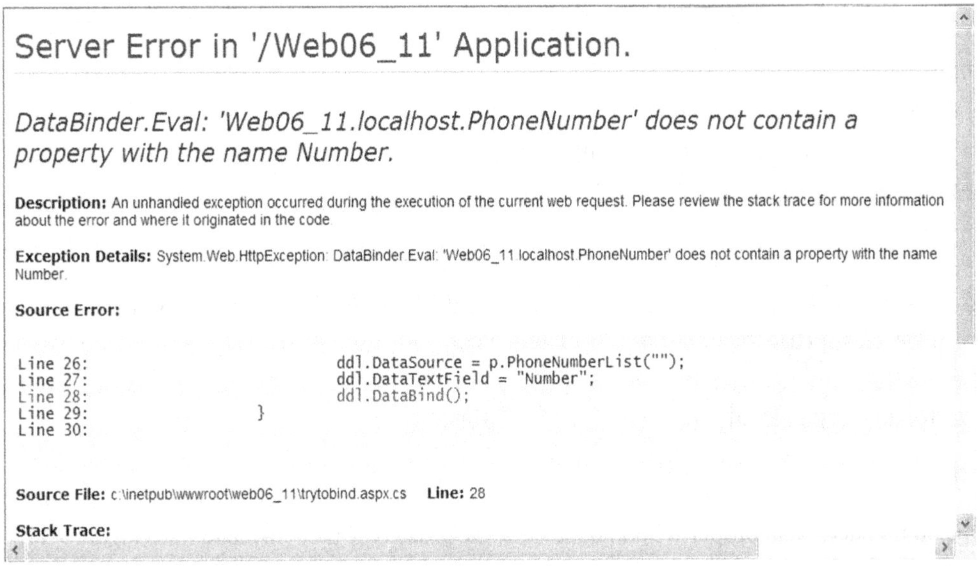

Server Error in '/Web06_11' Application.

DataBinder.Eval: 'Web06_11.localhost.PhoneNumber' does not contain a property with the name Number.

Description: An unhandled exception occurred during the execution of the current web request. Please review the stack trace for more information about the error and where it originated in the code.

Exception Details: System.Web.HttpException: DataBinder.Eval: 'Web06_11.localhost.PhoneNumber' does not contain a property with the name Number.

Source Error:

```
Line 26:                        ddl.DataSource = p.PhoneNumberList("");
Line 27:                        ddl.DataTextField = "Number";
Line 28:                        ddl.DataBind();
Line 29:                }
Line 30:
```

Source File: c:\inetpub\wwwroot\web06_11\trytobind.aspx.cs   **Line:** 28

Stack Trace:

Figure 6-15. *Exception that occurs when you try to bind to fields instead of properties*

This exception occurs because the data-binding engine is using reflection to find the properties named by DataTextField. It doesn't use reflection to look for *fields*, only *properties*. Your choices in this situation are to rewrite the proxy type manually, or create a different PhoneNumber type on the client that exposes this state information as properties instead of fields, and then accept an instance of the proxy type in a custom constructor and map the fields to the properties.

The 2.0 proxy generator solves this problem by using properties. Adding a reference to exactly the same service using Visual Studio .NET 2005 results in the following type declared in the generated proxy:

```
[System.SerializableAttribute()]
[System.Xml.Serialization.XmlTypeAttribute(Namespace="http://phoneNumber/")]
public partial class PhoneNumber {
```

```
    private string areaCodeField;

    private string numberField;

    private PhoneType numberTypeField;

    public string AreaCode {
        get { return this.areaCodeField; }
        set { this.areaCodeField = value; }
    }

    public string Number {
        get { return this.numberField; }
        set { this.numberField = value; }
    }

    public PhoneType NumberType {
        get { return this.numberTypeField; }
        set { this.numberTypeField = value; }
    }
}
```

The differences here are so subtle that you wouldn't notice them in most contexts. They do, however, appease the data-binding engine nicely.

1.x Problem: Type Fidelity Available Only for Datasets

Consider what you looked at earlier with the PhoneNumber and its proxy type. You established that the type on the server isn't at all the same as the type generated for the proxy. Where the type on the server had properties and behaviors, the proxy type had only fields (see Figure 6-11). Given this, how can the following service possibly work?

```
[WebMethod]
public DataSet getPubsData()
{
    string sql = "select * from authors "
        + "select * from titles "
        + "select * from publishers "
        + "select * from titleauthor";
    SqlConnection cn = new SqlConnection(WebStatic.ConnectionString);
    SqlCommand cm = new SqlCommand(sql,cn);
    DataSet ds = new DataSet();

    new SqlDataAdapter(cm).Fill(ds);

    ds.Relations.Add(
        ds.Tables[1].Columns["title_id"],
        ds.Tables[3].Columns["title_id"]);
```

```
    ds.Relations.Add(
        ds.Tables[0].Columns["au_id"],
        ds.Tables[3].Columns["au_id"]);
    ds.Relations.Add(
        ds.Tables[2].Columns["pub_id"],
        ds.Tables[1].Columns["pub_id"]);

    return ds;
}
```

Here's the some code consuming this method using a Web Service proxy.

```
void Page_Load(object sender, EventArgs e)
{
    Proxies.TypedService ts = new Proxies.TypedService();
    DataSet ds = ts.getPubsData();
    foreach (DataTable dt in ds.Tables)
    {
        DataGrid dg = new DataGrid();
        dg.DataSource = dt;
        dg.DataBind();
        this.FindControl("form1").Controls.Add(dg);
    }
}
```

What's going on here? Is this .NET type fidelity for a Web Service? This is accomplished with smarts that are built into the proxy generating code. This DataSet is still XML described by XML Schema on the wire. It's still interoperable. Another platform won't see this data as a DataSet, but as a complex hierarchal document described by XML Schema from the WSDL. The .NET proxy, however, has been taught to recognize this as a DataSet, and so when it comes in off the wire, the proxy creates a new instance of a real DataSet and merges this data into it from the SOAP body of the message.

In version 1.x of the Framework, the DataSet was the only type that supported this functionality. In version 2.0, Microsoft has added a point of extensibility so you can modify the proxy generator and affect the code it produces.

Understand that this is a modification to the design time behavior of a developer's environment and not a way to change the run-time behavior of Web Services. In cases where the assemblies contain types that are needed on both the client and server, it can be very tempting to long for the type affinity that the client and server share in an RPC environment. This isn't really even considered a Best Practice (or a good idea, depending on who you're listening to) in a service-oriented environment. It's a throwback to the tight coupling between client and server that service orientation is supposed to liberate us from. All these considerations aside, sometimes this is the behavior you need. Today, the only choice is to manually modify the generated client-side proxies. This is not a lot of fun, because you must apply whatever changes are made anew every time the service changes and the proxy needs to be regenerated.

So the new feature in 2.0 extends the pipeline that's generating the client-side proxy. This pipeline extension executes when your users choose to Add a Web Reference from within the IDE, or when they run the wsdl.exe command-line tool. Typically the proxy generator is going to look at each type as it's described by the schema in the WSDL and generate a proxy type to represent it. Now, before it does that, it gives you a chance to override that behavior and check what the proxy generating code is about to do. If you recognize the type represented in schema as one you already know, you can generate your own code instead of relying on the proxy generator to do this for you.

So in your case, when the proxy generator alerts you that it's about to generate a proxy type to represent the PhoneNumber, you'll intercede and say "No, no, I know this guy, here, here, use this type instead … ." Piece of cake.

The steps to affect this change are as follows:

1. Create a type that inherits from the SchemaImporterExtension type.

2. Override ImportSchemaType, a method that fires every time the proxy code generator is processing a type from the WSDL document.

3. Write code to check the name and namespace of the type described in the schema of the WSDL document, and when it's a type you know, generate the proxy code yourself instead of relying on the generated code.

4. Give your type a strong name and put it in the Global Assembly Cache (GAC).

5. Register the extension to the proxy generation process in the machine.config of the developer workstation where you're generating the client side proxy.

6. Use Add Web Reference or wsdl.exe to generate the proxy.

7. Stand back and marvel at your ingenuity.

In the example we've created, you're going to generate a proxy that uses the real NumberLib.PhoneNumber type instead of the generated proxy type. This allows you to call custom constructors and the methods available on this type, instead of just having the state of an instance represented within the proxy type. Keep in mind that the assembly containing the type you're substituting must get to the client via some means other than the Web Service. On the wire you're still passing plain old XML. You're modifying what the *client proxy* does with the XML once the SOAP message containing the response is pulled off the wire by customizing the process that generates the client-side proxy code.

First, let's take a closer look at the type definition you'll be replacing the proxy code for. You control the namespace of the type on the wire using the XmlRoot attribute on the type definition. You'll search for the same namespace used here in your proxy generator extension.

```
[XmlRoot("phoneNumber", Namespace = "http://phoneNumber/", IsNullable = true)]
public class PhoneNumber
{
...
```

Next, you create a type that inherits from SchemaImporterExtension. This type lives in the System.Xml.Serialization.Advanced namespace. You're searching in this code for the PhoneNumber type as it's represented on the wire.

```
public class PhoneNumberSchemaImporterExtension : SchemaImporterExtension
{
    public override string ImportSchemaType(string name,
        string ns,
        XmlSchemaObject context,
        XmlSchemas schemas,
        XmlSchemaImporter importer,
        CodeCompileUnit compileUnit,
        CodeNamespace mainNamespace,
        CodeGenerationOptions options,
        CodeDomProvider codeProvider)
    {

        //Searching for the type name and the namespace we set with XmlRoot
        if (name.Equals("PhoneNumber") && ns.Equals("http://phoneNumber/"))
        {
            compileUnit.ReferencedAssemblies.Add("SchemaImp.dll");
            mainNamespace.Imports.Add(new CodeNamespaceImport("NumberLib"));
            return "NumberLib.PhoneNumber";
        }
        else
            return null;
    }
}
```

The ImportSchemaType method will be called for every type processed by the proxy generator. Only when you find your type do you take action by adding a reference to the assembly where the PhoneNumber type lives, adding an imports for the namespace, and returning the fully qualified name of the type to the proxy generator. For all other types you return null, which causes the generator to continue with its default behavior.

Assign a license file so your type gets a strong name, compile the code, and put the resulting assembly in the GAC. It has to be in the GAC, because you're not modifying behavior within the context of a project, you're modifying it on the entire machine. The type has to be in the GAC so that wsdl.exe or Visual Studio .NET can find it from wherever the developer is generating proxy code.

Because it's a machine-wide behavior you're changing, you also have to make an entry in the machine.config. Make this entry as a child of the configuration element, but after configsections.

```
<system.xml.serialization>
    <schemaImporterExtensions>
        <add name="PhoneNumber"
         type="SchemaImp.PhoneNumberSchemaImporterExtension, SchemaImp, Version=...
    </schemaImporterExtensions>
</system.xml.serialization>
```

The type attribute is truncated, but it must include a full description of your type, including its version, culture, and public key token. In our case, the string looks like this, but your public key token (and maybe your version) will be different:

```
SchemaImp.PhoneNumberSchemaImporterExtension, SchemaImp,
Version=1.0.0.0, Culture=neutral, PublicKeyToken=caebdbe3a168b171
```

You can copy some of this information from the assembly's property page in the GAC.

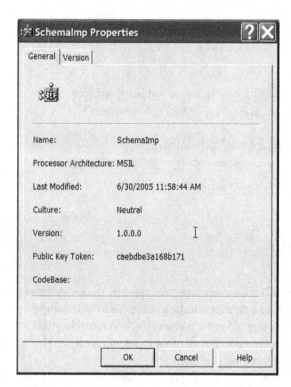

Figure 6-16. *Assembly property page from the GAC*

Now you can add a reference to a WSDL document that's using an instance of the PhoneNumber type. The code that you just wrote executes *while this proxy code is being generated*. When the proxy is created (named localhost.Dialer in this case), you can call a method that accepts an instance of the PhoneNumber type. Instead of being a proxy type (which would be named localhost.PhoneNumber in this example), it's a fully qualified instance of NumberLib.PhoneNumber, shown via IntelliSense in Figure 6-17.

```
{
    protected void Page_Load(object sender, EventArgs e)
    {
        localhost.Dialer d = new localhost.Dialer();
        d.SendSMS(
        bool Dialer.SendSMS (NumberLib.PhoneNumber phoneNumber, string Message)
    }
}
```

Figure 6-17. *IntelliSense reveals the type built into the proxy code by your extension*

Keep in mind that the assembly containing NumberLib.PhoneNumber must be present on the developer's workstation. The Web Service won't send it to you; it deals only in XML. You could make these changes on a single development box and generate all of the proxies on that box. Any time a service changes, you'd then have to regen the proxies using the specially configured workstation and get the new proxies out to all of the developers on the team using the proxies. You could also make these configuration changes on each developer's workstation, which is only feasible if you have a relatively small team. This introduces a tight coupling between the Web Service server and the consuming process, because the same assembly must be present on both machines. The Web Service is simply your mechanism for marshaling state information across the wire. Also keep in mind that other platforms could still use the service with their SOAP Stack of choice. This doesn't modify the server-side implementation of the service *in any way*. The coupling is limited to the developer's workstation and other machines using the custom-generated proxy.

1.x Problem: Custom Serialization Lacks Adequate Extensibility

You've seen how type fidelity is provided between client and server for DataSets, and how you can use schema importer extensions to provide similar behavior for your own types. The other facet of the DataSet that makes this possible is the format it uses to represent itself within XML. The DataSet object actually provides its own XML Schema format to pass in the SOAP message, one that better facilitates rehydrating an instance of the DataSet when it arrives at the client as a SOAP message. The DataSet accomplishes this by implementing the IXmlSerializable interface, the methods of which the ASMX infrastructure calls when putting the document onto the wire. Using this custom extension of the XML serializer, the DataSet is able to add metadata to the XML representing it on the wire. The proxy uses this additional information to re-create the DataSet when taking messages off the wire.

There is no support for implementing this interface on your own types in version 1.x of the Framework. This isn't to say it hasn't been done, but it hasn't been a sanctioned activity, and is more difficult than it needs to be due to some hard-coded dependencies on the DataSet object. This changes in version 2.0 of the Framework. This interface is exposed and there's full support for implementing it with your own types. When you do so, the ASMX infrastructure calls a method of your type to get the XML Schema for how your type should be represented in the SOAP message, and calls a method on the interface to actually get the XML stream representing your type. This gives you very precise control over how your type is represented on the wire. By implementing a schema importer extension, you can also control how an instance of the type is created by the proxy, and how the XML is used to restore the state information of the type on the client.

Microsoft has added an implementation of this interface for a number of types in the Framework. They include the DataTable, the XPathDocument, and the types from the System.Data.SqlTypes namespace. This means that .NET clients get type affinity for instances of these types returned from a service, although the DataTable does get wrapped in a DataSet.

In some cases you'll want to take control of the XML on the wire for your own types. Let's examine the definition of our own custom type, BookDetails (see Figure 6-18).

- BookDetails()
- BookDetails(int)
- Save()
- SaveNewBook()
- UpdateBook()
- Authors
- Binding
- BookID
- BookImage
- ISBN
- ListPrice
- LocationID
- LowestPrice
- PageCount
- PublicationDate
- Publisher
- Review
- ScanDate
- Subjects
- Title
- Weight

Figure 6-18. *The* BookDetails *type as viewed in the Object Browser*

The property named BookImage is an instance of type Bitmap, which holds an image of the book cover. The Bitmap type is not serializable, and has no default constructor. This means the following simple Web Service is invalid:

```
[WebMethod]
public BookDetails getABook(int BookID)
{
    return new BookDetails(BookID);
}
```

An attempt to invoke this operation results in the following error displayed in Figure 6-19. You could work around this problem by making the following code change to the definition of the BookDetails type:

```
[XmlIgnore()]
public Bitmap BookImage
{
    get { return m_BookImage; }
    set { m_BookImage= value; }
}
```

This causes the default serializer to ignore this property. Now you can use the type as a return value and invoke the Web Method that was failing above. The BookDetails type now produces the following XML on the wire (see Figure 6-20).

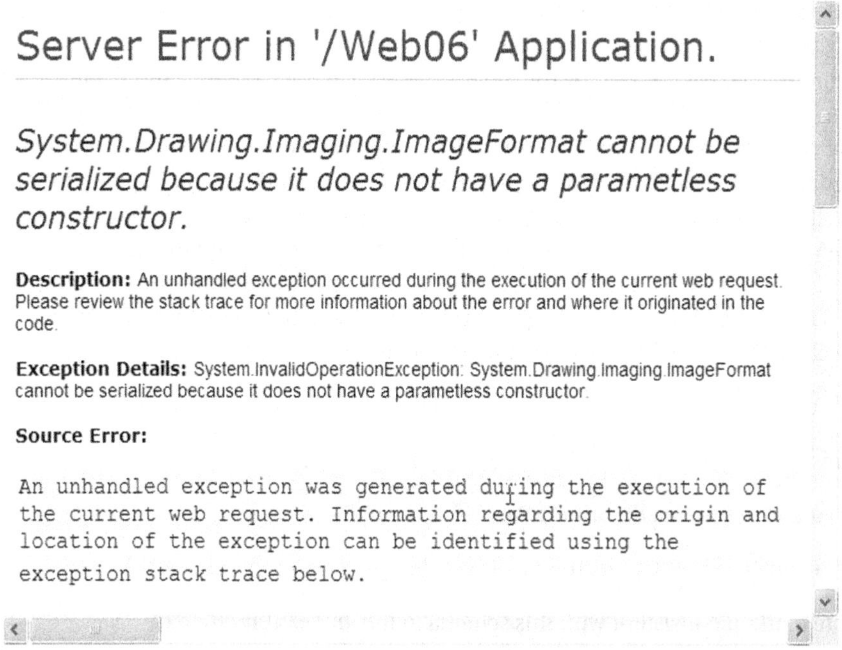

Server Error in '/Web06' Application.

System.Drawing.Imaging.ImageFormat cannot be serialized because it does not have a parametless constructor.

Description: An unhandled exception occurred during the execution of the current web request. Please review the stack trace for more information about the error and where it originated in the code.

Exception Details: System.InvalidOperationException: System.Drawing.Imaging.ImageFormat cannot be serialized because it does not have a parametless constructor.

Source Error:

An unhandled exception was generated during the execution of the current web request. Information regarding the origin and location of the exception can be identified using the exception stack trace below.

Figure 6-19. *BookDetails cannot be returned by a Web Service because it contains a bitmap*

```xml
<?xml version="1.0" encoding="utf-8" ?>
- <BookDetails xmlns:xsi="http://www.w3.org/2001/XMLSchema-instance"
    xmlns:xsd="http://www.w3.org/2001/XMLSchema" xmlns="http://tempuri.org/">
    <BookID>102</BookID>
    <ISBN>0688082742</ISBN>
    <LocationID>1</LocationID>
    <Title>Four Arguments for the Elimination of Television</Title>
    <Publisher>Perennial</Publisher>
    <PageCount>376</PageCount>
    <PublicationDate>1978-03-01T00:00:00</PublicationDate>
    <Weight>0</Weight>
    <LowestPrice>2</LowestPrice>
    <ListPrice>13</ListPrice>
    <ScanDate>2004-11-14T12:05:28.057</ScanDate>
    <Review>0</Review>
    <Binding>Paperback</Binding>
  - <Authors>
      <anyType xsi:type="xsd:string">Jerry Mander</anyType>
    </Authors>
  - <Subjects>
      <anyType xsi:type="xsd:string">Entertainment</anyType>
      <anyType xsi:type="xsd:string">Media Studies</anyType>
      <anyType xsi:type="xsd:string">Nonfiction</anyType>
      <anyType xsi:type="xsd:string">Social Sciences</anyType>
      <anyType xsi:type="xsd:string">Sociology</anyType>
      <anyType xsi:type="xsd:string">Television</anyType>
    </Subjects>
  </BookDetails>
```

Figure 6-20. *BookDetails with the bitmap excluded by applying the XmlIgnore attribute*

This works, but only at the expense of excluding your image! What if you need that image? There's nothing preventing you from encoding the binary information into the result message; it's just not supported "out of the can" by the tools. You'll have to take matters into your own hands.

To take full control of the XML and schema used to represent your own types on the wire, you need to add the XmlSchemaProvider attribute to your class declaration and implement the two methods required of you by the IXmlSerializable interface. You'll create a type that uses this custom SOAP serialization pattern to put a collection of BookDetails on the wire.

You're also going to need to control how the client takes instances of the type off the wire. To do this you'll create another XmlSchemaImporter and register it in the machine configuration file on the client. Your steps for this solution will be to

1. Create a type that builds a collection of BookDetails objects.

2. Have this type implement the IXmlSerializable interface.

3. Invent your own schema describing BookDetails on the wire.

4. Add a static method that emits this XmlSchema for the type on the wire.

5. Generate markup consistent with this schema in the WriteXml method of IXmlSerializable.

6. Create instances of the BookDetails types based on this markup in the ReadXml method.

7. Create a SchemaImporterExtension that maps the collection type on the wire back to your implementation of IXmlSerializable.

8. Register this type in the machine configuration file on the client.

9. Generate a proxy and code against it.

Let's start by looking at the code to implement IXmlSerializable. First, we'll take a peek at the code that provides its base functionality. (This code can be found in BookCollection.cs of the Library project.)

```
public class BookCollection : IEnumerable, IXmlSerializable
{
    public Hashtable ht = new Hashtable();
    private static string ns =
        "http://www.intertechtraining.com/Library/BookCollection";

    public int Add(BookDetails book)
    {
        ht.Add(book.BookID, book);
        return ht.Count - 1;
    }

    public int Count
    {
        get { return ht.Count; }
```

```
    }
    public void Remove(int BookID)
    {
        ht.Remove(BookID);
    }
    public void Remove(BookDetails book)
    {
        ht.Remove(book.BookID);
    }
    public IEnumerator GetEnumerator()
    {
        return ht.GetEnumerator();
    }
...
```

As you can see, this type just provides a simple wrapper around a Hashtable, accepting only instances of the BookDetails type, and keying the entries with the book IDs.

To implement IXmlSerializable, you must provide code for three methods. The first of these is GetSchema, but GetSchema has been deprecated, and so you need only to simply return a null:

```
public System.Xml.Schema.XmlSchema GetSchema()
{
    return null;
}
```

This method stays on the interface for backwards compatibility. The actual schema that describes your type as it will appear on the wire is provided via another method, one of your choosing. This needs to be a static method on your type that accepts a single argument of type XmlSchemaSet and returns an XmlQualifiedName. You can choose any name for this static method. You tell the serializer the name you've chosen using an attribute on your type. You'll modify the class to name this method with the XmlSchemaProvider attribute, and then add this static method to the type. Given the name of the method, it gets invoked using Reflection. Here we do this with a method we've chosen to name BookCollectionXsd:

```
[XmlSchemaProvider("BookCollectionXsd")]
public class BookCollection : IEnumerable, IXmlSerializable
{
    public static XmlQualifiedName BookCollectionXsd(XmlSchemaSet xss)
    {
        string xsdPath = HttpContext.Current.Server.MapPath("BookCollection.xsd");
        XmlSchema xs = XmlSchema.Read(new XmlTextReader(xsdPath), null);

        xss.XmlResolver = new XmlUrlResolver();
        xss.Add(xs);
        return new XmlQualifiedName("BookCollection_Type", ns);
    }
...
```

The static method named with the XmlSchemaProvider attribute must accept an instance of the XmlSchemaSet class as an argument. The XmlSchemaProvider attribute names the method in the class that the serializer will call when serializing an instance of the class. This is the change that breaks compatibility with the interface and introduces the need to use an attribute to name the method the serializer will call to get the schema. Here the method is named BookCollectionXsd. This method loads the schema from the file system, adds it to the schema set, and returns a qualified name of the complex type in the schema that provides the definition of what goes into the SOAP message.

The next method on IXmlSerializable is WriteXml. This code must create an XML stream based on the object instance that matches the schema returned by the XML Schema provider. It gets handed an XmlWriter as an argument that you can use to generate this stream:

```
public void WriteXml(System.Xml.XmlWriter writer)
{
    BinaryFormatter b = new BinaryFormatter();
    MemoryStream ms;
    BookDetails book;
    ASCIIEncoding ascEnc = new ASCIIEncoding();

    writer.WriteStartElement("books", ns);
    foreach (int i in ht.Keys)
    {
        writer.WriteStartElement("book", ns);
        book = (BookDetails)ht[i];

        writer.WriteElementString
            ("bookID", ns, book.BookID.ToString());
        writer.WriteElementString
            ("binding", ns, book.Binding);
        writer.WriteElementString
            ("isbn", ns, book.ISBN);
        writer.WriteElementString
            ("listPrice", ns, book.ListPrice.ToString());
        writer.WriteElementString
            ("lowestPrice", ns, book.LowestPrice.ToString());
        writer.WriteElementString
            ("pageCount", ns, book.PageCount.ToString());
        writer.WriteElementString
            ("publicationDate", ns, book.PublicationDate.ToString());
        writer.WriteElementString
            ("publisher", ns, book.Publisher);
        writer.WriteElementString
            ("review", ns, book.Review);
        writer.WriteElementString
            ("scanDate", ns, book.ScanDate.ToString());
        writer.WriteElementString
            ("title", ns, book.Title);
```

```
        writer.WriteElementString
            ("weight", ns, book.Weight.ToString());
        writer.WriteStartElement
            ("authors", ns);
        foreach (string s in book.Authors)
            writer.WriteElementString("author", ns, s);
        writer.WriteEndElement();
        writer.WriteStartElement("subjects", ns);
        foreach (string s in book.Subjects)
            writer.WriteElementString("subject", ns, s);
        writer.WriteEndElement();

        writer.WriteStartElement("image", ns);
        ms = new MemoryStream();
        book.BookImage.Save(ms, ImageFormat.Jpeg);
        int size = Convert.ToInt32(ms.Length);
        writer.WriteAttributeString("size", "", size.ToString());

        ms.Position = 0;
        writer.WriteBase64(ms.ToArray(), 0, size);
        writer.WriteEndElement();

        writer.WriteEndElement();
    }
    writer.WriteEndElement();
}
```

The code in bold is where the real customization to how this type will appear on the wire has been added. This is where you create an image element, add the image size as an attribute, and then use Base 64 encoding to pack the binary data for the image into the XML as text content of the element.

The last method is the ReadXml method, which, of course, must take the stream off the wire and rehydrate a proper instance of BookCollection:

```
public void ReadXml(System.Xml.XmlReader reader)
{
    BookCollection bc = new BookCollection();
    BookDetails book;
    BinaryFormatter bf = new BinaryFormatter();
    string val;

    reader.Read();
    reader.ReadStartElement("books");
    while (reader.NodeType != XmlNodeType.EndElement)
    {
        book = new BookDetails();
        reader.ReadStartElement("book", ns);
```

```
book.BookID =
    Convert.ToInt32(reader.ReadElementContentAsInt("bookID", ns));
book.Binding =
    reader.ReadElementString("binding", ns);
book.ISBN =
    reader.ReadElementString("isbn", ns);
book.ListPrice =
    reader.ReadElementContentAsDouble("listPrice", ns);
book.LowestPrice =
    reader.ReadElementContentAsDouble("lowestPrice", ns);
book.PageCount =
    reader.ReadElementContentAsInt("pageCount", ns);
val =
    reader.ReadElementContentAsString("publicationDate", ns);
book.PublicationDate =
    DateTime.Parse(val);
book.Publisher =
    reader.ReadElementString("publisher", ns);
book.Review =
    reader.ReadElementString("review", ns);
val =
    reader.ReadElementContentAsString("scanDate", ns);
book.ScanDate =
    DateTime.Parse(val);
book.Title =
    reader.ReadElementString("title", ns);
book.Weight =
    reader.ReadElementContentAsDouble("weight", ns);
reader.ReadStartElement("authors");
while (reader.NodeType != XmlNodeType.EndElement)
{
    book.Authors.Add
        (reader.ReadElementContentAsString("author", ns));
    reader.MoveToContent();
}
reader.Read();
reader.ReadStartElement("subjects");
while (reader.NodeType != XmlNodeType.EndElement)
{
    book.Subjects.Add
        (reader.ReadElementContentAsString("subject", ns));
    reader.MoveToContent();
}
reader.Read();
```

```
        int size = Convert.ToInt32(reader.GetAttribute("size"));
        byte[] bytes = new byte[size];
        reader.ReadElementContentAsBase64(bytes, 0, size);
        book.BookImage = new Bitmap(new MemoryStream(bytes));
        reader.Read();
        reader.MoveToContent();
        bc.Add(book);
    }
}
```

Once again, the customization is in bold. The bold code is where you pull the Base 64 encoded string out of the element, and reconstitute the `Bitmap`, assigning it back to the `BookImage` property for the current instance. The rest of the code, while still custom, performs work that any generated proxy would do by default with the type.

This obviously requires type affinity on the server and client, necessitating the need for another `SchemaImporterExtension`. It will be very similar to the one you looked at in the last section. As a Web Service proxy is generated, you'll swap out the proxy type information with a full-blown instance of `BookCollection`:

```
class LibraryImporterExtension : SchemaImporterExtension
{
    public override string ImportSchemaType(string name,
        string ns,
        XmlSchemaObject context,
        XmlSchemas schemas,
        XmlSchemaImporter importer,
        CodeCompileUnit compileUnit,
        CodeNamespace mainNamespace,
        CodeGenerationOptions options,
        CodeDomProvider codeProvider)
    {
        System.Diagnostics.EventLog.CreateEventSource("Library", "Application");
        System.Diagnostics.EventLog.WriteEntry("Library", "Fired:" + name);
        if (name.Equals("BookCollection"))
        {
            compileUnit.ReferencedAssemblies.Add("Library.dll");
            mainNamespace.Imports.Add(new CodeNamespaceImport("Library"));
            return "Library.BookCollection";
        }
        else
            return null;
    }
}
```

The assembly containing the definition of `BookDetails`, `BookCollection`, and `LibraryImporterExtension` must be installed on the client machine. You must also modify the machine configuration file to create the strong type affinity during the proxy generation:

```
<system.xml.serialization>
  <schemaImporterExtensions>
    <add name="Library" type="Library.LibraryImporterExtension, Library, Version=...
  </schemaImporterExtensions>
</system.xml.serialization>
```

Now, when the client adds a Web Reference to a service returning an instance of BookCollection, you use your own type to control the collection's markup on the wire, and have type affinity at the client, with a fully restored instance of the book cover stored in the BookImage property.

Other Enhancements

There are a handful of other enhancements to the ASMX infrastructure in ASP.NET 2.0. These include an attribute-based approach to enforcing conformance with the WS-I Basic Profile, a simplification of the asynchronous invocation model, and the ability to use a Windows Forms application as a host for receiving Web Service requests, which is convenient when you need a *call back* infrastructure, or for an *event*-based one-way messaging scenario. Consult the SDK docs for more details on these features.

WS-I and WSE

The need to solve problems of interoperability across platforms doesn't stop once you agree on public specifications and create them. Even with industry-wide adoption of the WS-I group's Basic Profile (as we've discussed), major hurdles need to be overcome to facilitate compatibility across languages, platforms, and Enterprises. Many common business problems still loom. The obvious ones are security and transaction management. But there are many other problems. How can binary information be packed away into an XML document in a standard format? How can a message be routed across several network endpoints? Do you always need to write code to determine Web Service behavior?

The WS-* specifications solve these requirements in a standard manner. These specifications dictate common SOAP headers you can use to address these different concerns. By standardizing on the structure of the SOAP header for a given problem, different companies can exchange security information in a common wire format, while also processing these credentials against their back-end user data stores in proprietary ways. In a secure system, someone is always going to have to send you credentials for access to your system. The question becomes *how* does that information get sent? What exactly do you expect it to look like? Without a specification for this and other common problems, you'd have "interoperability," in theory, but everyone would have to reinvent the wheel (and do some custom coding) to accommodate the security descriptors of different partners, or divisions, or departments.

Another benefit of a standards-based approach to solving these problems is that you can leverage a vendor-supplied implementation of the specification. This saves you from writing any custom code at all. You can just extend your SOAP Stack with a package from a vendor that provides the code for the requirements you need. This is where Microsoft's Web Service Enhancements (WSE) package comes into the picture.

WSE is an add-on package for the Windows operating system. It's available as a free download from Microsoft. The group that provides WSE isn't tied to any product or release schedule, so, for example, it doesn't have to wait until the next version of Visual Studio ships to provide a new version of its functionality. This is intentional, so that the group can respond to and provide implementations of new specifications as they become available from the various standards bodies involved in inventing these things. WSE 3.0 will contain features specifically designed to leverage version 2.0 of the .NET Framework. See http://msdn.microsoft.com/webservices/building/wse for the most current version information.

Operational Requirements

We'll take a quick look at some of the WS-* specifications that are met by the current version of WSE, and examine a little bit about how it fits into the ASMX SOAP Stack. Keep in mind that as these standards evolve, WSE will provide new and current implementations.

Most of the implementations of these specifications are provided as *Pre* and *Post* request processors that extend the default ASMX pipeline. This concept is very similar to the concepts we discussed in Chapter 2 about the ASP.NET pipeline. The big difference in the case of Web Services (see Figure 6-21) is that request processing needs to be extended on both the server (similar to ASP.NET) and on the client (no equivalent in ASP.NET). Requests for Web Forms come in from web browsers. Requests for services come in from Web Service proxies.

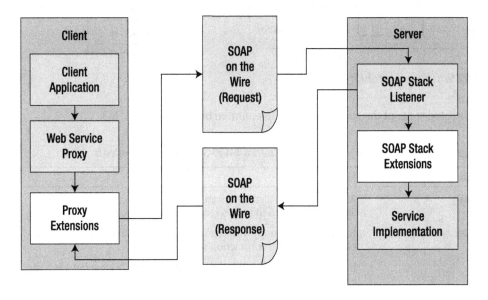

Figure 6-21. *Extensions to the Web Service processing pipeline*

This doesn't mean that the implementations provided by WSE are .NET-specific. On the contrary, they're more interoperable than any custom solution would be, as they're based on public specifications that other vendors can implement for other platforms. This means that WS-Security can be used from a .NET client to a J2EE server, or it can be used from a J2EE client and a .NET Server (see Figure 6-22).

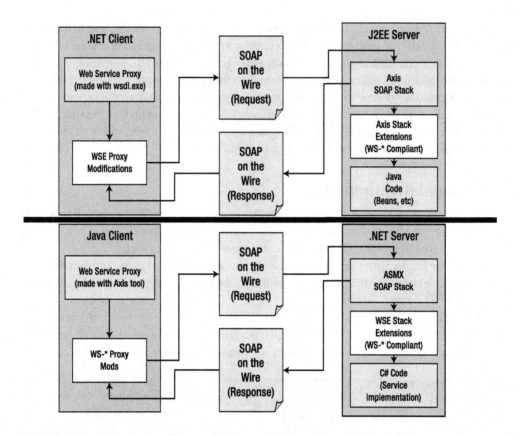

Figure 6-22. *WS-* Interoperability*

We've listed some of the specifications implemented by WSE 3 in Table 6-3.

Table 6-3. *Specifications Implemented by the Microsoft Web Service Enhancements*

Specification	Meaning in Life
WS-Security	Allows you to encrypt and sign SOAP messages as well as bind security tokens to the message.
WS-SecureConnection	Extends WS-Security with the capability for a caller and service to establish a secure connection using keys.
WS-Trust	Extends WS-Security with the capability to verify trust between the caller and service.
WS-Policy	Provides a way for the caller and service to agree upon how SOAP messages must be crafted to be accepted.
WS-Addressing	Provides a way to forward and intercept SOAP messages.
WS-Referral	Provides a way to forward to a new XML Web service while preserving the current message.
WS-Attachment/DIME (Direct Internet Message Encapsulation)	A new message encoding format that allows SOAP messages to include additional attachments (for example, binary files).

A discussion of all of these is beyond the scope of this chapter. Here, we present a high-level overview, summarizing where WSE fits into the "Big Picture." We'll also take a look at an implementation of WS-Security in action.

Once WSE 3.0 is installed, from within Visual Studio .NET 2005, you can configure a project to leverage the functionality by right-clicking on the project and choosing WSE Settings 3.0… (see Figure 6-23).

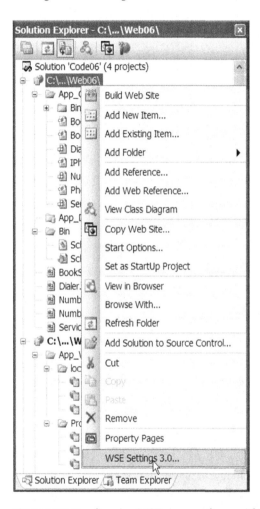

Figure 6-23. *Configuring WSE support from within Visual Studio .NET 2005*

Selecting this option brings up a dialog with many tabs. Support for WSE is enabled when you select the check boxes (see Figure 6-24).

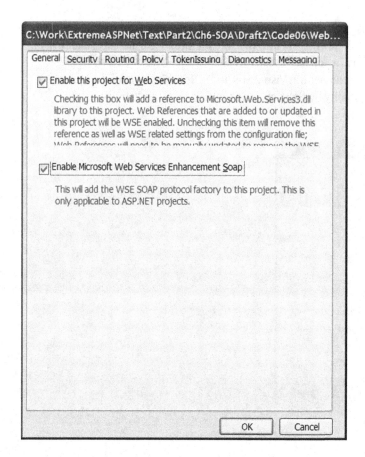

Figure 6-24. *Enabling WSE within a project*

When this dialog is dispatched, Visual Studio adds a reference to the WSE 3.0 assembly, `Microsoft.Web.Services3`. Modifications will also be made to your `Web.Config` file to enable support for the SOAP Extensions where the WS-* specifications are implemented:

```
<configSections>
  <section name="microsoft.web.services3"
           type="Microsoft.Web.Services3.Configuration.WebServicesConfiguration,
                 Microsoft.Web.Services3, Version=3.0.0.0, Culture=neutral,
                 PublicKeyToken=31bf3856ad364e35" />
</configSections>
<system.web>
  <webServices>
    <soapExtensionImporterTypes>
      <add type="WseSettings.WseExtensionImporter, WseSettings3, Version=3.0.0.0,
                 Culture=neutral, PublicKeyToken=97707682dce9a66b" />
    </soapExtensionImporterTypes>
    <soapServerProtocolFactory type="Microsoft.Web.Services3.WseProtocolFactory,
                 Microsoft.Web.Services3, Version=3.0.0.0,
                 Culture=neutral, PublicKeyToken=31bf3856ad364e35" />
  </webServices>
```

```
<compilation>
  <assemblies>
    <add assembly="Microsoft.Web.Services3, Version=3.0.0.0, Culture=neutral,
                      PublicKeyToken=31BF3856AD364E35" />
  </assemblies>
</compilation>
</system.web>
<microsoft.web.services3>
  <tokenIssuer>
    <statefulSecurityContextToken enabled="true" />
  </tokenIssuer>
</microsoft.web.services3>
```

Each specification that's supported by WSE 3.0 has corresponding types exposed in the Microsoft.Web.Services3 namespace that allow you to control the implementation programmatically. Table 6-4 provides a summary of some of the types found in the assembly.

Table 6-4. *Summary of Namespaces in the* Microsoft.Web.Services3 *Assembly*

Namespace	Meaning in Life
Microsoft.Web.Service3	This root namespace defines core types to interact with the incoming and outgoing WSE-enabled request/response and SOAP payload.
Microsoft.Web.Service3.Addressing	Types that implement the WS-Addressing specification.
Microsoft.Web.Service3.Dime	Types that implement the DIME specification.
Microsoft.Web.Service3.Messaging	Types that implement the WS-Referral specification.
Microsoft.Web.Service3.Security	Types that define the core WS-Security types. There are several subnamespaces here that cover specific security models.

Table 6-4 is just a summary of the namespaces in the assembly. There are others that relate to other parts of the WSE 3.0 implementation.

WSE 3.0 actually contains an implementation of a complete SOAP Stack. This stack can be used in concert with the ASMX SOAP Stack exposed by the ASP.NET Framework, or it can be used on its own. The WSE SOAP Stack has an option to listen to a TCP/IP port for incoming SOAP messages. When you use this option, IIS isn't even required. With WSE 3.0, it's also much easier to host the ASMX stack in your own process, removing the need to rely on IIS.

When used in concert with the ASMX SOAP Stack running under IIS, WSE intercepts all incoming and outgoing SOAP messages. This is where the SOAP extensions added in the configuration file step in and create or examine the SOAP headers that are needed for the specification's required functionality (see Figure 6-25). There's also a client component to the WSE functionality. When WSE support is enabled in a project, all Web Service proxies that are generated when you add a Web Reference will be modified and extended to account for the WSE functionality.

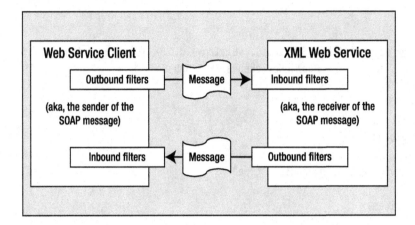

Figure 6-25. *Message interception as provided by the WSE infrastructure*

As incoming messages are intercepted on the server, WSE moves the SOAP headers off the wire and creates instances of corresponding objects as defined in the WSE name-spaces. These objects are added to, and made available to, the rest of the request processing via the SoapContext object. A reference to the current SOAP context can be obtained from anywhere in the request processing pipeline by referencing the Current property of the RequestSoapContext:

```
SoapContext myCtx = RequestSoapContext.Current;
```

This concept is very similar to the HttpContext available in the ASP.NET request processing pipeline. Details of the request (SOAP headers in this case) are made available as instances of managed types. Another similarity to ASP.NET is the notion of a request and a response. Again, the big difference is that this can be used from both the client and the server, instead of just the server. Request context can be used to modify requests on the client and to examine details of the request on the server. It can be used to modify the results that are going back in a message to the client.

On the client-side of the equation, you must also enable support for WSE 3.0 via the same dialog available from the context menu of the project. Once it's enabled, adding a Web Reference results in the generation of two proxies: the standard .NET proxy and a WSE-enabled proxy. The WSE-enabled proxy will be named after the .NET proxy, but will have a wse suffix tacked on. Using this proxy, clients will be able to obtain a reference to the SOAP context:

```csharp
using System;
using WSEWebServiceClient.localhost;
using Microsoft.Web.Services3;

namespace WSEWebServiceClient
{
  class ClientApp
  {
    static void Main(string[] args)
    {
        SampleWebServiceWse wsWSE = new SampleWebServiceWse();
```

```
        // Get current SOAP context to augment the response.
        SoapContext ctx = wsWSE.RequestSoapContext;
    }
  }
}
```

SOAP context is central to processing of the WSE functionality. This context contains properties that reference the different objects providing the implementation of a WSE specification. This context is leveraged from both the client and the server when the SOAP Stack extensions are processing WSE-specific headers. Each specification implemented by WSE has a corresponding object model available and is exposed by this context. The client uses this context to create the SOAP headers to send to the server with the request message, and the server uses this object model to process the headers once they arrive at the server.

Let's take a look at how this is done, specifically by examining the WS-Security implementation.

WS-Security

The WS-Security specification provides a number of standard ways to use SOAP headers to pass authentication and authorization information. These range from simple user name and password tokens to X-509 certificates. The specification also spells out how messages can be signed using digital signatures, and how portions of a SOAP message can be encrypted on the wire.

The header of a SOAP message leveraging WS-Security may include any of a number of elements to describe details of the specification's functionality that it's leveraging. The root element of a WS-Security header is named `<Security>`. It has a number of allowable child elements, listed in Table 6-5.

Table 6-5. *SOAP Headers Defined in the WS-Security Specification as Children of the Security Element*

WS-Security SOAP Header Element	Meaning in Life
`<UsernameToken>`	Contains user name/password data for authentication purposes.
`<BinarySecurityToken>`	Contains binary security data such as X-509 certificates.
`<KeyInfo>`	Contains key data derived from an XML signature.
`<Signature>`	Contains signing details of a SOAP message.
`<ReferenceList>`	Contains data that references the encrypted elements of a SOAP message.
`<EncryptedKey>`	Contains data for any encrypted keys.
`<EncryptedData>`	Contains any additional encrypted data.
`<Timestamp>`	Contains timestamp data. This can help prevent a hacker from attempting to reuse outdated messages for evil-doings.

Using WS-Security requires coding on both the client and the server. The server is expecting authentication information to be packed into the SOAP header. The client has to take steps to create this header with the user's credentials. The server needs to validate these credentials against a user data store before executing the service request.

On the server, a SOAP extension runs to process the SOAP header when the message arrives with the authentication information packed into the Security element. This is done by an instance of a class deriving from SecurityTokenManager. There is an implementation of this class that ships with WSE for authenticating the user information against the Windows domain the service is running within. To use your own user data store, you'll need to create an instance of a type that inherits from UsernameTokenManager and looks the credentials up against your own user database. UserNameTokenManager derives from SecurityTokenManager.

You can do the work of authentication by overriding the virtual AuthenticateToken method on the base class. This method gets passed the user name that the client sent, and your job in implementing this method is to look up the user's password and send it back as a return value of the method call. The WSE code then compares the passwords and decides if the caller should be authenticated or not:

```csharp
using System;
using System.Data;
using System.Data.SqlClient;
using Microsoft.Web.Services3;
using Microsoft.Web.Services3.Security;
using Microsoft.Web.Services3.Security.Tokens;

public class CustomAuthManager : UsernameTokenManager
{
  private string ConnStr = "server=.;database=...";
  protected override string AuthenticateToken( UsernameToken token )
  {
    string password = "";

    // Extract user name from the token.
    string username = token.Username;
    SqlCommand cm = new SqlCommand
        ("select Password from UserTable WHERE UserName = @UserName",
         new SqlConnection( ConnStr));
    cm.Parameters.Add("@UserName", SqlDbType.VarChar, 30).Value = username;
    cm.Connection.Open();
    Object o = cm.ExecuteScalar();
    cm.Connection.Close();

    if (o != null)
        password = o.ToString();

    return password;
  }
}
```

Once this class is created and compiled, it must be registered as a security token manager using the WSE configuration utility. Let's say, for example, that your CustomAuthManager class is defined in the WSECode namespace, and lives in an assembly named WSECode. You would deploy this assembly into the bin directory of your web application and fill out the Security tab in the WSE configuration dialog to point to your custom CustomAuthManager type (see Figure 6-26).

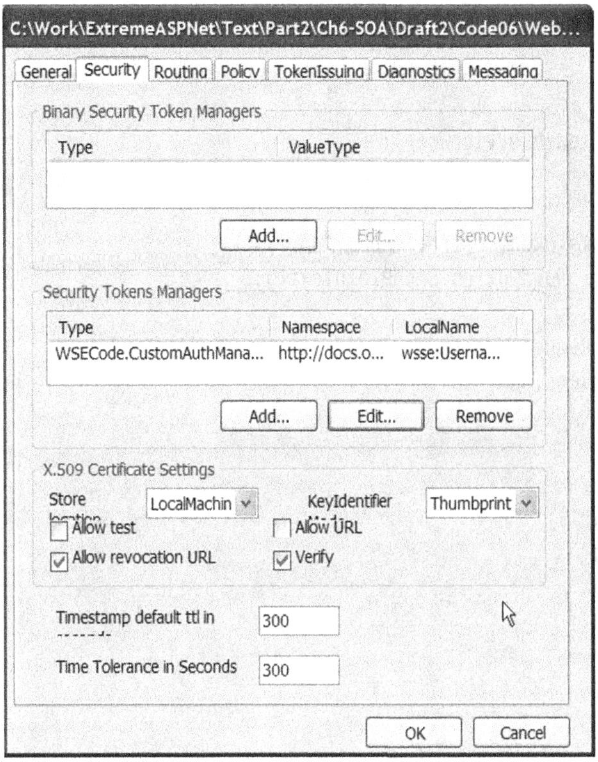

Figure 6-26. *The Security tab on the WSE configuration dialog*

As you may have already suspected, this dialog is nothing more than a friendly editor that makes entries in the Web.Config (or app.config) file of the project you're using it from. Here's the entry in the Web.Config made by the dialog displayed in Figure 6-26.

```
<microsoft.web.services3>
  <tokenIssuer>
    <statefulSecurityContextToken enabled="true" />
  </tokenIssuer>
  <security>
    <securityTokenManager>
      <add type="WSECode.CustomAuthManager, WSECode"
           namespace="http://docs.oasis-open.org/wss/2004/01/..."
           localName="wsse:UsernameToken" />
    </securityTokenManager>
  </security>
</microsoft.web.services3>
```

The type attribute lists your fully qualified type name, followed by the assembly name. The namespace declaration and the qname attribute must be listed exactly as shown.

The server is now correctly wired to authenticate requests coming into this application using a WS-Security-compliant implementation that leverages your own custom user data store. Any request for Web Services coming into this application must now include the appropriate SOAP security header. You can do this on the client using the custom WSE proxy that's generated when a Web Reference is added to your service:

```
static void Main(string[] args)
{
  SampleWebServiceWse w = new SampleWebServiceWse();

  // Create a UsernameToken
  UsernameToken token = new UsernameToken( "atroelsen", "abc",
                        PasswordOption.SendPlainText );

  // Add the SecurityToken to the Request Context
  w.RequestSoapContext.Security.Tokens.Add( token );

  try
  {
    BookDetails book = w.GetBook(101);
    Console.WriteLine(book.Title);
  }
  catch(Exception ex)
  {
    Console.WriteLine(ex.Message);
  }
}
```

After creating an instance of your WSE proxy, you use the UsernameToken object provided by the WSE object model. Its constructor accepts a user name, a password, and an encryption option for the password as arguments. After creating this instance, you instruct the proxy to create a SOAP security header and add it to the request by adding the instance of UsernameToken to the collection of tokens exposed by the SOAP security context.

Everything else flows from here. When you invoke the service, the security token is added to the SOAP header as a WS-Security-compliant element. When the request arrives at the server, the user name is handed off to your custom authentication type, and you return the password for the user name passed to you. If someone passes you invalid credentials, the service operation never executes, and the caller receives a SOAP Fault instead.

In this example you instructed the proxy to send the password as plain text. You could also have it encrypted on the wire by using the SendHashed value of the PasswordOption enum.

You can see in this example that by leveraging the SOAP extensions on the server and the custom WSE proxy on the client, you can easily pass WS-* compliant headers and process them when servicing requests. The other WSE features are exposed via similar models of the other objects in the WSE library. While we're out of bandwidth for examining them here, you can consult the WSE documentation for details on using them.

Summary

Service orientation in the .NET Framework as exposed via the ASMX call stack lends a lot of power and flexibility to your application design and development process. Web Services, as they ship with the .NET Framework, create a seamless, attribute-based model for exposing methods on your classes as service operations. You can use the WSDL generation features of ASMX, or you can take control of our WSDL and its underlying XML Schema and have a server-side interface defining the service generated for you, and then simply create a class that implements the interface.

Version 2.0 adds many new features to the ASMX call stack, including the ability to control the XML used to represent your types in a SOAP message, and customize the types created during proxy generation.

When you need greater interoperability you can extend the features added to the ASMX stack using Web Services enhancements, which provide implementations of many specifications in the WS-* family of Web Service architecture. This add-on package of technology affects the behavior of both the server-side processing pipeline and the client-side proxy generation.

CHAPTER 7

■■■

Enterprise Services

The hosting environment that was originally shipped as Microsoft Transaction Server (MTS) has a lot of names nowadays. Some call it Component Services. Some call it Enterprise Services. Some prefer the brevity of just COM+.

Whatever you call it, Component Services is the original aspect-oriented application server for Windows. Support for Component Services has been extended into the .NET Framework, so even though it's still a COM-based technology, you can create types in .NET that can be configured and hosted in the COM+ environment.

In this chapter we'll take a look at the features provided by this hosting environment, and then examine what you do exactly to create .NET types that can benefit from this feature set.

Component Services

Component Services provides a hosting environment and configuration registry for exposing software assets as services. Originally called Microsoft Transaction Server, these services were designed to be exposed in an RPC manner via DCOM. Over time, it became as common (if not more common) to leverage configured components from Internet Information Server (IIS). This was the standard architecture for ASP-based applications. Creating COM types and hosting them as configured services in COM+ provided many benefits, including compiled code (as opposed to interpreted script) and a type system (as opposed to one type: the VBScript Variant). Figure 7-1 shows the original common architectures.

Many powerful features of Component Services worth leveraging from managed code still exist. Support for running managed code within the COM environment of COM+ is accomplished via highly specialized interoperability code that has been added to the Component Services infrastructure. Because of this, not just any .NET type can be configured and hosted in this environment. Not only do you need to make special considerations for the design of these types, but the types must also inherit from a special base class and adhere to special run-time behaviors.

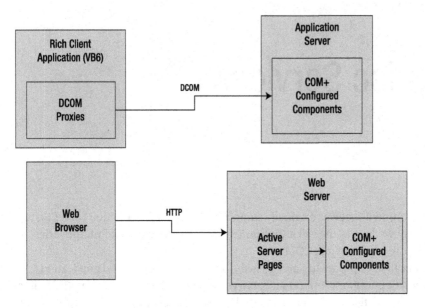

Figure 7-1. *The original common architectures for Component Services*

We'll take a look at how support for Component Services is grafted onto the .NET Framework over the course of the chapter. First, let's take a quick look at why you would be tempted to create configured components in the first place. Table 7-1 lists some of the features of COM+.

Table 7-1. *Features You Can Leverage from the Components Services Hosting Environment*

COM+ Feature	Meaning in Life
Thread Management	COM+ allocates thread pools to manage higher loads and service many requests concurrently. Combined with Just-in-Time Activation (JITA) and object pools, COM+ can greatly reduce the overhead of object instantiation and destruction, and can effectively manage object lifetimes in a highly scalable environment.
Transaction Management	Leveraging the features of the Microsoft Distributed Transaction Coordinator (MSDTC), types can be made to have their work participate in transactions declaratively. That is, transactional behavior becomes an aspect of the type, in many cases eliminating the need for special considerations while coding. Transactions can also be managed across disparate servers, even across different database vendors.
Queued Components	This feature set creates a perfect layer of abstraction between a developer and Message Queuing (MSMQ). Method calls become messages, benefiting your code by making your method calls asynchronous, which provides peak load balancing and guaranteed delivery. All of the details of creating a message, putting it in a queue, and processing it on the receiver are managed by the hosting environment.
Security	Applications, classes, and even methods can be declared as requiring the executing user be in a predefined role. This is declarative security, eliminating the need to modify imperative code to meet your authorization requirements.

These services are all provided with the concept of a call context. Objects that share run-time requirements will share context; objects with different run-time requirements will be created in different contexts. Contexts provide an interception boundary for the hosting environment. As code from a method in type A calls into code of a method in type B, execution does not immediately move from A to B. COM+ code intercepts the call, and additional work is done before execution moves to the code in type B. This interception boundary does things like enable COM+ to retrieve an object of type B from the pool to service the request. When the method call is done, the context interception code is fired again before control returns to the instance of A. COM+ can, at this point, put the object back into the pool, as would be the case with JITA, for example.

While contexts are invisible to the developer consuming these services, the presence of contexts in COM+ is ubiquitous; they are the mechanism via which all of its services are implemented. They also provide an additional layer of overhead, which you should always consider before you make the decision to move to COM+. We'll discuss some of these considerations in detail later in the chapter. First, let's take a look at what you have to do specifically to your managed code so that it will play nicely within the Component Services environment.

COM+ in .NET

Before we dig into the .NET-specific bits, let's take a minute to look at some terms listed in Table 7-2.

Table 7-2. *Names and Titles Used to Talk about COM+*

Term	Meaning in Life
Microsoft Transaction Server (MTS)	An application hosting environment that provides services to components via aspects, determining the behavior of the components with declarations rather than requiring imperative code. This is the predecessor to COM+.
COM+	The name given to the environment for hosting configured components. COM+ has some new features that were not present in MTS. It could have been called "MTS version 2.0", but Microsoft renamed it COM+ instead.
Component Services	Another name for COM+. This is the name given to the Microsoft Management Console (MMC) snap-in used for creating and configuring COM+ applications, and so has become another name for COM+.
Configured Component	When you register a class into COM+, it is said to be a configured component. The act of installing it into COM+ is the act of configuring it. This is true for COM types as well as .NET types, although you use different means to configure each of these types of components.
Enterprise Services	The set of features baked into the .NET Framework that enable you to create managed types that can live in COM+ (aka that can be configured). The namespace of the types supporting these features is System.EnterpriseServices, and so the term is frequently used to describe managed COM+ components.
Serviced Component	This is the name of a type built into the .NET Framework Class Library (the full name is System.EnterpriseServices.ServicedComponent). It is, therefore, used frequently to refer to a specific managed type designed to be hosted under Component Services (aka "Is the CustomerService object a Serviced Component?").

The managed functionality of COM+ is exposed in the .NET Framework via the assembly named System.EnterprisesServices (which lives in System.EnterprisesServices.dll). This assembly is part of the Framework class library, but you still have to explicitly add a reference to it from the project you'll be creating configured components in (see Figure 7-2).

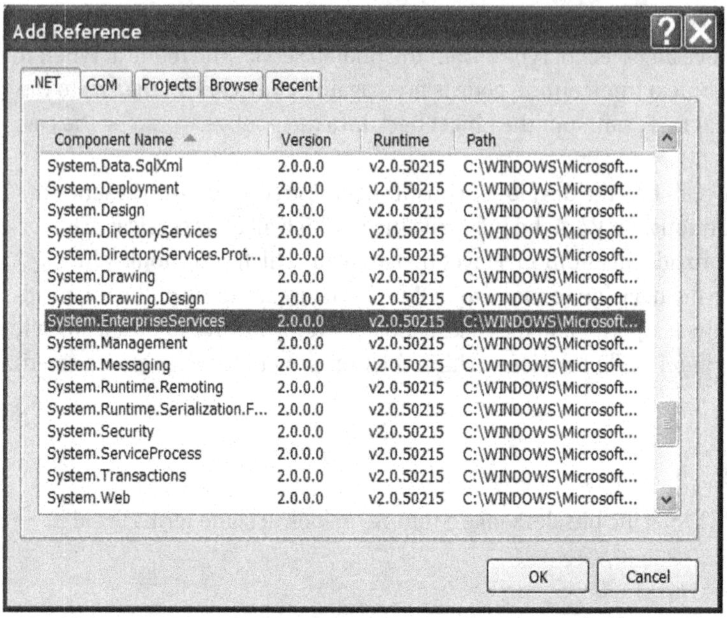

Figure 7-2. *Adding a reference to* System.EnterpriseServices

This will make the ServicedComponent class available to your class library project. All managed components that you want to configure to run under COM+ must use this type as their base class. Here's a simple implementation of a Serviced Component. (You can find this type in the Serviced project of the Code07 solution.)

```
// All the important enterprise service types are contained here.
using System.EnterpriseServices;

namespace CarLibrary
{
    // Set the transaction mode to "supported"
    [Transaction(TransactionOption.Supported)]
    public class CarService : ServicedComponent
    {
        // If method raises exception, tx is automatically aborted.
        [AutoComplete(true)]
        public void InsertCar(DataSet carData)
        {
            // Insert the car data into the database
        }
    }
}
```

This type will now be hosted in Component Services, by virtue of the fact that it inherits from the ServicedComponent base class. It's configured to leverage transactions within Component Services. This is done via attributes applied to the type at the class and method level: Transaction and AutoComplete. These attributes determine the default configuration of the component when it's registered into COM+. We'll cover these attributes in detail as we examine specific functional areas of Component Services, for now just realize the *default* configured behavior of Serviced Components is always determined declaratively by .NET attributes (see Figure 7-3).

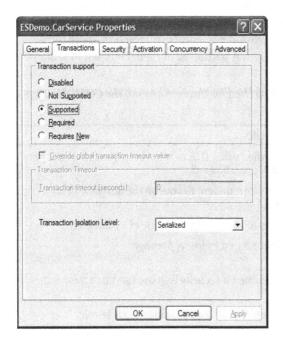

Figure 7-3. *The configuration of the* CarService *type as determined by its attributes*

The ServicedComponent base class deals with the underlying details of hosting a managed component in a COM environment. This is interoperability between .NET and COM, but it is not the same type of "COM Interop" you're used to when, for example, you use the Office interop assemblies or your own COM proxy created with tlbimp.exe. This is more specialized interop code, designed and optimized specifically for interacting with Component Services. While its performance is better than standard COM Interop, it's still a layer of abstraction, which will invariably cause a performance hit you must consider before you decide to adopt Enterprise Services. Keep in mind that when your Serviced Component is registered in COM+, a type library will be generated and the registry will be populated with information about it. Although this happens automatically behind the scenes, it's important to realize you have these dependencies on traditional COM infrastructure.

Usually, the features that are needed from Component Services will offset the performance hit your application will incur by leveraging Enterprise Services. Perhaps you have scalability concerns as traffic increases to your application, and you know object pooling will help address it. Remember, many of the nonfunctional requirements you have to meet in your applications need to be done at the expense of performance. For scalability, moving your code into Component Services by adopting Enterprise Services will make the application more scalable so it can deal with a higher number of concurrent users, but the experience of a single user will not be as fast.

Frequently it's the distributed transaction features that drive the adoption of Enterprise Services. If your application has complex transactional requirements, the management and services provided by COM+ will certainly justify the loss in performance incurred by using this COM environment. There's likely no way you could code this yourself and have it perform any better, much less be as reliable (or even work, for that matter).

You can determine most of the details of configuration under COM+ using .NET attributes to decorate your Serviced Components. There are some instances, though, when you need write code to interact with the hosting environment. For this interaction, there is the ContextUtil class, and its stable of static members. A partial list of them is shown in Table 7-3.

Table 7-3. *Static Members of the* ContextUtil *Type Used for Interacting with the COM+ Hosting Environment*

Static Member of ContextUtil	Meaning in Life
DeactivateOnReturn	Set to true when using JITA to return the instance to the pool at the end of a method call.
EnableCommit, DisableCommit	Enables your component to vote on the outcome of a transaction.
MyTransactionVote	Another way to vote on the outcome of a transaction.
GetNamedProperty SetNamedProperty	Access to the Shared Property Manager.
IsSecurityEnabled	Boolean indicated if security is in use for the current call context.
IsCallerInRole	Checks to see if a user is in a specified COM+ role.
IsInTransaction	Boolean indicating whether the work being done is transactional or not.

We'll take a look at more details of these ContextUtil members as they're relevant in the discussion of COM+ features that follows. Serviced Components must also always be strongly named.

COM+ Applications

Classes are deployed into COM+ using the abstraction of an *application*. A COM+ application can be thought of as simply an aggregation of configured classes that share run-time requirements. Once configured within COM+, these classes are also called *components*.

Components are aggregations of interfaces, and interfaces are aggregations of methods. Aspects of the run-time behavior that can be controlled at the application level will be shared across all components, all the way down to the method level. Some aspects can be added or overridden at each level in the hierarchy.

The most important configuration aspects at the application level are security and activation. *Security* controls what identity the components run under. When deciding what components should be grouped in an application, consider that cross-application calls can cross a security boundary, so you should logically group them for optimum performance.

Activation is the other prominent aspect. This aspect controls whether components are created in their own process, or whether they are created in the process of their caller. Applications created in their own process are called *server applications*, and while calling these components incurs the performance hit of crossing a boundary, you also gain the benefits of isolation. This can affect pool allocation and the identity of the process.

Applications created in the process of the caller are called *library applications*. They lose the capability to specify their run-time identity, as they will run under the identity of their caller. They will also have pools created for each application from which they're invoked (see Chapter 8 for more details of library versus server applications).

When you're creating Serviced Components, you can control these aspects of a COM+ application using assembly level attributes (these attributes can be found in `AssemblyInfo.cs` in the `Serviced` project).

```
[assembly: ApplicationName("Serviced")]
[assembly: ApplicationAccessControl(false)]
[assembly: ApplicationActivation(ActivationOption.Library)]
```

These attributes are then read via reflection and applied when the component is being configured. We'll examine configuration more closely after we look at the specific features you can leverage from within Component Services.

Just-In-Time Activation

This feature (abbreviated as JITA), enables an instance of an object to survive for the span of only a single method call. Even if a consumer of this type holds a reference to an instance of it for a long period of time, instances will only be created when the consumer actually calls a method.

JITA is configured on a class using the `JustInTimeActivation` attribute, as in the following class declaration.

```
[JustInTimeActivation(true)]
public class JITA : ServicedComponent
{
    //Class Implementation
}
```

The only other thing necessary to have COM+ destroy the object after a call is to apply the `DeactivateOnReturn` attribute. To illustrate the effect JITA has on object lifetimes, examine it via this simple service method. (This class can be found in the `Serviced` project of the `Code07` solution.)

```
//[JustInTimeActivation(true)]
public class JITA : ServicedComponent
{
    private DateTime m_CreateStamp;
    public JITA()
    {
        m_CreateStamp = DateTime.Now();
    }
}
```

```
public DateTime GetCreateStamp()
{
    //ContextUtil.DeactivateOnReturn = true;
    return m_CreateStamp;
}
}
```

Notice the JITA specific code is commented out. Now exercise this code with the following loop, and examine the output it generates. (You can find test code in the TestHarness project of the Code07 solution.)

```
static void Main(string[] args)
{
    JITA j = new JITA();

    for (int i = 0; i < 5; i++)
    {
        Console.WriteLine(j.GetCreateStamp());
        Thread.Sleep(3000);
    }
    Console.ReadLine();
}
```

With the JITA attribute commented out, the dates on the output all match (see Figure 7-4). This makes sense, because the consumer is holding a reference to the same instance across all calls, and so the object is only created a single time.

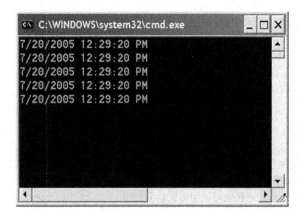

Figure 7-4. *The timestamp matches across all method calls without JITA.*

Look at what happens if you remove the comments around the JITA-specific code and rerun the client (see Figure 7-5).

Now, obviously the churn involved in object creation and destruction will, in most cases, consume the benefit gained by not keeping extraneous instances around between a client's method calls. For this reason, JITA usually makes the most sense when it's combined with object pooling. We'll take a look at object pooling in the next section.

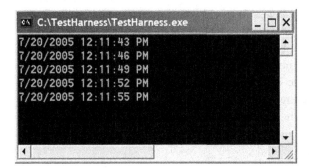

Figure 7-5. *With JITA, each iteration of the loop is actually calling a new instance of the service object.*

The goal of JITA is to optimize the efficiency of stateless components. Since classes designed to be used within COM+ should generally be stateless, JITA has broad applicability in this environment. Enabling this feature removes control of the object lifetime from the client, and puts the server component in control of its own lifetime. This is going to increase scalability if you have clients that are holding references to your components, even when they should be creating instances late and releasing them as soon as possible (a best practice in distributed, stateless programming environments).

It could be argued then, that if your client is stateless (like it is when the "client" is an ASP.NET web application), JITA is not needed because the lifetime will only ever last as long as the lifetime of the Web Form holding the reference. This is theoretically true, but even if your client is stateless, enabling JITA can guard against bad coding practices, like putting a reference to a COM+ component into the ASP.NET web cache. In larger environments where you may not necessarily be in a position to review the code that's consuming your components, JITA can still be worthwhile.

The only time JITA should not be considered is when your component is maintaining state information across method calls. When this is necessary, the lifetime of the component must be managed by the client, and JITA-enabling this component will cause the state information to be lost.

We'll be looking at COM+ transactions in a following section. It's worth noting that enabling transactions on your type automatically causes it to be JITA-enabled.

Object Pooling

A pool of objects increases the scalability of an application by avoiding expensive object instantiation and destruction overhead, and it is able to service the requests of many times more clients than can be served with an instance per client. Coupling pools with JITA can dramatically increase the load your application can withstand.

A *pool* is nothing more than a number of active instances of a type that COM+ maintains in memory, and then dynamically allocates as clients request instances of the type. With JITA configured, these allocations occur on a *per method call* basis. When the method is finished executing, the instance is returned to the pool to service the next request. Not only are instances of the type more readily available, but also precious resources are saved by not instantiating an instance per client reference, and by avoiding the expensive process of allocating additional blocks of memory to hold the instance.

For this to work, the object *must be stateless*. Any field-level information designed to be maintained across method calls will not necessarily be maintained. These types must be entirely autonomous at the method level. They need to accept all of the parameters required to do their work, do the work within the method call, and release any resources used to do the work before returning results to the caller.

Pooling behavior is controlled with the ObjectPooling attribute, seen as follows. (You can find this class in the Serviced project of the Code07 solution.)

```
[ObjectPooling(5, 500)]
public class Poolable : ServicedComponent
{
    public DataSet GetSomeData(string sql)
    {
        SqlConnection cn = new SqlConnection(ConnStr);
        SqlCommand cm = new SqlCommand(sql, cn);
        DataSet ds = new DataSet();

        new SqlDataAdapter(cm).Fill(ds);
        return ds;
    }
    protected override CanBePooled()
    {
        return true;
    }
}
```

The ObjectPooling attribute controls the default configuration of the component when it's registered with COM+ (see Figure 7-6). As objects are deactivated, the COM+ runtime calls the CanBePooled method to verify that it has permission to return the instance to the pool. This method returns false from the base class, so you need to override it and return true in order to get instances into the pool.

Pooling should always be used in combination with JITA, for highly available instances that are returned to the pool after each method completes.

```
[ObjectPooling(5, 500)]
[JustInTimeActivation(true)]
public class Poolable : ServicedComponent
{
    public DataSet GetSomeData(string sql)
    {
        SqlConnection cn = new SqlConnection(ConnStr);
        SqlCommand cm = new SqlCommand(sql, cn);
        DataSet ds = new DataSet();

        cn.Open();
        new SqlDataAdapter(cm).Fill(ds);
        cn.Close();
```

```
    ContextUtil.DeactivateOnReturn = true;
    return ds;

  }
}
```

Notice that in this case, we've added not only the JustInTimeActivation attribute back on to the class definition, but also added a call to DeactivateOnReturn into the method body, to ensure COM+ knows the instance can be returned to the pool when the method call is complete.

Finally, you can use object pooling to throttle access to a limited resource. By minimizing the maximum pool size, you can control the number of concurrent requests that can be processed by the pooled object. For example, you might have a document management system with a ten-connection license. In order to avoid having more than ten concurrent connections, you can pool the object with a maximum pool size of ten, and a peak in load will be serialized after the tenth instance is served from the pool.

Figure 7-6. *An object configured for pooling within Component Services*

Transactions

COM+ can also manage transactions. Transactions can span methods, components, databases, and even servers running database products from different vendors. All code enlisted in the transaction gets to "vote" on the outcome of the transaction. It's more like veto power though, because any vote of "no" causes the entire transaction to be rolled back.

Each class configured in COM+ sets an attribute determining its transactional behavior. This attribute is designed so that a transaction can be dynamically composed of many different components, in a way that may not be known when the autonomous components are designed. Table 7-4 is a summary of the options for transactional behavior.

Table 7-4. *Options for Configuring the Transactional Behavior of COM+ Components*

Transaction Option	Meaning In Life
Requires	COM+ will create a new transaction if none exists, or the object will be enlisted in the transaction of the object that created it.
Requires New	COM+ will create a brand new transaction. The object will not participate in the transaction of its creator, if one exists.
Supports	The object will be enlisted in the transactional support of the creating object (if it has any) or else will run without a transaction.
Does Not Support	This is the default. The object does not care about, and does not participate in, any transactions.
Disabled	This is like Does Not Support, but it requires no COM+ context. This choice is nearly equivalent to a nonconfigured component.

Transactions are always kicked off by a *root object*, which is a component flagged as either requiring a transaction or requiring a new transaction. This root object acts as the manager of the transaction, enlisting the appropriate set of autonomous methods to accomplish the transactional work. If any single method enlisted in the transaction votes "no," the entire transaction is doomed to fail. All of the other objects enlisted in the transaction are called *secondary objects*. They need to be flagged with the Supports or Requires option. If they are flagged with Requires New, they become a new root object in a new transaction that will succeed or fail independently from the transaction that created it. This allows for a very flexible design of the transactions to reflect complex business processes (see Figure 7-7).

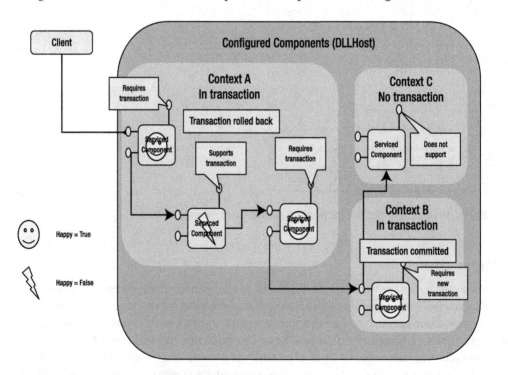

Figure 7-7. *A complex set of transactions, where one transaction failed and another succeeded, while a third component did its work outside of the context of any transaction*

There are a couple of options for a component to vote on the outcome of a transaction from code. One is declarative and the other imperative. The declarative method is very easy. A method can be flagged with the AutoComplete attribute, and as long as the method body does not throw an exception, the method's vote will be to commit the transaction. The method must be coded such that if something goes wrong, an exception is thrown. If an exception is thrown by the database, it must be left to ascend the call stack, or be trapped, wrapped, and rethrown. Any violation of business rules that results in the method being unable to complete its work must also be handled by throwing an exception. (You can find this code in XActional.cs in the Serviced project.)

```
[Transaction(TransactionOption.Required)]
public class CustomerService
{
    [AutoComplete(true)]
    public void IncreaseCreditLimit(
                        int customerNum,
                        double increaseAmount)
    {
        try
        {
            Customer cust = new Customer(customerNum);
            double max = cust.MaxAllowableCredit;
            double current = cust.CreditLimit;

            if (max < current + increaseAmount)
            {
                throw new Exception("Max Credit Limit Exceeded");
            }
            cust.CreditLimit += increaseAmount;
            cust.Save();
        }
        catch (Exception ex)
        {
            throw new Exception(
                    "Attempt to increase limit failed", ex);
        }
    }
}
```

Notice the explicitly thrown exception captures the violation of a business rule. The try/catch block traps and wraps the explicitly thrown exception, or any other exception that bubbles up the call stack from your calls into the Customer object.

The other option is to explicitly vote on the transaction outcome from within the body of your method. In this case, you would omit the AutoComplete attribute, and use the ContextUtil properties to indicate the success or failure of the work that's been done.

```
[Transaction(TransactionOption.Required)]
public class CustomerService
{
    public void IncreaseCreditLimit(
                        int customerNum,
                        double increaseAmount)
    {
        try
        {
            Customer cust = new Customer(customerNum);
            double max = cust.MaxAllowableCredit;
            double current = cust.CreditLimit;

            if (max < current + increaseAmount)
            {
                ContextUtil.MyTransactionVote = TransactionVote.Abort;
            }
            else
            {
                cust.CreditLimit += increaseAmount;
                cust.Save();
                ContextUtil.MyTransactionVote = TransactionVote.Commit;
            }
        }
        catch (Exception ex)
        {
            ContextUtil.MyTransactionVote = TransactionVote.Abort;
            throw new Exception(
                        "Attempt to increase limit failed", ex);

        }
    }
}
```

It's only necessary to use this option when you do not want to throw exceptions when a component is unable to finish its work. Generally, unless it interferes with a larger error-handling strategy, you should use the AutoComplete attribute, as this results in much cleaner code overall.

Transactions are managed under the hood of COM+ by the Distributed Transaction Coordinator, a separate Windows Service. This service must be running for COM+ transactions to work. It is an expensive resource, and you must make considerations for the overhead your application will incur when you decide to use it. MSDTC is not the only technology available to manage transactions; you should consider other less-expensive options before deciding to go into COM+. A few bars for entry into COM+ for transactional management exist.

- Your transaction spans data sources, especially if it spans different relational databases. For example, if your transaction is moving information from Microsoft SQL Server into an Oracle database, MSDTC is an excellent option for managing the transaction.

- Your application has complex requirements around transactional composition. In this case, your services are designed to do different, autonomous pieces of work. Transaction coordinators are written that call these different services to accomplish a specific business process. The number of ways these services can be combined is high, or the requirements change and evolve often, and you anticipate introducing new transaction coordinators as newer versions of the product are introduced.

- Your application has customizable functionality, such that an end user, power user, or administrator has a tool that can affect how services are combined to do transactional work.

As a corollary to these guidelines, if you can meet your transactional requirements with another resource manager, your solution will probably perform better. One option may be using transactions within SQL Server Transact-SQL (TSQL). This limits the transaction to a single command execution from your data access code. A stored procedure can call other stored procedures to enlist in the work of the transaction. Another option is to use ADO.NET transactions. These transactions are tied to a connection so that many commands can be executed against a single data store and enlisted in a single transaction. You can use this to dynamically generate SQL or to combine multiple stored procedure calls. These options are not nearly as flexible as COM+ transactions, but they are much better performers; thus, you should leverage them when they can do the job.

See Chapter 12 for information on the transactional infrastructure built into the .NET Framework 2.0, which gives you options for "upgrading" transactions dynamically; this way, only the resource managers needed get enrolled on an as-needed basis.

Queued Components

Queued Components (QC) provide a layer of abstraction between the COM+ developer and MSMQ. Configuring a component as queued gives you all of the benefits of message queuing, including asynchronous method invocation, without having to worry about the underlying details of preparing MSMQ messages and placing them in queues.

When a component is configured as queued, a call to the message prompts COM+ to prepare a MSMQ message and place it in a private queue. Another COM+ process acts as a listener to that queue, pulls the message out when it arrives, and invokes the method described by the message (see Figure 7-8).

QC provides a fire-and-forget model of service invocation. For this reason, methods that are configured as queued cannot have a return value. The caller does not wait for a return value; instead, the caller continues execution as soon as COM+ prepares the message and gets it into the queue. The actual work the method does occurs asynchronously with whatever code path the caller continues with after the method call.

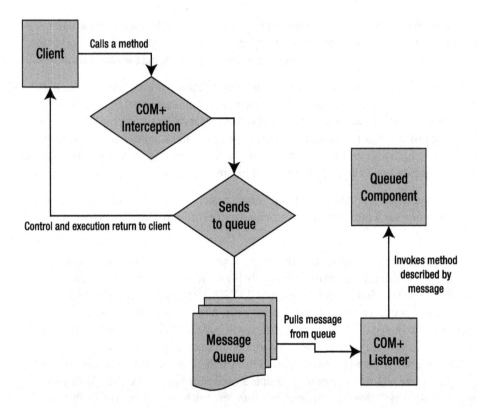

Figure 7-8. *The process of a method call to queued component*

Creating queued components is a little more involved than some of the other features of COM+. You'll need to do specific configurations on the server and on the client. You must add an assembly-level attribute to the assembly containing your components to queue. Finally, you must define an interface with all the methods you're planning to queue for a component, and then your Serviced Component must implement the interface.

When a client creates an instance of the component, it won't automatically call it using queuing. The good part about this is that the client has the flexibility to call the component in a queued manner or not. The downside is the need to write some specific code to leverage the queuing functionality. (You can find this queuing code in the Client and Server projects in the QCDemo directory of the Code07 solution.)

Let's start by taking a look at the assembly-level attribute that must be present.

```
[assembly: ApplicationQueuing(Enabled = true, QueueListenerEnabled = true)]
```

This sets up the application containing the component so that it can be queued. You can control the maximum number of listener threads with the attribute as well. The default is 16 per processor on the hosting machine.

Next you need to define an interface that you'll bind your queued messages to. An interface is necessary because you're using a COM-based technology, and all COM objects implement at least one interface. Queuing is, therefore, exposed on an interface-specific level of scope. So your Serviced Component must explicitly implement an interface, which your client will use to bind to and leverage the queued behavior.

You'll define an interface containing a single method. Remember that methods on this interface will not be able to return values; therefore, any method used with queuing must be declared as returning void.

```
public interface IQueuable
{
    void executeSQL(string sql);
}
```

Now you'll create a Serviced Component that implements this interface:

```
[InterfaceQueuing(Interface = "IQueuable")]
public class QCDemo : ServicedComponent, IQueuable
{
    public QCDemo() {}

    public void executeSQL(string sql)
    {
        try
        {
            SqlCommand cm = new SqlCommand(sql, new SqlConnection(ConnStr));
            cm.Connection.Open();
            cm.ExecuteNonQuery();
        }
        finally
        {
            cm.Connection.Close();
        }
    }
}
```

Notice you have decorated the type with the InterfaceQueuing attribute. With this attribute you're declaring your intent to use the named interface with in a queued manner. This will affect how the component gets configured (see Figure 7-9).

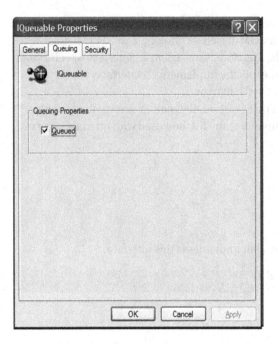

Figure 7-9. *An interface configured for queuing*

Your class is then declared as inheriting from ServicedComponent and implementing IQueuing. Clients will now have the choice of invoking this type via queuing or not. Here's a simple application to test your component:

```
static void Main(string[] args)
{
    string sql = "insert into jobs ( job_desc, min_lvl, max_lvl) "
             + "values ('Some job',10,250)";
    QCDemo o = new QCDemo();
    o.Dispose();
    Console.Write("Component registered.  Press enter to invoke");
    Console.ReadLine();
     IQueuable qable;
     try
     {
       qable = (IQueuable)Marshal.BindToMoniker
                           ("queue:/new:Server.QCDemo");

       for(int i = 0; i < 100; i++)
           qable.executeSQL(sql);
     }
     finally
     {
        Marshal.ReleaseComObject(qable);
     }
}
```

Configuration of a queued component can take a long time. Since you're relying on *lazy registration* (see the "Configuration" section a bit later in this chapter), your first block of code creates an instance of the type specifically for the purpose of registering it in COM+. You then declare an instance of the IQueuable interface and instantiate by using the Marshal.BindToMoniker method. This method lives in the System.Runtime.InteropServices namespace, which must be imported with a using statement. The string passed to it has the fully qualified name of the type built into the tail end of it, which is how the BindToMoniker method knows the proper type to create. The Serviced Component infrastructure takes care of the rest. Your code proceeds to call the executeSQL method 99 times. These method calls do not wait for the work of the insert statements to get done. Execution continues (and in our case, the application terminates) while the database work is picked up off the queue by the COM+ listener and executes asynchronously independently from our application. The last thing you do is explicitly destroy the COM object by calling ReleaseComObject (another static method on the Marshal type).

Role-Based Security

COM+ has its own infrastructure for enforcing role-based security. You can apply roles at the component, interface, or method level.

From Serviced Components, the .NET developer has two main tasks: creating COM+ roles and enforcing security at the appropriate level to make sure a caller is in the required role for the service it's attempting to call. Role creation is done with an assembly-level attribute:

```
[assembly: SecurityRole("Executive")]
[assembly: SecurityRole("Director")]
[assembly: SecurityRole("Manager")]
[assembly: SecurityRole("Grunt")]
```

These attributes result in the corresponding COM+ roles that are created (see Figure 7-10).

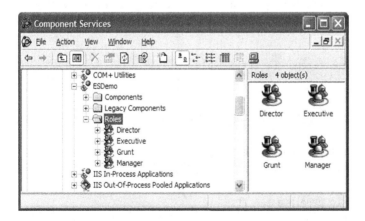

Figure 7-10. *Roles created in COM+ with .NET assembly-level attributes*

Role membership can now be enforced via either declarative aspects or imperative code. The declarative option is attractive, as it saves you from pushing complex conditional logic into the code, and enables you to simply decorate your types with declarations of their security requirements. You use the SecurityRole attribute for this purpose as well. (This code is in the Serviced project of the Code07 solution.)

```
[SecurityRole("Manager")]
public class RBDemo
{
    public RBDemo() {}

    public DataSet GetManagerData()
    {
        //implementation
        return new DataSet();
    }

    [SecurityRole("Executuve")]
    public DataSet GetExecutiveData()
    {
        //implementation
        return new DataSet();
    }
}
```

In this class, callers to any method must be in the Manager role. You've further restrained access to the GetExecutiveData method, requiring that callers to that method are in the Executive role. You could also apply the attribute to an interface declaration.

Sometimes you need a finer grain of control over your role-based security implementation. For example, you may want to render a list of reports, and user roles determine access to the reports. In these cases, you'll need programmatic access to the roles information. This is exposed to use via the SecurityCallContext type. While this may at first appear to be similar to ContextUtil, security context is different, so using SecurityCallContext is required in this case.

```
public void GetReportData(DataSet reportCriteriaData)
{
    // Get the current security call context
    SecurityCallContext callCtx = SecurityCallContext.CurrentCall;

    // Verify role based security is enabled (optional)
    if (callCtx.IsSecurityEnabled)
    {
        // Only allow managers to generate reports
        if (callCtx.IsCallerInRole("Manager"))
        {
            // proceed with report generation
        }
        else
        {
```

```
        // security error
    }
  }
}
```

Using imperative coding enables you to introduce different flow-of-control scenarios into your code based on the role of your calling users.

Configuration

Once you get your classes inheriting from the Serviced Component base class written and compiled, you'll need to configure them within the Component Services environment. You can be lazy or proactive about this.

The lazy approach enables the runtime to do this the first time someone creates an instance of the type. Seriously, it's called *lazy loading*. The nice thing about this approach is that there's no additional setup or installation step that needs to occur. The first time the component is requested, the runtime makes sure the COM+ application exists and checks all of the other assembly-level attributes (such as role declarations) to make sure they're present as well. Anything that doesn't exist will be created. If the application already exists, it will be shut down and the changes applied. Components and their interfaces then get registered and configured with COM+. The best reason to use this type of registration is right in its name: laziness. This approach should be avoided if at all possible.

The downside to lazy registration is that there's a significant performance hit on the first request to your application. Especially if your app is using queued components, this delay can last as long as a few seconds. The other, probably more serious, drawback is that the user running the process has to be an administrator to have the appropriate permissions to do this. So when you're running Serviced Components from ASP.NET, the user running the ASP.NET Framework must be configured as an administrator. This is usually a show stopper for folks, and leads them to your second option: registering the components yourself using a command line tool (seen with its options displayed in Figure 7-11).

```
C:\WINNT\System32\cmd.exe                                          _ □ ×

D:\>regsvcs
Microsoft (R) .NET Framework Services Installation Utility Version 1.0.3705.0
Copyright (C) Microsoft Corporation 1998-2001.  All rights reserved.

USAGE: regsvcs.exe [options] AssemblyName
Options:
    /? or /help      Display this usage message.
    /fc              Find or create target application (default).
    /c               Create target application, error if it already exists.
    /exapp           Expect an existing application.
    /tlb:<tlbfile>   Filename for the exported type library.
    /appname:<name>  Use the specified name for the target application.
    /parname:<name>  Use the specified name or id for the target partition.
    /extlb           Use an existing type library.
    /reconfig        Reconfigure existing target application (default).
    /noreconfig      Don't reconfigure existing target application.
    /u               Uninstall target application.
    /nologo          Suppress logo output.
    /quiet           Suppress logo output and success output.
    /componly        Configure components only, no methods or interfaces.

D:\>_
```

Figure 7-11. *The help screen for the* regsvcs *(register services) command line utility*

To use this utility, you simply feed the tool the name of the assembly containing classes you need to configure with the /c switch for "configure." You can also use /fc if there's a possibility that the application already exists, and you just want to add your types to it.

After registration with COM+, the .NET attributes applied to your types will determine the default configuration of the components. You (or an administrator) can always go in and use the MMC snap-in for Component Services to change and further refine them.

Some Practices Worth Observing

There are a lot of details to keep in mind when you're using component services. While a comprehensive discussion of the details of contexts, COM Interop, and an exhaustive list of best practices is out of scope for the summary we present in this chapter, we advise you keep some simple things in mind as you move into development in this space.

Component Design

First and foremost, create your applications with a stateless design. Don't use field-level information that creates a dependency across method calls. Have each method be truly autonomous and isolated. If and when you need to maintain state, do so in the database, and pass a session ID to the user that he can use to later retain the state information. Don't initialize connections in the constructor of your type to use it from the different methods of your type. Don't assume your user is going to be responsible in the use of your type by creating late, and destroying early; use JITA-enabled components instead.

To more explicitly separate the interface of your component from the implementation, you should always create an interface for your Serviced Component to implement.

An interface will be created under the hood to represent your class. By default, it will have the name _ClassName. You might as well create your own interfaces, and have your Serviced Component implement them. This means the interfaces listed within COM+ will be known types you've intentionally created; this will also ease the deployment of metadata if you're using COM+ in a distributed architecture.

Do not use static methods on types that inherit from ServicedComponent. These are not designed to work within COM+.

Also, always use the ContextUtil and SecurityCallContext to get to the underlying COM+ functionality. Do not call directly into the native COM+ libraries, as the behavior here will be volatile or perhaps merely unpredictable at best. The Enterprise Services assembly has been created with a layer of interoperability specifically designed and optimized for Serviced Components. Use it.

Security Contexts

You generally want to avoid using impersonation. This is true for Component Services, but is more generally true for the middle tier. Impersonation means that a unique user is used to execute the code for each session of the application. There is a security context involved here, and so pooled objects will not be shared across users. This can largely defeat the whole purpose of pooling in the first place. It can actually make things worse, as a pool per user may create far more instances than are actually needed.

Object Lifetime

As a consumer of Serviced Components, always call Dispose on an instance when you're finished with it. The easiest way to do this is to use the using statement. This guarantees Dispose gets called on the type, regardless of your error-handling semantics.

```
private static void ExPool()
{
    string[] tables =
        { "authors", "employee", "titles", "publishers","sales" };
    Random r = new Random();
    using (Poolable p = new Poolable())
    {
        for (int i = 1; i < 10; i++)
        {
            string s = string.Format(
                "select * from {0}", tables[r.Next(tables.Length - 1)]);
            DataSet ds = p.GetSomeData(s);
        }
    }
    //Dispose called automatically when 'using' goes out of scope
}
```

If you're creating Serviced Components you can control instance lifetimes by using JITA (see previous section on JITA). Instead of explicitly calling DeactivateOnReturn from each method implementation, you also have the option of simply flagging your class with the AutoComplete attribute. This attribute will guarantee instances are disposed of after a method completes. If your type is not JITA-enabled, the AutoComplete attribute will be ignored.

Configuration and Deployment

Only use the attributes from the Enterprise Services assembly that you really need. Each of the features we've looked at is configured with attributes. Each incurs some overhead. Leaving a component unconfigured for a given feature means no overhead will be incurred for leveraging that feature. Be conscious and deliberate about which of these you need.

For production deployments, you should always use Regsvcs.exe to register your Serviced Components in COM+. Lazy registration is a convenient feature, but one that should only be enjoyed during development.

Regsvcs.exe will automatically put your Serviced Components into the Global Assembly Cache (GAC). While this is convenient, any assemblies your Serviced Component is dependant upon will not enjoy the same convenience. This could cause a problem at runtime. For this reason, your deployment should also explicitly register your components and their dependencies in the GAC.

Summary

Component Services exposes a rich set of features that you can consume from .NET by having your types inherit from ServicedComponent and decorating your types with attributes that determine how they'll be configured when they're registered with COM+.

Because this is still a COM-based technology, a layer of interop is used; therefore, you must be sure the benefits of the features you're leveraging outweigh the performance hit you'll incur by using the environment. Many of the features of COM+, when needed, will be worth this performance hit.

Once your components are created and configured within COM+, calling processes will need to get to them. This may happen in process from IIS, it may happen via DCOM from a Windows Forms application, or it may happen via Web Services. In the next chapter, we'll examine some of the different options that are available for invoking Serviced Components from within different application architectures.

CHAPTER 8

■■■

Hosting and Communications

You use a lot of the services, available at different tiers, to define autonomous pieces of your application. How you build them determines the public interface exposed by those services. You may use interface types to describe these services, or you may use a public standard such as Web Service Description Language (WSDL). Once services are written, deciding how to expose those services to other layers, which may or may not span different physical tiers of your application, is another, somewhat separate, set of decisions.

Some of the technologies we've looked at in this book are coupled to a particular mechanism for exposing them. For example, creating Web Services by decorating your methods with the WebMethod attribute couples them to using WSDL for metadata, schema for type definition, and SOAP for invocation.

However, you must keep in mind that someone could still add a reference to the assembly where your service is implemented and invoke it in-process. Sometimes the coupling is not nearly as clear. Deciding to leverage the features of Enterprise Services by creating types that inherit from ServicedComponent does not in any way couple those types to a particular method of exposure. They may be created in-process with your ASPX pages, exposed directly as Web Services, or exposed via a remoting listener installed as an NT Service (to name just a few options).

A lot of the time people will discuss making a choice between using Remoting, Web Services, or Enterprise Services. We think this "choice" is artificial; the decision to use any of these technologies is not mutually exclusive from using the others. You can use all three technologies from different contexts to get to the same method on a single type. Further, this is not an exhaustive set of the choices you have.

In this chapter, we'll examine some of the different ways these different types of services can be exposed to other logical layers and other physical tiers of your application. The services you select become the "plumbing" of your application.

Processes and Marshaling

The sets of choices we present in this chapter revolve around two fundamental decisions you must make about the different tiers of your application.

- What process will be used to host a given tier? Whenever out-of-process communication takes place within a distributed application, a facility to start and "pin" in memory a process that's "listening" for incoming requests has to exist. This process acts as the "host" of your listener process. Frequently this host is expecting messages to arrive via the network; however, the same concepts apply when the communication is between two processes on the same machine. When this machine is part of the architecture of a distributed application, it's commonly called an *application server*.

- How will communication occur between those tiers? This second question directly follows, and is closely related to, the first. What is the host listening *for*? The answer to this question determines what is marshaled between the processes of the distributed application. Sometimes the answer to this question is determined by the choice made for hosting; sometimes it's independent of that choice.

A process host can provide a number of services to your application. It can provide automatic startup for your application. It enables you to establish and control an identity that will be used to execute the process, and, therefore, can provide a security boundary between tiers of an application. It can provide complex pooling behaviors, such as the automatic allocation of thread pools or automatic establishment of database connection pools. And it can directly affect maintainability. COM+, which we discussed in the Chapter 7, is an example of a process host. You can also create your own custom hosting processes. Deployment of components within a given host dictate the lifetime of, the availability of, and how recycling happens for the process hosting the components. Table 8-1 provides you with a look at the options you have available to address the question of where your processes will be hosted.

Table 8-1. *Processes You Can Use as "Listeners" in a Distributed Application*

Process	Meaning In Life
Internet Information Server (IIS)	If you use IIS as a process host, you expose the functionality of your application via the HTTP protocol. IIS provides many features as a host, including many built-in security models, thread pool management, and a flexible model of process isolation via the abstractions of virtual directories and IIS applications. The functionality of IIS can be extended via an Internet Server Application Program Interface (ISAPI) application. An ISAPI application enables third-party code libraries to be configured to extend the functionality of the server. ASP and ASP.NET are both implemented as ISAPI applications. We'll take a look at some others in the sections that follow.
Component Services	As you saw in Chapter 7, you can configure Component Services to run in a dedicated process. This happens when the `ApplicationActivation` attribute is set to `Server`. This process is named `DLLHost.exe`, and provides and manages many features of the COM+ infrastructure, including thread pool management, object pools, and interacting with the Distributed Transaction Coordinator for transaction management. Keep in mind that when a COM+ application has its `ApplicationActivation` attribute set to `Library`, the services are created in the process of the caller. This is commonly the case when using COM+ from IIS. Setting this attribute to `Server` is done when you decide to run these components in their own dedicated process. As you'll see in the section that follows, this is also the model in use when calling Component Services via DCOM.

Process	Meaning In Life
Windows Service	A .NET application can be created to run as a Windows Service. This enables the operating system to automatically start the process in the background when Windows boots; allows for background execution, even when there is no user logged in; and allows you to control the identity the process is running as. Windows Services are commonly created to listen for incoming Remoting requests or monitor a message queue. This host has many fewer features than IIS or Component Services. It is very much a "roll-your-own" environment.
User Interface Processes	These are what we commonly think of when we're talking about processes. They're kicked off by a user double-clicking on an EXE, or console applications and Windows applications. While console applications are generally not suited for hosting the types of components you're considering, they can be very handy during development for easily creating a listener application, and making its invocation and activation very visible. We'll take a look at an example of this for a Remoting listener.

When you've chosen more than a single process to use to host your software, you have to decide how you'll communicate between them. Marshaling information between processes takes on many forms and can traverse many boundary types. One thing is constant, and that is that marshaling is expensive. There will always be a performance hit on your application, whether you're moving pieces of a system into different physical tiers or across processes on the same physical tier.

Marshaling can occur across application domains within a process, across processes on the same machine, across machines within a LAN, or across machines distributed on the Internet. Different types of communication work best for different scenarios. Performance is not always the most important consideration when you're deciding how to communicate between processes. Most often, the decision to introduce another physical tier has already been made (a prerequisite for needing to select a communication technology), and other non-functional requirements, such as the need to use a pool of database connections, are larger considerations than performance (see Chapter 1 for several examples of these decisions).

Communication and marshaling breaks down into two facets: What am I sending out of process (or out of the application domain), and how am I sending it? What you're sending out of process can be a SOAP-formatted document, binary data, or a Message Queuing (MSMQ) message. How you'll send it involves a protocol, be it HTTP, HTTPS, named pipes, or TCP. We summarize the options in Table 8-2.

With Web Services, what you're sending is always a SOAP message. Many people have the misconception that SOAP messages must always be sent via HTTP or HTTPS, but the SOAP specification intentionally leaves the question of protocol open. This means that SOAP messages can be send via TCP, Simple Mail Transfer Protocol (SMTP), MSMQ, or a custom protocol. HTTP and HTTPS are still the most common way to send Web Service requests.

Remoting breaks the questions of how and what into two extensible layers of abstraction: channels and messages. The Remoting infrastructure is specifically designed to enable someone to plug into his own channel (protocol) and provide his own message format (what's getting passed over the protocol). Remoting ships with implementations of both channels and formatters; HTTP, IPC, and TCP for channels, and SOAP and binary for message formats.

Table 8-2. *Communications Options with Different Applications Servers*

Application Server	Communications Options		
	Web Services	**Remoting**	**DCOM and Interop**
Component Services	Can be exposed directly via configuration from COM+; otherwise, expose via IIS.	Component Services should be exposed to clients using Remoting via IIS when using HTTP. To use TCP, a custom listener must be created and installed as an NT Service.	A DCOM proxy can be generated, and a .NET client can use it via an interop assembly. Custom interop is used internally by COM+ to communicate between managed and unmanaged stacks.
IIS	Deploy an ASMX file pointing at the .NET class type containing any WebMethod attributes on class method (or on methods of interfaces implemented in the class).	Deploy a configuration file specifying URL to use to reach exposed type into the root of the web application. Must use HTTP as a channel, but any formatter can be chosen. .NET includes SOAP and binary formatters.	N/A
Legacy COM Servers	You can use the COM SOAP stack to expose these as Web Services. You could also use ASMX and an interop assembly to expose them via IIS.	N/A	Use an interop assembly to expose functionality, or use vendor provided interop assemblies, such as the Office interop assemblies from Microsoft.

You can write a custom listener process that accepts requests from a TCP channel or via HTTP. You can also program it to expect binary or SOAP messages over your chosen channel. These choices are independent. It's only when you're hosting a remoted component within ASP.NET that you're limited in these choices, as you are bound to the HTTP channel. However, this channel can still be used to send binary or SOAP messages. We'll take a look at all of these scenarios in the sections that follow.

Remote objects can also be used to pass messages across application domains within a managed process. This is what Remoting is most highly optimized to accomplish, and is what Microsoft says is the best reason to adopt Remoting. See Chapter 6 and Chapter 9 for a discussion of some of the issues relating to Remoting versus Web Services (which is really a debate of RPC versus Service Oriented Architecture, or SOA).

With the introduction of the Windows Communication Foundation (WCF), Microsoft is moving this concept of an extensible layer of transport and messaging into all out-of-process calls that are done in the operating system (see Chapter 9 for a preview of WCF). This is why WCF is called the "unified out-of-process call stack." Today with WCF, Web Services requests can get passed via MSMQ as easily as they are via HTTP. There are really a lot of valid combinations.

Internet Information Server

Internet Information Server (IIS) is *the* application server for the Windows platform. This application server has been evolving for the past 10 years, and will continue to evolve into the foreseeable future. IIS has gone from serving static markup to a full-featured application hosting environment. ISAPI applications have been available as a point of extensibility for years. A number of the technologies you'll be looking at in this chapter are implemented as ISAPI applications: ASP.NET, SQLXML, and SOAP exposure of Enterprise Services. Others, such as the COM SOAP stack, are beyond the scope for this book.

Note As IIS continues to evolve, you can expect to see ASP.NET leveraged for more and more functionality, as this is the ISAPI extension of choice for extending the behavior of IIS using the .NET Framework. We provide full coverage of ASP.NET as an application pipeline in Chapter 2.

ASP.NET Framework

With the ASP.NET Framework, Microsoft has created an ISAPI application that enables the functionality of IIS to be extended using the .NET Framework. We examined a number of ways this is done within the Framework Class Library in Chapter 2. In this section, we'll focus on some of these implementations, and how they enable you to leverage IIS as a network endpoint for cross boundary and cross machine communication.

Web Services

In addition to serving requests for Web Forms, the ASP.NET Framework also acts as the .NET SOAP Stack. (We examined some details of the generalized concept of a SOAP Stack in Chapter 6.) A SOAP Stack is a process that listens to a well-defined network endpoint for incoming SOAP messages posted to the server. It maps these requests to a service implementation, and translates the results of the service into a SOAP response.

In the .NET Framework, Web Services are so well integrated into IIS and ASP.NET that most people don't even realize they're using a SOAP Stack at all if they learn Web Services using the .NET Framework. For any other platform, you'd have to go out and pick a SOAP Stack, install it, and take specific steps to map types to service operations you want to expose. This is true for Java platforms, and it is even true for exposing COM types as Web Services.

Visual Studio .NET and ASP.NET make this so easy that it can be taken for granted by most developers. By mapping asmx files to types, by automatically handling requests for asmx documents in ASP.NET, by auto-generating WSDL documents, and by auto-generating client-side proxies, the Web Service handler built into ASP.NET hides all of the standards-based details of the underlying protocols and wire format in use.

This can be a good thing or a bad thing. A service-oriented purist would shudder at the thought of it, and would advocate a "WSDL first" approach to service development. The other extreme would be to acknowledge the simple fact that if you need a method on a type exposed across your network, you can slap the WebMethod attribute on it, put an asmx document in front of it, and you're done (as long as chunky statelessness is a given for the method design).

Exposing your .NET types as Web Services vastly increases the reach of your managed code. If you're in an environment where there are several platforms and languages in use, Web Services dramatically decreases the amount of time and churn spent integrating packages and applications. By hosting your Web Services within IIS, you can also give them exactly the reach you want them to have. You may have services within a department, services exposed to the entire enterprise, and services exposed over the Internet to partners and vendors. You can even publish public services for general consumption. These can be subscription based or free (see www.xmethods.net). The broader the reach of your Web Services, the greater the chances you'll want to adopt some of the WS-* specifications for functionality such as authentication, message routing, and transactions. You can do this with the Web Service Enhancements add-on available for free and supported by Microsoft (see Chapter 6 or http://msdn.microsoft.com/webservices/webservices/building/wse/default.aspx).

Remoting

ASP.NET also acts as a host for remoted components. The Remoting handler is automatically mapped to requests of files with extensions of .soap or .rem via a configuration document that gets added to the root of your web application, requests of specific network endpoints are mapped to types living in assemblies in the application's bin directory.

Discussions about Remoting internals are beyond the scope of this book (see Tom Barnaby's book, *Distributed .NET Programming in C#* (Apress, 2002) for excellent coverage). However, in this chapter, we'll still take a look at a couple of ways .NET types can be exposed via Remoting. Here's a simple type that by inheriting from MarshalByRefObject is pinned in the process it's created within; and so it can be called via Remoting.

```
class BookService : MarshalByRefObject
{
    public DataTable getBookList()
    {
        SqlConnection cn = new SqlConnection(connStr);
        SqlCommand cm = new SqlCommand(
            "select BookID, Title From Book Order by Title", cn);
        DataTable dt = new DataTable();
        try
        {
            cn.Open();
            dt.Load(cm.ExecuteReader());
            return dt;
        }
        catch { }
        finally
        {
            if (cn.State == ConnectionState.Open) cn.Close();
        }
    }
}
```

This component then can be exposed via ASP.NET using the following entry in the web.config of an IIS application:

```
<system.runtime.remoting>
    <application>
        <service>
            <wellknown mode="Singleton"
                        type="BookLib.BookService, BookLib"
                        objectUri="BookService.soap" />
        </service>

        <channels>
            <channel port="13101" ref="http" />
        </channels>

    </application>
</system.runtime.remoting>
```

The client requires a configuration file to use the remoted type. Here's a configuration file you can use as the app.config for a simple console application:

```
<system.runtime.remoting>
    <application>

        <client displayName="BookService">
            <wellknown type="BookLib.BookService, BookLib"
                url="http://localhost:13101/BookHost/BookService.soap" />
        </client>

        <channels>
            <channel ref="http" />
        </channels>

    </application>
</system.runtime.remoting>
```

And here's the code for a console application consuming this remoted type:

```
static void Main(string[] args)
{
    // Load the remoting config file
    RemotingConfiguration.Configure("BookClient.exe.config");

    // Now connect to the remote object by simply using its constructor!
    BookLib.BookService b = new BookLib.BookService();

    DataTable dt = b.getBookList();
    foreach (DataRow dr in dt.Rows)
        Console.WriteLine(dr["Title"]);
}
```

The limitation of exposing remoted types via ASP.NET is that you must use HTTP as the transport protocol. If you want to use TCP, you have to write your own listener instead of relying on ASP.NET. See the section "Custom Listeners" later in this chapter for an example of doing this with a Windows Service.

Serviced Components

When you're using Serviced Components, you'll want to consider how they'll be exposed. You can do this via *either* Web Services or Remoting. These choices are independent from one another; that is, there is nothing in a decision to use Serviced Components that ties you to using either Web Services or Remoting. These are your choices when exposing your Serviced Components via ASP.NET. However, they are not your only choices. As you'll see in the sections that follow, you still have the option of using traditional DCOM and COM interop to get to Serviced Components; and with Windows XP and Windows 2003, they can be exposed directly as Web Services.

The salient point in hosting Serviced Components always comes back to the `ApplicationActivation` attribute. This is the assembly-level attribute we discussed in Chapter 7.

```
//Use this for DllHost.exe
[assembly: ApplicationActivation(ActivationOption.Server)]
//or this for hosting in the process of the creator
[assembly: ApplicationActivation(ActivationOption.Library)]
```

This is the attribute that determines how your Serviced Components will be hosted. Keep in mind that a server application can call components in a library application, and those types will then be created in the DllHost process dedicated to the server application. `DllHost.exe` actually hosts an instance of the Common Language Runtime (CLR), within which it can execute Serviced Components.

When calling a Library application from IIS, types are created in process with the calling worker process (`w3wp.exe` for IIS6, `aspnet_wp.exe` for IIS5.x). If you have several IIS applications calling library applications in COM+, they will each be created in the process of the caller, resulting in thread pools, connection pools, and object pools for each of your IIS applications.

Windows Communication Foundation

As you'll see in Chapter 9, ASP.NET will also be the hosting environment of choice for services created using Microsoft's new unified out-of-process class stack named Windows Communication Foundation (WCF). While this won't be your only choice for hosting WCF services, it will be the "path of least resistance choice" as WCF is being designed from the ground up to be a first-class (and well-behaved) citizen within ASP.NET.

Component Service SOAP

Windows XP and Windows Server 2003 add the option of exposing Component Services directly via SOAP. This SOAP Stack is implemented as another IIS application that acts as a dedicated listener for SOAP requests and maps them to your COM+ application. This technology is not limited to .NET. It can be used to expose your Enterprise Services (.NET types that inherit from ServicedComponent; see Chapter 7), but also can be used to expose Component Services written in a COM language. If your COM+ application is written with a COM language, interop assemblies are automatically generated that act as a front end for the SOAP stack.

Setting this up is very easy. The Activation tab of the property page of a COM+ application is displayed in Figure 8-1.

Figure 8-1. *The Activation tab of the property page of a COM+ application*

Notice we've checked the Uses SOAP check box and provided a name for a virtual directory. When you click OK, Component Services does the rest of the work. A directory is created in the System32\COM\SOAPVRoots subdirectory within the Windows installation directory. This directory is automatically configured as an IIS application. The directory has a few files, but the important one is an automatically generated copy of a web.config, where the mapping of incoming SOAP requests to the type contained in Component Services is set up.

For this to work, .NET types must be installed in the Global Assembly Cache (GAC). If a COM type is exposed via this method, interop assemblies will be generated and added to the bin subdirectory of this virtual directory.

WSDL can be retrieved from this directory using fully qualified type names. For example, the ESDemoSOAP application you've just exposed contains a number of types in the ESDemo namespace. On of them is a class named Poolable. These types are exposed via a handler that responds to requests for documents with a .soap extension. The general form is:

```
http://servername/ApplicationName/Namespace.TypeName.soap
```

Tacking on a query string of ?wsdl causes the handler to generated the WSDL document. The URL for the WSDL document of the type named JITA in the ESDemo namespace would be formed as:

```
http://localhost/ESDemoSOAP/ESDemo.JITA.soap?wsdl
```

So a request for this URL causes the WSDL describing the type to be generated and returned, as displayed in Figure 8-2.

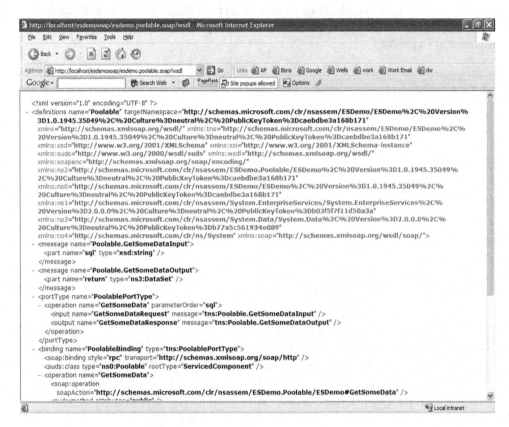

Figure 8-2. *The auto-generated WSDL describing a Serviced Component*

Any of the types in the application can now be exposed via a Web Service proxy. Now use the Add Web Reference feature of Visual Studio .NET to generate a proxy in your console application, as shown in Figure 8-3.

And now you can use this type just like any other Web Service. In the following code you use a proxy to the Just-in-Time Activation (JITA) service (from the TestApp project in the Code08 solution):

```
static void Main(string[] args)
{
    Proxies.JITA j = new Proxies.JITA ();

    for (int i = 0; i < 10; i++)
    {
        DateTime t = j.GetCreateStamp();
        Console.WriteLine(t);
    }
}
```

Furthermore, any platform supporting Web Services can now use it, too.

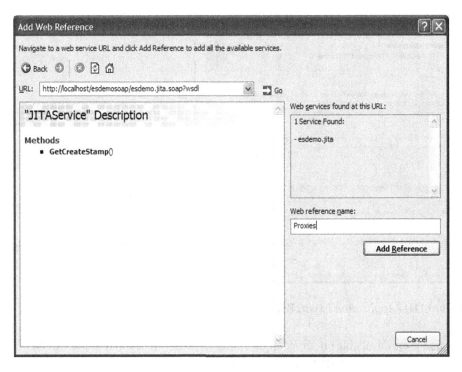

Figure 8-3. *Adding a Web Reference to the Serviced Component*

Stored Procedure SOAP

The SQLXML add-on for SQL Server exposes very similar functionality for stored procedures. This mechanism uses its own ISAPI application and is not dependent upon the .NET Framework. The tool will interrogate the schema of a Transact-SQL (T-SQL) Stored Procedure and automatically generate the WSDL to expose the procedure directly via SOAP. See the SDK docs on SQLXML for a walk-through of this functionality.

DLLHost and DCOM

The debate of performance versus maintainability always exists on a continuum. In this environment, way off to the side of this continuum that favors performance at the expense of maintainability is DCOM. Oddly enough, exporting DCOM proxies and invoking them via an interop assembly from the client is still the best-performing option for remote procedure calls.

A DCOM package can be exported from COM+ using the Export option on the context menu of a COM+ application, as shown in Figure 8-4.

Notice we've selected the Application proxy radio button. This causes the wizard to create an installable package of COM+ *proxies*, which are wrapper types that expose the interface of the configured components on the client, but marshal the actual method call across the network to the Component Services server using the DCOM RPC mechanism.

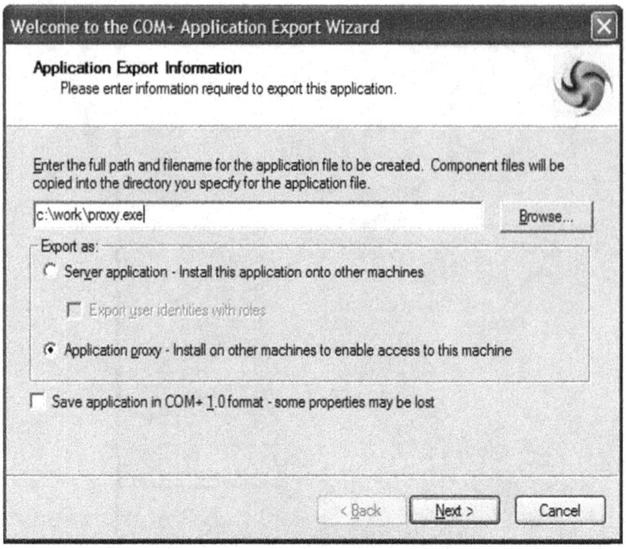

Figure 8-4. *The COM+ Application Export Wizard*

This option is only available on server applications, because when you're using DCOM you're relying on DLLHost.exe to act as your host. Remember that a library application is created in the process of the caller. Since you're not using ASP.NET as the host, there is no server-side process within which to create the library application types. DLLHost.exe provides the dedicated process, listening for requests coming in from the network.

Managed clients need to access these proxy types via a COM interop assembly, as they are exported as COM libraries. It's hard to believe this performs twice as fast as the fastest Remoting configuration, considering you're introducing two layers of interoperability between managed and unmanaged code: one on the client to go from managed code to the COM proxy, and another on the server to move from the COM-based Component Services call stack to the managed call stack of our Serviced Components.

This performance comes at a high price for maintainability. DCOM is notoriously difficult to configure correctly, especially if there are firewalls or complex security requirements in place. We won't be digging into the details here. This technology has been around for a decade, so there are volumes of information and references available for its usage. Hosting in ASP.NET should be considered as a first option if it will meet the performance demands of your environment. The DCOM option should really only be on the table for rich client applications; with a web application, it almost always makes more sense to host COM+ in-process on the web server. Possible exceptions to this would show up in environments with a lot of web servers running a lot of different applications. In these cases, it may be possible, for example, that you want the data access layer isolated on a single server to pool connections to the database. You should still consider ASMX for exposing this data access layer via SOAP before using DCOM. Remoting may even be a better option. It's not as easy to configure as ASMX, but it's still significantly simpler than DCOM. When performance is the primary concern, however, DCOM is still about twice as fast as Remoting for crossing machine boundaries.

Message Queuing

Message Queuing (MSMQ) is Microsoft's messaging solution. Access to queues is exposed in the Framework via types in the System.Messaging namespace. This is one of the two main ways in .NET to leverage MSMQ. The other is to use Enterprise Services, which provides a layer of abstraction on top of queues and their messages by automatically transforming method calls into messages when they're configured as Queued Components (QC) (see Chapter 7 for details on Queued Components).

There are many tangible benefits to a message queuing infrastructure. Client functionality is not tied to server availability. Since message queuing is done asynchronously from the perspective of the client, if the server is unavailable or under a heavy load, the client is not required to wait for the server to become available before continuing processing. This is very handy for dealing with times of high load on the server. Requests for services are serialized in the message queue, and clients continue to work without waiting for their requests to be processed. You also get guaranteed delivery of your service request. Since the message is persisted to disk when it arrives at the server, even if the server is unavailable, the message will be processed when it comes back online.

The downside is that there can be no response returned from the service request. This is intrinsic in the design of any asynchronous messaging infrastructure, and it seriously limits the number of operations that are viable for service requests. In some situations the client/server paradigm can be flipped around, and the client can have its own queues exposed to receive messages back from the server (see Figure 8-5). We'll show you an example of this later in the chapter.

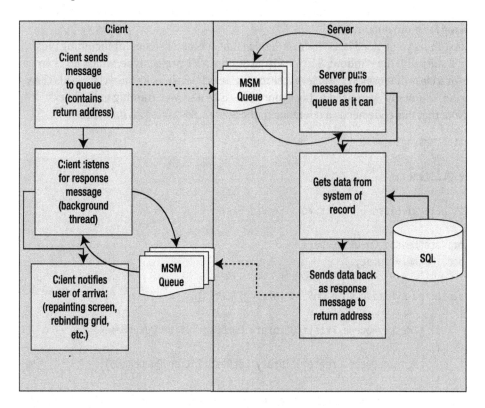

Figure 8-5. *Using the client as the server for message-based callbacks*

When you're comparing MSMQ to the ASMX style of message processing, the big difference is the wire format and protocol. While you *can* pack SOAP into the body of MSMQ messages, you still need the MSMQ stack on both the client and the server. This necessitates Windows-to-Windows communication (or the use of some translation layer). ASMX, on the other hand, does not know and does not care what platform is on the other end of the communication because it is based on open, industry-standard specifications (see Chapter 6). Conversely, you have much more control over what goes into the message with MSMQ, liberating you from the constraints of SOAP and XML Schema.

When you're not using Queued Components, you must write code to create messages and place them in queues. You must also create a listener process, one that is listening for messages arriving in the queue, pulls them out, and processes them. This alone is a strong argument in favor of using Component Services. Many features of COM+ can be leveraged automatically via adherence to some design principles and some details of configuration (thread pools and object pools, for instance). See Chapter 7 for a detailed look at Queued Components.

Let's take a look at a custom message pump for MSMQ. Here's the premise: The enterprise you work for has decided it needs a complete inventory of all of the Word documents that exist on all of the workstations. You're going to push an application to the users' machines that will scan their hard drive for Word docs, and send them to the server, which will insert them into the database. Because this application will run first thing in the morning when users log in, you know there will be a huge spike in traffic doing inserts into this database table. In order to avoid coupling the efficiency of the document search to the availability of the database, you'll have the client post messages into a queue, and then they can be pulled out and processed as the server can get to them, without forcing the update to succeed before the client can continue looking for more documents.

The first thing you'll need is a Windows Service that acts as a listener for incoming messages. You'll start with the Windows Service Visual Studio .NET project type, which gives you a template for a class that uses `System.ServiceProcess.ServiceBase` as its base class. This class gives you the "plumbing" you need to host your process as a service running in the background. Note that this code needs a reference to the `System.Messaging.dll` assembly.

```
using System.Messaging;

namespace QListener
{
    public partial class ListenerSvc : ServiceBase
    {
        private MessageQueue queue;
        bool bDone = false;

        protected override void OnStart(string[] args)
        {
            if (!MessageQueue.Exists(QLibrary.DocDescription.QueueName))
            {
                MessageQueue.Create(QLibrary.DocDescription.QueueName);
            }
            queue = new MessageQueue(QLibrary.DocDescription.QueueName);
```

```
        Thread t = new Thread(MonitorQueue);
        t.Start();
    }

    protected override void OnStop()
    {
        bDone = true;
    }
//Class Definition Continues…
```

The overridden onStart method is called when the Service is started, either at system startup or when an administrator starts it manually from the Services applet. This code ensures that the queue you'll be using exists, and then starts a listener thread using the address of the MonitorQueue method. You'll look at the code for monitor queue shortly. The QLibrary.DocDescription type contains some types that you'll use from both the client and the server, so it lives in its own assembly. The definition of the string QueueName (used above) looks like this:

```
public const string PrivateQ = @"\private$\";
public const string LocalQName = "queuetest";
public static readonly string QueueName =
                    string.Format("{0}{1}{2}",
                    System.Net.Dns.GetHostName(),
                    PrivateQ,
                    LocalQName);
```

This builds up the full name of the queue you'll be monitoring. The overridden OnStart method instructs your code to create a private queue named queuetest that you'll monitor from the service. MonitorQueue is the process that waits for messages to come into the queue, and then processes them. There are a couple of different ways you can monitor a queue. You can set up a *trigger*, which relies on another Windows Service to monitor the queue and then pass the messages to a component of your choosing. Using this results in code that looks more like "event trapping" code. The downside of this approach is that you must set up the trigger on the server hosting the queue, resulting in more complex deployment and configuration. The other method is to write your listener as a *polling* application. The algorithms used to do this can become quite complex. You can create your own thread pools, and you're also in control of the polling frequency used on each thread. Further, you may have many queues involved. What you need will depend upon the type of processing the listener will be doing and the expected load patterns of messages coming into the queue. The example here is quite simple: It uses a single thread that's listening for incoming messages and then processes them (from Program.cs in the ConsoleHost project of the Code08 solution).

```
private void MonitorQueue()
{
    Message msg;
    while (!bDone)
    {
        try
        {
```

```
                msg = queue.Receive(new TimeSpan(0, 0, 1));
                msg.Formatter = new BinaryMessageFormatter();
                QLibrary.DocDescription d = (QLibrary.DocDescr)msg.Body;
                QLibrary.DocDescription.SendToDatabase(d);
            }
            catch { Thread.Sleep(1000); }
        }
    }
}
```

This code sets up a single loop that will iterate as long as the bDone Boolean variable remains true. This value is set to false in the overridden OnStop method (shown in the preceding code), and so when the system shuts down or an administrator stops the service, this loop will terminate and the process hosting the thread will be torn down.

Within the loop, we use the MessageQueue instance to monitor the thread for incoming messages. The call to the Receive method does this, and we're using a TimeSpan to specify that the operation should time out if no message arrives within one second. If the timeout occurs, the Receive method throws an exception, at which point we're putting the thread to sleep for one second before monitoring the queue again. This keeps the listener quiet in times when no messages arrive in the queue.

When a message does arrive, execution continues in the body of our try block. Anything can be packed away into a message body. For our application, we're packing away an instance of the DocDescription object. We obtain a reference to this object by casting the Body of the message into the DocDescription type. We'll show you the client code that sends an instance of this type into the message body in a bit. First take a look at the definition of the instance portions of the DocDescription type itself. (We'll cover the static methods later. This code is from the QLibrary project in the Code08 solution.)

```
[Serializable()]
public class DocDescription
{
    //Static methods omitted for brevity

    public DocDescription() { }

    public DocDescription(string docIP, string docPath, string docName)
    {
        this.DocIP = docIP;
        this.DocPath = docPath;
        this.DocName = docName;
    }

    private string docName;
    public string DocName
    {
        get { return docName; }
        set { docName = value; }
    }
    private string docIP;
```

```
    public string DocIP
    {
        get { return docIP; }
        set { docIP = value; }
    }
    private string docPath;
    public string DocPath
    {
        get { return docPath; }
        set { docPath = value; }
    }
}
```

This is a simple type, which contains three properties: an IP, a path, and a name. You use this object to pass state information over the wire in the body of the message. The listener application sends the object on to the database by calling a static method on DocDescription that uses ADO.NET to call a stored procedure (not shown here, as this could be any data access layer call).

On the client, you need to write code that will place messages into the queue. This code could run on an end user's machine for a rich client Windows Forms application, or could be executed from ASP.NET for a Web-based application (resulting from a Web Service call from the client, for example). This code is also in DocDescription.cs of the QLibrary project.

```
public static void SendToQueue(DocDescr d)
{
    MessageQueue q = new MessageQueue(QueueName);
    Message msg = new Message(d, new BinaryMessageFormatter());
    q.Send(msg);
}
```

This code accepts an instance of the DocDescription type and serializes it into the message body using the binary message formatter. Note that this is the same formatter used in the listener to pull the instance out of the message body (as seen in the code for MonitorQueue).

The client code then simply surfs the hard drive of your user, creating an instance of DocDescription and posting it to the queue whenever a Word document is found. (This code is Form1.cs of the QClient project in the Code08 solution.)

```
bool bDone = false;
int count;
string ip = System.Net.Dns.GetHostAddresses
            (System.Net.Dns.GetHostName())[0].ToString();

private void btnScan_Click(object sender, EventArgs e)
{
    count = 0;
    bDone = false;
    btnScan.Enabled = false;
    btnCancel.Enabled = true;
    Thread t = new Thread(FindDocs);
```

```
        t.Start();
}

private void FindDocs()
{
    FindDocs(new DirectoryInfo(@"c:\"));
    btnCancel.Enabled = false;
    btnScan.Enabled = true;
}

private void FindDocs(DirectoryInfo dir)
{
    QLibrary.DocDescription doc;
    string name;
    string path;
    if (bDone) return;
    try
    {
        foreach (FileInfo fi in dir.GetFiles("*.doc"))
        {
            name = fi.Name;
            path = fi.FullName.Substring(0, fi.FullName.LastIndexOf(@"\"));
            doc = new QLibrary.DocDescription(ip, path, name);
            QLibrary.DocDescription.SendToQueue(doc);
            label1.Text = string.Format("{0} documents found", ++count);

            if (bDone) break;
        }

        foreach (DirectoryInfo d in dir.GetDirectories())
        {
            FindDocs(d);
            if (bDone) break;
        }
    }
    catch {  }
}
private void btnCancel_Click(object sender, EventArgs e)
{
    bDone = true;
    btnCancel.Enabled = false;
    btnScan.Enabled = true;
}
```

Since this code is placing messages into queues, there is no blocking that occurs to wait for the row to actually get inserted into the databases. This leaves the client free to search the drives of the users, regardless of how many concurrent instances are posting messages to the queue.

Realize also that you would want to have the client application use a Web Service proxy and send the document information to ASP.NET, where it could be serialized into the queue. This enables you to have several instances running on many machines across the network, and use a single centralized queue to aggregate the requests. This example is coded to run on a single user's machine, which simplifies the composition of the demo, and still leaves the pertinent code intact.

Custom Listeners

The other time you'll need to create your own custom listener is when you want to use a TCP channel to send binary encoded requests in Remoting. This can be as simple as a console application with an application configuration file.

```
<system.runtime.remoting>
    <application>
        <service>
            <wellknown mode="Singleton"
                        type="BookLib.BookService, BookLib"
                        objectUri="BookService.soap" />
        </service>

        <channels>
            <channel port="8080" ref="tcp" />
        </channels>

    </application>
</system.runtime.remoting>
```

You can see in this configuration that the Remoting infrastructure is being directed to listen to port 8080 for incoming TCP requests. The code for the listener application simply calls into the Remoting infrastructure to start listening for requests on that port.

```
class Program
{
    static void Main(string[] args)
    {
        // Load the remoting configuration file
        RemotingConfiguration.Configure("RListener.exe.config");

        // Keep server alive until enter is pressed
        Console.WriteLine("Press Enter to end");
        Console.ReadLine();
    }
}
```

Notice that this application blocks and therefore keeps the process alive by making a call to Console.Writeline. A background thread, spawned by the Remoting infrastructure when you call Configure, will listen to the configured port for incoming requests for remoted components as long as this process stays running.

This is fine for development and testing, but it is obviously no solution for a production environment. You would generally want to install a custom listener as an NT Service. This can be done by leveraging the Windows Service project type in Visual Studio .NET, and then using a command line tool to install the service on the server (see Figure 8-6).

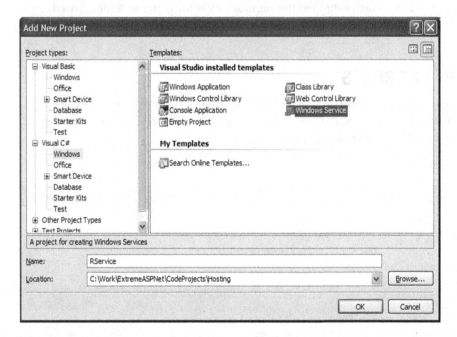

Figure 8-6. *The Windows Service project type dialog box*

You'll simply move your configuration code from the console application into the implementation template provided by the Windows Service project type:

```
public partial class Service1 : ServiceBase
{
    private bool bDone = false;
    public Service1()
    {
        InitializeComponent();
    }

    protected override void OnStart(string[] args)
    {
        Thread t = new Thread(PulseService);
        t.Start();
    }

    private void PulseService()
    {
        RemotingConfiguration.Configure("RService.exe.config");
        while (!bDone)
        {
```

```
        Thread.Sleep(1000);
    }
}

protected override void OnStop()
{
    bDone = true;
}
}
```

After compiling this assembly, you'll need to install it on the server using a command-line tool that ships with the Framework: InstallUtil.exe, which executes the Install method implemented on the ServiceBase class to configure your type as a Windows Service (see Figure 8-7).

Figure 8-7. *The output of a call to InstallUtil.exe. The name of the service executable and the* -i *parameter (for install) are passed to it as command line arguments.*

We also need to copy the configuration file, RServer.exe.config, to the System32 subdirectory of the Windows installation directory so it can be found when the operating system starts the service. Now the service is available in the services applet of the Administrative Tools menu (see Figure 8-8).

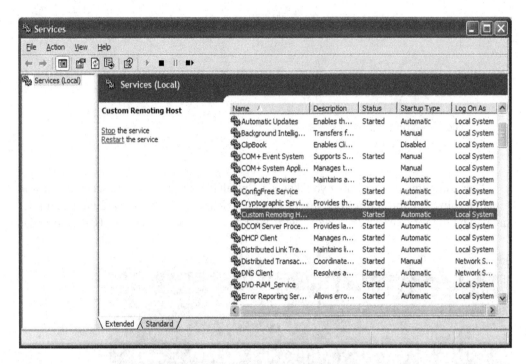

Figure 8-8. *Your service in the Services Applet. Choosing Start causes your onStart override to execute.*

Things are not that different in the client application from our previous example, where the components were hosted in ASP.NET. Because the channel and format of the message is completely abstracted away from the consumer of the remoted component, the only thing that needs to change is the configuration file:

```
<system.runtime.remoting>
    <application>

        <client displayName="Server">
            <wellknown type="BookLib.BookService, BookLib"
                       url="tcp://newton:8080/BookService.soap" />
        </client>

        <channels>
            <channel ref="tcp" />
        </channels>

    </application>
</system.runtime.remoting>
```

Newton is a machine name. You will need to replace this with the name of the server hosting the component. You now can easily call the BookLibrary methods from a Windows Forms application:

```
public partial class Form1 : Form
{
    public Form1()
    {
        RemotingConfiguration.Configure("RClient.exe.config");
        InitializeComponent();
    }

    private void button1_Click(object sender, EventArgs e)
    {
        BookLib.BookService b = new BookLib.BookService();
        dataGridView1.DataSource = b.getBookList();
    }
}
```

Your calls to the BookService type are now automatically marshaled to the Remoting server on TCP port 8080 (see Figure 8-9).

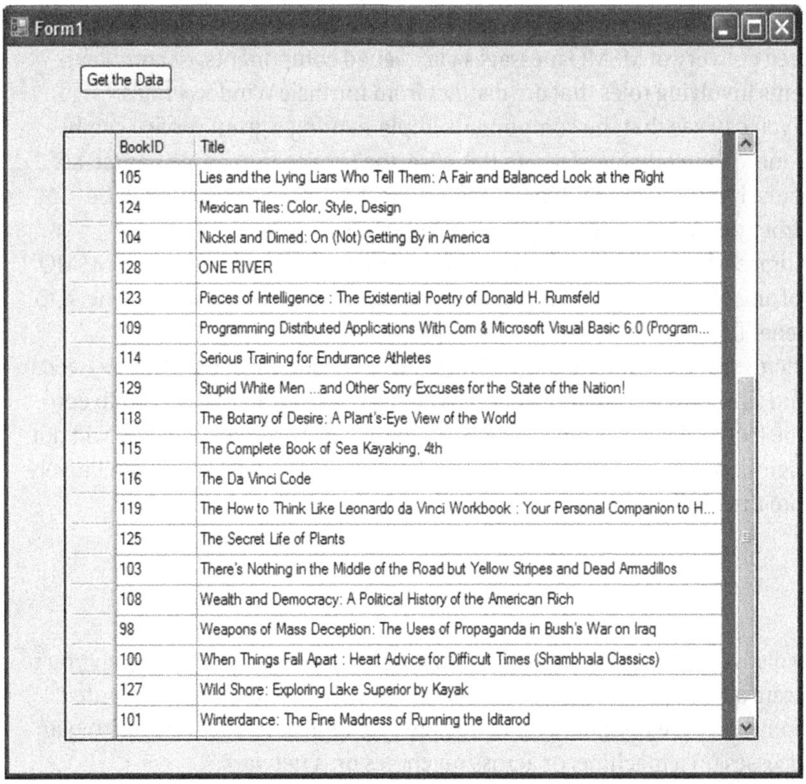

Figure 8-9. *Data retrieved from the remoted component and bound to a* GridView

Permutations

With all these choices, it helps to know the direction is Microsoft is going. Their advice? Use ASMX and WSE 3.0 (if you need the additional features). This will provide the easiest migration path into WCF, and is the area where you're guaranteed the best future support from Microsoft. Looking out even further, Windows Vista will have WCF baked right into it, and will be the messaging stack the OS is heavily dependent upon. Planning for interoperating with and migrating into WCF is discussed extensively in Chapter 9.

You only need to adopt WSE if you need the feature set. This is the package that contains the implementations of some of the WS-* specifications (see Chapter 6).

OOP is not the next "legacy" technology. Traditional object-oriented techniques should still be used within service boundaries. Objects are no longer what get passed around on the wire, but they're still perfectly valid for use within a process. To adopt Service Oriented Architecture (SOA) is to acknowledge that RPC is conceptually flawed, and messages should be passed across boundaries instead of passing instances of types.

Enterprise Services is a separate and independent package of functionality. The choice to use Enterprise Services does not hinge on your choice of hosting environment or communication mechanism. This decision should be based entirely on your application's need for any element of the feature set. This can include dynamic composition of transactions, the asynchronous guaranteed delivery of MSMQ messages via queued components, or complex security requirements involving roles that are distinct from intrinsic Windows roles.

In Figure 8-10 you can see that the components implementing a given service can be implemented with more than one interface. In this case, the services are implemented as Serviced Components, but this would not be necessary. Each of these decisions can be made in isolation from decisions about adopting the other mechanisms.

There may be times when you need the asynchrony and guaranteed delivery of MSMQ but have no need of any of the other Enterprise Services features. In this case, you'll need to write a custom listener for a queue, as outlined above.

And what is Microsoft's recommendation for when to use Remoting? Use it if you need to communicate within a process across application domains. This is where they plan to continue support for the technology. This is also the only technology we've covered that will not have a seamless migration path into WCF. ASMX, MSMQ, and COM+ will all have a relatively painless journey into the WCF call stack.

Summary

When you're doing distributed application development, you must always decide how you're going to communicate across boundaries. When you're using .NET to do your distributed application development, these boundaries can be between application domains within a process, across processes on a machine, or across machines on a network.

In order to decide how to communicate across these boundaries, you must decide two things: what will be used as a listener, and what the listener will be listening for? There are many answers to these questions when using the .NET Framework. The answer to one question doesn't necessarily dictate the answer to the second question, so you have many valid combinations of choices.

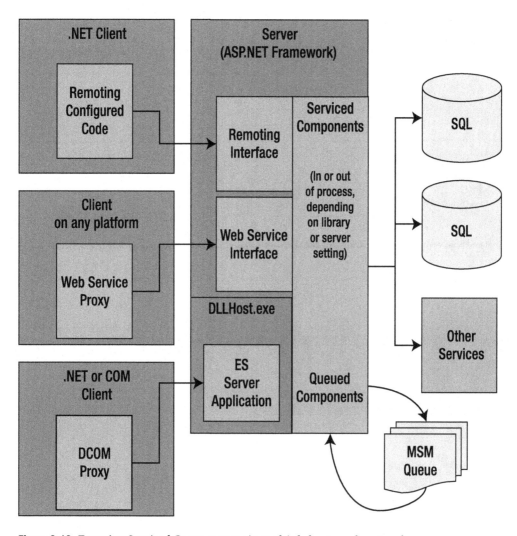

Figure 8-10. *Exposing Serviced Components via multiple hosts and protocols*

ASP.NET should be your first choice as a listener because it can deal with requests for Web Services, can handle requests for remoted objects, can expose Enterprise Services, and can be used in concert with MSMQ.

Microsoft is attempting to simplify this entire landscape with the WCF. In the next chapter, we examine the WCF and see how it will reign in some of this complexity.

CHAPTER 9

■■■

Windows Communication Foundation

Not too long ago, many web applications were deployed as a single unit on a single machine. That is, the presentation, business, and data access logic all executed on the same machine and within the same process. Typically, only the database server would be on a different physical machine. As business needs became more and more complex, however, businesses required more out of their web applications—more performance, more scalability, more flexibility, and more integration with other systems.

This, in turn, has lead to the present era, where a given web application may need to communicate with several applications running on a variety of different machines and platforms. In Chapter 5, we discussed the distributed technologies that .NET currently provides to help you meet these challenges. In this chapter, however, we look at a future distributed technology—Windows Communication Foundation (WCF)—that will eventually supersede the technologies of today.

Introducing Windows Communication Foundation

To begin, we describe the nature of the new technology and why it is different from the current set of technologies. Then we dive into some of the issues surrounding the current distributed technologies to establish why something this unique was required in the first place.

What Is Windows Communication Foundation?

Windows Communication Foundation (WCF) is Microsoft's next-generation distributed systems technology. It provides a single API and a single infrastructure on which you can build, deploy, and operate distributed applications WCF takes the best features from the existing .NET distributed technologies and unifies them under a single programming model. As if this weren't ambitious enough, it also promotes service orientation to a first-class citizen, while also supporting the best practice usage of conventional Distributed Object and Remote Procedure Call (RPC) technologies.

WCF ships within WinFX—a redistributable that contains the .NET Framework 2.0, Windows Communication Foundation, and Windows Presentation Foundation (Microsoft's next-generation UI technology). The WinFX release is planned for the second half of 2006 alongside Windows Vista. WinFX for Windows XP (SP2+) and Windows Server 2003 (SP1+) will also ship at the same time.

Understanding the WCF Motivations

As with any new technology, having a good understanding of WCF begins with having an appreciation for its underlying motivations. After all, .NET currently has several effective technologies that enable you to build distributed applications: .NET Remoting, MSMQ, Enterprise Services, and, of course, Web Services. What is the point of having yet another distributed technology? In this section, we tackle this all-important question.

Problem: Distributed Technology Soup

In the previous paragraph, we mentioned the many distributed technologies that are already available to .NET developers. To save syllables and trees, we'll collectively refer to these four technologies—.NET Remoting, MSMQ, Enterprise Services, and Web Services—as the "Big Four."[1] Although it's usually nice to have many options, in this case, the number of options combined with large amounts of overlapping functionality make it extremely difficult to choose the right technology for the job. Of course, each of the Big Four exhibits distinct advantages and disadvantages relative to the others. But deciding the right technology based on them may require application and infrastructure knowledge that you may not yet have. For example, you may choose Web Services to leverage its loose coupling advantage, only to find out much later that the actual application load requires the performance advantage of Enterprise Services. Given that the programming models for each of the Big Four differ greatly, switching to another technology midstream in the development cycle proves difficult and costly.

To better understand the nature of the problem, take a look at Table 9-1. This table details each technology's characteristics, advantages, and disadvantages. Looking at this, it's no wonder that news groups and forums are flush with which, when, where, and why questions regarding the Big Four.

WCF's Solution to Distributed Technology Soup

WCF solves the distributed technology soup problem by incorporating the best of each Big Four technology into one programming model. For developers, this eases the burden of having to remember four extremely different models. It also simplifies the task of switching midstream to another distributed technique.

In terms of a programming model, WCF actually supports three levels of "programming": API, declarative attributes, and configuration. The extensive WCF API exposes all of its functionality including low-level plumbing and extensibility points. Although the API is powerful, WCF also defines many attributes that are much simpler to use and that support most scenarios. Finally, WCF's configuration support enables you modify many settings without even touching your source code.

Beyond providing a simple programming mode, WCF's attribute-based approach also enables you to expose a component on the wire without deriving from a special base class. In contrast, .NET Remoting and Enterprise Services require that you derive your remote object from `MarshalByRefObject` and `ServicedComponent`, respectively. Because .NET allows only one base class, this makes it difficult to incorporate your own custom base class.

---

1. We're including Web Service Enhancements (WSE) with Web Services.

Table 9-1. *Summary of the Big Four Distributed Technologies*

Technology	Characteristics	Advantages	Disadvantages
Web Services	RPC style[1] XSD type fidelity Schema/WSDL integration	Great for interoperability Resilient	Issues with performance and immature specifications in the WS-* space.
Remoting	RPC style CLR type fidelity Code-based integration	Lean and mean	Fragile No built-in services such as hosting or security Poor interop
Enterprise Services	RPC style Code integration Declarative services: transactions, pooling concurrency	Proven technology Very fast Provides many services	COM-isms leak out and present COM hassles Poor interop
MSMQ	Message style Schema or code integration Robust messaging support (guaranteed deliver, transacted messaged, etc.)	Great when robust messaging is required	Poorly understood

1. By this, we're referring to the .NET tools that assume every developer wants an RPC façade over the SOAP messages.

Problem: Current Focus on Distributed Objects and RPC

Currently, most of the Big Four provide a distributed object programming model. In other words, they try to apply the principles of object orientation to the world of distributed applications. The problem, unfortunately, is that while object orientation is extremely successful in many types of applications, it does not translate well to distributed applications. In fact, to achieve acceptable performance and scalability out of a distributed object, you must violate some core principles of object orientation. Examples of this include creating stateless objects (an oxymoron by many object standards) and exposing a chunky interface rather than the chatty interface recommended by object orientation. Furthermore, many distributed object technologies assume a homogeneous environment and atomic deployment—both of which are exceedingly rare in the real world.

Despite these issues, .NET Remoting and Enterprise Services rely heavily on the object metaphor. The same can also be said for .NET Web Services in that the Web Service code generated by Visual Studio .NET implements a logical RPC interface on top of a document-based wire format. This leaves MSMQ as the only Big Four technology that eschews the distributed object mentality in favor of a pure messaging approach.[2]

WCF's Solution to the Distributed Object/RPC Focus

In light of the limitations of a distributed object mindset, the industry is beginning to adopt a new approach called *service orientation* (SO). In the next section, we provide a detailed

---

2. Unless you are one of the few who has forged a contract-first Web Service design and implementation despite the lack of tooling.

explanation of this approach and why it's a better fit for a distributed application. For now, simply remember this: SO addresses the unique characteristics and requirements of a distributed application in a cleaner way than distributed objects do. The problem today, however, is that most distributed technologies and tools favor the classic distributed object approach. Obviously, this makes a service-oriented approach much more difficult to implement than it should be.

WCF addresses this situation by making SO a first-class citizen. Its primary focus is to provide the tools and infrastructure necessary to ease a developer's learning curve and implementation burden when applying a service-oriented solution. That said, WCF also supports the best practice use of distributed objects.

YASOE: Yet Another Service Orientation Explanation

The terms service orientation (SO) and Service Oriented Architecture (SOA) are clearly the new buzzwords leading us into the next generation of distributed applications and shaping the stack of technologies that enable developers to implement them.

Note The terms SO and SOA are often interchanged despite being two distinct ideas. Later, you'll see the difference, but until then we'll simply use the SO/A acronym to represent the union of the two concepts.

Despite (or maybe because of) the huge amount of cyberspace real estate dedicated to SO/A explanations, debates, and marketing, the SO/A semantics still remain unclear. Line up ten SO/A enthusiasts and ask each "What is SO/A?" and you'll get ten different answers, each with varying degrees of overlap and conflict. These discussions, frankly, are becoming more and more tedious and at the same time less and less fruitful.

That said, we still feel compelled to convey our SO/A point of view within this chapter. Not because we believe ours is the canonical one, but because:

- Not everyone has had the luxury of reading the hundreds of SO/A related articles, slides, and presentations. For these folks, this section serves as a nice overview of the concepts.

- Those who are already veterans of the SO/A definition wars may benefit from this section because it explains what we mean when we refer to SO/A. Hopefully, this will ward off confusion (not to mention a few angry e-mails) based purely on semantics.

SO/A: Revolution, Evolution, or Neither?

One of the many complaints we often hear regarding SO/A is that it offers nothing that sophisticated and successful distributed implementations aren't already doing. To which we simply say: "That's the point." We've all learned many hard lessons over the past few years by watching distributed applications deliver disappointing results or completely fail. The primary goal of SO/A is to take those lessons to heart and document the characteristics of the most successful distributed systems. The hope is that this information will help future developers avoid the same mistakes that crippled many early attempts at building distributed applications.

Therefore, we see SO/A as a meta-pattern. Like any pattern, it defines a proven approach that incorporates the experience of architects and developers as they struggled to build these systems. Or, as Joe Long of Microsoft succinctly said: "Service orientation is all about building distributed systems the right way."

Objects vs. Services: The Metaphor Matters

If you compare object orientation with service orientation, the first obvious distinction is the use of the object metaphor versus the service metaphor. The object metaphor is simply an abstraction to help humans better understand the machine code underneath. This, in turn, makes it easier for humans to reason about and organize the larger system.

By nature, a metaphor implies characteristics. An object, for example, has attributes and behaviors, and maintains its own state. In the context of software development, an object implies chatty interfaces and support for encapsulation, inheritance, and polymorphism. Objects and their implied characteristics have proved extremely helpful when you're designing and implementing local systems. However, in the early '90s, high-speed LAN networks became more common, making it feasible to create applications that were distributed across several physical machines. Later, the emergence of the Web made it possible to communicate with business partners over this common networking infrastructure rather than using a costly propriety infrastructure.

Given the success of objects in the local context, it seemed natural to also apply the object metaphor in the distributed context. Unfortunately, the characteristics that worked so well in the local context were ineffective and even destructive in the distributed context. Specifically, chatty interfaces caused an object-based distributed solution to perform poorly and stateful objects made it extremely difficult to scale the system out. When you think about it, that's a fatal combination. Over time, many developers learned these issues and began developing "objects" that were stateless and exposed chunky interfaces. But, of course, the resulting entity was not an object at all. The bottom line is that the object metaphor actually hindered, rather than helped, developers in gaining an understanding of the best way to develop a distributed system.

Unlike past distributed approaches, which tried to take the round object metaphor and fit it into the square distributed world, SO/A introduces a new metaphor—the service, whose characteristics are much better aligned with the realities of the distributed world. The service metaphor helps humans reason about the communication that occurs between two distributed applications. It also implies the characteristics that help make that communication as efficient, flexible, and open as possible.

The Four Tenets of Service Orientation

So what exactly are the characteristics that make services a better metaphor for describing distributed applications? This is where the well-traveled "Four Tenets of Service Orientation" come into play. Understand, these are Microsoft-defined tenets, so they describe how Microsoft views SO/A. Also, these tenets have been bouncing around cyberspace for quite some time, so in-depth discussions and arguments about each one are only an Internet search away.

With that last point in mind, our goal in this section is to cover each tenet in just enough detail to satisfy the curiosity of someone fairly new to the SO/A discussion. Others may (and likely will) skip this section.

Tenet One: Boundaries Are Explicit

Many current distributed technologies boast of a feature called *location transparency*. This is the notion that the code you write to invoke a procedure is the same regardless of where that function actually lives. For example, it may be executing in process, out of process but on the same physical machine, or out of process and running on a different machine. Of course, in the distributed object paradigm, the procedure is really a method within an object, so the location of the method follows the object. And that, of course, brings us back to the issues around the object metaphor. An object assumes that all communication with its consumer is simple and local. In other words, it assumes the best case scenario. These assumptions caused a lot of pain, particularly in the early days of DCOM and CORBA, as developers took their local, chatty, and stateful objects and relocated them to a remote server without modification.

Services, on the other hand, take an entirely different approach. Around any service implementation lies a logical boundary that separates the service from the outside world. From the service point of view, the mechanisms used beyond this boundary to communicate with its consumers are completely unknown. The communication may need to cross large physical distances, multiple networks, various trust boundaries, etc. Or the communication may simply need to cross the service boundary to an in-proc consumer. Since these communication details are unknown to the service, *it assumes the worst case scenario*. That is, it assumes that each communication between it and the consumer is extremely costly. Therefore, SO ensures that each boundary crossing does as much work as possible. To that end, a service uses explicit message passing to communicate outside of its boundary, where each message contains all the data required to complete the operation.

Tenet Two: Services Share Schema and Contract

No matter what distributed technology you use, each one must provide some way for the consumer to know what operations are available, what inputs are needed and what their structure is, and what the structure of the return is. In .NET Remoting, for example, this information is deployed to the consumer in the form of a shared .NET assembly that contains the remote object interfaces or even their concrete classes. This complicates versioning and makes interoperation with non-.NET platforms impossible without bridging tools.

In contrast, services follow the Web Service approach and provide their structural and operational details using schemas and contract. In Web Service implementations, the schema and contract are typically contained within a Web Service Description Language (WSDL) document that the consumer can retrieve. And although SO doesn't require the use of WSDL, early implementations do use it.

Tenet Three: Service Compatibility Is Based on Policy

In certain cases, the service consumer may need to make specific demands on the service before engaging in any conversation (or vice versa). For example, the consumer may be a service itself and running within the context of a larger transaction. Therefore, the consumer must ensure that the remote service supports transactions. This transaction requirement represents a policy.

A given policy may indicate a service capability (for example, "I support transactions") or a service requirement (for example, "I require transaction support from other services"). In the case of WCF, each policy assertion adds the appropriate interceptor on both sides of the communication link. These interceptors actually apply the policy. Therefore, policy negotiation must occur before any real communication commences.

Tenet Four: Services Are Autonomous

Quite honestly, this tenet is probably the most nebulous one for developers as they learn the service-oriented concepts. In fact, of the four tenets, the majority of questions and discussions tend to focus on this one. The concept itself is simple to explain: services are self-governed and contain resources that cannot be modified by any external entity. The completely logical question that typically follows this, however, is the confusing aspect. That question is "How practical is a service that is completely autonomous?" The answer, of course, is not at all.

To help resolve this apparent contradiction, it's best to consider this tenet as a driving principle that a service should strive to achieve, rather than a hard and fast rule that a service must follow. In that sense, this tenet is similar to the encapsulation principle in object orientation. Total encapsulation would dictate that the object has no public members, which, of course, is a completely useless object. However, it still is an important principle that you should violate only when necessary. Likewise, you should use the autonomy principle to drive the design and factoring of your services. This will help you create services that are as independent, robust, and resilient to change as possible.

Service Orientation vs. Service Oriented Architecture

New technologies and development paradigms typically come attached with a barrage of new terminology, acronyms, and jargon. SO/A is no exception. To make things even more confusing, some terms are often lazily interchanged despite being different in subtle but important ways. But this is hardly unique to SO/A. In writings about object orientation, for example, the term *object* is often used where *class* would be more appropriate, or vice versa.

The terms that are most confused in the service space are service orientation (SO) and Service Oriented Architecture (SOA). *Service orientation* refers to a mindset that centers on the four SO tenets. These principles can drive activities across the entire spectrum of development tasks: architecture, design, requirement gathering, and coding. In contrast, the term *Service Oriented Architecture* is more specific in that it refers to the activity of developing an architecture or can be used to describe and existing architecture.

When the service notion first appeared within the developer world, it was commonly referred to as SOA. The problem with the SOA term, however, is that it implies that service orientation is simply an architectural approach. Therefore, the industry is slowly adopting SO as the generic term and using SOA in the context of discussing architectures.

Programming with WCF

While the previous sections paint a high-level picture of WCF, if you are anything like us, then a few lines of code speak a thousand words. So after providing you with an overview of some core WCF concepts, we'll show you several code examples that demonstrate the "look and feel" of programming WCF.

Caution At the time of this writing, WCF has been released only as an early beta. Therefore, take all code examples with a pound of salt—many of the details will likely change by the time WCF is officially released.

The ABCs of WCF: Address, Binding, and Contract

Concisely stated, a WCF service is a collection of endpoints where each endpoint implements a service contract and contains a binding and an address. Crystal clear, right? Probably not, so in this section, we elaborate on this definition by illustrating what is meant by contracts, bindings, and addresses.

Defining Service Contracts

Defying convention, a good place to start is with the *C*, which actually represents *service contract*. A service contract defines the service operations and the input and output parameters of each operation. In fact, this notion is extremely similar to the <portType> section in WSDL today. A service contract is typically defined by applying attributes to a class or interface:

```
using System.ServiceModel

[ServiceContract]
class MathService
{
    [OperationContract]
    public int Add(int n1, int n2)
    {
        return n1 + n2;
    }

    [OperationContract]
    private int Subtract(int n1, int n2)
    {
        return n1 - n2;
    }
}
```

In this example, note the ServiceContract and OperationContract attributes. These attributes combine to create the service contract. The OperationContract attributes are analogous to the familiar WebMethod attribute in that each attribute defines the attached method as an exposed operation. However, notice that the Subtract method is private. In WCF, the access modifiers are orthogonal to the service contract and, therefore, have no bearing on what can or cannot be exposed outside the service.

These attributes can also be applied to an interface to create the service contract. For example:

```
using System.ServiceModel

[ServiceContract]
interface IMathService
{
   [OperationContract]
   int Add(int n1, int n2);

   [OperationContract]
   int Subtract(int n1, int n2);
}
class MathService : IMathService
{
   public int Add(int n1, int n2)
   {
      return n1 + n2;
   }

   public int Subtract(int n1, int n2)
   {
      return n1 - n2;
   }
}
```

In this example, notice how the implementing class needs no attributes; its only concern is to implement the IMathService interface. Since it's desirable to keep the contract separate from the implementation, using an interface to define the service contract is the preferred approach.

Specifying the Address and Binding

In addition to implementing a contract, each endpoint also contains an *address* and a *binding*. The address is essentially a URL that defines the location of the endpoint (and the service by extension) in the network.

Bindings are a little more interesting. The endpoint binding defines what protocols, transport, and encoding the endpoint will use for all its communication. You can create a custom binding, but WCF provides several useful built-in bindings. Table 9-2 shows a partial list of these.

Table 9-2. *A Few of WCF's Standard Bindings*

Binding	Description
BasicProfileBinding	WS-I Basic Profile conformant binding that provides seamless interoperability with any other Basic Profile conformant Web Service. Use this binding to communicate with Web Services.
WSProfileBinding	Provides the same features as BasicProfileBinding, but also includes support for the full WSE 3.0 stack of protocols.
NetProfileNamedPipeBinding	Provides extremely fast communication between processes running on the same machine.
MsmqIntegrationBinding	Use to interoperate with MSMQ applications.

Although you can configure the address and binding programmatically, it's much easier (not to mention more flexible) to configure these in the app.config file (or web.config file) as we show here:

```
<configuration xmlns="http://schemas.microsoft.com/.NetConfiguration/v2.0">
  <system.serviceModel>
    <services>

      <service serviceType="IndigoServer.MathService">
        <endpoint bindingSectionName="wsProfileBinding"
                  address="http://localhost:13101/MathService"
                  contractType="IndigoServer.MathService, IndigoServer">
        </endpoint>
      </service>

    </services>
  </system.serviceModel>
</configuration>
```

As you can see, the <endpoint> element provides several attributes. With these, you can set the address, binding, and contract type.

Remember, by definition a service can contain multiple endpoints. Here's the configuration for this scenario, where multiple endpoints are applied to one service:

```
<configuration xmlns="http://schemas.microsoft.com/.NetConfiguration/v2.0">
  <system.serviceModel>
    <services>

      <service serviceType="IndigoServer.MathService">
        <endpoint bindingSectionName="wsProfileBinding"
                  address="http://localhost:13101/MathService"
                  contractType="IndigoServer.IMathService, IndigoServer">
        </endpoint>

        <endpoint bindingSectionName="basicProfileBinding"
                  address="http://localhost:13102/MathService"
                  contractType="IndigoServer.IMathService, IndigoServer">
        </endpoint>
      </service>

    </services>
  </system.serviceModel>
</configuration>
```

In this example, the second endpoint configures a slightly different binding, thus enabling the service to communicate using two different protocol stacks.

Hosting the Service

A WCF service can be hosted in many types of applications: Windows Service, Windows Forms, ASP.NET, and even a simple console application. Although ASP.NET will likely be the most popular host for services, for the sake of simplicity the following example demonstrates how to host a service within a simple console application.

```
static void Main(string[] args)
{
   using (ServiceHost<MathService> service =
      new ServiceHost<MathService>())
   {

      // communication infrastructure set up on call to open
      service.Open();

      //Stay alive to process requests
      Console.WriteLine("Hit [Enter] to exit");
      Console.ReadLine();
   }
}
```

The points of interest in this simple example are the ServiceHost constructor call and the call to Service.Open method. By constructing the generic ServiceHost class with the MathService parameter, the runtime generates a hosting environment for the MathService service. The ServicedHost.Open method establishes the communication infrastructure required by each endpoint based on its binding. Each opened ServicedHost consumes its share of resources, so it's important to close the service to release those resources. You could do this explicitly by calling the Close method on the ServiceHost, but the previous example implements a using block that implicitly closes the ServiceHost once the thread leaves the scope of the using block.

Calling the Service

WCF supports several ways to create and configure a client to call a service. First, as was the case with hosting a service, the calling code can exist within any type of application—web application, Windows application, even another WCF service.

Regardless of the client application type you choose, the client requires several bits of information to successfully call the service.

- *The service contract*: This can be any local type (class or interface) that adheres to the contract published by the service endpoint.

- *The service address*: This should be the same address configured in the service endpoint.

- *The service binding*: The client must use the same protocols, transport, and encoding as the service endpoint.

Notice that these three pieces of information match the information exposed by the service endpoint exactly. In fact, the client must use this information to establish a client-side endpoint. Similar to the service endpoint, the client-side endpoint establishes the communication plumbing going up to the service and also manages the message exchange.

WCF does not care exactly how all this information gets to the client. You could, for example, manually code the contract type into the client and set the proper address and binding in the configuration file. Here's what this might look like:

```
// In the client code
// This must adhere to the service contract, but does NOT need
// to be named the same.
[ServiceContract]
interface INotTheSameNameAsService
{
    [OperationContract]
    int Add(int n1, int n2);

    [OperationContract]
    int Subtract(int n1, int n2);
}
```

```
<!-- In the client's configuration file -->
<system.serviceModel>
  <client>
      <endpoint bindingSectionName="wsProfileBinding"
              address="http://localhost:13101/MathService"
              contractType="INotTheSameNameAsService">
  </client>
</system.serviceModel>
```

In this example, notice that the client-side contract (INotTheSameNameAsService) is, as its name suggests, not named the same as the service-side contract (IMathService). WCF will validate that the service contract at each endpoint (client and service) is *structurally* equivalent, but unlike some distributed technologies, such as .NET Remoting, WCF does not require full type fidelity down to the type name and assembly name. This is an important difference between a distributed object approach and a service-oriented approach because the latter leads to easier versioning and, therefore, more resilient systems. That said, you shouldn't radically change the name of the contract for no good reason.

Although the technique shown in the previous listing is a valid way to represent the address, binding, and contract, most developers would rather avoid all the manual coding and tedious configuring in favor of a more automated approach. Thankfully, WCF ships with the Service Metadata Utility tool (Svcutil.exe) that can query a service, retrieve its metadata, and create the appropriate client-side address, binding, and contract. It also creates a service proxy that, similar to a Web Service proxy, enables the client code to call the service by calling the proxy's methods.

The Svcutil.exe tool has many options, but the following example demonstrates a simple, common usage:

```
svcutil.exe http://localhost:13101/MathService /config:app.config
```

In this case, the Svcutil.exe tool generates a configuration file with all the appropriate address and binding settings. It also generates a client-side service contract type and a proxy class, as we show here:

```
[ServiceContract()]
public interface IMathService
{
    [OperationContract( ... )]
    int Add([MessageBody(...)] int n1, [([MessageBody(...)]int n2);
    [OperationContract( ... )]
    int Subtract([MessageBody(...)] int n1, [([MessageBody(...)]int n2);
}


public partial class MathServiceProxy : ProxyBase<IMathService>, IMathService
{
    public MathServiceProxy() {}

    public MathServiceProxy(string configurationName) :
            base(configurationName) {}

    public MathServiceProxy(System.ServiceModel.Binding binding) :
            base(binding){}

    public MathServiceProxy(EndpointAddress address, Binding binding) :
            base(address, binding) {}

    public int Add(int n1, int n2)
    {
        return base.InnerProxy.Add(n1, n2);
    }

    public int Subtract(int n1, int n2)
    {
        return base.InnerProxy.Subtract(n1, n2);
    }
}
```

Now that the proxy, contract, and configuration are complete, the client code can simply use the proxy to call operations on the service. We demonstrate this here:

```
class Program
{
    static void Main(string[] args)
    {
        using(MathServiceProxy math = new MathServiceProxy("IMathService"))
        {
            Console.WriteLine(math.Add(5, 2));
            Console.WriteLine(math.Add(3, 3));
        }
    }
}
```

Revisiting WCF Contracts

The concept of a contract is a core foundation to WCF. Address and binding are also important pieces, but they track closer to an administrator's set of responsibilities. Contracts, on the other hand, are firmly rooted in the developer's space.

WCF defines three different types of contracts:

- *Service contract*: As we mentioned earlier, this defines the service operations and the input and output parameters of each operation. Every service must have one associated service contract and may have more.

- *Data contract*: This defines the data structure WCF uses to serialize and deserialize an instance of a complex type. Data contracts must be associated with every complex type exposed by a service operation as parameters or return values.

- *Message contract*: This enables you to explicitly define the layout of a message; for example, what goes in the header versus what goes in the body of the message.

The following sections provide some more details about each of the contract types.

Using Service Contracts

WCF provides three attribute types that together allow you to define a service contract: ServiceContract, OperationContract, and BindingRequirements.

You've already seen simple examples of ServiceContract and OperationContract. Understand that each of these provides additional parameters that allow you to further refine the contract. For example, consider this service contract, which shows some ServiceContract and OperationContract settings:

```
[ServiceContract(Namespace="http://indigorocks/", Name="CustomerService")]
interface ICustomerService
{
    [OperationContract()]
    CustomerData GetCustomerByEmail(string email);

    [OperationContract(IsOneWay=true)]
    void SaveCustomer(CustomerData cust);
}
```

In this example, first notice the additional parameters set in the `ServiceContract` attribute. `Namespace` and `Name` together enable you to explicitly specify the namespace and name of the contract. By default, WCF uses the full interface or class name. Also notice the `IsOneWay` parameter is set in the `OperationContract` to indicate that the `SaveCustomer` method is a one-way operation with no return values.

Using Data Contracts

Data contracts describe the structure of data passed in and out of the service. In the case of simple, known types such as integers and strings, WCF applies a default contract; if your service exposes only simple types, you do not need to define a data contract. The `CustomerService` contract shown in the previous listing, however, exposes a `CustomerData` type, which is a complex type and, therefore, requires a data contract.

Again, WCF makes it easy to define a data contract by providing several attributes that you can use to decorate the `CustomerData` type:

```
// Also need a reference to System.Runtime.Serialization.dll
using System.Runtime.Serialization;

[DataContract]
public class CustomerData
{
    [DataMember] public string FirstName;
    [DataMember] public string LastName;
    [DataMember] public string Email;
}
```

As you can see, the data contract attributes are analogous to the XML serializer attributes such as `XmlElement` and `XmlAttribute`. However, unlike today's Web Services, WCF does not by default use the `XmlSerializer` to serialize complex types. Instead it uses `XmlFormatter`, which has better support for versioning and understands these new `DataContract` and `DataMember` attributes. You can explicitly specify the desired formatter using the `FormatMode` parameter of the `ServiceContract` attribute as we show in the following example.

```
[ServiceContract(Namespace="http://indigorocks/", Name="CustomerService",
    FormatMode = ContractFormatMode.XmlFormatter)]
interface ICustomerService
{ ... }
```

Using Message Contracts

Future WCF developers will frequently define service and message contracts, but using message contracts to explicitly define the message structure will likely be less common. This can prove useful if you need to interoperate with another (non-WCF) service, which requires a particular message format.

To define a message contract, you use the `MessageContract`, `MessageHeader`, and `MessageBody` attributes as shown here:

```
[MessageContract]
public class CustomerMessage
{
    [MessageHeader]
    public int CustomerId;

    [MessageBody]
    public CustomerData Customer;
}
```

This message contract can now be used as a parameter in a service operation. For example:

```
 [ServiceContract()]
interface ICustomerService
{
    [OperationContract()]
    void SaveCustomer(CustomerMessage customerMsg);
```

Instancing, Transactions, and Much, Much More

The previous examples are meant to provide a sneak preview of the WCF programming look and feel. Of course, WCF provides many more features and so this is by no means an exhaustive look at WCF programming.

To help fill some gaps, Table 9-3 lists several important features and which WCF API or attribute enables each one. Use this as a self-study starting point.

Table 9-3. *Other WCF Features*

WCF Feature	Attribute or API	Notes
Transactions	OperationBehaviorAttribute	Provides AutoEnlistTransaction parameter
Instancing	ServiceBehaviorAttribute	InstanceMode parameter accepts values such as PerCall, Singleton, etc.
Asynchronous calls	OperationContract ServiceContract	Both provide parameters for declaring an asynchronous task and a valid callback interface on the client.
Message Queuing	NetProfileMsmqBinding	Sends message to queues.

Preparing for WCF

WCF and SO represents a huge shift both in how we reason about distributed applications and how we implement them. The benefits, however, are significant, so it's no wonder that architects and developers are anxious to adopt WCF as soon as possible. On the other hand, most of these folks also have systems that need to be developed today using today's technologies and, therefore, they cannot afford to wait for Microsoft to release WCF. So the question on everyone's mind then is, "What can I do today to make the future migration to WCF easier?" In particular, you need to know which of the Big Four technologies to choose and what features of the chosen technology you should use or avoid. To answer this question, we must break it down into three more specific questions:

1. Will installing WCF break my application because it uses a particular Big Four technology?

2. Will my chosen Big Four technology interoperate with WCF services?

3. Will my chosen Big Four technology easily port to WCF?

This section discusses each of these questions as it applies to each of the Big Four technologies.

Will WCF Break My Current Application?

Of the three, this is probably the most important question. It also has the most welcomed answer: WCF will *not* break an existing application using any of the Big Four technologies. WCF will be deployed as an entirely distinct technology with its own protocol stacks and, therefore, it neither changes nor depends on anything from the Big Four stacks.

This is great news, particularly for folks who have already heavily invested in current technologies. It also contradicts some of the talk around .NET Remoting, a technology that should steal a famous line from Mark Twain: "The rumors of my death have been greatly exaggerated." Although it's true that Remoting presents some issues in terms of porting to and interoperating with WCF, like all the other Big Four technologies it will continue working as normal after you install WCF.

Will My Implementation Interoperate with WCF?

As we stated in the previous section, all of the Big Four technologies are equal in that they won't break after you install WCF. In terms of interoperating with WCF, however, the Big Four technologies are clearly not equal; most interoperate, but one simply does not.

Before getting to that detail, however, let us clarify the question. Each of the Big Four relies on a distinct stack of protocols that define serialization, wire format, object lifetime semantics, and so on. It should be no surprise, therefore, that these technologies generally do not interoperate well. For example, a Web Service cannot directly communicate with a .NET Remoting object or vice versa because (among a few other issues) it accepts and sends different message formats across the wire. However, since WCF incorporates the best of each Big Four technology, it achieves "wire interoperability" with three of the Big Four technologies.

The one exception is .NET Remoting. Some, unfortunately, have misinterpreted this to mean that WCF breaks Remoting. In reality, it simply means that your existing Remoting code will not communicate with your new WCF-based services (and vice versa). This is certainly an important limitation that you'll need to consider carefully before you adopt a solution based on .NET Remoting. That said, it doesn't signal the death of .NET Remoting.

Remoting aside, the overall WCF interoperability story is outstanding. It does achieve wire interoperability with your current Enterprise Service, MSMQ, and .NET Web Service code. In addition, WCF services can interoperate with any non-.NET Web Service if it conforms to the WS-I Basic Profile specification.

Finally, WCF can also interoperate with a Web Service that uses Web Service Enhancements (WSE) for WS-Security, WS-Policy, and other new Web Service specifications. This WSE interoperability, however, comes with one big caveat: It is true for WSE version 3.0 only. To keep up with the dynamic nature of the Web Service specification space, Microsoft must constantly produce updated versions of their WSE tool. Because of this, the WCF team decided to target a WSE version that, hopefully, contains a much more stable set of specifications.

How Easily Will my Application Migrate to WCF?

Like the interoperability question, this question also helps to distinguish the current Big Four technologies. The answer to the ease of migration question centers on the programming model; if your current technology uses a programming model based primarily on declarative attributes rather than code, it will be easier to port the code to WCF.

Before diving into the details for each technology, however, let us address another question that has likely crossed your mind. Given WCF's great interoperability story, why would you endure the hassle of migrating a Web Service that has proven to be reliable and functional? The answer, simply, is that migrating allows you take full advantage of all the WCF capabilities. WCF is built upon the latest and greatest protocols, brings SO to the masses, and provides a single, simple programming model. But migrating existing code to WCF is the only way to realize all of its functionality.

The following sections discuss the migration details of each Big Four technology and give each a rating of either "trivial" or "non-trivial" where:

- *Trivial* means that the required changes are simple and can be expressed in a cookbook-style document or can be reliably automated via a tool.

- *Non-trivial* means that the required changes are generally too complex for reliable automation and, therefore, require human intervention.

In the non-trivial cases, Microsoft intends to publish whitepapers to help guide developers through the migration process. Also understand that even in these non-trivial cases, a little WCF foreknowledge can help you implement solutions with WCF in mind and, thus, ease that migration. To that end, in each of the following sections we provide usage suggestions that will minimize your migration task.

Migrating Web Services to WCF

Not surprisingly, Web Services are easily migrated to WCF. This is true for a couple reasons. First, the .NET Web Service programming model is based primarily on attributes rather than code. Second, the underlying protocols and standards already support, if not embrace, a service-oriented mindset. Because of this, Web Services enjoy a *trivial* migration.

That said, if you're writing a Web Service today but know it will eventually be ported to WCF, here are a few suggestions for ensuring a seamless transition.

- *Avoid or abstract custom SOAP extensions.* SOAP extensions enable you to intercept incoming and outgoing SOAP messages and execute custom logic before the message lands within the Web Service or at the client. This can be useful when you're implementing a custom security mechanism, custom logging, etc. However, WCF provides its own interception and extensibility mechanism, so all SOAP extensions must be rewritten as WCF behaviors or channels.

- *Avoid or abstract calls to* HttpContext. The HttpContext class provides access to the intrinsic ASP.NET objects such as Session, Application, and Server. You can rely on this to work because .NET Web Services are always hosted in ASP.NET. However, WCF services may run within several types of hosts, including a simple console application. So you can no longer assume the WCF service is hosted by ASP.NET and, therefore, has an HTTP context.

Currently, WSE 2.0 is a popular way to provide security and other required enterprise abilities to Web Services. Unfortunately, Web Services that leverage WSE 2.0 experience a decidedly *non-trivial* migration path. In fact, Microsoft warns that it may cost significant developer time. This is a particularly problematic given that WCF also doesn't support wire-interoperability with WSE 2.0 either. The good news, however, is that the port from WSE 3.0 to WCF should be trivial. So if you use WSE 2.0, be prepared to migrate to WSE 3.0 as soon as possible to provide a much smoother path to WCF.

Moving Enterprise Services to WCF

Like Web Services, the Enterprise Services programming model is based on attributes. Despite this, there are several issues that prevent the Enterprise Services migration from achieving a trivial rating. First, the attribute names and settings are extremely different from those you've come to know in Enterprise Services. For example, the familiar Requires Transactions, Supports Transactions, etc. settings are replaced by an attribute setting named AutoEnlistTransaction. Furthermore, the Enterprise Services technology is tightly bound to the distributed object mindset, and has few facilities for a serviced-oriented implementation. Therefore, the migration path is rated as *non-trivial*.

That said, understand that migrating an Enterprise Service implementation promises to be much easier than a WSE 2.0 implementation primarily because of its attribute-based programming model. But there are too many caveats to call it a truly simple migration. These caveats include:

- *Different attribute names and settings.* WCF not only changes the attributes for transactional behavior, but it also uses different attributes for lifetime and security settings.

- *Loosely Coupled Events (LCE).* Depending on the scenario, LCE code may require significant modifications.

- *Implicit Reference Passing.* In classic distributed object programming, it's common to pass a reference back to the client that provides direct access to another object on the server. However, this practice violates the autonomous tenet of SO, and, therefore, is not allowed in WCF. Instead, WCF supports the notion of explicitly returning endpoint references—essentially URLs that the client can use to access another service, but only through a service boundary layer.

If you're writing Enterprise Service code today, you obviously cannot avoid the attribute name issue. However, if you can avoid using LCE or returning objects by reference, then you can greatly simplify your future migration to WCF.

Migrating Remote Objects to WCF

Given that .NET Remoting does not provide an attribute-based programming model and that it *fully* embraces the distributed object mindset, it is no surprise that it also presents a *non-trivial* migration path to WCF. Much like Enterprise Services, however, if you carefully implement your Remoting solutions by avoiding specific features of .NET Remoting, you'll enjoy a much easier migration to WCF in the future. Here are a few suggestions:

- *Avoid using .NET Remoting extensibility*. .NET Remoting's channel, sink, and formatter objects allow you to extend its behavior. For example, many have used these objects to implement a secure channel that automatically encrypts and decrypts the messages. To migrate to WCF, however, all of this code will need to be rewritten against WCF's extensibility model, which has similar object names but different interfaces and behaviors. Also note that a lot of functionality, such as security, is already implemented in WCF so custom extensions may not be required.

- *Use interfaces for all remoted classes*. Split each remoted class into an interface and a class implementation. This not only simplifies deployment today, but it also eases migration to WCF in the future.

- *Strive for a service oriented solution*. Although it's difficult if not impossible to implement a pure SO solution using Remoting, taking a few small steps toward SO is relatively easy and can greatly simplify a future migration. These steps include using chunky interfaces, using stateless objects, avoiding Remoting events, and avoiding implicitly returning object references.

Migrating System.Messaging Code to WCF

Although the MSMQ technology is well-suited to the service-oriented mindset, its programming model is different enough to warrant a *non-trivial* migration rating. Keep in mind that it's extremely easy to interoperate between WCF and MSMQ. Given this, plus given MSMQ's already rich messaging infrastructure, migrating MSMQ code will likely be a low priority.

MSMQ offers a few different APIs: a Win32 unmanaged API, a COM-based API, and a managed API named System.Messaging. The best approach you can take today to ease future MSMQ migration is to work exclusively through the managed System.Messaging API.

Interoperability and Migration Summary

You've now seen how the Big Four technologies compare in terms of interoperability and migration and how to best utilize each for the smoothest path to WCF. You can find a convenient summary of the key facts in Table 9-4.

Table 9-4. *WCF Interoperability and Migration Summary*

Technology	Interop with WCF?	Migration?
Web Services	Yes	Trivial
WSE 2.0	No	Non-trivial
WSE 3.0	Yes	Trivial
Enterprise Services	Yes	Non-trivial
.NET Remoting	No	Non-trivial
System.Messaging (MSMQ)	Yes	Non-trivial

Overall Guidance for Choosing the Best Technology

One Big Four technology stands out as providing the best migration path to WCF: Web Services. This is true not only for simply migrating code, but also more importantly for migrating your frame of mind from objects to services. The best way to understand SO is to do service orientation, and Web Services allow you to do just that—right now. If you're currently using WSE 2.0, plan to migrate to WSE 3.0 as soon as possible. This will provide interoperability with WCF and a simpler migration path to WCF.

While the above is the recommended approach straight out of Redmond, no one—including Microsoft—is foolish enough to believe that one technology is always the right answer for every situation. For example, some applications may have performance requirements that a Web Service-based solution cannot meet. Or the situation may require distributed transactions or involve a proprietary protocol. For all these reasons and more, the other technologies still play important roles.

If Web Services are ruled out, particularly for performance reasons, Enterprise Services is the next recommended technology. Enterprise Services use DCOM as the communication protocol, which, somewhat surprisingly, remains the fastest distributed wire protocol—faster even than .NET Remoting over the network. Enterprise Services also provide critical services such as distributed transactions, object pooling, and a proven hosting environment. However, Enterprise Services is currently built upon COM+ technology. This may seem like a minor detail except that it leaks through the Enterprise Service abstraction in serious ways. For example, all Enterprise Service assemblies must be strong named, and configured within COM+.

So that brings us to .NET Remoting, which performs extremely well when using binary serialization with the TCP protocol. In fact, it's actually faster than DCOM when communicating between application domains within a single process. It's also a pure managed code solution that doesn't suffer from registration and deployment hassles like Enterprise Services. Finally, .NET Remoting allows you to get extremely close to the underlying wire protocols. So much so that you can use .NET Remoting to implement or interact with a proprietary wire protocol. The downside, however, is that Remoting is strongly biased toward distributed object approaches, which can potentially make your code difficult to migrate into WCF. Because of this and because Remoting is not wire interoperable with WCF, it's recommended to use it only for cross-application domains, in process calls, or when you need to implement custom protocols.

Compared to the other three technologies, the decision to use MSMQ is a simple one. If you need robust messaging with guaranteed delivery, transacted queues, built-in security, and more, you must use MSMQ because it's the only current Microsoft technology that provides these features.

Summary

WCF is a future technology that promises to unify the current distributed technologies under one programming model and technology stack. It also promises to bring SO to the mainstream. Microsoft has already released and continues to release a large amount of WCF-related information. This is a testament to the impact it's expected to have.

Of all the current .NET distributed technologies, Web Services will enjoy the easiest transition to WCF. The migration story for the rest of the Big Four is a mixed bag. However, the best way to ensure a smooth migration path is to learn everything you can about SO and apply its ideas now to guide how you build a distributed application.

PART 3

■■■

Data Access Layer

The third part of the book is about how the data access layer manifests in the .NET Framework.

Every business application has requirements to retain information across a user's sessions with the application. These requirements are called the persistence requirements for the application. Although there are scores of persistence mediums, one has come to dominate: the relation database server. Relational databases store information using rules described by a schema; these rules are based on the tenets of information theory and are implemented using Structured Query Language, or SQL. It has also become widely accepted that isolating access to this persistence medium yields great benefits in the design and maintenance of complex applications. This isolation layer is called the data access layer.

Chapter 10

The third part of the book starts with an overview of ADO.NET, with a focus not so much on the "hows" of using a managed provider for data access, but rather on when to use different types and techniques and some best practices for each scenario.

Chapter 11

Several features of the Framework are designed for the data access layer, yet they don't directly pertain to managed providers. We'll examine some of these key services here, including data source controls, database-dependent cache entries, and the data access layer application block.

In the last section of this chapter, we'll examine some of the radical new features of SQL Server 2005, which change some of our fundamental suppositions about distributed applications, and force us to learn new ways to think about what runs in-memory with the database engine.

Chapter 12

The next version of the Framework introduces a more elaborate transaction model, enabling you to have a transaction manage work that gets done in memory, so it can be rolled back the same way transactional database work can be. We'll examine this and see how a transaction can start as you make modifications to business objects, and then be promoted to do database work, and get promoted again if the transaction becomes distributed across databases. We'll also show you how to implement your own resource manager, which can do work that will participate in these transactions.

CHAPTER 10

■ ■ ■

Managed Providers of Data Access

The data access model that you've used for your .NET development is called ADO.NET. This is a marketing name, as the technology has very little to do with ADO, and nothing to do with ActiveX (which is what the A in the acronym ADO stands for). A more descriptive name would be Managed Providers of data access. In this chapter, we've made the assumption that you've used Managed Providers in your .NET development efforts. We examine some specific techniques for optimizing data access, compare and contrast the data access models available when using Managed Providers, and provide a summary of some of the new features in ADO.NET 2.0. A Managed Provider is really just a set of types that implements a known set of interfaces.

ADO and OLEDB, Microsoft's COM-based data access technology, was designed when the client-server model of application development was at its peak. As the Web caused distributed application development to move to the fore, ADO had to be modified to account for architectural differences that worked well in a client server environment, but were not scalable enough for distributed applications. ADO.NET was designed from the ground up for distributed architectures, formalizing a disconnected model of data access into the object model.

One of the major drawbacks of working with Recordsets (the type for working with result sets with COM-based ADO) was that it was hard to know in what situations you should use which cursor and locking models. Furthermore, there was very little discernable difference in how the developer interacted with the result set regardless of the cursor model used. In short, it was very easy to use ADO result sets in a way that could negatively impact performance and scalability. A developer needed to understand the internals of the Recordset cursor model in order to choose the cursor and locking models most appropriate in specific circumstances.

ADO.NET gives you a choice of how to work with result sets with two different data access models. One is an in-memory model, and the other is a low memory footprint, row-based approach. Each of these models is implemented with different classes, meaning you work with different objects depending on which method you employ. The programming models between the two methods are different, and this makes it clear to the developer which technique he's using. This clear differentiation should reduce the number of times the incorrect model gets used. However, choosing the correct model still requires a clear understanding of the differences, the features, and trade-offs of each one.

The low memory footprint model of data access in ADO.NET provides a row-based approach to processing a result set. With this approach, a single row of data is loaded into memory at a time; you process the data for your specific operation, and then the row is discarded from memory when you move on to the next row. This means the memory consumed on the web server (or the physical tier where the result set is being processed) is minimized to the memory needed to hold a single row of the result set, and that footprint is bounded throughout the processing of the set. This is ideal for operations that are common to web applications such as transforming a result set into an HTML table. The type that provides this functionality is called a *data reader*. We'll examine data readers in some detail shortly.

The in-memory type for processing data is called a DataSet. A DataSet is like a collection of ADO-style Recordsets. The actual type the DataSet carries a collection of is a DataTable. The DataSet provides a complete layer of abstraction between you and the data that you're working with. That is, a DataSet does not know and does not care where its data comes from. It can come from SQL Server, some legacy ODBC source, or even an XML file; the programming model stays the same. There can even be a layer of indirection between the schema used at the database and the schema used in memory by the DataSet.

Because all of the data for a DataSet is loaded into memory when a command is executed against the database, more features are available than with a data reader. With a DataSet, you can sort data, modify data, apply filters to the data, even establish relationships between different result sets. DataSets can be stored in the Session, squirreled away in the Web Cache, or marshaled to a client via a Web Method. We'll show you how to put the DataSet through its paces after we delve into the data readers.

Managed Providers

There are many different database vendors with strong offerings on the market. A data access model must be designed to generalize the functionality of a relational database, so that the data access model is relevant regardless of the database of choice. With ADO.NET, you access a specific vendor's database using a Managed Provider of data access specifically created for that vendor. There are also providers implemented that allow backwards compatibility with OLEDB and ODBC.

When a vendor decides to create a Managed Provider for .NET Framework users to employ to access their database, they implement a series of interfaces (see Figure 10-1). Since all Managed Providers consist of classes implementing this common set of interfaces, the programming model is the same or very similar, regardless of which vendor's product you're using.

These interfaces are what provide the layer of abstraction between the developer and the database. For many providers, this removes a software layer between your code and the database that was present in the ADO model. This can provide better performance, as the types that are used to talk to SQL Server, for example, are coded to communicate directly with that database. For native providers such as SQL Server and Oracle, a layer of abstraction that was present in OLEDB and ODBC has been removed in the ADO.NET model. For backwards-compatibility providers, such as OLEDB and ODBC, no performance gains are realized.

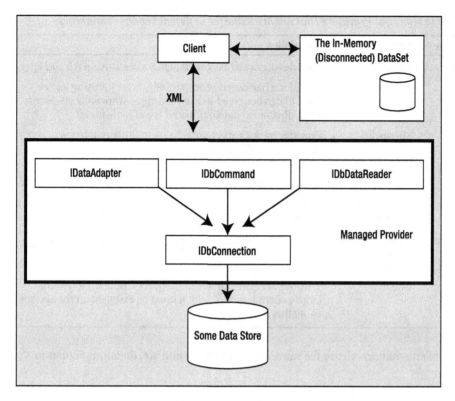

Figure 10-1. *The interfaces underlying a Managed Provider of data access*

This gain in performance is at the expense of reuse. In ADO, you could change a connection string and use the same code to access different databases (as long as the SQL statements used were compatible across the systems). This was a model commonly used by software vendors to write applications that could use either SQL Server or Oracle as a backend database, for example. Because each Managed Provider is implemented as a set of different types, to get this type of reuse is a bit trickier in version 1.x of the .NET Framework than it was in ADO (where all you needed to do was change a connection string). Microsoft has acknowledged the need to simplify this type of reuse in certain situations and has introduced a new set of features in 2.0 that addresses this specifically. We'll take a look at these features in the upcoming section on data provider factories.

There are many Managed Providers available (see Table 10-1). Microsoft ships several with the Framework, there are open source implementations, and several vendors have written providers for their own products, as well.

Table 10-1. *Some Managed Providers That Are Available for Different Vendor's Databases*

Provider Name	Vendor	Description
SQL Server	Microsoft	Provides access to Microsoft SQL Server, version 6.5 and later.
OLEDB	Microsoft	Provides a backwards-compatibility layer for using legacy OLEDB drivers. Need to use this one to work with MS Access or FoxPro, as no native provider is available for Jet.
ODBC	Microsoft	Provides backwards compatibility to those databases supporting ODBC drivers.
Oracle	Microsoft	Provides access to Oracle data sources. Built on top of the Oracle client libraries, which must be installed on the system using this provider.
Interbase	Borland	Access to Borland's Interbase relational database product.
mySQL	Source Forge Open source Others	Access to the open source implementation of mySQL.
Oracle	Oracle	Provides access to Oracle data sources. Built on top of the Oracle client libraries, which must be installed on the system using this provider.

These implementations all use the same set of interfaces, and are, therefore, similar to one another.

System.Data Namespace

The core namespace of the Framework class library for data access is System.Data. Table 10-2 is a survey of the namespaces contained within this namespace.

Table 10-2. *Survey of Namespaces from the* System.Data *Assembly*

Namespace	Meaning in Life
System.Data	This is the core namespace of ADO .NET. It defines types that represent tables, rows, columns, constraints, and the almighty DataSet. Be aware that this namespace does not define types to connect to a data source. Rather, it defines the interfaces implemented by specific Managed Providers and the types that represent the data itself.
System.Data.OleDb	This namespace defines the types that allow you to connect to an OLE DB-compliant data source, submit SQL queries, and fill DataSets. These are the types you must use to talk to Access or FoxPro data sources. They are also provided for backwards compatibility to vendors that do not have a native provider available.
System.Data.ODBC	This namespace defines the types that allow you to connect to an ODBC providers of data access. These types are provided for backwards compatibility and will usually not perform as well as a native provider.

Namespace	Meaning in Life
`System.Data.SqlClient`	This namespace defines the types that constitute the SQL Managed Provider. Using these types, you can talk directly to Microsoft SQL Server and avoid the level of indirection associated with the OleDb equivalents.
`System.Data.OracleClient`	These are types to talk directly to Oracle8i and later databases. These types ship in a stand-alone assembly. You must also have MDAC 2.6 and Oracle Client installed. There is also a native Managed Provider available directly from Oracle.
`System.Data.SqlServerCe`	Provides access to SQL Server CE Edition, which is part of the .NET Compact Framework, and is designed to run on hand-held devices.

In addition to the subnamespaces that are defined the in `System.Data` namespace, a number of types are also housed in the namespace (see Table 10-3). The core object from this namespace is the `DataSet`. The `DataSet` object can hold a collection of result sets in memory, providing random access to the data for sorting, filtering, and modifying the data. A number of types contained by the `DataSet` object are also defined in `System.Data`.

Table 10-3. *A Sampling of Types That Live in the* `System.Data` *Namespace*

`System.Data` Type	Meaning in Life
`DataSet`	Represents an in-memory cache of data, which may consist of multiple related `DataTables`.
`DataTableCollection` `DataTable`	The `DataTableCollection` type represents all the tables (`DataTable` types) for a particular `DataSet`.
`DataRelationCollection` `DataRelation`	This collection represents all relationships (`DataRelation` types) between the tables in a `DataSet`.
`ForeignKeyConstraint` `UniqueConstraint`	`ForeignKeyConstraint` represents an action restriction enforced on a set of columns in a primary key/foreign key relationship when a value is changed or deleted. The `UniqueConstraint` type represents a restriction on a set of columns in which all values must be unique.
`ConstraintCollection` `Constraint`	The `ConstraintCollection` represents all constraints (foreign key constraints, unique constraints) assigned to a given `DataTable`. `Constraint` represents a single constraint assigned to one or more `DataColumns`.
`DataColumnCollection` `DataColumn`	`DataColumnCollection` represents all of the columns used by a `DataTable`. `DataColumn` represents a specific column in a `DataTable`.
`DataRowCollection` `DataRow`	These types represent a collection of rows for a `DataTable` (`DataRowCollection`) and a specific row of data in a `DataTable` (`DataRow`).
`DataRowView` `DataView`	`DataRowView` allows you to carve out a predefined "view" from an existing row. The `DataView` type represents a customized view of a `DataTable` that can be used for sorting, filtering, searching, editing and navigation.

These types are all contained by instances of the `DataSet` object. We'll look at `DataSets` after we examine the data access model that's built for speed: data readers. Data readers expose a forward-only, read-only, low memory footprint architecture for data access. The choice between a data reader and a DataSet is a choice between performance and functionality. Which you choose depends on what you're trying to accomplish. We'll take a look at the details of data access with data readers and with the DataSet, and then we'll examine some of the trade-offs and differences between these methods. But first, we'll examine the fundamental requirement of any data access toolset, the Connection class.

Connections

Connections are the fundamental abstraction needed in a data access technology. A Connection object deals with the underlying technical details of establishing a network path of communication with the database server, and is also responsible for presenting the credentials of the user requesting the data to the database. This is one of the most expensive parts of communicating with the database, and is, therefore, one of the most critical resources in data access technology. For this reason, an environment that establishes a pool of connections to the database is usually desired, so that each request for data does not have to incur the overhead of knocking on the door of the database, making an introduction, and getting permission to come in and wander around.

Pools

Connection pooling is implemented by the Managed Providers of data access. The discussion in the section pertains to the SQL- and Oracle-managed providers from Microsoft. The ODBC- and OLEDB-managed providers are backwards compatibility layers, and so rely on the native pooling functionality provided by the driver or provider, respectively.

Connections are established on a per-user basis. That is, two different users cannot share a connection to the database. This is true whether you're using integrated security or a database-specific security model. This works fine when a web application is executing as a dedicated user (such as ASPNET, the user the ASP.NET Framework runs as by default). When you're using impersonation and integrated security, though, code is executed with the credentials of the user that has requested the page. This leaves connection pools virtually useless, which can seriously impair the scalability of your application. For this reason, impersonation in the data access tier is not highly recommended. Instead, you should use a dedicated user account or a database user defined for the application.

Pooling behavior is controlled using attributes in the connection string. You can control the minimum pool size, control the maximum pool size, or opt out of pooling altogether.

When designing your application to leverage connection pools, the most important thing to keep in mind is that there is a pool allocated for each connection string and for each security context. For example, when you're using impersonation within ASP.NET, and using integrated security against the database, you can connect to the database with the following connection string:

```
Server=YourServerName;Integrated Security=SSPI;database=Library;MinPoolSize=5
```

When 100 users show up, how many connection pools are there? How many connections? Since all users are using the same connection string, you might hope that there would be one pool. The default maximum pool size is 100, but your actual connection count will, hopefully, be much lower, as many of the users will be able to share the connections—that is, they're not *all* going to be accessing the database at *exactly* the same time. This, after all, is the whole point of connection pooling.

Table 10-4. *Connection String Attributes That Control the Managed Provider's Connection Pooling Behavior*

Attribute	Defaulted Value	Meaning in Life
Pooling	true	Set this value to `false` to avoid having connections pooled at all.
MinPoolSize	0	You can control the minimum pool size with this value. Smaller minimum pool sizes will incur less overhead when the first connection to the database is established. Larger minimums incur more of a hit on the first request, but subsequent users connect more quickly, as connections are already in the pool for them.
MaxPoolSize	100	You can lower this to throttle connections to the database; if it does not have the capacity to bear the load, requests to connect will begin to pool on the web server. The default value is overkill in almost all cases. This value will enable connections to trend up over time if your application has a connection leak.

Unfortunately, your hopes are dashed when you learn of the sad reality of the situation. Since pools are sensitive to security context, and you're using impersonation and integrated security, each user has her own context, and so each user is actually allocated her own pool. Since you've established a minimum pool size of 5, with 100 users on your site, you have 100 pools with 5 connections each in them—500 connections total!

This is the reason why connection pools, impersonation, and integrated security don't mix very well. To best leverage connection pooling, you should use SQL Server logins in connection strings when using impersonation from the web server. This can throw a wrench in plans to meet a common requirement, which is that all changes and additions to the data must record who made the change. With integrated security, this information is present and can be used in the SQL statement. With SQL Server security, you must pass this information from the web server to the database server when executing a command. The best way to do this is to make data modifications with stored procedures, and add a username as a parameter to the procedure footprint.

For this reason, connection pools are also not very helpful in a two-tiered application; though by leaving the minimum pool size at zero, they also don't hurt anything. Each user gets a pool on the client, and each pool has a connection in it (after the first time a connection is opened from the code). The only way another connection could get added is if the client application uses two connections and holds them both open at once. You may wonder what the point of using the pool at all is. Instead of leveraging the pool, which keeps the connection open, why not just open a connection when the process spins up and leave it open until the user tears it down? The answer is that there's no real difference. However, the coding practice of opening connections late and closing them early allows the pool to manage the number of connections and their lifetimes. This can be especially important when you start doing transactional work on a connection. Since there's no difference between using the pool and holding the connection open with application scope, you might as well use the pool, saving you from rewriting the data access layer if you should ever choose to move to an n-tiered architecture by adding a dedicated physical data access tier.

In ADO.NET 2.0, the capability to tear down a pool has been added. In 1.x, almost the only way the pool would release its connections was to end the process. There was also a bug in the perfmon tool that showed this connection count, leaving many people believing that connections remained open even after a process was torn down. These new methods give you the ability to choose when these connections close, by calling `ClearPool` to tear down a specific pool, or `ClearPools` to tear them all down. These are both static methods on the `SqlConnection` and `OracleConnection` types.

Connection Strings

Where to store the connection string is a challenge that every application using a relational database has to solve. This is a simple persistence problem, with a "chicken and an egg" twist. When a relational database is the chosen source of persistence, it's the default location for storing information. The connection string, however, is needed to get to your location of persistence. This, coupled with the fact that sensitive security information is often stored in the connection string, and that the string frequently needs to change as you move from development to staging to production, presents a problem that needs some careful consideration to solve.

You can hard code the connection string in a public, static string of some type in the application. This means the string becomes compiled into the application, which can have the feel of being more secure than storing somewhere in a flat file. Keep in mind, though, that .NET libraries are compiled to Common Intermediate Language (CIL) code, which can easily be decompiled.

Here's a line of code from a data access layer containing sensitive authentication information:

```
SqlConnection cn = new
  SqlConnection("server=.;database=pubs;uid=sa;pwd=password");
```

And here's the resulting, compiled, CIL code (viewed via ILDASM):

```
IL_0007:  ldstr       "server=.;database=pubs;uid=sa;pwd=password"
IL_000c:  newobj      instance void
[System.Data]System.Data.SqlClient.SqlConnection::.ctor(string)
```

Not really secure. Don't fool yourself into thinking that it is. To show you how connection strings can easily be secured, we're first going to look at a new feature—the `connectionStrings` element—in the Framework for connection string management. You need to see this feature in order to work your way back to how to protect connection strings. Take a look at the `connectionStrings` element in the configuration file:

```
<connectionStrings>
    <add name="localPubs"
        connectionString="server=.;database=pubs;uid=sa;pwd=123123"/>
    <add name="productionPubs"
connectionString="server=prodBox;database=pubs;uid=web_db_user;pwd=ab@2de3"/>
</connectionStrings>
```

This gives you a dedicated place in the configuration file for storing connection strings. The feature just acknowledges the fact that today a lot of folks are storing these strings in the `appSettings` element. By breaking it out into its own section, you separate the sensitive connection information from any other values you're storing within `appSettings`. Later you'll see how this enables you to encrypt this sensitive information, without having to also encrypt other less sensitive information in appSettings.

There's also now a dedicated method for retrieving connection strings from configuration. It's a static method of the ConfigurationManager type named ConnectionStrings (you can see this code in UseConnStr.aspx of the Web10 project).

```
protected void Page_Load(object sender, EventArgs e)
{
    string sConn = ConfigurationManager.ConnectionStrings["localPubs"].ToString();
    SqlConnection cn = new SqlConnection(sConn);
    SqlCommand cm = new SqlCommand("select * from authors", cn);
    GridView gv = new GridView();

    cn.Open();
    gv.DataSource = cm.ExecuteReader(CommandBehavior.CloseConnection);
    gv.DataBind();
    this.form1.Controls.Add(gv);
}
```

Changing a connection string in a configuration file as you move from environment to environment (QA to staging, for example) can be a dicey proposition. Someone could make a typo and the system would fail to connect in the new environment. It would be better to change a simple string describing the environment as the application moves through the development process.

```
<appSettings>
    <add key="EnvironmentName" value="local"/>
</appSettings>

<connectionStrings>
    <add name="local"
        connectionString="server=.;database=pubs;uid=sa;pwd=123123"/>
    <add name="production"
        connectionString="server=prodBox;database=pubs;uid=db_user;pwd=ab@2de3#"/>
</connectionStrings>
```

Now the connection strings portion of the configuration file can remain constant as the application moves across environments. The only thing that needs changing is the EnvironmentName value in appSettings. You then change the code to use the appSetting as the key for retrieving the connection string (see this code in UseConnStr.aspx of the Web10 project).

```
string Environment = ConfigurationManager.AppSettings["EnvironmentName"].ToString();
string Conn = ConfigurationManager.ConnectionStrings[Environment].ToString();
SqlConnection cn = new SqlConnection(Conn);
SqlCommand cm = new SqlCommand("select * from authors", cn);
```

This also better isolates the connection strings, making it easier to encrypt this portion of the configuration document and leave it encrypted, leaving the only thing that needs to be changed in the unencrypted appSettings portion of the file.

You can also use these connections strings from the markup in your page. Here's the declaration of a SqlDataSource control, which we'll be looking at in Chapter 11. With this code, though, notice how the connection string attribute is being set.

```
<asp:SqlDataSource Runat=server ID=sdsAuthors
    ConnectionString= '<%$ ConnectionStrings:localPubs %>'
    SelectCommand="select * from authors" />
```

This looks like a data-binding expression, but it is a new, hybrid syntax that can be embedded into your markup, and will be evaluated even when DataBind is not called on the Page.

Encrypting this section is very simple in 2.0. The capability to do encryption of any section of your configuration file has been added to the aspnet_regiis command-line tool. This feature of configuration is really nice, because it's completely transparent to the consumer of the encrypted information. Even with the connectionStrings section encrypted, all of the code you've looked at in this section will continue to work, with no changes. Doing the encryption is simple as well. The name of the web application you've been working on is Web10. Here's the call to aspnet_regiis that will encrypt the connection strings section of the configuration file:

```
aspnet_regiis -pe connectionStrings -app /Web10
```

This transforms the connectionStrings element of the web.config for the Web10 application into the following (abbreviated a bit):

```
<connectionStrings>
    <EncryptedData Type="http://www.w3.org/2001/04/xmlenc#Element"
        xmlns="http://www.w3.org/2001/04/xmlenc#">
        <EncryptionMethod Algorithm="http://www.w3.org/2001/04/..." />
        <KeyInfo xmlns="http://www.w3.org/2000/09/xmldsig#">
            <EncryptedKey Recipient="" xmlns="http://www.w3.org/2001/04/xmlenc#">
                <EncryptionMethod Algorithm="http://www.w3.org/2001/04/..." />
                <KeyInfo xmlns="http://www.w3.org/2000/09/xmldsig#">
                    <KeyName>Rsa Key</KeyName>
                </KeyInfo>
                <CipherData>
                    <CipherValue>c/2jOF+gayZtHeusqvsHkiEPeHzLOliKjo3eRkJUmI/Af+3Q...
                </CipherData>
            </EncryptedKey>
        </KeyInfo>
        <CipherData>
            <CipherValue>k2bGkbrLexSN8cz4iN8PgJF4qxy1OddDMJCU6EUe2+kboIdYf9Nwh...
        </CipherData>
    </EncryptedData>
</connectionStrings>
```

All of the code that uses these connection strings continues to work. To decrypt these values, use the same command with the -pd switch instead of -pe.

Data Readers

The data reader is the low memory footprint, forward-only, read-only method of data access. What it lacks in functionality, it makes up for in performance. By maintaining a low memory footprint, rather than loading the entire result set into the memory space of the web server, you greatly increase the scalability of data access operations using a data reader. It is ideally suited for generating HTML. When the data is being transformed directly into an HTML form or an HTML table, there's no real need to have random access to it in memory. Instead, the data is transformed into markup a row at a time. The markup is retained, but each row of data is discarded after it's processed. You can do almost all data-binding operations with the data reader.

Working with Data Readers

Data readers are created by an object factory built into the `Command` object. This is always how a reference to a reader is obtained. There are no data reader types with any public constructors, so it's impossible to create an instance of it directly. Instead, the `Command` type's `ExecuteReader` method uses the `Connection` property and `CommandText` property to execute the command against the database, and then returns a reference to an instance of a specific data reader type, which is ready and waiting to stream the results back as quickly as they can be consumed.

Data readers are designed to be executed and consumed as quickly as possible. Because they are forward-only, once the code has moved through the result set, the data is no longer available. Readers should be closed as soon as they've been consumed, freeing the connection to execute other commands. They do not inherit from `MarshalByRefObject`, nor are they flagged with the `Serializable` attribute, meaning they are bound within the application domain where they are created. References to readers should not be cached, marshaled across processes, or held as a field level variable. If you need any of this behavior with your result set, then you need to use a `DataSet` and not a reader.

Because data readers are read-only, when it comes time to move data back to the database, you must use something other than the data reader. You can use the `ExecuteNonQuery` method of the command object, which you should employ whenever you aren't expecting a result set back from the database. This can be for simple `insert`, `update`, or `delete` commands, but it can also be for calls to stored procedures that don't return a result set.

Even when dynamically generating SQL instead of using stored procedures, you should use the `Command`'s parameter collection instead of building values right into strings. The following code will work just fine to insert a row into a table. (You can see this code in app_Code\ DataReaderIE.cs of the Web10 project.)

```
public void InsertWithGenSql(string JobDescr, int MinLvl, int MaxLvl)
{
    string sql = string.Format(
        "INSERT INTO Jobs "
        + " (job_desc, min_lvl, max_lvl)"
        + " ('{0}', {1}, {2})",
        JobDescr, MinLvl, MaxLvl
    );
```

```
    SqlCommand cm =
        new SqlCommand(
        sql,
        new SqlConnection(
        "server=.;data6base=pubs;uid=sa;pwd=123123")
    );

    cm.Connection.Open();
    cm.ExecuteNonQuery();
    cm.Connection.Close();
}
```

But you should increase the scalability of this code by using parameters in the SQL string, and then creating parameter objects to hold the values. This is just a matter of being kind to your database. When you send in the hard-coded values in the string, the server has to parse the command, compile it, and then come up with an execution plan. When you send a new command string the next time a row is inserted, the server has to repeat the whole process. When a parameter is used, the server recognizes the second execution of the command as being fundamentally the same as the first. Instead of sending two different command strings, you're sending the same command strings that differ only by the values of the parameters built into the string. Here's the same insert logic implemented using parameters. (You can see this code in app_Code\DataReaderIE.cs of the Web10 project.).

```
public void InsertWithParams(string JobDescr, int MinLvl, int MaxLvl)
{
    string sql = "INSERT INTO Jobs "
        + " (job_desc, min_lvl, max_lvl)"
        + " ('@descr', @min, @max)";

    SqlCommand cm =
        new SqlCommand(
        sql,
        new SqlConnection(
        "server=.;database=pubs;uid=sa;pwd=123123")
    );

    cm.Parameters.Add(
            new SqlParameter(
            "@descr",
            SqlDbType.VarChar, 50)
        ).Value = JobDescr;

    cm.Parameters.Add(
            new SqlParameter(
            "@min",
            SqlDbType.TinyInt)
        ).Value = MinLvl;
```

```
    cm.Parameters.Add(
        new SqlParameter(
        "@min", SqlDbType.TinyInt)
        ).Value = MaxLvl;

    cm.Connection.Open();
    cm.ExecuteNonQuery();
    cm.Connection.Close();
}
```

When you can use them, stored procedures are your best option for data access. They live within the database server, and, thus, are always going to outperform other methods. Stored procedures are compiled and optimized internally, and they create a layer of abstraction between the consumer of the data and the actual data being consumed. They also simplify security, as you can grant execute permissions to the stored procedure without granting direct access to the underlying database tables. This enables the stored procedures to enforce a final layer of validation on the work being done on the database, making these rules impossible to circumvent with the credentials granted to an application.

You can use the facility of the DataReader to return multiple result sets with stored procedures as well. Here's a simple TSQL stored procedure that returns publisher details, authors, and titles that pertain to a specified publisher ID. (You can find a script to create this stored procedure in usp_GetPublisherDetails.sql in the Code10 project.)

```
create procedure usp_GetPublisherDetails
@pubid char(4)
as
select * from publishers
where pub_id = @pubid

select * from titles
where pub_id = @pubid

select * from authors
where au_id in
(select au_id from titleauthor
inner join titles on
titleauthor.title_id = titles.title_id
where titles.pub_id = @pubid)
```

Here's the code to execute this stored procedure and output the data as HTML tables to a web browser.

```
public partial class CallSproc_aspx : System.Web.UI.Page
{
    protected void Page_Load(object sender, EventArgs e)
    {
        bool bDone = false;
        SqlDataReader dr;
        string pubid;
```

```
        if (Request.QueryString["pubid"] == null)
            pubid = "0736";
        else
            pubid = Request.QueryString["pubid"].ToString();
        SqlCommand cm =
            new SqlCommand(
            "usp_GetPublisherDetails",
            new SqlConnection(ConfigurationManager.
            ConnectionStrings["localPubs"].ToString())
        );
        cm.CommandType = CommandType.StoredProcedure;
        cm.Parameters.Add(
            new SqlParameter(
            "@pubid",
            SqlDbType.Char, 4)
        ).Value = pubid;
        cm.Connection.Open();
        dr = cm.ExecuteReader();
        while (!bDone)
        {
            GridView gv = new GridView();
            gv.DataSource = dr;
            gv.DataBind();
            form1.Controls.Add(gv);
            bDone = !dr.NextResult();
        }
        dr.Close();
        cm.Connection.Close();
    }
}
```

By using output parameters and return values, you can use stored procedures in combination with the ExecuteNonQuery method of the Command object to quickly retrieve data from the server that's not in a tabular form. For example, you may have a procedure that calculates total sales for a given day and returns the amount as an output parameter. The code to execute this procedure would look like this. (This procedure is in app_Code\DataReaderIE.cs in the Web10 project.)

```
public double DailySalesTotal(DateTime day)
{
    SqlCommand cm =
        new SqlCommand(
        "usp_GetDailySalesTotal",
        new SqlConnection(
        "server=.;database=pubs;uid=sa;pwd=123123")
    );
```

```
cm.Parameters.Add(
        new SqlParameter(
        "@dayToCalc",
        SqlDbType.DateTime)
    ).Value = day;

cm.Parameters.Add(
        new SqlParameter(
        "@total",
        SqlDbType.Money)
    ). Direction = ParameterDirection.Output;

cm.Connection.Open();
cm.ExecuteNonQuery();
cm.Connection.Close();

return Convert.ToDouble(cm.Parameters["@total"].Value);
}
```

The advantage to this is that your process doesn't incur the overhead of preparing to retrieve a result set that you're not actually planning on getting back. Tabular data is a memory hog. Aside from the actual size of the data, there's a lot of metadata describing the result set that gets created in preparation for the set. This involves many allocations to the managed heap; therefore, it should be avoided when results aren't going to be processed as tabular data.

Even when retrieving a single row from the database, output parameters will perform better than a select statement. Here's a stored procedure that queries on the primary key of the publishers table; given this, it will always only return a single row of data (or none). (A script for this procedure is in usp_GetPubDetails.sql in the Code10 project.)

```
create procedure usp_GetPubDetails
@pub_id char(4),
@pub_name varchar(40) OUTPUT,
@city varchar(20) OUTPUT,
@state char(2) OUTPUT,
@country varchar(30) OUTPUT
as
SELECT
@pub_name = pub_name,
@city = city,
@state = state,
@country = country
FROM publishers
WHERE (pub_id = @pub_id)
```

Instead of incurring the overhead of using a data reader, this procedure is executed with ExecuteNonQuery, and the data is retrieved from the values of the output parameters. Here, the stored procedure is used from the custom constructor of a business object. (You'll find this business object in the app_Code\PublisherBO.cs file of the Web10 project.)

```csharp
public PublisherBO(string pubId)
{
    SqlCommand cm =
        new SqlCommand(
        "usp_GetPubDetails",
        new SqlConnection(ConfigurationManager.ConnectionStrings
                                        ["localPubs"].ToString())
    );

    cm.CommandType = CommandType.StoredProcedure;

    cm.Parameters.Add(
        new SqlParameter(
        "@pub_id",
        SqlDbType.Char,4)
    ).Value = pubId;

    cm.Parameters.Add(
        new SqlParameter(
        "@pub_name",
        SqlDbType.VarChar,10)
    ).Direction = ParameterDirection.Output;

    cm.Parameters.Add(
        new SqlParameter(
        "@city",
        SqlDbType.VarChar,10)
    ).Direction = ParameterDirection.Output;

    cm.Parameters.Add(
        new SqlParameter(
        "@state",
        SqlDbType.VarChar,10)
    ).Direction = ParameterDirection.Output;

    cm.Parameters.Add(
        new SqlParameter(
        "@country",
        SqlDbType.VarChar,10)
    ).Direction = ParameterDirection.Output;

    cm.Connection.Open();
    cm.ExecuteNonQuery();
    cm.Connection.Close();
```

```
        this.pubId = cm.Parameters["@pub_id"].Value.ToString();
        this.pubName = cm.Parameters["@pub_name"].Value.ToString();
        this.city  = cm.Parameters["@city"].Value.ToString();
        this.state = cm.Parameters["@state"].Value.ToString();
        this.country = cm.Parameters["@country"].Value.ToString();
}
```

When you need to retrieve a single value from a single row, an execute method for an even more specific type of query exists. This is basically a database lookup, where the select statement being used has a single column in the column list and is querying on a primary or unique column in the where clause. You can use ExecuteScalar as a programming convenience in this instance. It returns an instance of a System.Object, and, therefore, must always be cast into the return type expected. (You can find this code in app_Code\DataReaderIE.cs of the Web10 project.)

```
public int GetBookCount(string pubid)
{
    string sql = "select count(title_id) from titles "
        + "where pub_id = @pubid";

    SqlCommand cm =
        new SqlCommand(
        sql,
        new SqlConnection(ConfigurationManager.ConnectionStrings
                                        ["localPubs"].ToString())
    );

    cm.Parameters.Add(
        new SqlParameter(
        "@pubid", SqlDbType.Char, 4)
    ).Value = pubid;

    cm.Connection.Open();
    int count = Convert.ToInt32(cm.ExecuteScalar());
    cm.Connection.Close();

    return count;
}
```

A data reader should always be closed after the result set (or sets) are processed. Close the data reader before closing the Connection the reader is on. Also, be sure to understand the role and function of each of the different execute commands in the previous section, and use the one appropriate to the command being executed.

CommandBehavior

The ExecuteReader method has an overloaded footprint that accepts an instance of a CommandBehavior enumeration value. CommandBehavior enables you to influence the reader in many different ways. We list the different values of the CommandBehavior enumeration in Table 10-5.

Table 10-5. *Values of the* CommandBehavior *Enumeration and Their Effect on a Data Reader*

Enumeration Value	Meaning in Life
CloseConnection	Causes the connection used for the data reader to be closed when the data reader is closed.
Default	The default value used when no argument is specified and does not affect the behavior of the data reader.
KeyInfo	Returns only column and primary key information.
SchemaOnly	Gets only schema information from the database for the command, but executes the command against the database.
SequentialAccess	Causes a forward-only cursor to be placed over the columns, so that data not accessed by the program is not marshaled to the caller.
SingleResult	Use to inform the reader you're expecting only a single result set.
SingleRow	Use to inform the reader you're expecting only a single row. Managed Providers may use this to optimize the performance for returning a single row.

Let's talk about a scenario where you would use one of these behaviors: SequentialAccess. By default, a data reader loads an entire row into memory at once. It doesn't expose random access to rows of data, but random access is available for the columns within a single row. When you're working with a result set that has columns that can contain a lot of data (usually because of having a column of binary information in the result set), you can access only those large chunks of data on demand by setting the CommandBehavior to SequentialAccess.

When using SequentialAccess, the data reader grants forward-only access to the columns within a single row of data. If some criteria in the first few columns determine whether or not the large column will be accessed, you can use this option to avoid marshaling all of the data to the client for each and every row. There may not be many situations where this is actually necessary (hopefully you can apply the criteria at the database level and return only the binary-large objects you need), but it's a good technique to be aware of should the situation arise.

Final Notes on Data Readers

When executing several commands against the database, do not reuse the same instance of a Command object. Changing parameter values of a Command object is okay, but if the CommandText is changing, you should allocate a new instance of the Command object to the managed heap. This is a cheaper operation than the tear down and build up the Command object has to do when its CommandText changes.

Another peculiarity of data reader behavior occurs when there is a need to terminate the processing of the result before you get to the end of the result set. If a loop reads halfway through a result set and then calls the Close method, the rest of the results are marshaled to the caller before the reader is actually closed! To avoid this, call Cancel instead of Close to terminate processing the result set.

DataSets

The DataSet is a very feature-rich type for working with result sets in memory. Data can be modified, filtered, and sorted. It can be read from relational or hierarchical sources, and the DataSet provides a bridge between SQL and XML. Schema can be used from either a database or XML Schema document. Relationships can be established between result sets, which then enforce rules of referential integrity and can be used to navigate parent child relationships.

DataSets are always populated using the services of a DataAdapter. The DataAdapter is a provider-specific type, whereas there is only one DataSet, regardless of the provider being used. A DataSet actually neither knows nor cares where its data came from. Changes made to a DataSet exist only in memory until they are moved back to the database using a DataAdapter, or are sent to some form of persistence as a stream of XML.

We'll show you how put the DataSet through some of its motions. Here's a method that will try to retrieve a DataSet from the cache, and load it from the database if it's not already in the cache. (You can find this code in DataSetIE.aspx of the Web10 project.)

```
private DataSet GetSourceData()
{
    DataSet ds;

    ds = (DataSet)Cache["Pub_Title"];

    if (ds == null)
    {
        ds = new DataSet();
        SqlConnection cn = new
            SqlConnection
            ("server=.;database=pubs;uid=sa;pwd=123123");

        SqlCommand cm = new
            SqlCommand
            ("select * from publishers select * from titles", cn);

        SqlDataAdapter da = new SqlDataAdapter(cm);

        da.Fill(ds);

        ds.Tables[0].TableName = "Publishers";
        ds.Tables[1].TableName = "Titles";

        ds.Relations.Add(
            new DataRelation(
            "Pub_Title",
```

```
                ds.Tables["Publishers"].Columns["pub_id"],
                ds.Tables["Titles"].Columns["pub_id"]));

        Cache["Pub_Title"] = ds;

    }
    return ds;
}
```

Centralizing this functionality is a good idea, because any code that needs this data does not need to be concerned with where the data comes from or the caching policy applied to the data. Every place where this data is consumed simply calls the central function.

Notice also that you're using white space-separated select statements in the command text. This results in the data adapter retrieving both result sets and creating a DataTable for each of them. This technique can also be used with stored procedures that return multiple result sets. After the DataTables have been created and added to the DataSet, you provide them with string names. Now, another override of the Fill method that accepts a table name exists, but this name applies to the first table retrieved, leaving the rest of the tables with auto-generated names ("Table" for the first DataTable, then "Table1," "Table2," through "Table$n$"). Using the override where no name is provided, and then explicitly naming the tables after the fact provides for more readable code. Naming them is a good idea; they should be referred to in the rest of the code with explicit names instead of ordinal positions. Here's a case where the increased ease of maintenance using named tables exceeds the miniscule performance gain that would be gleamed by using ordinal positions.

You can then use the named tables to establish the relationship between them. This corresponds directly to the primary and foreign key relationship that exists between them in the database. A DataRelation will enforce the same rules on DataTables that a primary/foreign key relationship enforces within a database. At the point this relation is created, the DataSet checks the existing data to make sure the data complies with the rule, and then enforces the rule as changes are made to the data. You could not, for example, delete a publisher that had corresponding rows in the titles table. You'll use this relationship to find all of the titles that belong to the publisher your user selects.

Although this code is to be part of a code-behind for this example, this pattern will still work just fine when you're using a data access tier. The check in the cache can be done, and when it's not found, the DataSet can be retrieved by a call to a data access layer helper method (or a Web Service method).

The other common modification that you can make to this method is to break it out into a static method in a stand-alone helper class, so that it will be available from more than one page.

We're going to show you how to use this data to create a list of publishers, and when a choice is made from the list, render a GridView with all of the titles from the publisher. To do this, you'll leverage DataViews and DataSet relations.

Here's the simple markup for our page (from DataSetIE.aspx in Web10):

```
<%@ Page Language="C#"
CompileWith="DataSetIE.aspx.cs"
ClassName="DataSetIE_aspx" %>
<html xmlns="http://www.w3.org/1999/xhtml" >
```

```
<head runat="server">
    <title>DataSet IE</title>
</head>
<body>
    <form id="form1" runat="server">
        <asp:DropDownList Runat=server ID=ddlPub
            AutoPostBack=true
            OnSelectedIndexChanged="ddlPub_SelectedIndexChanged" />

        <asp:GridView Runat=server ID=gvTitle
            EnableViewState="false"
            BorderWidth="1px"
            BackColor="White"
            GridLines="Vertical"
            CellPadding="4"
            BorderStyle="None"
            BorderColor="#DEDFDE"
            ForeColor="Black">
            <FooterStyle BackColor="#CCCC99" />
            <PagerStyle ForeColor="Black"
                HorizontalAlign="Right"
                BackColor="#F7F7DE" />
            <HeaderStyle ForeColor="White"
                Font-Bold="True"
                BackColor="#6B696B" />
            <AlternatingRowStyle BackColor="White" />
            <SelectedRowStyle ForeColor="White"
                Font-Bold="True"
                BackColor="#CE5D5A" />
            <RowStyle BackColor="#F7F7DE" />
        </asp:GridView>
    </form>
</body>
</html>
```

Most of these attributes just establish the look and feel that the page will have. The important bits are the ones that determine that the DropDownList will automatically post back when a choice is made from the list, and the name of the method that will fire on the server when this occurs (AutoPostBack and OnSelectedIndexChanged).

From the code-behind, then, you have only to add the code that will bind the list, and the code that will bind the grid when the user makes a choice from the list. You'll bind the DropDownList when the page first loads (again, from DataSetIE.aspx in Web10):

```
protected void Page_Load(object sender, EventArgs e)
{
    if (!Page.IsPostBack)
    {
        ddlPub.DataSource = GetSourceData().Tables["Publishers"];
```

```
        ddlPub.DataTextField = "pub_name";
        ddlPub.DataValueField = "pub_id";
        ddlPub.DataBind();
        ddlPub.Items.Insert(0, "");
    }
}
```

Here you're drilling right into the reference of the DataSet's first table, and handing the reference straight to the data-binding engine. After the list is bound, you pop an empty item into the first position of the list, so that the page will not render with a "default" choice of publisher.

When the user makes a selection, you need to bind your GridView. Since you have the data cached, and you have a relationship established between publishers and titles, this will only take a few lines of code. For this operation, you'll use the DataView object, leveraging its intrinsic abilities to establish row filters and navigate relationships:

```
protected void ddlPub_SelectedIndexChanged(object sender, EventArgs e)
{
    DataView dv = new DataView(
        GetSourceData().Tables["Publishers"],
        string.Format("pub_id = '{0}'",
        ddlPub.SelectedValue), "",
        DataViewRowState.CurrentRows);
    if (dv.Count > 0)
    {
        gvTitle.DataSource = dv[0].CreateChildView("Pub_Title");
        gvTitle.DataBind();
    }
}
```

Although this is only a few lines of code, you're making the DataView do quite a bit of work in its constructor. The first parameter to the constructor is, of course, the DataTable you want to create a view on. The second is the RowFilter you're applying to the view. Here you use the value of the drop-down list to describe the publisher the user has selected. Since you're filtering on the primary key of the publishers table, you know you only ever have one row in the result set of the view. The next parameter is a sort, which you're leaving blank as there's no sense in sorting a single row, and the last is an enum indicating the state of the rows you want to query. CurrentRows should be the default, and there should be an overridden constructor that omits this argument. Since there is not, you provide it here.

After the constructor finishes its work, you'll have a DataView object with a single row in it, corresponding to the publisher the user has selected in the interface. To bind the grid, then, you'll use the CreateChildView method of the DataViewRow class, which allows you to navigate from a row of data in the parent view to its collection of children in a new view that gets created by the method. You can pass an instance of a relation to this method, or just name a relation, as you're doing here.

Another handy facility of the DataSet is the capability to bind a column to an expression. You can use this to create simple aggregates across relationships. You can add an OrderTotal

column to an Orders table that uses a relationship to calculate the total from the OrderItem
child table. This example adds an average price column to the DataSet used in the last example, and displays it at the top of the grid when a publisher is chosen. First you add a line of
code to the GetSourceData method, just after the relation is created.

```
ds.Tables["Publishers"].Columns.Add(
    new DataColumn(
        "AveragePrice",
        typeof(double),
        "Avg(Child.price)"));
```

Here you're adding a new DataColumn to the collection of columns for the publisher table.
The first two constructor parameters are the name and type of the column. The third is our
column expression. This string tells the DataTable to use the relation to get to its child table,
and compute an average of all the prices in its collection of child rows. Other simple aggregates are valid in these expressions as well. If there's more than one relation on the parent
table, you can also build the relation name into the expression.

```
Avg(Child(Pub_Title).price)
```

You can now use this column to output the average when the user makes a selection from
the publisher list. You've added a label control named lblAvgPrice next to the drop-down list
in the markup of the page. The output is then done from the SelectedIndexChanged event trap.

```
if (dv[0]["AveragePrice"] != DBNull.Value)
    lblAvgPrice.Text =
        Convert.ToDouble(dv[0]["AveragePrice"]).ToString("C");
```

Enhancements in 2.0

The DataSet gets a nice set of enhancements in version 2.0 of the Framework. The performance of the DataSet has been optimized for large row counts in a DataTable. Performance here
is typically twice as fast. The indexing engine is a complete rewrite, also to accommodate large
row counts. For Remoting, the DataSet can now be marshaled across processes as a binary
stream of information, greatly reducing the footprint of what gets passed on the wire. The
DataTable itself also gets a major facelift, reducing many of the dependencies it has on the
DataSet in version 1.x of the Framework. For example, with version 1.x of the Framework
there's no way you can read an XML document from the file system and create a DataTable
without using a DataSet, even if you know the DataSet will have only a single DataTable in it.
And a new method on the DataTable allows you to get a reference to a data reader for reading
the DataTable data using a cursor-based approach, without the aid of a DataAdapter.
    A very useful new feature of the DataTable allows you to read data from the database
using a data reader and create an instance of a DataTable without using the services of a
DataAdapter and without involving a DataSet. This would take a significant amount of coding
to do in 1.x, but in 2.0, it's built into the DataTable via the Load method. Here you use the new
Load method on the DataTable to load the author's data into memory (see DataTableIE.aspx in
the Web10 project).

```
public DataTable GetAuthorData()
{
    string conn = ConfigurationManager.ConnectionStrings["localPubs"].ToString();
    SqlConnection cn = new SqlConnection(conn);
    SqlCommand cm = new SqlCommand("select * from authors", cn);
    DataTable dt = new DataTable();

    cn.Open();
    dt.Load(cm.ExecuteReader());
    cn.Close();
    return dt;
}
```

The benefit here is twofold. First, you don't have to create a DataAdapter. The smarts of the adapter have been built into the DataTable, making the coding model much simpler. Second, you don't need to create a DataSet. Creating an instance of a DataSet is pure wasted overhead whenever you're expecting a single result set. What good is it with a single result set? "It can write out the data as XML," you may say. "It can write out schema for the data, too!" you may add. Well the DataTable can now do those things, too. The ReadXML and WriteXml methods from the DataSet have been added to the DataTable, along with the corresponding methods for reading and writing schema information, so you can do single table transformations from hierarchical to relational data and back again. Here you see a method that will write a DataTable out to disk (in DataTableIE.aspx from Web10).

```
public void SaveDataTableToDisk(DataTable dt)
{
    string schemaFile = string.Format("{0}.xsd",dt.TableName);
    string xmlFile = string.Format("{0}.xml",dt.TableName);

    schemaFile = Server.MapPath(schemaFile);
    xmlFile = Server.MapPath(xmlFile);

    dt.WriteXmlSchema(schemaFile);
    dt.WriteXml(xmlFile);
}
```

This code may seem familiar to you, because WriteXml and WriteXmlSchema have been available on the DataSet for years. This is their first appearance on the DataTable, though. You can read the DataTable back in from disk with other familiar methods adopted from the DataSet, as well (in DataTableIE.aspx from Web10).

```
public DataTable ReadDataTableFromDisk(string TableName)
{
    DataTable dt = new DataTable(TableName);
    string schemaFile = string.Format("{0}.xsd", TableName);
    string xmlFile = string.Format("{0}.xml", TableName);

    schemaFile = Server.MapPath(schemaFile);
    xmlFile = Server.MapPath(xmlFile);
```

```
    dt.ReadXmlSchema(schemaFile);
    dt.ReadXml(xmlFile);

    return dt;
}
```

Another very nice new feature of the DataTable is the addition of a data reader factory method. Here the DataTable learns a new trick from the Command object. Command objects have always exposed the ExecuteReader method, which serves as a factory for provider-specific data readers. The DataTable now exposes the CreateDataReader method, which will create a forward-only cursor for us to traverse the DataTable data with. The type it returns is a DataTableReader, which implements the IDataReader interface and so is type-compatible with data readers from other Managed Providers.

Let's say, for example, that you've made caching data in your site a configurable behavior. More specifically, you've added a UseCaching entry to the appSettings of the web.config. (This entry is in the web.config of the Web10 project.)

```
<appSettings>
    <add key="UseCaching" value="false" />
</appSettings>
```

When set to true, you're going to cache data on the web server so you don't need to go back to the database for it with every request. When false, you're going to go back to the database with every request. This strategy can be used effectively in combination with SQL Cache Dependencies (see Chapter 11). In either case, you want to bind to a data reader instead of a DataTable, so when you're not caching you don't take the hit of loading the entire result set up in memory. Because the DataTable now returns a data reader-compatible cursor, a single method can account for both of these scenarios (from DataTableIE.aspx in Web10).

```
public IDataReader GetTitleReader()
{
    bool caching = Convert.ToBoolean(
        ConfigurationManager.AppSettings["UseCaching"]);
    DataTable dt = null;
    IDataReader dr;

    if (caching) dt = (DataTable)Cache["TitleData"];

    if (dt == null)
    {
        string conn =
                ConfigurationManager.ConnectionStrings["localPubs"].ToString();
        SqlConnection cn = new SqlConnection(conn);
        SqlCommand cm = new SqlCommand("select * from titles", cn);
        dt = new DataTable();

        cn.Open();
        if (caching)
        {
```

```
            dt.Load(cm.ExecuteReader());
            Cache.Insert("TitleData", dt);
            cn.Close();
            dr = dt.CreateDataReader();
        }
        else
        {
            dr = cm.ExecuteReader(CommandBehavior.CloseConnection);
        }
    }
    else
    {
        dr = dt.CreateDataReader();
    }

    return dr;
}
```

This method deals with three main possibilities. When caching is off, you return a SqlDataReader streaming data straight from the database. Or caching can be on. If it's on, the DataTable may be in the cache. If so, you'll call the CreateDataReader method and return it to the caller. If not, you use the Load method of the DataTable to load the data, and then call CreateDataReader to return to the caller.

Code calling this method doesn't need to be concerned with where the data is coming from and whether or not it's being cached. It just binds (also from DataTableIE.aspx).

```
gv = new GridView();
gv.DataSource = GetTitleReader();
gv.DataBind();
this.form1.Controls.Add(gv);
```

While the DataSet continues to be a very powerful object, you can largely retire it to the work it's good at, which is dealing with multiple result sets. The DataAdapter may make less frequent appearances as well. With these upgrades to the DataTable, this type moves into the primary role when the focus is on a single result set, shedding its former limitations that forced you to unnecessarily tangential instances.

DataSets vs. DataReaders

The choice between a DataSet and a data reader is one of functionality versus performance. The DataSet is very full-featured, but these features come at the price of resource consumption and performance. The data reader, on the other hand, is a very fast, very low footprint method for processing a result set.

So choose which one to use based on the requirements of the data processing that's being done. Understanding what can be done with each data access method is the key to consistently making this choice quickly and correctly.

A data reader cannot sort your result set. You can build sorting into a SQL statement or a stored procedure, but when you're using a stored procedure, it cannot be dynamically built into the procedure definition itself. A stored procedure that dynamically generates the statements it is going to execute is not much better than dynamically generated SQL. What gets compiled and optimized is the code that generates the statement, not the actual execution of that statement. All the work that has to be done with dynamically generated SQL passed in as command text has to also be done with statements that are generated within a stored procedure and executed using sp_executesql or a similar facility built in to your database.

This can become a problem when you're allowing your users to pick which columns they want to sort on. Either you need a stored procedure for each possible sort value or you need to dynamically generate the statement.

Using a GridView, we'll show you some of the differences in solving this problem with a data reader and a DataSet. The GridView itself is very simple (see SortIE.aspx in Web10).

```
<asp:GridView Runat=server ID=gvAuthors
    EnableViewState=false
    AllowSorting=True
    OnSorting="gvAuthors_Sorting"
    BorderWidth="1px"
    BackColor="White"
    GridLines="Vertical"
    CellPadding="3"
    BorderStyle="Solid"
    BorderColor="#999999"
    ForeColor="Black">
    <FooterStyle BackColor="#CCCCCC" />
    <PagerStyle ForeColor="Black"
        HorizontalAlign="Center"
        BackColor="#999999" />
    <HeaderStyle ForeColor="White"
        Font-Bold="True"
        BackColor="Black" />
    <AlternatingRowStyle BackColor="#CCCCCC" />
    <SelectedRowStyle ForeColor="White"
        Font-Bold="True"
        BackColor="#000099" />
</asp:GridView>
```

The grid is bound by a method named BindGrid. You'll be implementing several different versions of this method. This code will be common to all of the examples (see SortIE.aspx in Web10).

```
protected void gvAuthors_Sorting(object sender, GridViewSortEventArgs e
{
    BindGrid(e.SortExpression);
}

protected void Page_Load(object sender, EventArgs e)
{
    BindGrid("au_id");
}
```

The grid, when rendered, will be a simple dump of the author data (see Figure 10-2). The column headers, however, will be rendered as hyperlinks because you set `AllowSorting` to `true` in the declaration of the grid. Clicking on the column header is what causes the gvAuthors_Sorting event to fire on the server. The name of the column the user has clicked on will be passed along to this event trap as `SortExpression`.

au_id	au_lname	au_fname	phone	address	city	state	zip	contract
172-32-1176	White	Johnson	408 496-7223	10932 Bigge Rd.	Menlo Park	CA	94025	☑
213-46-8915	Green	Marjorie	415 986-7020	309 63rd St. #411	Oakland	CA	94618	☑
238-95-7766	Carson	Charlie	415 548-7723	589 Darwin Ln.	Berkeley	CA	94705	☑
267-41-2394	O'Leary	Michael	408 286-2428	22 Cleveland Av. #14	San Jose	CA	95128	☑
274-80-9391	Straight	Dean	415 834-2919	5420 College Av.	Oakland	CA	94609	☑
341-22-1782	Smith	Meander	913 843-0462	10 Mississippi Dr.	Lawrence	KS	66044	☐
409-56-7008	Bennet	Abraham	415 658-9932	6223 Bateman St.	Berkeley	CA	94705	☑
427-17-2319	Dull	Ann	415 836-7128	3410 Blonde St.	Palo Alto	CA	94301	☑
472-27-2349	Gringlesby	Burt	707 938-6445	PO Box 792	Covelo	CA	95428	☑
486-29-1786	Locksley	Charlene	415 585-4620	18 Broadway Av.	San Francisco	CA	94130	☑
527-72-3246	Greene	Morningstar	615 297-2723	22 Graybar House Rd.	Nashville	TN	37215	☐
648-92-1872	Blotchet-Halls	Reginald	503 745-6402	55 Hillsdale Bl.	Corvallis	OR	97330	☑
672-71-3249	Yokomoto	Akiko	415 935-4228	3 Silver Ct.	Walnut Creek	CA	94595	☑
712-45-1867	del Castillo	Innes	615 996-8275	2286 Cram Pl. #86	Ann Arbor	MI	48105	☑
722-51-5454	DeFrance	Michel	219 547-9982	3 Balding Pl.	Gary	IN	46403	☑
724-08-9931	Stringer	Dirk	415 843-2991	5420 Telegraph Av.	Oakland	CA	94609	☐
724-80-9391	MacFeather	Stearns	415 354-7128	44 Upland Hts.	Oakland	CA	94612	☑
756-30-7391	Karsen	Livia	415 534-9219	5720 McAuley St.	Oakland	CA	94609	☑
807-91-6654	Panteley	Sylvia	301 946-8853	1956 Arlington Pl.	Rockville	MD	20853	☑
846-92-7186	Hunter	Sheryl	415 836-7128	3410 Blonde St.	Palo Alto	CA	94301	☑
893-72-1158	McBadden	Heather	707 448-4982	301 Putnam	Vacaville	CA	95688	☐

Figure 10-2. *The authors data displayed in a grid for sorting*

First you'll dynamically generate the SQL (see `SortIE.aspx` in Web10).

```
private void BindGrid(string sortExpr)
{
    SqlConnection cn = new
        SqlConnection ConfigurationManager.ConnectionStrings
        ["localPubs"].ToString());

    SqlCommand cm = new
        SqlCommand
        (string.Format(
            "select * from authors order by {0}",
            sortExpr),
        cn);
```

```
    cn.Open();
    gvAuthors.DataSource = cm.ExecuteReader();
    gvAuthors.DataBind();
    cn.Close();
}
```

When this page is put under load, it serves about 106 requests per second. Of course, this is specific to the machine that it's running on, but in the following examples, you'll be changing nothing except the data access method, so you should get a good relative gauge as to how these sorting methods compare. Next, you'll move the dynamic generation of the SQL into that database, using this stored procedure (script for this can be found in usp_SortAuthors.sql in the Code10 directory).

```
create procedure usp_SortAuthors
@sortExpr varchar(25)
as
declare @sql varchar(100)

set @sql = 'select * from authors order by ' + @sortExpr

EXEC(@sql)
Go
```

The BindGrid method of your test page will be modified to call this stored procedure instead of generating the SQL itself. The sort expression will be passed as a parameter to the stored procedure (see SortIE.aspx in Web10).

```
private void BindGrid(string sortExpr)
{
    SqlConnection cn = new
            SqlConnection ConfigurationManager.ConnectionStrings
            ["localPubs"].ToString());

    SqlCommand cm = new
        SqlCommand("usp_SortAuthors", cn);

    cm.CommandType = CommandType.StoredProcedure;
    cm.Parameters.Add(
        new SqlParameter(
            "@sortExpr",
            SqlDbType.VarChar,
            25)).Value = sortExpr;

    cn.Open();
    gvAuthors.DataSource = cm.ExecuteReader();
    gvAuthors.DataBind();
    cn.Close();
}
```

This method yields about 104 requests per second. Clearly, you're not getting the gains you'd expect to by moving to a stored procedure. You're simply not saving the database any work; you're just moving the SQL generating logic into another process.

Next you'll try a dedicated stored procedure for each column the user can sort by. You'll dynamically generate these stored procedures (see SortIE.aspx in Web10).

```
private void GenSprocs()
{
    SqlConnection cn = new
            SqlConnection ConfigurationManager.ConnectionStrings
            ["localPubs"].ToString());

    SqlCommand cm = new
        SqlCommand("select * from authors", cn);

    DataSet ds = new DataSet();

    cn.Open();
    SqlDataAdapter da = new SqlDataAdapter(cm);

    da.Fill(ds);

    foreach (DataColumn dc in ds.Tables[0].Columns)
    {
        string sql = "create procedure usp_SortAuthors_{0} as "
            + "select * from authors order by {0}";
        sql = string.Format(sql, dc.ColumnName);
        cm = new SqlCommand(sql, cn);

        cm.ExecuteNonQuery();

    }
    cn.Close();
}
```

Now you'll modify the BindGrid method to dynamically build the name of the stored procedure you'll call (see SortIE.aspx in Web10).

```
private void BindGrid(string sortExpr)
{
    SqlConnection cn = new
            SqlConnection(ConfigurationManager.ConnectionStrings
            ["localPubs"].ToString());

    SqlCommand cm = new SqlCommand
        (string.Format("usp_SortAuthors_{0}",sortExpr), cn);

    cm.CommandType = CommandType.StoredProcedure;
```

```
    cn.Open();
    gvAuthors.DataSource = cm.ExecuteReader();
    gvAuthors.DataBind();
    cn.Close();
}
```

This method bears about 110 requests per second. This improvement isn't much, and you may expect more because you've moved away from dynamically generated SQL and are using stored procedures. However, the statements are not that complex, and the lion's share of the work is the actual sorting of the data. With this in mind, an improvement this size is almost surprising. This method is not very maintainable. Each of these stored procedures now has to be maintained. In a real application, the logic retrieving the data is going to be more complex than select * from a table. Any change to this logic will have to be propagated across all of these stored procedures. This is probably just not a reasonable, realistic solution.

The real way to help this situation is to index all of the columns you're sorting by. Here, though, you're allowing the user to sort by *all* of the columns, and this many indexes is probably not a reasonable option. This is something to consider when designing an interface that enables users to pick what they sort by. It may be better to pick a subset of the columns that are most common to sort by and add indexes to those.

The best thing to increase the performance of this page is going to be to cache the data in the memory of the web server, instead of going back to the database for it on each request. You already know that a data reader cannot be sorted, and you've examined several strategies for doing the sorting at the database. Take a look at what happens when you move the data to the client. First, you'll pull that data access out into a helper method, centralizing the command and caching logic (see SortIE.aspx in Web10).

```
private DataSet GetAuthors()
{
    DataSet ds;

    ds = (DataSet)Cache["AuthorData"];

    if (ds == null)
    {
        ds = new DataSet();
        SqlConnection cn = new SqlConnection
            ("server=.;database=pubs;uid=sa;pwd=123123");

        SqlCommand cm = new
            SqlCommand("select * from authors", cn);

        new SqlDataAdapter(cm).Fill(ds);

        Cache.Insert("AuthorData", ds);

    }
    return ds;
}
```

Then you'll modify BindGrid to use the cached data from the DataSet instead of a data reader. You'll use the construction semantics of the DataView to apply the sort the user has requested (see SortIE.aspx in Web10).

```
private void BindGrid(string sortExpr)
{
    gvAuthors.DataSource = new DataView(
        GetAuthors().Tables[0], "",
        sortExpr,
        DataViewRowState.CurrentRows);

    gvAuthors.DataBind();
}
```

This method yields an average of about 126 requests per second, but from the chart displayed in Figure 10-3, you can see this processing is really erratic. The server can handle about 145 requests per second; there are just consistent drops in the processing.

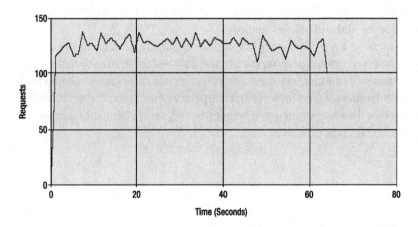

Figure 10-3. *Results per second when caching data and sorting with a* DataView

The problem is the number of allocations you're making to the managed heap. Every time a request occurs, you're allocating a DataView to the heap. With all the requests coming in, this forces the garbage collector to do frequent sweeps and reclaim the memory you've used for previous requests. This leads to the up and down peak load the server can handle. Instead of creating a view for each user, you'll want to get more aggressive in the use of the cache. In this version, you'll cache each DataView; thus, all users will share the same instance of the DataView, and there will only be one per sort in the cache (see SortIE.aspx in Web10).

```
private void BindGrid(string sortExpr)
{
    DataView dv;
    string sCacheEntry =
        string.Format("Author_Sort_{0}", sortExpr);

    dv = (DataView)Cache[sCacheEntry];
```

```
    if (dv == null)
    {
        dv = new DataView(
            GetAuthors().Tables[0], "",
            sortExpr,
            DataViewRowState.CurrentRows);
        Cache.Insert(sCacheEntry, dv);
    }

    gvAuthors.DataSource = dv;
    gvAuthors.DataBind();
}
```

Here, you get 136 requests per second, making this the best performing option. This also consumes fewer resources than the previous example, as you only have one DataView per sort instead of one per request.

In-memory filtering of the data is another example of a task that the DataSet and DataViews are particularly suited for. Again, you could implement this at the database tier, but if you're giving the user control over the column they're querying on, once again you're looking at having to use dynamic SQL generation. Sorting on a column using a DataView causes the DataView to index that column under the hood, so you get an optimized structure for applying the filter.

For this example, you'll display a list of states, and when the user selects one, display a grid of the authors from that state. You'll once again use a DropDownList and a GridView (the code for this demo can be found in Filtering.aspx of the Web10 project).

```
<asp:DropDownList Runat=server ID=ddlState
    AutoPostBack="True"
    OnSelectedIndexChanged="ddlState_SelectedIndexChanged" />
<asp:GridView Runat=server ID=gvAuthors
    EnableViewState=False
    BorderWidth="1px"
    BackColor="LightGoldenrodYellow"
    GridLines="None"
    CellPadding="2"
    BorderColor="Tan"
    ForeColor="Black">
    <FooterStyle BackColor="Tan" />
    <PagerStyle ForeColor="DarkSlateBlue"
        HorizontalAlign="Center"
        BackColor="PaleGoldenrod" />
    <HeaderStyle Font-Bold="True"
        BackColor="Tan" />
    <AlternatingRowStyle BackColor="PaleGoldenrod" />
    <SelectedRowStyle ForeColor="GhostWhite"
        BackColor="DarkSlateBlue" />
</asp:GridView>
```

The list gets bound upon the first request of the page.

```
protected void Page_Load(object sender, EventArgs e)
{
    if (!IsPostBack)
    {
        SqlConnection cn = new SqlConnection(
                ConfigurationManager.ConnectionStrings
                ["localPubs"].ToString());

        string sql =
        "select state from authors group by state order by state";
        SqlCommand cm = new
            SqlCommand(sql, cn);

        cn.Open();
        ddlState.DataSource = cm.ExecuteReader();
        ddlState.DataTextField = "state";
        ddlState.DataBind();
        cn.Close();
        ddlState.Items.Insert(0, "");
    }
}
```

All postbacks are then fired by a change made to the DropDownList. Here's where you'll use a cached DataView that already has an index prepared for the state column of the authors table. By applying a row filter to the view, you're leveraging the index on the column you sorted by when creating the view. By keeping it in the cache you are once again using only a single instance of the data instead of returning to the database each time the user selects a state.

```
private DataView GetAuthors()
{
    DataSet ds;
    DataView dv;

    dv = (DataView)Cache["AuthorData"];

    if (dv == null)
    {
        ds = new DataSet();
        SqlConnection cn = new SqlConnection(
                ConfigurationManager.ConnectionStrings
                ["localPubs"].ToString());
```

```
        SqlCommand cm = new
            SqlCommand("select * from authors", cn);

        new SqlDataAdapter(cm).Fill(ds);

        dv =
            new DataView
            (ds.Tables[0], "",
            "state",
            DataViewRowState.CurrentRows);

        Cache.Insert("AuthorData", dv);

    }
    return dv;

}
protected void ddlState_SelectedIndexChanged(object sender, EventArgs e)
{
    DataView dv = GetAuthors();

    dv.RowFilter =
        string.Format("state = '{0}'", ddlState.SelectedValue);

    gvAuthors.DataSource = dv;
    gvAuthors.DataBind();
}
```

Here again, you could go back to the database with each request that comes into the server, but you'll be much better off keeping a cache of this data in memory and using the DataView to create an index on the data you'll be querying upon. If the users can choose the column they want to apply the filter to, you can apply a strategy similar to the one you used in the sorting example, creating a cached DataView per column being queried upon.

The problem with an in-memory cache is, of course, concurrency and dirty data. When someone comes along and makes a change to the data, the cache entry is no longer useful to you. In Chapter 11, we take a look at the new facility that's been added to 2.0 to create a dependency between a cache entry and the relational database where the entry came from, the SqlCacheDependency.

We also examine some overall strategies for managing latency and concurrency when modifying data.

Managed Provider Factories

Version 2.0 of the Framework introduces a factory model for creating instances of data access objects. Using this factory enables you to write code that's generic across different database vendors. This feature is available through ADO, but to write vendor-neutral code in .NET requires using an interface-based late bound programming model or one of the backwards compatibility Managed Providers, such as OLEDB or ODBC. The interface-based approach involves programming against the interfaces common to all Managed Providers, and then using Reflection or a custom-written factory to actually load instances of types at runtime. The backwards compatibility layer introduces a serious performance hit to your managed applications. This is particularly painful if the databases you're supporting do provide Managed Providers coded specifically for those vendors' platforms. You don't ever want to, for example, use the OLEDB Managed Provider to talk to SQL Server 2000.

So in 2.0, there's a Provider Factory model. This factory enables you to let configuration entries drive what database you're to use, but get instances of types from specific Managed Providers at runtime. So if you're using SQL Server, you get a SqlConnection object to use from your code. If you're using Oracle, you get an OracleConnection.

The services of the Provider Factory are exposed through a couple of types that Microsoft added to the System.Data.Common namespace. DbProviderFactories exposes a couple of simple shared methods (see Table 10-6).

Table 10-6. *The Shared Methods of the* DbProviderFactories *type*

Shared Method	Meaning in Life
GetFactoryClasses	This method returns a DataTable with metadata about all of the installed providers on the system.
GetFactory	This method returns an instance of a DbProviderFactory type. It accepts an argument that describes the factory—either a DataRow from the DataTable returned by GetFactoryClasses, or an "invariant name" of the provider, which is a column returned in the DataTable.

All of the configured Managed Providers are available through the services of the Provider Factory. To get a list of installed providers on a system, you can use the GetFactoryClasses method on the DbProviderFactory type (see Default.aspx in Web10).

```
protected void Page_Load(object sender, EventArgs e)
{
    GridView gv = new GridView();
    gv.DataSource = DbProviderFactories.GetFactoryClasses();
    gv.DataBind();
    form1.Controls.Add(gv);
}
```

By binding this DataTable to a grid, you can see the information it returns, and a list of the installed providers on the machine, shown here in Figure 10-4.

Name	Description	InvariantName	AssemblyQualifiedName
Odbc Data Provider	.Net Framework Data Provider for Odbc	System.Data.Odbc	System.Data.Odbc.OdbcFactory, System.Data, Version=2.0.0.0, Culture=neutral, PublicKeyToken=b77a5c561934e089
OleDb Data Provider	.Net Framework Data Provider for OleDb	System.Data.OleDb	System.Data.OleDb.OleDbFactory, System.Data, Version=2.0.0.0, Culture=neutral, PublicKeyToken=b77a5c561934e089
OracleClient Data Provider	.Net Framework Data Provider for Oracle	System.Data.OracleClient	System.Data.OracleClient.OracleClientFactory, System.Data.OracleClient, Version=2.0.0.0, Culture=neutral, PublicKeyToken=b77a5c561934e089
SqlClient Data Provider	.Net Framework Data Provider for SqlServer	System.Data.SqlClient	System.Data.SqlClient.SqlClientFactory, System.Data, Version=2.0.0.0, Culture=neutral, PublicKeyToken=b77a5c561934e089
SQL Server CE Data Provider	.NET Framework Data Provider for Microsoft SQL Server 2005 Mobile Edition	Microsoft.SqlServerCe.Client	Microsoft.SqlServerCe.Client.SqlCeClientFactory, Microsoft.SqlServerCe.Client, Version=9.0.242.0, Culture=neutral, PublicKeyToken=89845dcd8080cc91

Figure 10-4. *The data returned by* GetProviderFactories, *listing the installed Managed Providers on the system*

In Figure 10-4, you can see the data contained in the DataTable returned by GetObjectFactories, including all of the invariant names of the providers, which you can use to create instances of the factory for a specific provider. All of the installed providers are registered in the machine.config under a new element named DbProviderFactories.

```
<system.data>
  <DbProviderFactories>
    <add name="Odbc Data Provider"
         invariant="System.Data.Odbc"
         description=".Net Framework Data Provider for Odbc"
         type="System.Data.Odbc.OdbcFactory, System.Data, Version=..." />
    <add name="OleDb Data Provider"
         invariant="System.Data.OleDb"
         description=".Net Framework Data Provider for OleDb"
         type="System.Data.OleDb.OleDbFactory, System.Data, Version=..." />
    <add name="OracleClient Data Provider"
         invariant="System.Data.OracleClient"
         description=".Net Framework Data Provider for Oracle"
         type="System.Data.OracleClient.OracleClientFactory, System.Data..." />
    <add name="SqlClient Data Provider"
         invariant="System.Data.SqlClient"
         description=".Net Framework Data Provider for SqlServer"
         type="System.Data.SqlClient.SqlClientFactory, System.Data, Version=..." />
    <add name="SQL Server CE Data Provider"
         invariant="Microsoft.SqlServerCe.Client"
         support="3F7"
```

```
        description=".NET Framework Data Provider for Microsoft SQL Server ..."
        type="Microsoft.SqlServerCe.Client.SqlCeClientFactory, Microsoft...." />
    </DbProviderFactories>
  </system.data>
  <system.web>
```

If you want to use a new or third-party provider with the Provider Factory, you must register it in configuration using the DbProviderFactory element. You can make this entry in the machine.config, or if you only plan to use the provider from a specific application, you can enter into the web.config.

The other method on DbProviderFactories returns an instance of DbProviderFactory. This type exposes eight factory methods for creating instance of connections, commands, parameters, and whatever other objects you need for interacting with your database. Here, you create an instance of the SQL Server Managed Provider factory and use it to execute a parameterize query against the database using the generic types served by the DbProviderFactory. (You can find this code in UseFactory.aspx of Web10.)

```
protected void Page_Load(object sender, EventArgs e)
{
    DbProviderFactory factory =
        DbProviderFactories.GetFactory("System.Data.SqlClient");
    DbConnection cn = factory.CreateConnection();
    cn.ConnectionString =
        ConfigurationManager.ConnectionStrings
        ["localPubs"].ToString();
    DbCommand cm = factory.CreateCommand();
    cm.Connection = cn;
    cm.CommandText = "select * from authors where [state] = @state";
    DbParameter pm = factory.CreateParameter();
    pm.ParameterName = "@state";
    pm.Value = "CA";
    cm.Parameters.Add(pm);

    GridView gv = new GridView();
    cn.Open();
    gv.DataSource = cm.ExecuteReader(CommandBehavior.CloseConnection);
    gv.DataBind();
    form1.Controls.Add(gv);
}
```

The code listed previously generates the Web Form displayed in Figure 10-5.

Notice the types you're using aren't SQL Server-specific. You're not using a SqlConnection object; you're using a DbConnection object. There is a whole set of these new types in the System.Data.Common namespace. They're created by the factory to represent a specific provider, but expose a generic type and programming model to the developer using the types (see Table 10-7).

au_id	au_lname	au_fname	phone	address	city	state	zip	contract
172-32-1176	White1	Johnson	408 496-7223	10932 Bigge Rd.	Menlo Park	CA	94025	☑
213-46-8915	Green	Marjorie	415 986-7020	309 63rd St. #411	Oakland	CA	94618	☑
238-95-7766	Carson	Charlie	415 548-7723	589 Darwin Ln.	Berkeley	CA	94705	☑
267-41-2394	O'Leary	Michael	408 286-2428	22 Cleveland Av. #14	San Jose	CA	95128	☑
274-80-9391	Straight	Dean	415 834-2919	5420 College Av.1	Oakland	CA	94609	☑
409-56-7008	Bennet	Abraham	415 658-9932	6223 Bateman St.	Berkeley	CA	94705	☑
427-17-2319	Dull	Ann	415 836-7128	3410 Blonde St.	Palo Alto	CA	94301	☑
472-27-2349	Gringlesby	Burt	707 938-6445	PO Box 792	Covelo	CA	95428	☑
486-29-1786	Locksley	Charlene	415 585-4620	18 Broadway Av.	San Francisco	CA	94130	☑
672-71-3249	Yokomoto	Akiko	415 935-4228	3 Silver Ct.	Walnut Creek	CA	94595	☑
724-08-9931	Stringer	Dirk	415 843-2991	5420 Telegraph Av.	Oakland	CA	94609	☐
724-80-9391	MacFeather	Stearns	415 354-7128	44 Upland Hts.	Oakland	CA	94612	☑
756-30-7391	Karsen	Livia	415 534-9219	5720 McAuley St.	Oakland	CA	94609	☑
846-92-7186	Hunter	Sheryl	415 836-7128	3410 Blonde St.	Palo Alto	CA	94301	☑
893-72-1158	McBadden	Heather	707 448-4982	301 Putnam	Vacaville	CA	95688	☐

Figure 10-5. *An HTML table generated using the generic data Provider Factory to talk to SQL Server*

Table 10-7. *Generic Database Types, the Factory Method on* DbProviderFactory *That Creates Them, and Their Role in Life*

System.Data.Common Type	Factory Method	Meaning in Life
DbCommand	CreateCommand	A generic command object, exposing Connection, CommandText, CommandType, a Parameters collection, and Execute methods for sending queries to the database.
DbCommandBuilder	CreateCommandBuilder	A generic object that will build the Insert, Update, and Delete Commands for a DataAdapter.
DbConnection	CreateConnection	A generic Connection object that uses a ConnectionString and Open method to establish communication with any database server.
DbConnectionStringBuilder	CreateConnectionStringBuilder	A helper type that abstracts away the details of the syntax of a connection string for a specific provider.
DbDataAdapter	CreateDataAdapter	A generic DataAdapter for manufacturing DataTables and moving DataSet changes back to the database.
DbParameter	CreateParameter	A generic Parameter for sending arguments to parameterized SQL statements or to procedures defined within the database.

Of course, the whole point of a Provider Factory is to select a Managed Provider at runtime instead of at design time. This can be especially helpful for software vendors who want to write applications that work against SQL Server or Oracle, for example; and their customers control this with the configuration when they install the application. You can change the last example to pull the name of the provider out of the connection information using the providerName attribute of the add element in the connectionStrings section of the configuration file.

```
<appSettings>
    <add key="EnvironmentName" value="localPubs"/>
</appSettings>
<connectionStrings>
    <add name=" localPubs"
        connectionString="server=.;database=pubs;uid=sa;pwd="
        providerName="System.Data.SqlClient"/>
    <add name=" OraclePubs"
        connectionString="Oracle Connetion String..."
        providerName="System.Data.OracleClient"/>
</connectionStrings>
```

By adding the provider name in your configuration file, you can change the code to have these configuration entries drive the provider, enabling users to dynamically select a provider when they deploy the application. You'll use the providerName setting to drive the invariant name of the provider you'll use (see ConfigFactory.aspx in Web10).

```
protected void Page_Load(object sender, EventArgs e)
{
    string EnvName =
        ConfigurationManager.AppSettings["EnvironemntName"].ToString();

    ConnectionStringSettings css =
        ConfigurationManager.ConnectionStrings[EnvName];

    DbProviderFactory factory =
        DbProviderFactories.GetFactory(css.ProviderName);
    DbConnection cn = factory.CreateConnection();
    cn.ConnectionString = css.ConnectionString;

    DbCommand cm = factory.CreateCommand();
    cm.Connection = cn;
    cm.CommandText = "select * from authors where [state] = @state";
    DbParameter pm = factory.CreateParameter();
    pm.ParameterName = "@state";
    pm.Value = "CA";
    cm.Parameters.Add(pm);
```

```
    GridView gv = new GridView();
    cn.Open();
    gv.DataSource = cm.ExecuteReader(CommandBehavior.CloseConnection);
    gv.DataBind();
    form1.Controls.Add(gv);
}
```

Adding the Provider Factory restores a feature of ADO that was lost when you moved to ADO.NET version 1.x: the ability to easily switch your backend database at deployment or even at runtime. Using these features won't be for everyone, but it will be very nice for those who do have the requirement of shipping code that can dynamically adjust to different vendor's databases.

Concurrency

Concurrency, or more specifically, the problem of what to do with a *dirty read* is always an issue in distributed application development. The problem is simple. User A reads a row of data, and begins to examine it within his browser window, contemplating changing it. Meanwhile, user B comes along and makes a change to the same row. User A finally applies a change, and posts it to the server for submission to the database. The row in the table has changed since user A first retrieved the data, so user A is said to have a dirty read of the data, and if user A posts those changes, it will result in a *dirty write* (see Figure 10-6).

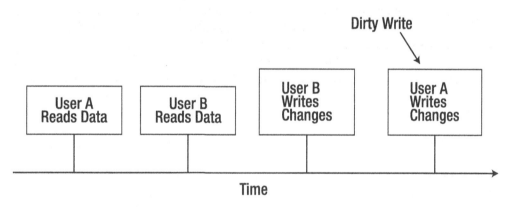

Figure 10-6. *A dirty read from the database*

The question is: How should the updating process deal with this situation? How can the updating process even learn of it? And once it does, what should be done? These questions must always be asked when inventing an application's architecture. How they are solved depends on the business requirements of the application, and the amount of control the development team has over the database whose data is being consumed. The problem is much different when it's a custom database than it is when the database is vendor supplied and changes cannot be made to it. These are the factors that determine which of the following solutions will be employed.

Blindly Overwrite Changes

Here, user A's changes overwrite the changes made by user B. This is the easiest solution to implement, as it requires that you do nothing other than squash the changes made by user B without telling either user about it. This is not acceptable under most circumstances. Users quite frequently confuse this "architectural solution" with something entirely different that they call a "bug."

Use Pessimistic Locking

Yeah. Right. That is so 1980s.

Query All Values in the where Clause

Here is the first solution worth serious consideration. In this case, when an update occurs, instead of finding the row to update by querying only on the columns that comprise the primary key, you query on all columns of the table that may have been changed since you did the read. In the case where a row has changed, the update will fail. What the application does in that circumstance is where the specific requirements of your application come in, but generally it involves informing the user that the data has changed since the time that she read it, and asking her if she'd like to overwrite the changes, cancel her update, or examine the differences between her data and the new data in the database.

The downside to this approach is that it can be extremely expensive for the database to perform these operations. When preparing the query, you need to send not only the updated values across the wire, but all of the original values as well. Evaluating the where clause will take the database much longer to do than it would if it were using only primary key or indexed columns. Also, it won't work for binary type columns (image, text, etc.). You must make special consideration for null values, as well (as the expression null = null evaluates to false).

Here's an example of what an update query using this strategy might look like:

```
update authors set
au_lname = @au_lname,
au_fname = @au_fname,
phone = @phone,
address = @address,
city = @city,
state = @state,
zip = @zip,
contract = @contract
WHERE     au_id = '123123' and
au_lname = @org_au_lname and
au_fname = @org_au_fname and
phone = @org_phone and
(address = @org_address or
(address is null and @org_address is null)) and
city = @org_city  or
(city is null and @org_city is null)) and
state = @org_state or
```

```
(state is null and @org_state is null)) and
zip = @org_zip or
(zip is null and @org_zip is null)) and
contract = @org_contract
```

The columns address, city, state, and zip allow nulls, so a separate comparison must be made to account for the case where the value was null when it was read out of the database and is still null when the update occurs. You can see this strategy is not pretty, and involves much more code.

When using a DataSet, this strategy is easily implemented from the data access layer code, as each row of a DataTable automatically tracks its current and original values. Code to move all updated rows from a DataTable to the database using the preceding command text follows (see Concurrency1.aspx from the Web10 project).

```
private bool UpdateAuthors(DataSet ds)
{
    string sql = "…statement from above…";

    SqlConnection cn = new SqlConnection(
        ConfigurationManager
        .ConnectionStrings["localPubs"].ConnectionString);
    SqlCommand cm = new SqlCommand(sql, cn);
    SqlDataAdapter da = new SqlDataAdapter
        (new SqlCommand("select * from authors",cn));
    SqlParameter pm;

    pm = new SqlParameter
        ("@au_lname", SqlDbType.VarChar, 40);
    pm.SourceVersion = DataRowVersion.Current;
    pm.SourceColumn = "au_lname";
    cm.Parameters.Add(pm);
    pm = new SqlParameter
        ("@au_fname", SqlDbType.VarChar, 10);
    pm.SourceVersion = DataRowVersion.Current;
    pm.SourceColumn = "au_fname";
    cm.Parameters.Add(pm);
    pm = new SqlParameter
        ("@phone", SqlDbType.Char, 12);
    pm.SourceVersion = DataRowVersion.Current;
    pm.SourceColumn = "phone";
    cm.Parameters.Add(pm);
    pm = new SqlParameter
        ("@address", SqlDbType.VarChar, 40);
    pm.SourceVersion = DataRowVersion.Current;
    pm.SourceColumn = "address";
    cm.Parameters.Add(pm);
    pm = new SqlParameter
        ("@city", SqlDbType.VarChar, 20);
```

```
pm.SourceVersion = DataRowVersion.Current;
pm.SourceColumn = "city";
cm.Parameters.Add(pm);
pm = new SqlParameter
    ("@state", SqlDbType.Char, 2);
pm.SourceVersion = DataRowVersion.Current;
pm.SourceColumn = "state";
cm.Parameters.Add(pm);
pm = new SqlParameter
    ("@zip", SqlDbType.Char, 5);
pm.SourceVersion = DataRowVersion.Current;
pm.SourceColumn = "zip";
cm.Parameters.Add(pm);
pm = new SqlParameter
    ("@contract", SqlDbType.Bit);
pm.SourceVersion = DataRowVersion.Current;
pm.SourceColumn = "contract";
cm.Parameters.Add(pm);
pm = new SqlParameter
    ("@org_au_id", SqlDbType.VarChar, 11);
pm.SourceVersion = DataRowVersion.Original;
pm.SourceColumn = "au_id";
cm.Parameters.Add(pm);
pm = new SqlParameter
    ("@org_au_lname", SqlDbType.VarChar, 40);
pm.SourceVersion = DataRowVersion.Original;
pm.SourceColumn = "au_lname";
cm.Parameters.Add(pm);
pm = new SqlParameter
    ("@org_au_fname", SqlDbType.VarChar, 20);
pm.SourceVersion = DataRowVersion.Original;
pm.SourceColumn = "au_fname";
cm.Parameters.Add(pm);
pm = new SqlParameter
    ("@org_phone", SqlDbType.Char, 12);
pm.SourceVersion = DataRowVersion.Original;
pm.SourceColumn = "phone";
cm.Parameters.Add(pm);
pm = new SqlParameter
    ("@org_address", SqlDbType.VarChar, 40);
pm.SourceVersion = DataRowVersion.Original;
pm.SourceColumn = "address";
cm.Parameters.Add(pm);
pm = new SqlParameter
    ("@org_city", SqlDbType.VarChar, 20);
pm.SourceVersion = DataRowVersion.Original;
pm.SourceColumn = "city";
```

```
        cm.Parameters.Add(pm);
        pm = new SqlParameter
            ("@org_state", SqlDbType.Char, 2);
        pm.SourceVersion = DataRowVersion.Original;
        pm.SourceColumn = "state";
        cm.Parameters.Add(pm);
        pm = new SqlParameter
            ("@org_zip", SqlDbType.Char, 5);
        pm.SourceVersion = DataRowVersion.Original;
        pm.SourceColumn = "zip";
        cm.Parameters.Add(pm);
        pm = new SqlParameter
            ("@org_contract", SqlDbType.Bit);
        pm.SourceVersion = DataRowVersion.Original;
        pm.SourceColumn = "contract";
        cm.Parameters.Add(pm);

        da.UpdateCommand = cm;
        da.Update(ds);

        return true;
}
```

Notice how you're mapping columns of the DataTable to parameters of the CommandText using the SourceColumn and SourceVersion attributes of the parameter object. For the parameters in the "set" portion of the SQL statement, you're pulling the current values from the DataTable. For columns in the where clause, you're pulling the original values from the DataTable. Realize that "select * from authors" is the SelectCommand of the DataAdapter. What you're building with this code is the UpdateCommand of the adapter, which you set just before calling the Update method.

Typically, when using an adapter for retrieving data from the database and later moving it back, you'll do a one-time creation of this adapter and cache it, as it's a lot of work. This code will also only work for updates to the DataSet; you'll also want to create and set an insert and delete command (for the InsertCommand and DeleteCommand properties of the adapter, respectively).

When the user gets into a "dirty read" situation using this approach, the error displayed in Figure 10-7 occurs.

In a full-blown application, this is the exception that would be caught and would kick off the rendering of whatever "concurrency resolution" interface was required by the business rules.

This strategy is good when modifications cannot be made to the database in use. Be sure to build only columns that could change into the where clause. The disadvantage to this approach is the amount of code it takes and the amount of work that must be done at runtime, including marshaling of data across the wire and the complexity of the database queries.

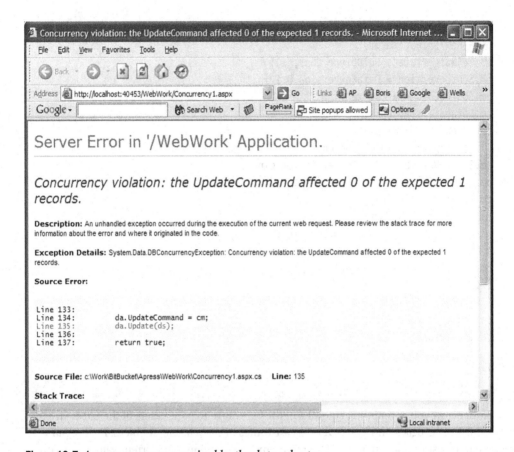

Figure 10-7. *A concurrency error raised by the data adapter*

Query On Only Changed Column Values

If you have no control over the database schema, but the overhead of the last approach is too much to bear, you can update and query on only those column values that have changed. Unfortunately, this approach requires dynamic generation of SQL statements, so it is generally frowned upon. For tables with high column counts, this approach may be worth the trade-off.

There is another business rule that must be present before adopting this approach. When user A moves a change to "address" back to the database, it must be irrelevant if user B has changed "state" in the meantime. Using this approach, "address" will get updated with the new value from user A, but "state" will remain the value that user B set it to. While technically both changes were based on "fresh" data, the combination of values might be invalid. You could end up with an author from Green Bay, MN. (East coasters: Green Bay is in Wisconsin.)

So, if your requirements can overlook all of the glaring deficiencies of this method, here's what it would look like (see Concurrency2.aspx in Web10).

```
private bool UpdateAuthors(DataSet ds)
{
    string sql = "";
    string sqlBase = " update authors set {0} where au_id = '{1}'{2}";
    string sqlUpdate = "";
    string sqlWhere = "";
```

```
    SqlConnection cn = new SqlConnection(
        ConfigurationManager
        .ConnectionStrings["localPubs"].ConnectionString);
    SqlCommand cm = new SqlCommand("", cn);
    foreach (DataRow dr in ds.Tables[0].Rows)
    {
        sqlUpdate = "";
        sqlWhere = "";
        foreach(DataColumn dc in ds.Tables[0].Columns)
        {
            if (dr[dc, DataRowVersion.Current] !=
                dr[dc, DataRowVersion.Original])
            {
                sqlUpdate += string.Format("{0} = '{1}', ",
                    dc.ColumnName, dr[dc]);
                sqlWhere += string.Format(" and {0} = '{1}'",
                    dc.ColumnName, dr[dc,
                    DataRowVersion.Original]);
            }
        }
        if (sqlUpdate.Length > 0)
        {
            sqlUpdate = sqlUpdate.Substring
                (0, sqlUpdate.Length - 2);
            sql += string.Format(sqlBase, sqlUpdate,
                dr["au_id", DataRowVersion.Original],
                sqlWhere); ;
        }
    }

    cm.CommandText = sql;
    cn.Open();
    int updates = cm.ExecuteNonQuery();
    cn.Close();

    return true;
}
```

The next thing to do with this method is to compare the number of rows that were updated to the number of rows that have changed in the DataSet, to make sure no concurrency errors occurred (in the limited definition you've implemented here). Then the DataSet would need to be refreshed by calling AcceptChanges.

```
if (updates != ds.Tables[0].GetChanges().Rows.Count)
    return false;
else
{
    ds.AcceptChanges();
```

```
        return true;
}
```

AcceptChanges doesn't move any data to the database (only an adapter can do that); it simply copies current values over original values. The same null checking logic you saw earlier needs to be built into this method as well.

Timestamp Column

When you have control of the schema of the database, your best option for managing concurrency is to add a timestamp column to the table, and then build a check of the value into the update query. The database automatically updates the timestamp value whenever a change is made to the data. So as long as the timestamp value that was read still matches it when an update is attempted, you can rest assured that the data has not changed in the interim.

A timestamp is binary data, so marshaling the value to and from a web browser requires some transformation along the way. You'll send the timestamp value to the browser in a hidden input. When the user sends changes back, you can retrieve it and use it in the where clause of your update. First, you'll need to modify the authors table and add a timestamp column to it. You'll do this on a copy of the authors table named authors_ts, as shown in Figure 10-8.

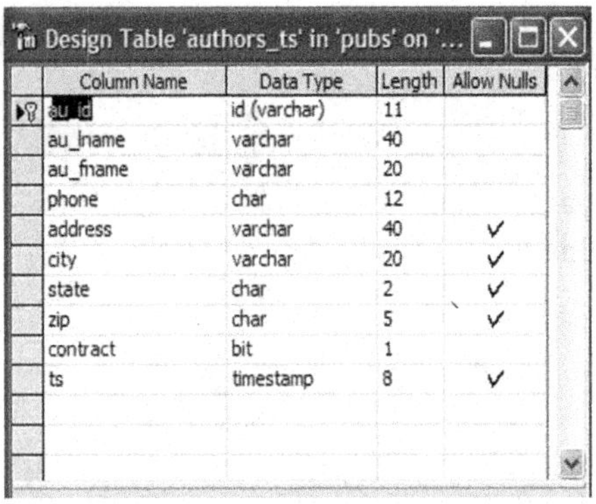

Figure 10-8. *The modified version of the authors table*

Here's the markup from the editing page. The user will pick an author for editing with the DropDownList. You're only creating an interface to edit the first and last name. Of course, usually you would create an interface for editing more of the data. What you're interested in for this demonstration, though, is the user control created just after the HTML table (see Concurrency3.aspx in Web10).

```
<asp:Panel Runat=server ID=pnEdit Visible=false>
    <table>
        <tr>
            <td>First Name</td>
            <td>
                <asp:TextBox Runat=server ID=txtFirstName />
            </td>
        </tr>
```

```
    <tr>
        <td>Last Name</td>
        <td>
            <asp:TextBox Runat=server ID=txtLastName />
        </td>
    </tr>
    <tr><td colspan=2 align=center>
        <asp:Button Runat=server ID=btnSave
            Text='Save'
            OnClick="btnSave_Click" />
    </td></tr>
</table>
<uc1:Timestamp ID="tsAuthor" Runat="server" />
</asp:Panel>
<br /><br /><asp:Label Runat=server ID=lblOutput />
```

To facilitate reuse of this logic across several tables, you'll encapsulate the timestamp value in a user control. You can also do this with a custom control, making it usable across different applications. Here's the markup for the user control. (This code is in Timestamp.ascx of the Web10 project.)

```
<%@ Control Language="C#"
CodeFile="Timestamp.ascx.cs"
Inherits="Timestamp_ascx" %>
<asp:TextBox Runat=server ID=txtTimestamp Visible=false />
```

It gets included on your edit page with the following register directive from Concurrency3.aspx:

```
<%@ Register TagPrefix="uc1"
TagName="Timestamp"
Src="Timestamp.ascx" %>
```

You can see there's not much to this control. It will have no visible rendering behavior; you're really just using it to store a value in the ViewState. The timestamp will be tracked by the user control with a public property named TimestampValue. It's implemented thusly in Timestamp.ascx.

```
public object TimestampValue
{
    get
    {
        byte[] ba = new byte[8];
        for(int indx = 0; indx < 8; indx++)
        {
            ba[indx] = Convert.ToByte(
                txtTimestamp.Text.Substring(indx * 3,2),16);
        }
        return ba;
    }
```

```
    set
    {
        txtTimestamp.Text = BitConverter.ToString((byte[])value);
    }
}
```

This code uses a BitConverter to transform the byte array received from the database into a string, and then uses the Convert.ToByte method to transform it back into a byte array for populating a parameter value to send to the database. By typing it as an Object, consumers of the control need not worry about their parameter values. They can set it with code like this (user control instance is named tsAuthor):

```
tsAuthor.TimestampValue = cm.Parameters["@ts"].Value;
```

And they can retrieve the value with this line of code:

```
pm = cm.Parameters.Add("@ts", SqlDbType.Timestamp);
pm.Value = tsAuthor.TimestampValue;
```

This is the type of programming ease you're designing for by encapsulating this logic in the user control.

So when the page first renders, you populate the author list. You've done this several times, so this code is omitted here for brevity. You can see from the markup that when the user chooses an entry from the list, a postback occurs (AutoPostBack=true), and the BindToAuthor method is executed (from Concurrency3.aspx).

```
protected void BindToAuthor(object sender, EventArgs e)
{
    SqlConnection cn = new SqlConnection(
            ConfigurationManager.ConnectionStrings
            ["localPubs"].ConnectionString);
    SqlCommand cm = new SqlCommand(
        "select @fname = au_fname, @lname = au_lname, @ts = ts "
        + "from authors_ts where au_id = @id", cn);

    cm.Parameters.Add("@id", SqlDbType.Char, 11)
        .Value = ddlAuthors.SelectedValue;
    cm.Parameters.Add("@fname", SqlDbType.VarChar,20)
        .Direction = ParameterDirection.Output;
    cm.Parameters.Add("@lname", SqlDbType.VarChar,40)
        .Direction = ParameterDirection.Output;
    cm.Parameters.Add("@ts", SqlDbType.Timestamp)
        .Direction = ParameterDirection.Output;

    cn.Open();
    cm.ExecuteNonQuery();
    cn.Close();
```

```
    txtFirstName.Text = cm.Parameters["@fname"].Value.ToString();
    txtLastName.Text = cm.Parameters["@lname"].Value.ToString();
    tsAuthor.TimestampValue = cm.Parameters["@ts"].Value;
    pnEdit.Visible = true;
}
```

Notice how you're retrieving values using output parameters built right into our command text. This statement is executed with ExecuteNonQuery, which means the overhead of creating a result set is never incurred. This data access method is screaming fast, especially for dynamically generated SQL.

You get the timestamp value back as an output parameter as well, and pass it right along to your user control, leaving it typed as an Object (basically untyped). This is fine, because the user control knows it's a byte array and converts to a string for streaming to the client.

The user can now edit to his heart's content, and when done, click the Save button. Here you're using dynamic SQL with parameters built in again, but this time they're all input parameters (again, from Concurrency3.aspx).

```
protected void btnSave_Click(object sender, EventArgs e)
{
    SqlConnection cn = new SqlConnection(
            ConfigurationManager.ConnectionStrings
            ["localPubs"].ConnectionString);
    SqlCommand cm = new SqlCommand(
        "update authors_ts set au_fname = @fname, "
        + "au_lname = @lname where au_id = @id "
        + "and ts = @ts", cn);

    cm.Parameters.Add("@id", SqlDbType.Char, 11)
        .Value = ddlAuthors.SelectedValue;
    pm = cm.Parameters.Add("@ts", SqlDbType.Timestamp);
    pm.Value = tsAuthor.TimestampValue;
    cm.Parameters.Add("@fname", SqlDbType.VarChar, 20)
        .Value = txtFirstName.Text;
    cm.Parameters.Add("@lname", SqlDbType.VarChar, 40)
        .Value = txtLastName.Text;

    cn.Open();
    int i = cm.ExecuteNonQuery();
    cn.Close();

    if (i == 1)
        lblOutput.Text = "Data saved";
    else
        lblOutput.Text = "Concurrency error";

    pnEdit.Visible = false;
    BindList();
}
```

You calibrate your success by the number of rows you've affected. Because the query is filtering on the primary key of the table, it will always affect, at most, only one row. So it either affects zero or one rows. If it affects one, your query has succeeded, which will only ever occur if a change has not been made to the row since it was read. If a change has been made (or the row has been deleted), the edit has been done with a *dirty read*, and you inform the user that there's been a concurrency error. This is a simplified example; in an actual application, you would use this branch of code to render whatever interface is required to deal with the concurrency error, enabling the user to resolve it.

Concurrency is a problem that must be solved in any distributed application. How the problem gets solved is going to depend on your business rules and how much control you have over the schema of the database you're interacting with. Hopefully some of the techniques we've gone over in this section will give you some ideas for meeting the requirements of your specific application.

Summary

There's a new data access model in the .NET Framework. This model is very different from ADO and OLEDB, because it dedicates types to specific databases. Vendors create a Managed Provider by implementing a known set of interfaces defined in the System.Data assembly.

There are two main data access models in .NET. One is a low memory footprint, read-only data access model, and the other is an in-memory result set model. Both are tailored for different tasks, and as a .NET database developer, you should be aware of which model to use in which circumstances.

Version 2.0 of the Framework adds many improvements to Managed Providers of data access, including a Provider Factory model, a configuration file entry dedicated to connection strings, and a very easy facility for encrypting these strings.

The DataTable object also has a lot of new functionality; new features enable it to do all of the operations for a single result set that used to require a DataSet and DataAdapter.

Finally, in a disconnected architecture, the problems of latency and concurrency must be handled. We examined a number of strategies for doing this in different circumstances.

There are many more features for data access in the .NET Framework in version 2.0. In Chapter 11, we'll examine some of these, including SQL cache dependencies and data source controls.

CHAPTER 11

■■■

Data Access Layer Services

Many features are available in managed code that you can put to use in the data access layer don't pertain directly to the Managed Providers of data access. In ASP.NET 2.0, a new set of controls enables you to use the markup of your ASPX page to declaratively bind a control to a data source. These are called the *data source controls*, and they are very advanced compared to the data-binding engine available in 1.x. Microsoft has also added one of the most requested features to the cache object: the capability to establish a dependency between a cache entry and a database table. This dramatically increases the usefulness of the cache, making it as dependable for purging dirty data as it always has been for XML documents. There's also a data access layer application block available from Microsoft, which simplifies a lot of the common tasks that need to be done within a data access layer. While this does not ship with the .NET Framework, it is available as a free download from Microsoft. We'll take a look at all of these features in this chapter. We'll wrap up with a preview of SQL Server 2005.

Declarative Data Access

ASP.NET 2.0 adds a suite of controls to the Framework called data source controls. These controls keep in line with Microsoft's migration from imperative code to declarative code. Data source controls allow data to be retrieved from a variety of sources using nothing but markup in the body of the ASPX page. If you're having flashbacks to the days of IDC and HTX, you're not entirely off base, but these controls are extremely flexible and powerful. Another benefit of the markup approach to declarative coding is that the XML DOM is much easier to use than the CodeDOM, and so there's really impressive support for these controls from within the Visual Studio IDE graphical editors. These tools generate the markup, exposing an interface that allows for some powerful expressions to be created without writing any code.

Still, as architects, our hunch is that you'll look at some of these tools and wince a little on the inside. They demo really well at the conferences, but for a lot of people, there's something about embedding data access code into markup that just somehow seems *wrong*. Data access belongs in a different logical layer of the application, and presentation code belongs in markup. This opinion may change over time, and XML Application Markup Language (XAML) may bring about changes in the way people think about coding and markup. But these are changes that may take many years to take hold, and, in the meantime, if these controls don't live up to their promise, they could undermine any eventual adoption of this model.

So we'll take a look at the data access controls in the first part of this chapter, drilling specifically into the SqlDataSource and ObjectDataSource controls (see Table 11-1). They may not represent the end of writing code to get to data sources, but in many cases they are a great way to dramatically speed a development effort. The ObjectDataSource adheres to a layered architecture better, whereas the SqlDataSource may prove itself suitable only for prototyping and quick fixes.

Table 11-1. *Data Source Controls in ASP.NET 2.0*

Data Source Control	Meaning in Life
AccessDataSource	Enables you to declaratively bind to an Access database file (MDB).
ObjectDataSource	Enables you to bind to an object model.
SitemapDataSource	Specialized XML format that describes the structure and hierarchy of your site. Used for binding to the site navigation controls.
SqlDataSource	Allows for binding to relational data sources.
XmlDataSource	Used to bind to an XML document.

None of these controls has visible rendering behaviors of its own. They can more logically be thought of as components rather than controls, but in order to avoid having to write code (as is common with components), they're implemented as controls.

When you're using a data source control, the creation of the interface is done by one of the new Web Controls that inherits from the DataBoundControl base class (or HierarchicalDataBoundControl) listed in Table 11-2.

Table 11-2. DataBoundControls *in ASP.NET 2.0*

Data Bound Control	Meaning in Life
AdRotator	This 1.x control has been redesigned to allow for binding to a data source control via the new DataSourceID property.
BulletedList CheckBoxList DropDownList ListBox RadioButtonList	These list controls have all been refactored to inherit from DataBoundControl and, thereby, expose the DataSourceID property for binding to data source controls. The bulleted list is a new addition to the list control family.
GridView	This is the replacement for the DataGrid control from 1.x, and is probably the "flagship" control for ASP.NET 2.0. This control overcomes scores of limitations of the DataGrid, allowing for editing, selecting, paging, and sorting features, all without writing a single line of code. Consider this the new version of the DataGrid. It is only packaged in a brand new type because the changes made to it are so extensive that they are not backwards compatible. Rather than breaking all existing implementations of the DataGrid, Microsoft wisely decided to just ship a new control.
DataGrid DataList Repeater	While these controls have not been changed to inherit from the DataBoundControl base class, they have been modified to support the DataSourceID property and do support data source controls.

Data Bound Control	Meaning in Life
DetailsView FormView	These great new additions to the Web Control collection provide a very easy facility for creating a form interface, where all columns of a table are displayed with a label on the left and a control on the right in a single column. The DetailsView provides a default rendering with VCR-style buttons to navigate through the result set, whereas the FormView provides more flexibility (and more work) by using a template-based approach (akin to the DataList). Realize that the fundamental difference with these controls, and the other data-binding controls, is that they focus on displaying a single row of data, whereas the others focus on displaying some output for each row in your data source.
Menu SiteMapPath TreeView	These advanced controls bind the HierarchicalDataSource controls to render their respective interfaces. The TreeView is an especially nice addition to the suite of tools. It's an advanced type of interface that leverages DHTML and out-of-band callbacks (see Chapter 4), but is still cross-browser compatible. The Menu and SiteMapPath work with a SiteMapDataSource to provide "easy-to-use" and "easy-to-code" navigation for your application, making you and your end users happier.

These controls have all been created specifically for binding to the data source controls. Each of them exposes a DataSourceID property, which points to a data source control also declared on the page. Using a combination of a DataSourceControl and a DataBoundControl enables you to do data binding declaratively, in place of setting the DataSource and calling DataBind from code. You see this strategy in use here with a GridView and a SqlDataSource. Here's our mantra: design goal = no code.

```
<asp:SqlDataSource Runat=server ID=sdsAuthors
 ConnectionString="server=.;database=pubs;uid=sa;pwd=123123"
 SelectCommand="select * from authors" />
<asp:GridView Runat=server ID=dvAuthors
 DataSourceID=sdsAuthors />
```

This dumps an HTML table with a border of one to the browser, which is the GridView's default rendering behavior. You can find this code in Simple.aspx of the Web11 project.

■Note This book does not provide "blow-by-blow" coverage of each new control provided in ASP.NET 2.0, as we focus on larger issues of architecture and design in an n-tiered application. You can find feature-level coverage in *Beginning ASP.NET 2.0 in C#* by Matthew MacDonald (Apress, 2005).

SQL Data Source Control

The SqlDataSource is designed to talk to the most common source of data: the relational database. It enables you to connect to, execute commands against, and update the database without writing a single line of code.

The SqlDataSource control also supports inserts, updates, and deletes. This markup will render a form interface for displaying, editing, and navigating to different rows in the authors table (see DetailsViewIE.aspx in the Web11 project). Figure 11-1 shows the output of the following control declarations.

```
<asp:DetailsView ID="DetailsView1" Runat="server"
    DataSourceID='sdsAuthors'
    AutoGenerateDeleteButton=true
    AutoGenerateEditButton=true
    AutoGenerateInsertButton=true
    AllowPaging="True"
    AutoGenerateRows="true"
    DataKeyNames="au_id">
</asp:DetailsView>

<asp:SqlDataSource Runat=server ID=sdsAuthors
 ConnectionString="server=.;database=pubs;uid=sa;pwd=123123"
 SelectCommand="SELECT * FROM [authors]"
 ProviderName="System.Data.SqlClient"
 DeleteCommand="DELETE FROM [authors] WHERE [au_id] = @original_au_id"
 InsertCommand="INSERT INTO [authors] ([au_id], [au_lname], [au_fname],
    [phone], [address], [city], [state], [zip], [contract])
    VALUES (@au_id, @au_lname, @au_fname, @phone, @address, @city,
    @state, @zip, @contract)"
 UpdateCommand="UPDATE [authors] SET [au_lname] = @au_lname,
    [au_fname] = @au_fname, [phone] = @phone, [address] = @address,
    [city] = @city, [state] = @state, [zip] = @zip,
    [contract] = @contract WHERE [au_id] = @original_au_id">
    <DeleteParameters>
        <asp:Parameter Type="String" Name="au_id"></asp:Parameter>
    </DeleteParameters>
    <UpdateParameters>
        <asp:Parameter Type="String" Name="au_lname"></asp:Parameter>
        <asp:Parameter Type="String" Name="au_fname"></asp:Parameter>
        <asp:Parameter Type="String" Name="phone"></asp:Parameter>
        <asp:Parameter Type="String" Name="address"></asp:Parameter>
        <asp:Parameter Type="String" Name="city"></asp:Parameter>
        <asp:Parameter Type="String" Name="state"></asp:Parameter>
        <asp:Parameter Type="String" Name="zip"></asp:Parameter>
        <asp:Parameter Type="Boolean" Name="contract"></asp:Parameter>
        <asp:Parameter Type="String" Name="au_id"></asp:Parameter>
    </UpdateParameters>
    <InsertParameters>
        <asp:Parameter Type="String" Name="au_id"></asp:Parameter>
        <asp:Parameter Type="String" Name="au_lname"></asp:Parameter>
        <asp:Parameter Type="String" Name="au_fname"></asp:Parameter>
        <asp:Parameter Type="String" Name="phone"></asp:Parameter>
```

```
        <asp:Parameter Type="String" Name="address"></asp:Parameter>
        <asp:Parameter Type="String" Name="city"></asp:Parameter>
        <asp:Parameter Type="String" Name="state"></asp:Parameter>
        <asp:Parameter Type="String" Name="zip"></asp:Parameter>
        <asp:Parameter Type="Boolean" Name="contract"></asp:Parameter>
    </InsertParameters>
</asp:SqlDataSource>
```

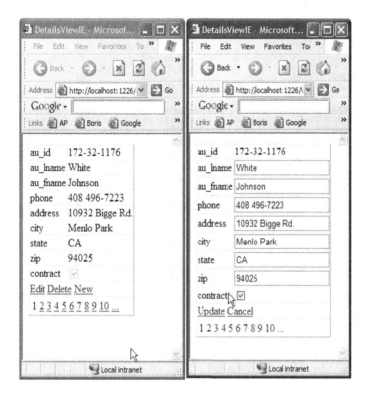

Figure 11-1. *An editable form created with no code using the* `SqlDataSource`

Queries can also be parameterized. This page uses a drop-down list to pick a publisher, and then renders a list of titles by that publisher when the user picks one (see `ParamIE.aspx` in the `Web11` project). Figure 11-2 shows the results.

```
<asp:SqlDataSource Runat=server ID=sdsPublishers
 ConnectionString="server=.;database=pubs;uid=sa;pwd=123123"
 SelectCommand="select pub_id, pub_name from publishers" />

<asp:DropDownList Runat=server ID=ddlPublishers
 DataSourceID='sdsPublishers'
 DataTextField='pub_name'
 AutoPostBack=true
 DataValueField='pub_id'  />
```

```
<asp:SqlDataSource Runat=server ID=sdsTitles
 ConnectionString="Server=.;database=pubs;uid=sa;pwd=123123"
  SelectCommand="select * from titles where pub_id = @id">
  <SelectParameters>
    <asp:ControlParameter
    ControlID=ddlPublishers
    PropertyName=SelectedValue
    Name="id" />
  </SelectParameters>
</asp:SqlDataSource>

<asp:GridView Runat=server ID=gvTitles
 DataSourceID=sdsTitles />
```

title_id	title	type	pub_id	price	advance	royalty	ytd_sales	notes	pubdate
BU2075	You Can Combat Computer Stress!	business	0736	2.9900	10125.0000	26	18722	The latest medical and psychological techniques for living with the electronic office. Easy-to-understand explanations.	6/30/1991 12:00:00 AM
PS2091	Is Anger the Enemy?	psychology	0736	10.9500	2275.0000	17	2045	Carefully researched study of the effects of strong emotions on the body. Metabolic charts included.	6/15/1991 12:00:00 AM
PS2106	Life Without Fear	psychology	0736	7.0000	6000.0000	17	111	New exercise, meditation, and nutritional techniques that can reduce the shock of daily interactions. Popular audience. Sample menus included, exercise video available separately.	10/5/1991 12:00:00 AM
PS3333	Prolonged Data Deprivation: Four Case Studies	psychology	0736	19.9900	2000.0000	11	4072	What happens when the data runs dry? Searching evaluations of information-shortage effects.	6/12/1991 12:00:00 AM
PS7777	Emotional Security: A New Algorithm	psychology	0736	7.9900	4000.0000	13	3336	Protecting yourself and your loved ones from undue emotional stress in the modern world. Use of computer and nutritional aids emphasized.	6/12/1991 12:00:00 AM

Figure 11-2. *A grid that gets queried with a drop-down list, created with no code using a* SqlDataSource

Here you're looking to another control on the page to provide you with a connection value. That's just one of many sources that can be used for parameters. Parameter values can also be pulled from the query string, the session, cookies, or the ASP.NET profile provider. Parameters can be built into the SQL declared with the SqlDataSource, or they can be parameters of a stored procedure, named by the SelectCommand, for example.

Table 11-3 shows a number of ways you can provide a value for the author ID column of the following SelectCommand. The table samples are all different ways to provide a value for this parameterized SQL statement.

```
SELECT * FROM authors WHERE (au_id = @au_id)
```

Table 11-3. *Parameter Sources, Syntax, and Meanings*

Parameter	Syntax	Meaning in Life

CookieParameter	`<asp:CookieParameter`
	`    CookieName="ID"`
	`    Name="au_id"`
	`    Type="String" />`
		This parameter enables you to pull a value from a named cookie. In this example, the cookie named "ID" will be passed to the select statement in place of the @au_id parameter in the statement.

ControlParameter	`<asp:ControlParameter`
	`    ControlID="ddlID"`
	`    Name="au_id"`
	`    PropertyName="SelectedValue"`
	`    Type="String" />`
		This parameter enables you to pull a named property from a control on the page. In this example, you're sending the selected value of the drop-down list control named ddlID as the @au_id value in the select statement.

FormParameter	`<asp:FormParameter`
	`    FormField="ID"`
	`    Name="au_id"`
	`    Type="String" />`
		This parameter can be used when another page is sending values to your page via an HTTP Post. You can use this to pass named values from the HTTP Post header right into the SQL statement. Here, you're passing the ID post value into the @au_id parameter of the select statement.

ProfileParameter	`<asp:ProfileParameter`
	`    Name="au_id"`
	`    PropertyName="ID"`
	`    Type="String" />`
		This parameter type enables you to pull values from the custom profile infrastructure provided in ASP.NET 2.0. You name any parameter configured as a property of the custom profile provider. Here you're moving the ID custom profile property into the @au_id value in the select statement.

Continued

Table 11-3. *Continued*

Parameter	Syntax	Meaning in Life

QueryStringParameter	`<asp:QueryStringParameter`
	`Name="au_id"`
	`QueryStringField="id"`
	`Type="String" />`
		The query string parameter enables you to pull any value that was tacked on to the end of your URL with a named value pair. Here, you're passing the named query string value of id along into the @au_id parameter of the select command.

SessionParameter	`<asp:SessionParameter`
	`Name="au_id"`
	`SessionField="id"`
	`Type="String" />`
		You can also pull values from the ASP.NET Session object. Here, you're pulling the session value named id and using it as the value for the @au_id parameter of the select command.

You can also move connection information into configuration files and referenced by name instead of being embedded directly in the markup, using the same techniques you learned in Chapter 10 on connection string management.

This entry would be in the `web.config`.

```
<connectionStrings>
    <add name="pubsConn"
    connectionString="database=pubs;server=.;uid=sa;pwd=123123" />
</connectionStrings>
```

And then you can use the `<%$ ConnectionStrings:ConnectionName %>` syntax from your markup.

```
<asp:SqlDataSource Runat=server ID=sdsAuthors
 ConnectionString= '<%$ ConnectionStrings:pubsConn %>'
 SelectCommand="select * from authors" />
<asp:GridView Runat=server ID=dvAuthors
 DataSourceID=sdsAuthors />
```

In these demos, you've seen pages that can display, query, modify, delete, and create your data. Doing so required no code. We're not going to bother showing you the Wizards and Designers that generate this markup (as there's about 100,000 screen shots of this on MSDN and the Web in general), but using these tools can eliminate the need to even learn the syntax and nuances of this markup. Creating pages like this is *extremely quick and easy to do*. This is powerful stuff. To reiterate, this control is great for a number of things.

- Evangelizing, and doing demos on, how easy Visual Studio is to use

- Prototyping/proof of concept/Requests for Proposals (RFPs)

- Internal tools or small solutions with simple requirements

- Any time doing something *quickly* is more important than any other architectural requirement

It is not, however, suited as a general purpose approach to providing a data access layer for a distributed application of any significant size, scale, or complexity. Embedding structured query language in the presentation tier is not maintainable for larger applications. Typically you want to see data access encapsulated within its own layer of the application, probably only exposed by a business object layer that sits between the presentation and data layers. Ideally, it's best to create a layer of abstraction between UI developers and relational databases. This lets developers focus on meeting functional requirements, and relegates database modeling and schema to the information architects and DBAs, where it belongs. When these architectural requirements are present, the ObjectDataSource provides a much better solution.

Object Data Source

Another control that may be viable in a wider range of applications is the ObjectDataSource. This type provides similar functionality to a SqlDataSource, but it allows for binding to an object model instead of injecting SQL or stored procedure calls directly into the markup.

This enables you to bind to, for example, a collection of business objects instead of the rows of a result set. Using this data source, you can have your pages declaratively bind to the middle tier of your application, instead of directly to the data tier. More specifically, these methods enable you to bind to methods rather than bind directly to database objects.

These objects do need to be designed in a specific manner so that they'll work correctly with the ObjectDataSource. This data source control does use a true late binding strategy, but there are a few rules for how the methods it binds to must be formed. For example, the SelectMethod must return a type that the data-binding engine can bind to. This means if you have your own custom CustomerCollection type, you cannot bind directly to that type; you must have another method that returns an instance of CustomerCollection. This subtle difference means you must create types (or at least methods on your types) that are tailored to the ObjectDataSource control.

Let's start with a very simple example. Here's the declaration of an ObjectDataSource that binds to a generic collection of BookDetail objects:

```
<asp:ObjectDataSource ID="odsBookList" runat="server"
    SelectMethod="GetBookList"
    TypeName="BookBinding" />
```

Note The code for the ObjectDataSource demo can be found in EditBook.aspx, EditBook.aspx.cs, BookBinding.cs, and BookDetails.cs, all of which are in the Web11 project.

This declaration names a type using the TypeName attribute, and a method on that type using the SelectMethod attribute. The data source control then uses Reflection and late binding to create an instance of the type and get the data when it's time to bind. Here's the first part of the code for the BookBinding type you're using with this ObjectDataSource control:

```
public class BookBinding
{
    public BookBinding()
    {}

    public SqlDataReader GetBookList()
    {
        String sql = "select BookId, Title From Book order by Title";
        SqlConnection cn = new SqlConnection(WebStatic.ConnectionString);
        SqlCommand cm = new SqlCommand(sql,cn);

        cn.Open();
        return cm.ExecuteReader(CommandBehavior.CloseConnection);
    }
    ...
```

The default constructor is required so that the control can create an instance of the type. You could omit it from this code, because you have no custom constructors, but if you have a custom constructor on your type, you must explicitly add the default constructor, even if it does nothing (like the preceding constructor).

The GetBookList serves as the select method of the binding operation. Here you're simply passing through a SqlDataReader. Using code like this, you're really using the ObjectDataSource to bind directly to a data access layer. This is still a vast improvement over putting the data access code directly in the markup, and it doesn't take much code do. You could call a stored procedure instead of using inline SQL, which would be even better.

You can use this control to bind any of the controls listed in Table 11-2. Here you'll create a ListBox bound to the ObjectDataSource:

```
<asp:ListBox ID="lbBookList" runat="server"
            DataSourceID="odsBookList"
            Width=600px
            DataTextField="Title"
            DataValueField="BookID"
            Rows=12 AutoPostBack="True" />
```

This renders a list of books displaying the title and carrying the BookID as the underlying value of the list items. It's really not much *less* code than it would take to do this in 1.x. The main differences here are that there's no code in the code-behind of our page (the BookBinding.cs file is in the app_code directory, but it could be in an external assembly), and the code that actually does the binding is contained in the ObjectDataSource control. In this example, that means the only thing you don't have to do is call DataBind. However, when you design and build an entire system using these controls, you'll likely get better reuse out of your object layer, and your individual page code will be much simpler.

This strategy is also much more powerful when it comes to editing data, as you can bind to a business object layer and have your business rules enforced. Let's take a look at another declaration of an ObjectDataSource:

```
<asp:ObjectDataSource ID="odsBookDetail" runat="server"
    DataObjectTypeName="BookDetails"
    SelectMethod="GetBook"
    UpdateMethod="UpdateBook"
    TypeName="BookBinding">
    <SelectParameters>
        <asp:ControlParameter ControlID="lbBookList" Name="BookId"
            PropertyName="SelectedValue"
            Type="Int32" />
    </SelectParameters>
</asp:ObjectDataSource>
```

Here you've added the DataObjectTypeName attribute. This enables you to use a business object and a collection of those objects, instead of using a DataReader or DataTable. Again, using Reflection, the ObjectDataSource is able to treat public fields and properties of the type named by DataObjectTypeName as bindable members instead of relying on columns from a result set. The BookDetails type is defined in BookDetails.cs of the app_code directory. It's a standard business object with public properties, private fields, and a Save method to commit changes to an underlying data store.

You've also added a SelectParameter to the declaration of this data source. All of the parameter types listed in Table 11-3 are also available on the ObjectDataSource. Instead of acting as parameters in a SQL statement or stored procedure, they're passed here as arguments to the corresponding methods they're declared for. For example, in this case because you declared a SelectParameter, the ObjectDataSource will automatically pass an Int32 to the SelectMethod, which in this case is GetBook.

Let's take a look at the code for GetBook, which is a method of BookBinding, the type named by the TypeName property. This is different than BookDetails, the type named by the DataObjectTypeName property. BookDetails is the type that BookBinding will create collections of and use for data updates.

```
public List<BookDetails> GetBook(int BookId)
{
    List<BookDetails> bookList = new List<BookDetails>();
    bookList.Add(new BookDetails(BookId));
    return bookList;
}
```

So GetBook returns a generic List of BookDetails objects. Because it accepts a BookId as an argument, there will only ever be one book in the list. This is by design. The ObjectDataSource associated with this method will bind to a DetailsView control, which only displays a single row at a time.

▓**Note** This method uses a new feature of the .NET Framework called *generics*, which enable you to create and use types that have some dynamic type information built into the definition. In this case, you're creating a collection of objects, but the type in the collection is declared at the same time you declare the list using the <TypeName> syntax. For a detailed discussion of generics, see *Pro C# and the .NET 2.0 Platform* by Andrew Troelsen (Apress, 2005).

Notice that for this method, there is a single argument that accepts an Int32. You declared the ObjectDataSource with an Int32 control parameter on the select statement. The control parameter points to the SelectedIndex property of the ListBox. This has the effect of passing the selected value of the ListBox into the GetBook method of the second ObjectDataSource, which you'll use to bind a DetailsView control to display the book. You can see the entire coil laid out in Figure 11-3. Keep in mind that at this point, there's not a single line of code in the code-behind the EditBook Web Form.

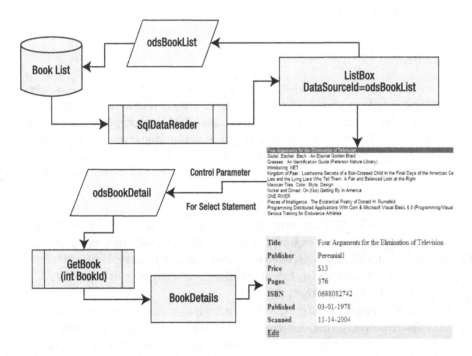

Figure 11-3. *Interdependent Object Data Sources used to feed values from a* ListBox *control to a* DetailsView *control*

Let's take a look at the declaration for the DetailsView control that displays the details of the selected book. All of the data and binding behavior for this control is already provided by the ObjectDataSource named odsBookDetail, which is, in turn, being fed a BookID value from the ListBox. This means the only thing left to specify with the declaration of the DetailsView is the look and feel you want to use to display the book data.

```
<asp:DetailsView ID="dvEditBook" runat="server" DataKeyNames='BookID'
    AutoGenerateRows="False" DataSourceID="odsBookDetail" Width=600px
    Height="50px" CellPadding="4" ForeColor="#333333" GridLines="None"
    OnItemUpdated="dvEditBook_ItemUpdated" >
    <Fields>
        <asp:BoundField DataField=BookID Visible=false />
        <asp:BoundField DataField="Title" HeaderText="Title"
                    ControlStyle-Width=420px />
        <asp:BoundField DataField="Publisher" HeaderText="Publisher"
                    ControlStyle-Width=420px />
        <asp:BoundField DataField="ListPrice" HeaderText="Price"
```

```
                              DataFormatString="{0:$#,###.##}"  />
        <asp:BoundField DataField="PageCount" HeaderText="Pages" />
        <asp:BoundField DataField="ISBN" HeaderText="ISBN" />
        <asp:BoundField DataField="PublicationDate" HeaderText="Published"
                      DataFormatString="{0:MM-dd-yyyy}" />
        <asp:BoundField DataField="ScanDate" HeaderText="Scanned"
                      DataFormatString="{0:MM-dd-yyyy}" />
        <asp:CommandField CancelText='x' UpdateText='ok' ShowEditButton="True"  />
    </Fields>

    <FooterStyle BackColor="#507CD1" Font-Bold="True" ForeColor="White" />
    <CommandRowStyle BackColor="#D1DDF1" Font-Bold="True" />
    <RowStyle BackColor="#EFF3FB" />
    <FieldHeaderStyle BackColor="#DEE8F5" Font-Bold="True" />
    <PagerStyle BackColor="#2461BF" ForeColor="White" HorizontalAlign="Center" />
    <HeaderStyle BackColor="#507CD1" Font-Bold="True" ForeColor="White" />
    <EditRowStyle BackColor=CornflowerBlue />
    <AlternatingRowStyle BackColor="White" />
</asp:DetailsView>
```

The single most important part of this declaration for this discussion is the DataSourceID property, which points the control at odsBookDetail. This causes the ObjectDataSource control to feed these control instances of BookDetails as they're selected from the ListBox. The BoundField declarations of this control then name public properties of that business object. Figure 11-4 displays the output generated.

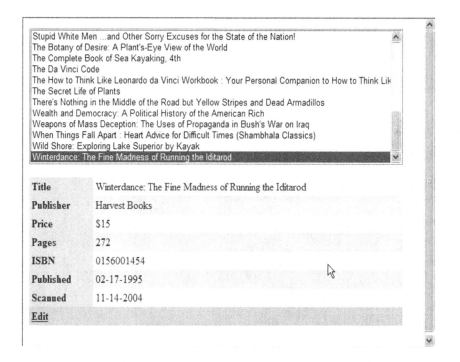

Figure 11-4. *A* ListBox *control and a* DetailsView *control bound to and tied together with* ObjectDataSource *controls*

Editing is also supported by the data source controls. In the declaration of odsBookDetails, notice that in addition to declaring GetBook as the SelectMethod, you're also declaring UpdateBook as the UpdateMethod.

```
UpdateMethod="UpdateBook"
```

This is another method on the BookBinding class. Let's take a look at this code.

```
public void UpdateBook(BookDetails b)
{
    b.Save();
}
```

Notice the type of the argument that it accepts is BookDetails. This is determined by the DataObjectTypeName property on odsBookDetails. The ObjectDataSource takes care of creating an instance of this type and moving values from the DetailsView to this instance of the business object, before passing it along as an argument to the UpdateBook method. Once in this method, you have only to tell the business object to move its values to persistence. This is work that the business object would usually delegate to a data access layer.

As far as the DetailsView is concerned, enabling editing involves a single element used in its declaration.

```
<asp:CommandField CancelText='x' UpdateText='ok' ShowEditButton="True"  />
```

This results in the Edit hyperlink being displayed (as shown in Figure 11-4). When the user clicks this link, the DetailsView automatically transforms its display from read-only into a data entry screen (see Figure 11-5).

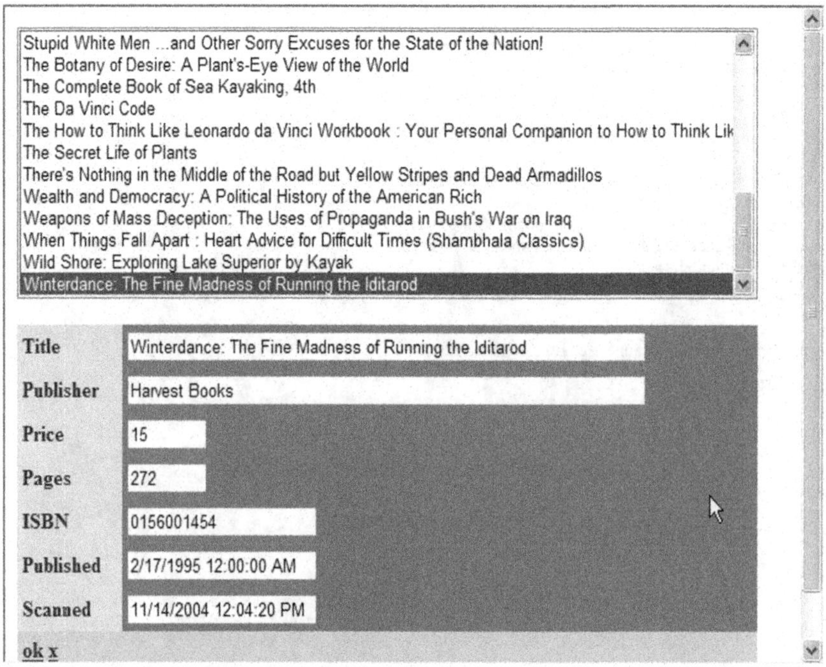

Figure 11-5. *The* DetailsView *in edit mode*

Now the user can apply changes, and when she clicks the ok link, the ObjectDataSource automatically creates an instance of the BookDetails object and passes it to the UpdateBook method of the BookBinding object.

And you still have no code in the code-behind the EditBook Web Form. As you begin to use these controls to implement real functionality, you'll find yourself in need of tweaking the interaction between these data source controls and the Web Controls they're bound to. Luckily there's a fairly rich event model exposed, enabling you to modify and extend the default behavior of these binding interactions (see Table 11-4).

Table 11-4. *Events Exposed by the* ObjectDataSource *Control*

Event	Meaning in Life
Deleting	Raised before a delete operation is executed
Deleted	Raised after a delete operation has completed
Filtering	Raised before a filter is applied to the underlying control data
Inserting	Raised before an insert operation is executed
Inserted	Raised after an insert operation has completed
ObjectCreating	Enables the developer to create his own custom object for the data source to use in binding operations
ObjectCreated	Raised after the data source's object is created, allowing for custom initialization
Selecting	Raised before a select operation is executed
Selected	Raised after a select operation has completed
Updating	Raised before an update operation is executed
Updated	Raised after an update operation has completed

In our example, the user may change the title of the book when editing. When they update the book, the DetailsView will automatically change back into a read-only view, but the ListBox will not be updated and so the title will be incorrect in the list. You can fix this by using the Updated event of the DetailsView. You can set up this trap with an attribute of the DetailsView declaration:

```
OnItemUpdated="dvEditBook_ItemUpdated"
```

In your code-behind, you can update the displayed value of the selected book:

```
protected void dvEditBook_ItemUpdated(
    object sender,
    DetailsViewUpdatedEventArgs e)
{
    lbBookList.SelectedItem.Text = e.NewValues["Title"].ToString();
}
```

Hopefully, you can see some of the benefits of the ObjectDataSource model over the model exposed by the SqlDataSource control. While you must take some consideration at the business object layer of the application, a set of types dedicated to feeding the data access controls still creates a better separation of these layers in your application architecture than using the code-behind for individual Web Forms will. You get a cleaner separation of layers with this model, where the specialized methods feeding the ObjectDataSource controls are concerned only with creating and returning appropriate instances of types for the methods they expose, and the data-binding logic is completely handled by the data source control. This looser coupling between layers leads to easier maintenance and better reuse across different presentation tier elements, and even across different applications.

Dependent Cache Entries

It is very easy to establish a dependency between a cache entry and an XML file. This is a great feature, as it enables you to load, parse, and cache an XML document for exactly as long as you need to: until you make a change to the document. Make a change to the doc, and the cache entry is automatically purged.

This type of dependency has very limited applications, though. It's very common to get XML data via a URL, or Web Service, or maybe even the database. In fact, it is still much more common to get data from the database than it is from XML in the first place. When it comes to loading data out of a database table and putting it into the cache, you have no similar capability to automatically purge the entry when a change is made to the data. The best you can do in 1.x of the Framework is to establish a timeout on the cache entry, and accept some level of latency. For example, if you put the data in the cache and have an absolute expiration of 60 seconds, any change you make to the data will take, at most, 59 seconds to show up.

This solution is not attractive for a couple of reasons. Sometimes this level of latency is not acceptable. A change to the data may need to show up on the site immediately. Conversely, sometimes your queries are so expensive that you don't want to go back to the database at 60-second intervals to refresh it, especially since there's no guarantee the data has even changed during that time.

What you'd really like to do is create a cache entry, and tell the cache that if, for example, the data in the authors table changes, then purge the cache entry so you'll know to go back to the database to refresh it. This feature has been added in version 2.0 of the Framework, but only for SQL Server 7 and later. The implementation for SQL Server 2005 is very different than it is for versions preceding it. Here, we'll examine the feature in SQL Server 7 and 2000.

Currently, XML file cache invalidation is done with the FileDependency class. SQL Server cache invalidation is done with a new class, named SQLCacheDependency. This type uses a combination of triggers on the database and polling from the client to determine when a cache entry has expired (see Figure 11-6).

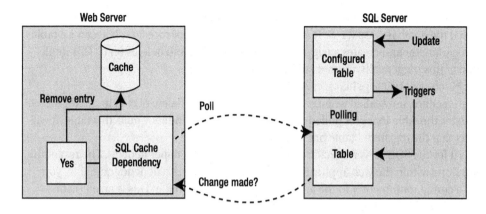

Figure 11-6. *SQL cache invalidation infrastructure*

SQL Cache Dependency Configuration

The first thing you must do to use SQL cache invalidations is set up a specific database to support the infrastructure. A command line tool, aspnet_regsql.exe, ships with version 2.0 of the Framework that automates a lot of the different database server setup that's required for different features of ASP.NET 2.0 (membership, personalization, session state, etc.). The tool supports a console window command line mode and a Win32 Wizard mode. To set up a specific database, you could use the following command line:

```
aspnet_regsql -S (local) -U sa -P 123123 -d Pubs -ed
```

Most of the switches are connection information. You could also use a connection string:

```
aspnet_regsql -C server=.;uid=sa;pwd=123123;database=pubs -ed
```

So you can see that, besides connection information, the only other switch you're passing is -ed. This tells the tool to enable the database you've specified for SQL cache invalidation, which creates a table named AspNet_SqlCacheTablesForChangeNotification in the database you've specified. This is the table that gets polled by the dependency, watching for changes. You'll see how changes get recorded in this table soon. There are also half a dozen stored procedures that get created. These are used for registering and unregistering tables, and polling and listing registered tables.

After a database is prepared for cache invalidations, you'll need to configure the tables you're interested in watching. This registration adds triggers to the tables that will record when something changes in the AspNet_SqlCacheTablesForChangeNotification table. This is the table that gets polled by ASP.NET, and is how the word gets back to the cache dependency that an entry needs to be purged.

The command line this time needs to specify the command, -et, for enable table, and then the -t switch to specify the table name:

```
aspnet_regsql -C server=.;uid=sa;pwd=123123;database=pubs -et -t authors
```

This time the command line tool simply calls the stored procedure that was created when you enabled the database, `AspNet_SqlCacheRegisterTableStoredProcedure`. It accepts a table name as a parameter and creates a trigger for inserts, updates, and deletes on it. This implementation of this trigger calls another stored procedure: `AspNet_SqlCacheUpdateChangeIdStoredProcedure`.

This procedure, now called whenever an insert, update, or delete occurs in the registered table, updates the table that gets polled. The next time the dependency polls this table, it will see the fact that the registered table has changed.

That's it for the SQL Server-specific setup needed for cache dependencies. The rest of the setup gets done within the web application that's going to declare a dependency. First, you must add a configuration entry to the application's configuration file. This is an element named `caching`, added as a child to the `system.web` element.

```
<caching>
    <sqlCacheDependency enabled="true" pollTime="10000">
        <databases>
                <add name="Publishers" connectionStringName="localPubs" />
        </databases>
    </sqlCacheDependency>
</caching>
```

The `SqlCacheDependency` element allows you to enable caching and set the default frequency of the database polling. This is a number of milliseconds, so here you're setting it to poll every ten seconds. If your DBA cringes at the thought of polling the database every ten seconds, remind her that it's a simple request of a very small table, and far better than having to go back to the database for the entire result set with every request. Even when polling, this strategy should result in a net *reduction* of overall database traffic. This presupposes, of course, that there is sufficient demand for (or expense in creating) the result set to warrant adoption of a caching strategy in the first place. A resource that isn't under high demand should not be cached with a database dependency. Polling might actually *increase* traffic in that case.

The databases element is where you map names of dependencies to connection strings the dependency will use to connect and poll. This dependency is named Publishers to illustrate that it is not actually a database, and does not even name anything you configured with a command line tool. It is arbitrary. You use this name when creating a dependency object, and it is nothing more than a convoluted way of giving the dependency object a connection string to use to poll the database (an alias for an alias for a connection string).

The `connectionStringName` attribute refers to a named connection from the `connectionString` element (covered in the Chapter 10 discussion on connection strings).

```
<connectionStrings>
    <add name="localPubs"
        connectionString="Server=.;Database=Pubs;uid=sa;pwd=123123" />
</connectionStrings>
```

Everything is now set up to use the dependency.

Programming with SQL Cache Dependencies

Let's add SQL cache invalidation to the sorting example we examined in Chapter 10. Here we showed you how to read the authors table, cache the dataset, and then create a DataView to represent each sort, and cache each of those. To make the dataset dependent upon the data changing, you have only to modify the line inserting the DataSet into the cache (you can find this code in SortIE.aspx of the Web11 project).

```
private DataSet GetAuthors()
{
    DataSet ds;

    ds = (DataSet)Cache["AuthorData"];

    if (ds == null)
    {
        ds = new DataSet();
        SqlConnection cn = new SqlConnection
            ("server=.;database=pubs;uid=sa;pwd=123123");

        SqlCommand cm = new
            SqlCommand("select * from authors", cn);

        new SqlDataAdapter(cm).Fill(ds);

        Cache.Insert("AuthorData", ds,
            new SqlCacheDependency("Publishers", "authors"));

    }
    return ds;
}
```

The third argument of the call to the Insert method is an instance of a CacheDependency object. Since SqlCacheDependency inherits from CacheDependency, you can create a new instance and configure it with its constructor. The first argument the constructor accepts is the name you gave the dependency entry in the configuration file. This maps back to the connection string the dependency will use for polling. The second parameter is the name of the table you want to watch. This table must be configured using the -et switch of the command line tool. The cache will now start polling the database every ten seconds.

As your user selects different sorts, different DataView instances are created and put in the cache as well. You'll make the same change to the line inserting these into the cache.

```
private void BindGrid(string sortExpr)
{
    DataView dv;
    string sCacheEntry =
        string.Format("Author_Sort_{0}", sortExpr);

    dv = (DataView)Cache[sCacheEntry];
```

```
if (dv == null)
{
    dv = new DataView(
        GetAuthors().Tables[0], "",
        sortExpr,
        DataViewRowState.CurrentRows);

    Cache.Insert(sCacheEntry, dv,
        new SqlCacheDependency("Publishers", "authors"));

}

gvAuthors.DataSource = dv;
gvAuthors.DataBind();
}
```

Now every time the user sorts, a new database-dependent cache entry gets created. The database does not, however, get polled by each dependency. One request is made to retrieve all change notifications.

These dependencies can also be used with output caching. The following OutputCache directive will make the page's output dependent upon a change to the authors table (see OutputCacheIE.aspx in the Web11 project).

```
<%@ OutputCache SqlDependency="Publishers:authors"
    Duration="9999" VaryByParam="none" %>
```

The first attribute names your cache entry in the configuration file, followed by a colon and the name of the table to watch. Keep in mind that the duration attribute determines the absolute expiration of the entry in the output cache. The polling time is still determined by the SqlCacheDepedency entry you made in the web.config using the aspnet_regsql command line tool.

Automating SQL Cache Dependency Administration

You can also perform the setup using an administrative helper type built into the Framework: SqlCacheDependencyAdmin. This type exposes a number of static methods (see Table 11-5). There are pairs for enabling and disabling databases and tables, and a method for retrieving a list of tables set up for notification. You can use these methods from an administrative tool during development as an alternative to the aspnet_regsql command line tool, or use them to dynamically set up and tear down dependencies at runtime.

You'll use this type to build a simple admin tool for setting up databases and tables for SQL cache dependencies. You'll use a drop-down list and a grid view to display databases and tables (see Figure 11-7). You can use this interface during project development to configure cache dependencies.

Table 11-5. *Static Methods of the SQL Cache Dependency Administration Class*

Method Name	Meaning in Life
EnableNotifications	Sets up a database for notifications. Same as the -ed command line switch.
DisableNotifications	Tears down the setup for notifications. Same as the -dd switch.
EnableTableForNotifications	Sets up a table for notifications. Same as the -et switch.
DisableTableForNotifications	Tears down the setup for notifications. Same as the -dt switch.
GetTablesEnabledForNotifications	Returns an array of strings naming the tables set up for notification.

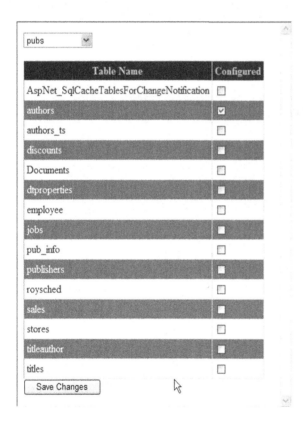

Figure 11-7. *A custom made adminstration interface for SQL dependencies*

Here's the markup for the drop-down list, the grid view, and the buttons needed to fire postbacks (see SetupSqlCache.aspx in the Web11 project).

```
<asp:DropDownList ID="ddlDatabase" Runat="server"
    AutoPostBack=true
    OnSelectedIndexChanged="ddlDatabase_SelectedIndexChanged" />
<br /><br />
<asp:GridView AutoGenerateColumns=false ID="gvTables" Runat="server"
```

```
        BorderWidth="1px" BackColor="White" CellPadding="4"
        BorderStyle="None" BorderColor="#3366CC">
        <FooterStyle ForeColor="#003399" BackColor="#99CCCC"></FooterStyle>
        <PagerStyle ForeColor="#003399"
                             HorizontalAlign="Left"
                             BackColor="#99CCCC" />
        <HeaderStyle ForeColor="#CCCCFF"
                               Font-Bold="True"
                               BackColor="#003399" />
        <SelectedRowStyle ForeColor="#CCFF99"
                                         Font-Bold="True"
                                         BackColor="#009999" />
        <RowStyle ForeColor="#003399" BackColor="White" />
        <AlternatingRowStyle ForeColor=White BackColor=DodgerBlue />
        <Columns>
            <asp:BoundField DataField='name' HeaderText='Table Name' />

            <asp:TemplateField HeaderText='Configured'>
                <ItemTemplate>
                <asp:checkbox  runat='server'
                    TableName='<%# Eval("name") %>'
                    Checked='<%# Convert.ToBoolean(Eval("Configured")) %>'
                    OnCheckedChanged='FlipBit' />
                </ItemTemplate>
            </asp:TemplateField>
        </Columns>
</asp:GridView>

<asp:button Runat=server id=btnSave
    Text='Save Changes'
    OnClick="btnSave_Click"
    Visible="False" />

<asp:Button ID="Button1" Runat="server"
    Text="Enable this Database"
    OnClick="Button1_Click"
    Visible="False" />
```

When the page first loads, the drop-down list will be populated with a list of databases for the server you're using.

```
protected void Page_Load(object sender, EventArgs e)
{
    if (!IsPostBack)
    {
        string sql =
        "SELECT name FROM sysdatabases ORDER BY name";
        SqlConnection cn = new SqlConnection
```

```
        (BuildConnStr("master"));
    SqlCommand cm = new SqlCommand(sql, cn);

    cn.Open();
    ddlDatabase.DataSource = cm.ExecuteReader();
    ddlDatabase.DataTextField = "name";
    ddlDatabase.DataBind();
    cn.Close();
    ddlDatabase.Items.Insert(0, "");
    }
}
```

A blank list item gets added to the top of the drop down, so there's no database selected when the page first renders. Since you're connecting to any number of databases for configuration, connections rely on a helper method to dynamically build the connection string.

```
private string BuildConnStr(string Database)
{
    return string.Format
        ("server=.;database={0};uid=sa;pwd=", Database);
}
```

When the user makes a selection from the list, the selected index changed event trap fires on the server (autopostback is set to true on the control). The trap calls the BindGrid method, which uses the name of the database the user has chosen to dynamically build a connection string, and queries the sysobjects table for all table names within the database.

```
protected void ddlDatabase_SelectedIndexChanged(object sender, EventArgs e)
{ BindGrid(); }

void BindGrid()
{
    string sql = "SELECT sysobjects.name, " +
        "sysobjects.type, case coalesce " +
        "(AspNet_SqlCacheTablesForChangeNotification.tableName, " +
        "'0') when '0' then 'false' else 'true' end AS Configured "+
        "FROM sysobjects LEFT OUTER JOIN " +
        "AspNet_SqlCacheTablesForChangeNotification " +
        "ON sysobjects.name = " +
        "AspNet_SqlCacheTablesForChangeNotification.tableName " +
        "WHERE (sysobjects.type = 'U') " +
        "ORDER BY sysobjects.name";

    SqlConnection cn = new SqlConnection(
        BuildConnStr(ddlDatabase.SelectedValue));

    SqlCommand cm = new SqlCommand(sql, cn);
```

```
    try
    {
        cn.Open();
        gvTables.DataSource = cm.ExecuteReader();
        gvTables.DataBind();
        btnSave.Visible = true;
    }
    catch
    {
        gvTables.Visible = false;
        btnSave.Visible = false;
        Button1.Visible = true;
    }
    finally
    {
        cn.Close();
    }
}
```

The query in use in this method also does on outer join to the polling table (AspNet_
SqlCacheTablesForChangeNotification). When this table is not present, the execution of the
query throws an exception. From this, you infer that the database is not configured for cache
dependencies, and display a button to let the user configure the database (see Figure 11-8).

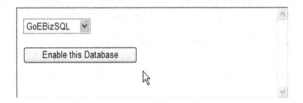

Figure 11-8. *The admin display when the selected database is not configured*

When the user clicks this button, you configure the database for cache dependencies and
render the grid.

```
protected void Button1_Click(object sender, EventArgs e)
{
    string sConn = BuildConnStr(ddlDatabase.SelectedValue);
    SqlCacheDependencyAdmin.EnableNotifications(sConn);
    Button1.Visible = false;
    gvTables.Visible = true;
    btnSave.Visible = true;
    BindGrid();
}
```

In the case where the database is configured (and so the polling table is present), the
outer join attempts to link the object name with the TableName from the polling table.

```
...FROM sysobjects LEFT OUTER JOIN
AspNet_SqlCacheTablesForChangeNotification
ON sysobjects.name =
AspNet_SqlCacheTablesForChangeNotification.tableName...
```

If the table name is present in the polling table, it's configured, and the outer join will succeed. If the table is not configured, it won't be present in the polling table, and the column value will be null. The query uses a case and a coalesce to translate these possible values into true or false, which you use to bind the checked value of the CheckBox on the grid.

```
case
coalesce (AspNet_SqlCacheTablesForChangeNotification.tableName ,'0')
when '0' then 'false'
else 'true' end
AS Configured
```

```
<asp:TemplateField HeaderText='Configured'>
    <ItemTemplate>
    <asp:checkbox  runat='server'
        TableName='<%# Eval("name") %>'
        Checked='<%# Convert.ToBoolean(Eval("Configured")) %>'
        OnCheckedChanged='FlipBit' />
    </ItemTemplate>
</asp:TemplateField>
```

The TableName attribute is not actually a property of the CheckBox control, but the rendering engine is smart enough to pass this value through into the markup and the ViewState, making it available for your use when the postback occurs. As the user makes changes to these CheckBox controls, the server-side OnCheckChanged events get queued up on the client, until the user clicks the submit button. Then a postback occurs, and the CheckChanged trap fires once for each CheckBox that has had its value altered. After all of the check-changed events are processed, the onclick of the button finally fires.

```
protected void FlipBit(Object sender, EventArgs e)
{
    CheckBox c = (CheckBox)sender;
    string sConn = BuildConnStr(ddlDatabase.SelectedValue);
    string tableName = c.Attributes["TableName"];

    if (c.Checked)
        SqlCacheDependencyAdmin.EnableTableForNotifications
            (sConn, tableName);
    else
        SqlCacheDependencyAdmin.DisableTableForNotifications
            (sConn, tableName);
```

```
}
void btnSave_Click(object sender, EventArgs e)
{
    BindGrid();
}
```

In the check-changed trap, you use the TableName attribute and the event sender to determine what table should be enabled or disabled. By the time the button click event fires, the only work left to do is to refresh the grid to ensure it matches the current caching configuration in the database.

SQL cache dependencies are a powerful new feature in ASP.NET 2.0. It's one people have been clamoring for for years, and is best suited for read-mostly data, or data where some latency is acceptable between changing the data and seeing the changes on the site. If the data is highly volatile and no latency is acceptable, then there's no sense in caching it, as it will constantly be invalidated as the data changes, and/or frequent polling will be required to get the latest version. For situations where the data is in high demand and it does not change constantly within the database, a caching strategy can increase the performance of your application by several orders of magnitude.

SQL Server 2005 has a notification infrastructure, which enables the database to call out to other processes as events occur. This eliminates the need for polling from the cache dependency, and results in less latency between changes and cache invalidations. See the last section of this chapter (on SQL Server 2005) for details.

Data Access Application Block

This is a set of assemblies from Microsoft designed to streamline, simplify, and supercharge data access code. This application block is in its third shipping version from Microsoft. The first two versions were stand-alone sets of assemblies that provided a generic data access layer. The original version of the Block was one of about a dozen different blocks available from Microsoft, each of which provided functionality covering a different set of requirements. There was a configuration block, an exception handling block, and a logging block, to name a few. Any block could be used in an application when its services were needed.

Microsoft's patterns & practices group created the application blocks. The goal of application blocks is to provide production-ready sets of functionality that you can add to your .NET Enterprise applications. Application blocks do not ship with the Framework; you have to download them separately. When you download them, you get all of the source code, the compiled assemblies, and project files for opening them in Visual Studio .NET and modifying them.

Note For a list of all application blocks and links for downloading, see http://msdn.microsoft.com/practices/AppBlocks/default.aspx

---

Problems came about when several application blocks were in use concurrently. Microsoft tested each of the blocks in isolation from one another, but in different combinations, the blocks had a tendency to step on one another's toes. Microsoft decided it would be easier to put them all into a single package, test them together, and just let folks leverage functionality out of specific assemblies as needed. And so the Enterprise Library was born.

The official name of this block is now the Enterprise Library Data Access Application Block Version 1.0, even though it's the third version of the block. Seven blocks have been rolled into the Enterprise Library. We discuss Enterprise Library v 1.0, which shipped in January of 2005, here. There will be a new version of the Enterprise Library shipped after the release of version 2.0 of the Framework, one that leverages some of the new Framework features. But if you're still using version 1.1 of the Framework, or until Microsoft ships a new version (as 2.0 will be backwards compatible and so Enterprise Library 1.0 will work with it), this data access layer can really give you a jump start on your data access code, and provide you with a few features that aren't present in the 1.x version of the Managed Providers.

Almost any application that accesses a relational database can benefit from this application block. The block results in less boilerplate code that has to be written to execute any command, and it manages opening and closing connections to the database, which maximizes the efficiency of the connection pool and reduces the chances of introducing a connection leak into an application. Code is simpler to maintain, and developers have a common model to use to execute commands against the database, simplifying the learning curve for someone working on an Enterprise suite of applications.

The block also introduces an object factory that creates a layer of abstraction between the consumer of the data and the database being used on the back end. This means the same code can use different databases, without any changes to the code. This was one of the biggest features lost in the move from ADO to Managed Providers. The Data Access Application Block restores this functionality for SQL Server, Oracle, and DB2. Since the source code is available, adding support for another Managed Provider is not hard. Instructions are included right in the block's documentation (note that the .NET Framework 2.0 adds this functionality to the Managed Provider model; see provider factories in Chapter 10).

Configuration and the Database Object

You use configuration files to name and provide connection information to the databases to be used from within the block. Within a configuration file you can name any number of logical databases, choose a database vendor for each, and establish connection strings. There's a configuration tool that ships with the Enterprise Library that will generate the appropriate entries for your application's configuration file. It's called "Enterprise Library Configuration."

The setup goes like this. You have any number of database types. The block supports SQL Server, Oracle, and DB2 by default. Within each type, you have a number of instances. These are specific databases you want to connect to of a specific type. This is the level of configuration where you establish a logical name of the database, which is all you need to use from your code to work with it. An instance is then associated with a named connection string. The connection entry in the configuration file has all of the named/value pairs that will be used to build the connection string at runtime.

Here you set the configuration for working with the pubs database from SQL Server. The name you'll use from code is PubsDatabase. The leaf nodes under the connection string contain all of the named values (see Figure 11-9).

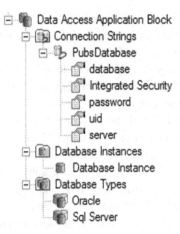

Figure 11-9. *The database node of the Enterprise Library configuration*

Although Oracle is set up here, you're not using it. The application block supports DB2 databases by default, but this option isn't compiled and built into the block's assemblies when you first install the Enterprise Library. The support for DB2 is dependent upon IBM's Managed Provider for DB2, so you must first install that, and then compile the DB2 project included with the application block's source code.

The configuration tool will still support DB2 databases, even though they are not present in the tool by default. The Type Selector dialog box sports a Load an Assembly... button. This dialog enables you to browse out to the assemblies created with the DB2 project, or to your own implementation of a Managed Provider for the block (see Figure 11-10). The tool does not care, just so the assembly chosen has a type that inherits from EnterpriseLibrary.Data.Database in it.

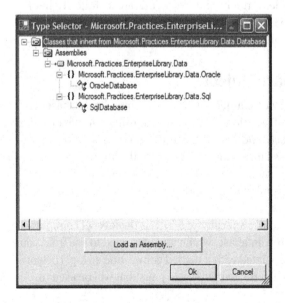

Figure 11-10. *The Type Selector dialog box*

When the configuration is saved, the tool writes out two files. One contains the elements that will be used from your application configuration file. It's basically just a verbose pointer to a file named dataConfiguration.config. This is the file that will be read by the block at runtime.

Here's the (slightly abbreviated) configuration file that will be used by the block:

```xml
<?xml version="1.0" encoding="utf-8"?>
<dataConfiguration>
  <xmlSerializerSection type="...">
    <enterpriseLibrary.databaseSettings
        defaultInstance="PubsDatabase" ...>
      <databaseTypes>
        <databaseType name="Oracle" type="..." />
        <databaseType name="Sql Server" type="..." />
      </databaseTypes>
      <instances>
        <instance name="PubsDatabase" type="Sql Server"
            connectionString="pubs" />
      </instances>
      <connectionStrings>
        <connectionString name="pubs">
          <parameters>
            <parameter name="database" value="pubs"
                isSensitive="false" />
            <parameter name="Integrated Security" value="false"
                isSensitive="false" />
            <parameter name="pwd" value="123123"
                isSensitive="true" />
            <parameter name="uid" value="sa"
                isSensitive="false" />
            <parameter name="server" value="localhost"
                isSensitive="false" />
          </parameters>
        </connectionString>
        <connectionString name="Sql Connection String">
          <parameters>
            <parameter name="database" value="database"
                isSensitive="false" />
            <parameter name="Integrated Security" value="True"
                isSensitive="false" />
            <parameter name="server" value="server"
                isSensitive="false" />
          </parameters>
        </connectionString>
      </connectionStrings>
    </enterpriseLibrary.databaseSettings>
  </xmlSerializerSection>
</dataConfiguration>
```

The ellipses all indicate omission of a full assembly name or a namespace. The important bits are retained. You can see from this configuration that a database named PubsDatabase is now mapped to a connection string to that database. You can create an instance of a database object that represents this connection with a single line of code.

```
Database db = DatabaseFactory.CreateDatabase("PubsDatabase");
```

Also, because the PubsDatabase is set as the default instance, you can simply create it with:

```
Database db = DatabaseFactory.CreateDatabase();
```

Naming the instance is only necessary when you're using more than one database from an application. You can still use a default in that case, but you'll be better off naming all instances explicitly to clarify the code and ease maintenance.

Now that you have an instance to a Database object, the rest of the work is done with its instance methods.

All of the code that follows requires a reference to the assembly named Microsoft.Practices.EnterpriseLibrary.Data.dll and the following using statement.

```
using Microsoft.Practices.EnterpriseLibrary.Data;
```

Data Access Methods

There are several scenarios this block specifically sets out to simplify (see Table 11-6). These data access methods require many lines of code when you're using a Managed Provider directly, but only a few when you're using the helper methods exposed by the block.

Table 11-6. *Different Data Access Scenarios the Data Access Application Block Assists With*

Data Access Scenario	Meaning in Life
Returning multiple rows	A couple of methods geared towards helping with a command that prepares and returns tabular data exist. Results can be returned with a data reader or a data set. Simple queries can be executed, and results returned, with two lines of code.
Executing commands that do not return result sets	A number of commands to send to a database that do not return a result set exist. Helper methods simplify several of these. You may be doing inserts, updates, and deletes; doing work within a transaction; or may expect output parameters or a single value.
Sending Dataset updates back to the database	After changes are applied in memory to data tables in a Dataset, the time comes to ship these back. The block can do this without a data adapter.
Getting XML data	The block will automatically transform result sets into XML.

These scenarios are all exposed via methods on the Database object. The snippet that follows connects to the pubs database (described as the default in the configuration file) and binds it to an instance of the GridView control:

```
protected void Page_Load(object sender, EventArgs e)
{
    Database db = DatabaseFactory.CreateDatabase();

    GridView1.DataSource = db.ExecuteReader(CommandType.Text,
                        "select * from authors");
    GridView1.DataBind();
}
```

You could do this just as easily by caching a DataSet:

```
void Page_Load(object sender, EventArgs e)
{
    GridView1.DataSource = GetAuthors();
    GridView1.DataBind();
}

private DataSet GetAuthors()
{
    DataSet ds;

    ds = (DataSet)Cache["Authors"];

    if (ds == null)
    {
        Database db = DatabaseFactory.CreateDatabase();

        ds = db.ExecuteDataSet(CommandType.Text,
                                    "select * from authors");
        Cache.Insert("Authors", ds);
    }
    return ds;
}
```

In both of these cases, the amount of code is reduced compared to what you'd need if you used a Managed Provider directly. Changes to the configuration file can switch the type of database in use. And the connection lifetime is managed by the block, creating consistently in your application's data access code.

Regardless of the data access method needed for a given result set, the block standardizes the code and the process that will be used to acquire resources, execute commands, and release those resources.

Dynamic SQL generation works fine for limited scenarios. Typically statements are more complex, or data access is being done with stored procedures, which usually require parameters. When parameters are in use, whether they're built into a dynamic SQL statement, or they're input or output parameters to a stored procedure, it is time to use a command wrapper.

The Command Wrapper Object

The command wrapper is a helper type for a `Command` object in a Managed Provider. It's created for you by a database object and automatically populates several properties of the wrapped `Command`. There are two main factory methods for retrieving an instance of a command wrapper (see Table 11-7).

Table 11-7. *Factory Methods for Command Wrapper Objects*

Factory Method	Meaning in Life
GetStringCommandWrapper	Creates a wrapper configured for `CommandType` of `Text`.
GetStoredProcCommandWrapper	Creates a wrapper configured for stored procedure execution.

Once returned, the wrapper exposes `AddXYZParameter` methods to define the parameters using simple names, types, and values. Consider this stored procedure again. (Recall that we used it in Chapter 10 to demonstrate calling a stored procedure with Managed Provider code.)

```
create procedure usp_GetPubDetails
@pub_id char(4),
@pub_name varchar(40) OUTPUT,
@city varchar(20) OUTPUT,
@state char(2) OUTPUT,
@country varchar(30) OUTPUT
as
SELECT
@pub_name = pub_name,
@city = city,
@state = state,
@country = country
FROM publishers
WHERE (pub_id = @pub_id)
```

The command wrapper code to execute this stored procedure is much simpler than in the Managed Provider code:

```
private PublisherBO GetPublisher(string PubID)
{
    PublisherBO boReturn = new PublisherBO();

    Database db = DatabaseFactory.CreateDatabase();

    DBCommandWrapper cw =
        db.GetStoredProcCommandWrapper("usp_GetPubDetails");

    cw.AddInParameter("@pub_id", DbType.String, PubID);
    cw.AddOutParameter("@pub_name", DbType.String, 40);
    cw.AddOutParameter("@city", DbType.String, 20);
    cw.AddOutParameter("@state", DbType.String, 2);
    cw.AddOutParameter("@country", DbType.String, 30);
```

```
    db.ExecuteNonQuery(cw);

    boReturn.PubID = PubID;
    boReturn.Name = cw.GetParameterValue("@pub_name").ToString();
    boReturn.City = cw.GetParameterValue("@city").ToString();
    boReturn.State = cw.GetParameterValue("@state").ToString();
    boReturn.Country = cw.GetParameterValue("@country").ToString();

    return boReturn;
}
```

While using the Database and command wrapper objects largely replaces constructor semantics of managed code with factory method calls, this example really shows how the amount of code is reduced, as it has a single line of code to deal with each property value in use at the business object layer. The structure of the code is much simpler than the constructor and indexing code the Managed Provider requires.

Parameters and the Parameter Cache

There is another option that's even simpler. The Get*XYZ*CommandWrapper methods have another overloaded method signature that accepts a parameter array as a second parameter. This parameter array will accept all the values for the procedure's input parameters.

The command wrapper factory then makes a request to the database for the schema definition of the procedure being executed. Using this information, it generates the set of parameters the procedure expects. Our last example could use this technique with the following code:

```
private PublisherBO GetPublisherParamCache(string PubID)
{
    PublisherBO boReturn = new PublisherBO();

    Database db = DatabaseFactory.CreateDatabase();

    DBCommandWrapper cw =
        db.GetStoredProcCommandWrapper("usp_GetPubDetails", PubID);

    db.ExecuteNonQuery(cw);

    boReturn.PubID = PubID;
    boReturn.Name = cw.GetParameterValue("@pub_name").ToString();
    boReturn.City = cw.GetParameterValue("@city").ToString();
    boReturn.State = cw.GetParameterValue("@state").ToString();
    boReturn.Country = cw.GetParameterValue("@country").ToString();

    return boReturn;
}
```

Here you've replaced all of the calls to create parameters and simply added the PubID as a second argument passed to the factory method. Notice that even though you haven't explicitly created them, the factory still creates all of the output parameters, which you use after executing the command. This simplifies your code, but comes at the cost of an extra round trip to the database to query the schema so the factory knows what parameters to create.

To compensate for this, the block uses a cache to keep the definition of the parameters present in memory after the initial round trip to retrieve the metadata. This means the penalty for the extra round trip is only incurred on the first request; subsequent requests will retrieve the parameters from the cache. This yields better performance for subsequent requests (after the first) than the previous example, which has to re-create all of the parameter objects with each request.

Ideally, you could create the parameters yourself on the first request (avoiding the extra round trip) and then cache the definition yourself for use on subsequent requests (avoiding the overhead of re-instantiating the collection of parameter objects with each request). Unfortunately, the parameter cache is not publicly exposed by the data access block, and so this would be a manual coding effort.

The parameter cache method is still good for late binding type of operations, where you don't know the footprint of the procedure you're calling in advance and therefore cannot possibly write code to create the parameter collection. In this situation, consumers of your data access layer could simply pass a list of values, and you would pass that list along to the command wrapper factory, and the appropriate parameter collection would be created using metadata.

```
public DataSet ExecuteProcedure(string ProcedureCall)
{
    Database db = DatabaseFactory.CreateDatabase();
    string SprocName;
    string ParamList;

    int iPos = ProcedureCall.IndexOf(" ");

    SprocName = ProcedureCall.Substring(0, iPos);
    ParamList = ProcedureCall.Substring(iPos + 1).Replace(" ", "");

    DBCommandWrapper cw =
        db.GetStoredProcCommandWrapper
        (SprocName, ParamList.Split(",".ToCharArray()));

    return db.ExecuteDataSet(cw);
}
```

Now stored procedures can be executed like the slackers used to do it with ADO!

```
void Page_Load(object sender, EventArgs e)
{
    GridView gv = new GridView();

    gv.DataSource =
        ExecuteProcedure("usp_SortAuthors au_fname");
    gv.DataBind();
    this.form1.Controls.Add(gv);
```

```
    gv = new GridView();
    gv.DataSource =
        ExecuteProcedure("AuthorTitleSales 500, 213-46-8915")
    gv.DataBind();
    this.form1.Controls.Add(gv);
}
```

This code executes these commands by passing a string naming the stored procedure first, and then white space separating parameter values. The consumers of this service do not need to be concerned with parameter names or types. You'd need more robust code to support parameter values containing spaces, and would need to add logic to parse the command text out to find values delimited with quotes or tics.

Keep in mind that there are trade-offs to this approach, and this will definitely not be the right method for any application. The round trip for parameter type discovery incurred on the first request is nontrivial, and there's not a lot of type safety built into this infrastructure. On the plus, side, it's extremely flexible and easy to use.

Using the Data Access Block for Transaction Management

Invariably, work must be done *transactionally*. You have many ways to do many types of transactions. We limit our discussion here to what you can accomplish with the Data Access Application Block, which is a transaction on a single connection to a single data store. The block leverages the transaction capabilities built into the Managed Providers.

The transaction model in the block is very simple. Many of the Execute*XYZ* methods you've already examined have a different overloaded method footprint that accepts an instance of an IDBTransaction instance. When this is present, the work is done in a transaction. This interface exposes the Commit and Rollback methods, which determine the fate of the work that's been done in the transaction. Transactions are created by another factory method of the Database object. Let's have a look.

Here you'll increase royalty paid to authors from the pubs database by 10 percent (a very fine idea indeed). First you'll update the royalty schedule. You'll then need to cascade this update to the titles table, where royalty (in a gross denormalization of the pubs schema) is carried as well. If this cascade update fails, you'll need to roll back the initial update of the royalty amounts.

```
private void UpdateRoyalties()
{
    Database db = DatabaseFactory.CreateDatabase();
    IDbConnection cn = db.GetConnection();

    string sql1 = "update roysched set royalty = royalty * 1.1";
    string sql2 = "update titles set titles.royalty = roysched.royalty " +
        "FROM roysched INNER JOIN " +
        "titles ON roysched.title_id = titles.title_id";

    DBCommandWrapper cwRoyal = db.GetSqlStringCommandWrapper(sql1);
    DBCommandWrapper cwTitle = db.GetSqlStringCommandWrapper(sql2);
```

```
IDbTransaction xaction = null;
try
{
    cn.Open();
    xaction = cn.BeginTransaction();
    db.ExecuteNonQuery(cwRoyal, xaction);
    db.ExecuteNonQuery(cwTitle, xaction);
    xaction.Commit();
}
catch
{
    if (xaction != null) xaction.Rollback();
}
finally
{
    cn.Close();
}
}
```

As you can see from the code, the Managed Provider transaction model has an *extremely* thin wrapper provided by the block. The preceding example takes control of the connection lifetime from the Database object. This works much the same way the DataAdapter.Fill method does. If the transaction is open when the Execute method is called, the Database object will use it and leave it open; otherwise, it opens, executes, and closes the connection.

This method of transaction management will work only when all work is being done on a single connection. For transactions that span databases or data providers, Microsoft Distributed Transaction Coordinator (MSDTC) must be enrolled via COM+.

For more information on transactions, see Chapter 7 for a discussion of distributed transactions, and Chapter 12 for an examination of the in-memory transaction model available in the .NET Framework 2.0 that automatically enrolls the resource managers needed as the scope of a transaction increases.

A Developer's Survey of SQL Server 2005

Traditionally, an ASP.NET developer's concern regarding the application architecture ends at the database. Sure, you may need to decide between using stored procedures or queries, or you may need to work with the data administrator to define the data schemas, but the brunt of the design and the implementation is normally passed to those who live and breathe tables, views, stored procedures, triggers, and Transact-SQL (T-SQL).

With the introduction of SQL Server 2005, however, come several new features that blur the sharp line between application and database concerns. Most notably, SQL Server 2005 provides a feature called Common Language Runtime (CLR) integration, which allows managed code to execute within the SQL Server 2005 process and interact directly with the data. Other new features of particular interest to application developers include Service Broker and XML as a native type. Although a detailed drill down of each of the features is beyond the scope of this book, this section provides an overview of each with the information you need to correctly position and leverage them in your architecture.

CLR Integration in SQL Server 2005

Perhaps the most anticipated new SQL Server 2005 feature (at least from a developer's perspective) is dubbed *CLR Integration*, and enables managed code to execute within the SQL Server 2005 process and interact directly with the data. This means that you can write stored procedures and user-defined functions using any .NET language while leveraging the rich set of functionality provided by the .NET Framework classes. You can even extend the SQL Server type system by creating your own custom data types.

But don't throw out all your T-SQL books yet! It turns out that CLR Integration is intended to complement traditional database development rather than replace it. So the real question regarding CLR Integration is when do you use it versus traditional database techniques such as T-SQL stored procedures? To help you answer this question, in this section, we'll go over the nature and capabilities of CLR integration and compare them with conventional database approaches.

Comparing Managed Code and Transact-SQL

Traditionally, SQL Server database development is done in Transact-SQL (T-SQL). This language is designed to make it easy to write database queries such as selects, inserts, deletes, and updates. In fact, such queries in T-SQL are syntactically similar to everyday English. Furthermore, T-SQL has many built-in functions that perform calculations on a particular column of a table for a set of selected rows. For example, this T-SQL query averages the unit price of all products in each category.

```
SELECT Categories.CategoryName, AVG(Products.UnitPrice)
FROM Products INNER JOIN Categories
ON Products.CategoryID = Categories.CategoryID
GROUP BY Categories.CategoryName
```

This demonstrates the power of T-SQL. In one statement, this code joins the Products and Categories tables by their respective CategoryID columns, computes the average Unit-Price for all products in each category, and then returns the calculated average UnitPrice for each category. That is quite a bit of work from one (albeit long) statement. Overall, this code demonstrates the effectiveness of T-SQL's *set-oriented* capabilities, which enable you to quickly and easily work with, filter, relate, and perform calculations on sets of data. Indeed, T-SQL excels at processing sets of data, which is not surprising given the fact that it is, after all, a database language.

T-SQL also has many language constructs that are similar to those of a typical procedural programming language. These include WHILE loops, variable declaration and assignment, cursors, decision branching (IF/ELSE, CASE), etc. However, although T-SQL excels at set-oriented processing, its procedural capabilities pale in comparison to most general purpose languages, particularly .NET languages such as C# or VB .NET. Furthermore, since T-SQL is an interpreted language, the execution of procedural logic is much slower than the execution of equivalent logic in a compiled language, such as C++, or even in a just-in-time (JIT) compiled language, such as any of those found in .NET. For these reasons, database programmers have always strived to fully leverage the set-oriented features of T-SQL, while resorting to its procedural constructs only when necessary.

In many cases, the required procedural logic isn't implemented within the database at all. Instead, it is placed within a .NET middle-tier component. This approach frees the SQL Server process to concentrate on what it does best: process sets of data. It also enables the .NET developer to leverage the rich procedural and object-oriented features of any managed .NET language and the full set of functionality provided by the .NET Framework classes. The downside to this approach, however, is that it results in more data marshaling costs as the data must be moved out of the SQL Server process and into the middle-tier component and vice versa.

Understanding the Role of CLR Integration

Before CLR Integration, the state of database programming was less than ideal. T-SQL works great for set-oriented tasks, but it is difficult to work with and slow for procedural tasks. .NET languages can provide the necessary procedural logic, but only at the expense of marshaling the data in and out of the SQL Server database.

CLR Integration provides an elegant solution to this problem. SQL Server 2005 can host the CLR and, therefore, can execute managed code in process. This provides the following benefits:

- Instead of struggling with the limited procedural constructs of T-SQL, database developers can take advantage of all the capabilities of a managed .NET language such as C# or VB .NET. These languages provide modern procedural and object-oriented features, making it much easier to develop and reuse complex procedural logic. The JIT compilation scheme these languages employ also performs much better than T-SQL interpretation.

- When writing database code in a managed language, you can access all the functionality of the .NET Framework. The Framework contains thousands of useful classes, many of which provide functionality that's missing from and difficult to implement in T-SQL. For example, the Framework provides rich string handling, regular expressions, cryptography, XML processing, image manipulation, file access, and much, much more.

- Since the managed code executes within the SQL Server process, there is no need to marshal data across process. Therefore, this is more efficient than using middle-tier components to implement the procedural logic. In fact, SQL Server 2005 has a new server-side ADO.NET data provider that enables you to use standard ADO.NET calls to access the data. In this way, you get the performance benefits of direct data access while using a familiar programming model.

Remember, despite all these advantages, T-SQL remains the preferred mechanism for implementing set-oriented logic. CLR Integration, on the other hand, provides a better approach to implementing tasks that require complex procedural logic or tasks that would benefit from the functionality found in the .NET Framework classes.

Choosing Between CLR Integration and Middle-Tier Components

As noted earlier, a common approach to implementing data-oriented procedural logic is to place it in middle-tier .NET components. Although this incurs the cost of data marshaling, it remains a viable option, even with the advent of SQL Server 2005 and CLR Integration.

The database server is typically the most heavily taxed server in the enterprise. So, although the marshaling of data causes overhead, it also unloads the procedural processing from the database server, thus freeing precious CPU resources to do other tasks. Understanding this tradeoff is key to making the right decision about where to execute the logic. Here are a few other factors that can influence the ultimate placement of any procedural logic:

- The procedural logic may already be contained within the database as a stored procedure. In this case, it's generally appropriate to take advantage of CLR Integration and port the logic to a managed language.

- The procedural logic may represent business logic that you wish to share with other applications. This is typically easier to do if the logic is in the middle tier.

- The procedural logic may represent business logic that requires data from other external data sources. Obviously, this is much easier if the code is in the middle tier and can use ADO.NET to access a variety of data sources.

- Related to the previous case, you may wish to allow an easy transition to another database server in the future. Clearly, having a significant amount of logic contained within a SQL Server 2005 database complicates any transition to another type of database. Again, in this scenario, placing the code in middle tier components is the better option.

As the preceding points show, SQL Server 2005's CLR Integration feature does not render middle-tier components obsolete. This question, though, of where best to place data-oriented procedural logic is not new; it is simply a continuation of the age-old debate between T-SQL stored procedures and middle-tier business objects. In other words, the issues and concerns that affect your choice between CLR Integration and the middle tier are essentially the same as those that affect your choice between T-SQL stored procedures and the middle tier. The primary difference when you're considering CLR Integration versus the middle tier is that you no longer need to factor the awkwardness, difficulty, and performance concerns of expressing the procedural logic in T-SQL. So, generally speaking, if you would otherwise feel comfortable implementing the logic in a T-SQL stored procedure, then using CLR integration and a managed language is an appropriate solution.

Surveying the CLR Integration Features

Now that we've established the role of CLR Integration, its time to look at the specific types of managed database items this new feature supports. CLR Integration provides five different types of managed database items:

- *Managed stored procedures*: The classic stored procedure in a managed language.

- *User-defined functions (UDFs)*: Return single scalar values and are generally called from queries.

- *Table-valued functions (TVFs)*: Like user-defined functions, but can return a result set.

- *User-defined aggregates (UDAs)*: Enable you to define your own custom aggregate function that behaves like SUM, AVG, MAX and other built-in functions.

- *User-defined types (UDTs)*: Enable you to extend the SQL Server type system with your own custom type.

In the rest of this section, we discuss each of these options in more detail and provide guidance on how to choose the best option for a particular task.

Note The examples provided in this section use the AdventureWorks sample database, which is available only as a separate download and install from SQL Server 2005 and SQL Server 2005 Express.

Managed Stored Procedures

A good way to introduce CLR Integration is to start by looking at the stored procedure functionality. With this feature, you can write a stored procedure using any .NET language. Once the stored procedure is completed and deployed to the database, you can invoke it like any standard T-SQL stored procedure.

The code within a managed stored procedure looks similar to any other code written in C# or VB .NET. The main difference, however, is that the logic must somehow access the internal database data and also must return result sets back to the caller. To facilitate this, SQL Server 2005 provides several interesting features.

- *In-proc ADO.NET*: This is a term used to describe the technology used to access SQL Server 2005 data from managed code running inside the database process. This technology provides data access through standard ADO.NET API calls. In other words, it contains classes like SqlCommand and SqlDataReader that you can use to query the database and read the results.

- SqlPipe: This class enables you to return the results of the stored procedure back to the caller.

- SqlContext: This class provides access to the current SQL context. Most notably, it contains a Pipe property that returns a SqlPipe object that you can use to return the results of a query to the caller.

For example, the following code defines a stored procedure that returns the title, first, and last name of every row in a Contacts table.

```
public partial class StoredProcedures
{
    [SqlProcedure()]
    public static void GetContactFullName()
    {
        // Note the connection string for an in-proc connection
        using (SqlConnection cnn = new SqlConnection("context connection=true"))
        using (SqlCommand cmd = new SqlCommand(
                "Select Title, FirstName, LastName From Person.Contact", cnn))
        {
            cnn.Open();
            SqlCommand cmd = new SqlCommand(
                "Select Title, FirstName, LastName From Person.Contact", cnn);
```

```
        SqlContext.Pipe.ExecuteAndSend(cmd);
    }
  }
};
```

In this example, you create the `SqlConnection` and `SqlCommand` much like you normally would. However, note the connection string passed to the `SqlConnection` constructor. Since this code is running within the SQL Server process, you simply use the `"context connection=true"` setting to connect to that SQL Server instance. Once the connection and command are established, the code uses the `SqlPipe.ExecuteAndSend()` to execute the command and return the results to the caller.

Note By default, SQL Server 2005 installs with CLR Integration disabled. To try out these examples, you'll need to explicitly enable CLR Integration by executing the query `sp_configure 'clr enabled', 1`.

This last code example is actually a little more complicated than it needs to be. If you don't explicitly provide a connection object in the `SqlCommand` constructor, it will use the context connection by default. Therefore, you could rewrite this managed stored procedure as:

```
[SqlProcedure()]
public static void GetContactFullName()
{
    // Look Ma - no connection!
    using (SqlCommand cmd = new SqlCommand
          ("Select Title, FirstName, LastName From Person.Contact"))
    {
        SqlContext.Pipe.ExecuteAndSend(cmd);
    }
}
```

Either way, once this stored procedure is deployed to a SQL Server 2005, you can call it like any other stored procedure. For example, you can call it using a T-SQL query:

```
exec GetContactSalutations
```

Or using ADO.NET in a managed language:

```
using (SqlConnection cnn = new SqlConnection(expressConnect))
{
    cnn.Open();
    SqlCommand cmd = new SqlCommand("GetContactSalutations", cnn);
    cmd.CommandType = CommandType.StoredProcedure;
    SqlDataReader reader = cmd.ExecuteReader();

    // Loop through the reader ...
}
```

Managed stored procedures are most useful when you need to retrieve a set of data, process each row (the procedural logic), and return the results. You can also use a managed stored procedure to encapsulate database update logic. In either case, remember that if there is little or no procedural logic to perform, then a T-SQL stored procedure will generally be easier to write and faster to execute. The sample stored procedure code, for example, can easily be expressed as a T-SQL stored procedure and, therefore, isn't a good example of a case where you should use a managed procedure.

User-Defined Functions and Table-Valued Functions

After managed stored procedures, the next logical place to apply CLR Integration is when creating managed user-defined functions (UDFs). A UDF is similar to a stored procedure in that it enables you to encapsulate data-oriented logic. However, there are a number of important differences.

- A UDF can only read data. Updates of any kind are not allowed.

- A UDF can return only a scalar value.

- A UDF can be invoked from nearly anywhere within a T-SQL query.

The last point highlights the primary reason why you might choose a UDF over a stored procedure. A stored procedure works best as a monolithic, atomic module that encapsulates all the data interaction required for a given request. In fact, a stored procedure is somewhat analogous to a service interface, in that a stored procedure typically sits at the data layer boundary and serves as the interface between the data tier and the middle tier.

On the other hand, UDFs are more analogous to components, in that they are intended to implement small, but useful, tasks that can be reused within queries as a part of a larger task. For example, the following code defines a simple managed UDF that returns a single full name from a given title, first name, middle name, and last name.

```
[SqlFunction()]
public static SqlString GetFullName(SqlString title, SqlString first,
   SqlString middle, SqlString last)
{
   StringBuilder fullName = new StringBuilder();
   if (!title.IsNull)
   {
      fullName.AppendFormat("{0} ", title);
   }
   fullName.AppendFormat("{0} ", first);
   if (!middle.IsNull)
   {
      fullName.AppendFormat("{0} ", middle);
   }
   fullName.Append(last);
   return fullName.ToString();
}
```

Now this UDF can be used within a T-SQL query in a variety of ways. For example, the following query displays the full names of each row in the Contact table:

```
SELECT dbo.GetFullName(Title, FirstName, MiddleName, LastName) As FullName
FROM Person.Contact
```

One of the disadvantages of a UDF is that it can return only a single scalar value. However, you can create another type of function, called a table-valued function (TVF) that returns a result set. Again, this is similar to the functionality of a stored procedure except that a TVF can be used within a query. Specifically, TVFs are typically found in the FROM clause of a SELECT query.

User-Defined Aggregates

For years, database developers have requested the ability to extend the set of built-in functions like COUNT, SUM, AVG, etc. with their own custom functions. Finally, you can now do exactly that by implementing a user-defined aggregate (UDA). UDAs are similar to UDFs, except that they are designed to compute a single value by operating on a given column over a set of rows.

Typically, you can also implement UDA functionality as a stored procedure or a UDF. The benefit of the UDA approach, however, is that you can use it in your queries like any of the built in aggregate functions. It will also perform better in most cases.

User-Defined Types

SQL Server 2005's new user-defined type (UDT) feature enables you to extend the SQL Server type system with your own custom scalar types. You simply define a custom type as a managed class and encapsulate all required data and behaviors within that class. Once the type is completed and deployed, you can use it just like any other SQL Server data type to define columns, declare variables, etc.

It is important to note, however, that this feature is not intended as a mechanism to turn SQL Server into an object-oriented database. This feature is meant for small and simple types only. If you attempt to use more complex types, you will soon run into the 8KB column size limit or various indexing restrictions. Therefore, complex business objects such as Customer, Product, Order, etc. are poor candidates for UDTs. On the other hand, a good example of where a UDT might be useful is if you have tables that use a custom date structure. With a UDT, you can encapsulate that custom date structure and its behaviors into a custom type.

SQL Server 2005 Service Broker

Service Broker is an enterprise-ready message queuing infrastructure that is fully integrated with the SQL Server 2005 data engine. This presents a radically different approach from the norm where products such as Message Queuing (MSMQ) provide this capability. In turn, this inevitably fosters many good questions: Why do you need messaging in the database? What are the scenarios where you would use this? How is this different from MSMQ? How do you choose between Service Broker and other messaging technologies such as MSMQ, Web Services, and BizTalk?

In this section, we address these questions, but let's begin by answering a more fundamental question...

Why Message Queuing?

Message queuing has long been a staple of highly scalable and robust systems. It is particularly useful for systems that must integrate disparate applications running on many different platforms, but its flexibility makes it an appealing solution for a wide variety of system scenarios where tasks must be executed asynchronously, correctly, and robustly.

So why aren't all distributed architectures based on messaging? Because building a messaging infrastructure with enterprise-level features is not a trivial task. In fact, it's plain hard. Messaging products such as MSMQ alleviate the implementation pain, but bring additional costs in terms of administration idiosyncrasies and mastering yet another fairly complex API. For many developers and architects building a small- to medium-sized system, these costs discourage the use of MSMQ and, thus, messaging in general (see Chapter 8 for a discussion and examples of MSMQ).

On the other hand, the industry is clearly shifting away from the Remote Procedure Call (RPC) and distributed object mindset in favor of messaging. A number of new and forthcoming technologies are enabling this shift by making message-based implementations more palatable in more scenarios. Web Services, BizTalk, and Windows Communication Foundation all treat a message as a first-class citizen rather than a network protocol detail to be abstracted into a method call. And now you can also add SQL Server 2005's new Service Broker feature to this ever-growing list of messaging tools.

Service Broker's Place in the Messaging World

Given the messaging capabilities of existing technologies, a common question surrounding Service Broker is what advantages it has, if any, over traditional messaging implementations such as MSMQ and BizTalk. Fundamentally, the primary difference between Service Broker and most other messaging technologies is its tight integration with a database engine. This provides a number of important benefits.

- *Unified programming model*: Service Broker adds message-related objects, such as message, queue, and service, to the standard set of database objects (table, stored procedure, trigger, etc.). It also enhances the T-SQL with the capability to read queues, write queues, and send messages to other Service Broker services. The result is a message programming model that is immediately familiar to database administrators and developers with T-SQL experience.

- *Improved transactional messaging support*: Many messaging scenarios call for a client application to perform a transactional read on a message queue. Unfortunately, several messaging infrastructures only support transactional reads on queues that are local to the receiving application. However, Service Broker allows any client, be it local or remote, to perform transactional reads. It also does not need to use expensive two-phase commit protocols to implement transactional messaging.

- *Integrated management and operations*: An organization's collected data is priceless, so it is usually protected with automated backup procedures and clustered hardware that ensures availability through failover. Since it's part of SQL Server 2005, the Service Broker message infrastructure automatically reaps these benefits.

Of course, Service Broker is not a messaging panacea. This tight integration with SQL Server 2005 comes at a steep price: Service Broker can only exchange messages with other Service Brokers (running in SQL Server 2005, of course). In contrast, MSMQ can send messages to any Windows machine running MSMQ and even some mainframes with the proper bridging software. And BizTalk, with its flexible adapter mechanism, can accept messages from just about anyone and send messages just about anywhere. Keep in mind, however, that even a single instance of SQL Server 2005 can make good use of Service Broker internally to provide reliable asynchronous interaction between it and the applications using the data—all without resorting to a general-purpose messaging technology like MSMQ. In fact, this may well describe the most common usage scenario.

Native XML Support

Another critical feature in SQL Server 2005 is the capability to store XML documents and fragments as a native type. In other words, XML joins the other common SQL Server types like `int`, `varchar`, `money`, etc. At first glance, this may seem like a minor upgrade. However, this fundamental feature provides an exceptional level of database engine integration and, in the process, opens a new world of possibilities by leveraging the best of the relational and XML data models.

Mixing XML and Relational Data

From the early days of XML, developers have tried to map data stored in XML documents to relational data structures. The subtle but fundamental differences between the two data models, however, create an impedance mismatch that is trumped only by the object/relational mismatch. Attempts to marry the two models fall into one of the following techniques.

- *Storing as a* `varchar`: In this case, the entire XML document is simply copied whole into a `varchar` typed column. However, from the database perspective, this `varchar` is nothing more than a blob of unstructured data, which means it can't be indexed nor can you query for individual pieces of information within the XML.

- *XML decomposition*: This approach, sometimes referred to as shredding, entails decomposing the XML document into one or usually more database tables. Although this technique is most faithful to the relational model, some of the XML goodness is stripped away in the process. Namely, XML document order is not preserved, which is extremely important in cases where the XML truly represents a document rather than a collection of data.

- *Partial decomposition*: This approach is a combination of the first two. It involves storing the entire XML document in a large `varchar` column and also copying some of the data from the XML into relational tables. This provides indexing and querying abilities on the extracted data plus preserves the document order in the original XML. However, choosing which part of the XML to decompose can be a difficult decision that requires a large amount of foresight. Who knows how future applications may need to use and query the data?

Clearly, none of the earlier solutions are ideal. What you need is a way to store XML data in its native form while also providing indexing and querying capabilities on *any* part of the data. This is exactly what SQL Server 2005 provides with the new XML native type and an integrated XML query language called XQuery.

Using the XML Type

Since XML is a native type like int, varchar, etc., adding an XML column to a table is the same as adding any other type of column. For example, the following script creates a table with an XML column:

```
CREATE TABLE Customer(
    CustomerId int NOT NULL,
    CustomerData xml NOT NULL,
)
```

This script creates a Customer table with two fields: CustomerId and CustomerData. Notice that CustomerData is typed as an XML column.

You can also define XML typed parameters in stored procedures. Again, as the following example shows, simply define it like any other type of parameter:

```
CREATE PROCEDURE SaveCustomer(
    @CustData xml
)
AS
--- stored proc code ...
GO
```

Untyped XML vs. Typed XML

The XML column created in the previous example is referred to as an *untyped XML* column because you did not associate an XML Schema. An untyped XML column can hold any well-formed XML document or fragment. This is useful if the column must accept several different types of XML documents or you do not have prior knowledge of the schema. SQL Server checks for well formedness before accepting XML into an untyped XML column, but it cannot validate the XML without an associated schema.

Although untyped XML columns are flexible, if possible, you should define a *typed XML* column by associating an XML Schema. This enables SQL Server to perform validation and optimize storage and queries. The following CREATE script demonstrates how to define a typed XML column:

```
CREATE TABLE Customer(
    CustomerID int,
    CustomerData xml (CustomerSchemaCollection)
)
```

As this example shows, you specify the schema information after the xml type keyword. SQL Server 2005 uses schema collections to contain and manage sets of related schemas. So for this to work, you must first define the customer schema and import the schema into CustomerSchemaCollection. The following example demonstrates this:

```
CREATE XML SCHEMA COLLECTION CustomerSchemaCollection AS
N'<?xml version="1.0" encoding="utf-16"?>
    <!-- Put your schema here! -->
</xs:schema>';
```

Content vs. Document Storage

Typed XML columns come in two varieties: content and document. Surprisingly, the default is content, which means that a column can store XML with multiple top-level elements. To explicitly define content storage, specify it when declaring the XML column:

```
CREATE TABLE Customer(
    CustomerID int,
    CustomerData xml (CONTENT CustomerSchemaCollection)
)
```

Alternatively, you can constrain the XML column to accept only XML documents that have a single top-level element. You do this using the DOCUMENT keyword, as we shown in the following example:

```
CREATE TABLE Customer3(
    CustomerID int,
    CustomerData xml (DOCUMENT CustomerSchemaCollection)
)
```

XML Methods and the Role of XQuery

Much like an object, the XML data type exposes several methods you can use to query and modify the XML data. These methods are listed in Table 11-8.

Table 11-8. *XML Data Type Methods*

Method Name	Meaning in Life
query	Executes a given XQuery expression on the contained XML and returns the result as an instance of XML type.
value	Executes a given XQuery expression on the contained XML and converts the result to a given SQL type (such as int, varchar, etc.) The XQuery expression must return a scalar value.
exists	Executes a given XQuery expression on the contained XML and returns 1 (representing true) if the query finds at least one matching XML node. Otherwise the method returns 0 (representing false).
modify	Updates the contained XML according to the given XML Data Manipulation Language (XML DML) expression.
nodes	Executes the given XQuery expression on the contained XML and returns the resulting nodes as a rowset. This is useful for shredding an XML document in to relational tables.

As you study these methods, you see a common theme: They all rely on XQuery expressions. XQuery is a relatively recent language created by the World Wide Web Consortium (W3C) to provide an SQL-like query language for XML data. Therefore, it makes an ideal language for querying XML data in SQL Server 2005. XQuery alone, however, can only query the data; it cannot modify it. So SQL Server 2005 also provides the XML Data Manipulation Language (XML DML) that extends XQuery with the capability to insert, update, and delete.

Here's an example of using the value method within a standard SELECT query to retrieve just the first name from the CustomerData column.

```
Select
    CustomerID,
    CustomerData.value(
        'declare namespace CUST="http://sql2005/Customer.xsd";
        /CUST:Customer/CUST:FirstName', 'varchar(30)') As FirstName
From Customer3
```

Remember that the value method accepts two arguments: an XQuery expression and an SQL data type. In this case, the XQuery expression is

```
declare namespace CUST="http://sql2005/Customer.xsd";
/CUST:Customer/CUST:FirstName
```

The first line of this expression establishes a namespace alias. The second, more interesting line, is an XPath expression that retrieves the FirstName element node, which the value method converts to a varchar(30) data type.

Full coverage of the XQuery language is well beyond the scope of this book. But remember, XQuery leans heavily on XPath, so past experience with XPath will drastically flatten the XQuery learning curve. In fact, many enhancements in XPath 2.0 were driven by the needs of the XQuery working group.

XML and ADO.NET 2.0

SQL Server 2005's integrated support for XML is truly impressive. However, an application developer's primary concern is moving data to and from the database, not how well the database handles XML. So all this XML integration means little if it doesn't also simplify retrieving XML data from the database into the application and saving XML data from the application to the database.

Thanks to enhancements in ADO.NET 2.0, it is, indeed, the case that moving XML data to and from the database is much easier. You'll find the clue that this is true in the System.Data.DbType and System.Data.SqlDbType enumerations, which both now include an XML value. Furthermore, the System.Data.SqlTypes namespace contains a new SqlXml class that is a client-side representation of XML typed database columns. The following code shows these new features in action.

```
private static void SaveCustomerXml()
{
    // Create an XmlReader using a customer data file
    using (XmlReader custReader = new XmlTextReader(
        "CustomerData.xml"))

    // Create a connection to the database
    using (SqlConnection cnn = new SqlConnection(cnnString))
```

```
// Create a command to insert the customer XML in the database table
using (SqlCommand cmd = new SqlCommand(
    "INSERT Customer(CustomerData) VALUES(@custData)",
    cnn))
{
    cnn.Open();

    // Create an SqlXml instance and pass it as a parameter
    SqlXml custXml = new SqlXml(custReader);
    SqlParameter param = cmd.Parameters.Add("@custData", SqlDbType.Xml);
    param.Value = custXml;

    // Execute the query (inserts the Customer XML)
    cmd.ExecuteNonQuery();

} // Dispose command, connection and XML reader
}
```

This example begins by creating an XmlReader to read the data from an external XML file named CustomerData.xml. Then, after creating and opening a database connection, it creates an SqlXml instance using the XmlReader. It then executes an INSERT command, passing the SqlXml instance as a parameter to the SqlCommand object. As a result, the XML data is saved in the CustomerData column of the Customer table.

Retrieving the XML data into your application is also straightforward. To handle this scenario, the SqlDataReader class provides a new GetSqlXml method that returns the data at the given column as a SqlXml instance. In addition, the SqlXml.CreateReader method creates and returns an XmlReader instance that you can use to navigate the XML contents. The following code demonstrates how to use these new methods to display the contents of an XML typed column.

```
static void DisplayCustomerData()
{
    using (SqlConnection cnn = new SqlConnection(cnnString))
    using (SqlCommand cmd = new SqlCommand(
        "SELECT * FROM Customer", cnn))
    {
        cnn.Open();

        // Use the standard ExecuteReader method to retrieve data reader
        SqlDataReader reader = cmd.ExecuteReader();

        while(reader.Read())
        {
            // Use GetSqlXml to retrieve the CustomerData column as an
            // SqlXml instance.
            SqlXml customerXml = reader.GetSqlXml(1);
```

```
        // Create and use an XML reader to navigate the customer data
        XmlReader xmlReader = customerXml.CreateReader();
        xmlReader.Read();
        Console.WriteLine(xmlReader.ReadOuterXml());
    }
  }
}
```

This example leverages the SqlXml.CreateReader method to retrieve an XmlReader, which is one of the common ways to read XML. In this particular case, however, it proves to be overkill since the next two lines of code simply write the entire XML content as one large string. You can achieve this more easily using the SqlXml.Value property, which returns the XML content as a string.

In general, ADO.NET 2.0 provides many ways to navigate, convert, read, and write XML data types. The overall combination of the ADO.NET SqlXml type, enhancements in the SQL Server data provider, and the tight data engine integration provided by the SQL Server XML data type promises to unify XML and relational data like never before. This, in turn, should accelerate the adoption of XML as the most common mechanism to represent business oriented data.

Summary

You have a lot of choices for putting a data access layer together. Some are useful in more situations than others. Data source controls are useful in some circumstances, while the Data Access Application Block is a likely boon to just about any application of decent size. Cache dependencies are a very powerful facility that can be leveraged to super-charge performance of applications in many situations that have historically been very difficult to address.

SQL Server 2005 introduces a new era in relational database technology by providing an integrated asynchronous messaging system, hosting the CLR in the same process as the database engine, and treating XML as a first class data type. Taken individually, these are powerful new features. Taken together, however, these features elevate SQL Server 2005 from a database to an application platform in its own right. Personally, we're excited to see how innovative developers will combine these features to elegantly address problems that have traditionally been daunting.

CHAPTER 12

Transactions

Virtually all business applications require some level of transaction support. You can largely maintain data integrity in a static view using the rules of schema that a relational database provides. In dynamic processes, however, a transaction can guarantee that all or none of the changes applied during the process are persisted when the process is complete. ACID properties (atomicity, consistency, isolation, and durability) are the cornerstone of any transaction infrastructure. In Chapter 7, you saw the attribute-based transactional behavior of Enterprise Services provided by COM+. These transactions are specific to a database, and it's common to think of work done with a database whenever you're considering transactions. Transactional behavior can be supplied for any resource, however, be it an in-memory hash table, a file on the disk, or an XML document. One of the design goals of the transactional engine built into version 2.0 of the .NET Framework is to make creating these resource managers much easier for any type of resource you want to participate in a transaction.

The problem with COM+ transactions is that they rely on the Distributed Transaction Coordinator (DTC), which is a feature-rich transactional engine, but those features come at a price. The DTC consumes a lot of resources and can introduce a performance penalty to your application. This is fine when transactional work occurs across relational database systems, but it can be a large price to pay if the transaction is isolated to a single database. For a single database, you're better off using T-SQL Transactions, or ADO.NET connection-based transactions. Another benefit of the transactional system in COM+ is the capability to dynamically compose transactions. An atomic method can be declared as requiring a transaction context. Sometimes you call that method on its own, where an ADO.NET transaction would completely suffice. Sometimes, however, you call that method as a step of a larger transaction, one in which you may need the distributed services of the DTC. Ideally the transaction would use the less-expensive resource manager of ADO.NET, and the transaction context would recognize when the services of a more robust resource manager such as the DTC were needed, and then automatically "promote" the transaction and enlist the more resource intensive manager. This automatic transaction promotion is the second big design goal of transactions in .NET 2.0.

Transactions in 1.x

A number of technologies that support transactions are available for use in version 1.x of the .NET Framework. Which one you select depends on the requirements of the transactional infrastructure. Because of the resource expense and performance hit incurred by introducing a transaction into a process, you should select the cheapest technology that does the job.

The first of these are transactions that you can create and manage from within a stored procedure. We'll examine Transact-SQL running on SQL Server, but other database vendors' products expose similar functionality for whatever language is available for coding procedures (e.g., PSQL in Oracle).

Building transactions right into the database stored procedures results in transaction logic that is managed by the database server, is optimized by the database engine, and runs in the same process space of the server. A stored procedure can start a transaction and call other stored procedures in the database and their work will be included in the transaction.

The downside to this approach is that it tends to move business logic coding into the database layer. Transactions frequently reflect business rules, so to code the transaction within the stored procedure code naturally introduces business logic into this tier of your application. You're also limited to a single database within which to do your transactional modifications. You can overcome this in SQL Server using *linked servers*, but you're definitely limited to modifying SQL Server data.

■**Note** A linked server in SQL Server is a server that is "virtualized" locally. That is, a linked server acts as an alias for an external database, and makes the database look like it's on the local SQL Server, even though it's located on an entirely different server.

T-SQL is an unmanaged language that lacks the eloquence and clarity of C# code. Stored procedure support for exception handling is also limited (these limitations can be overcome with SQL Server 2005, which enables you to write stored procedures using C#, see the last section of Chapter 11). You also lose the ability to dynamically compose a transaction, as whatever work is being done in the stored procedure becomes the work done in the transaction. Any attempt to overcome this will invariably result in more business logic in your database layer.

You can do transactions on a single connection with ADO.NET transactions. This overcomes some of the problems using T-SQL transactions, as it moves the transaction management logic into your C# code, where structured error handling and the other niceties of managed code execution can be leveraged. It's also easier to dynamically compose transactions by calling an arbitrary set of stored procedures determined by business logic (although this still requires some design consideration and coding and is not as easy as the attribute-based system available in COM+).

Here's a simple procedure doing some database work in a transaction. (See XActionIE.aspx in the Web12 project.)

```
public static void SingleDBUpdate(Hashtable ht)
{
    using (SqlConnection cnn = new SqlConnection(WebStatic.ConnectionString))
    {
        string sql;

        cnn.Open();
        SqlTransaction tx = cnn.BeginTransaction();
        try
```

```
    {
        foreach(string key in ht.Keys)
        {
                    sql = "INSERT INTO Tuples (keyValue, dataValue) " +
                "VALUES ('{0}', '{1}') ";

            sql = string.Format(sql, key, ht[key]);
            SqlCommand insert = new SqlCommand(sql, cnn, tx);
            insert.ExecuteNonQuery();
        }
        tx.Commit();
    }
    catch (Exception e)
    {
        tx.Rollback();
        HttpContext.Current.Response.Write(e.Message);
    }
    finally
    {
        cnn.Close();
    }
}
}
```

Here you're explicitly tied to a single connection. You can pass this connection around to dynamically compose the commands that make up the connection, but are still tied to a single data source. To span data sources, you must enlist the services of the DTC via COM+. (See Mover.cs in the App_Code directory of the Web12 project.)

```
[Transaction(TransactionOption.Required)]
public class Mover : ServicedComponent
{
    [AutoComplete]
    public void Move()
    {
        using(SqlConnection cnnDB1 = new SqlConnection(Database1),
                cnnDB2 = new SqlConnection(Database2))
        {
            SqlCommand cmdDeleteDB1 =
                new SqlCommand("DELETE ...", cnnDB1);
            SqlCommand cmdInsertDB2 =
                new SqlCommand("INSERT ...", cnnDB2);
            // ADO.NET connections automatically enlist into
            // the DTC transaction
            cnnDB1.Open();
            cnnDB2.Open();
            cmdDeleteDB1.ExecuteNonQuery();
```

```
        cmdInsertDB2.ExecuteNonQuery();
    }
  }
}
```

Here you're not only spanning databases, but also if you want to dynamically compose the steps of the transaction, any method you called on the class would also automatically be enrolled. You could even call out to methods on other types flagged with `TransactionOption` as `Required` and their work would automatically be enlisted in the transaction. You can clearly see the power available in this model when there are requirements to compose transactions dynamically. (See Chapter 7 for more details on COM+ transaction composition.)

The trade-off for this amount of flexibility is costly, though. Your type must inherit from the `ServicedComponent` base class. And regardless of how your transactions are composed, you'll always incur the overhead of invoking the DTC, even if you're updating a single row in a single table. This is a high price to pay, especially if most of your transactions are against a single data source and a distributed transaction is rare, as is normally the case.

This is a real bummer, because it puts you in the situation where if you *ever* need to dynamically compose transactions, then you *always* have to use the DTC.

Transactions in 2.0

The transaction management system in version 2 of the .NET Framework sets out to address the problem of excessive overhead for dynamic composition of transactions by enlisting only the resource managers required for the type of transactional work being done. It also provides an infrastructure where you can roll in more volatile resources into the "commit" and "roll-back" model of transactions.

This means that if your transaction starts by modifying a hash table in memory, there is a resource manager that will manage that memory. If you commit the transaction, the changes will be committed to the hash table. If you roll it back, the hash table will revert to the state it had when the transaction started. In 1.x, the following code results in the loss of the entry from the hash table, even though the transaction is rolled back. (See `Mover.cs` in the `App_Code` directory of the `Web12` project).

```
[AutoComplete]
public void Move2(object key)
{
    object val = hashTable[key];
    hashTable.Remove(key);
    using(SqlConnection cnnDB2 = new SqlConnection(Database2))
    {
        // Insert value from hash table into DB
        SqlCommand cmdInsertDB2 =
            new SqlCommand("INSERT ...", cnnDB2);
        cnnDB2.Open();
        cmdInsertDB2.ExecuteNonQuery();
    }
}
```

In 2.0, however, you can use a *transacted hash table* that would automatically participate in the transaction present.

Furthermore, if on another path of code dynamically composing a different transaction, you start again by modifying the hash table but then modify a file from the hard drive, the transaction will automatically be "promoted" to enlist the file-based transaction manager. If your code continues and uses ADO.NET to modify a database table, the transaction is promoted again, to one that can handle the database transaction.

Notice at this point in the scenario you have enlisted a transaction manager that is much more of an expensive resource than one that simply manages the memory consumed by a hash table. You have done so only on an as-needed basis, however. If your process continues and modifies a table from a different database, then and only then is the DTC enlisted to manage the distributed transaction.

This is a far superior model to the one available in 1.x of the .NET Framework. You can dynamically compose your transactions, and the DTC will not be involved until you need for it to be. In fact, only the resource managers that need be involved will be, giving you a much better cost-to-feature ratio than was available in 1.x.

The volatile management of memory and the file system is provided to you by the Lightweight Transaction Manager (LTM), which we look at next.

Lightweight Transaction Manager

The LTM is a very fast, very inexpensive resource manager for transactions occurring in a single application domain. It's the starting point of all transactions in the Framework, and it monitors the resources being touched by a transaction and enlists the services of more robust resource managers on an as-needed basis.

When the transactional work goes out-of-process (i.e., you start modifying database data), the LTM will automatically use a resource manager that supports the Promotable Single Phase Enlistment (PSPE) model of transaction management. This is a new transactional infrastructure that knows and understands the "pay as you go" mechanism of the LTM. If there is no PSPE manager available, the LTM enlists the DTC. And then, of course, the DTC is enlisted any time multiple remote data sources are modified.

When the PSPE model can do the job, then your transactions will perform as well as an ADO.NET Transaction would in version 1.x. Why use the PSPE model if you get the same performance as you would with ADO.NET transactions? It's used so that the transaction is automatically promoted to the DTC when more than one database is touched.

In version 2.0 of the .NET Framework, you will automatically get a PSPE transaction when working with SQL Server 2005. If the transactional work touches another server or another database, it automatically uses the DTC. Volatile transactions automatically participate in the PSPE without invoking the DTC.

Programming Transactions

The new functionality of transactions is made available in the System.Transactions namespace of the Framework class library. There a few ways to create transactions and enlist resources to do work within them, but the best and most common way is to use the TransactionScope object.

Here's a method that uses TranasactionScope to do its work in a transaction. (See XAction.cs in the App_Code directory of the Web12 project.)

```
public bool UpdateQuantity(int itemId, int quantity)
{
    using (TransactionScope tx =
        new TransactionScope(TransactionScopeOption.Required))
    {
        AuditItemUpdate(itemId, quantity);

        string sql = "UPDATE Inventory SET OnHand = OnHand - @quantity "
                    + "WHERE InventoryID = @inventoryID and "
                    + "OnHand - @quantity >= 0";

        SqlConnection cn = new SqlConnection(connStr);
        SqlCommand cm = new SqlCommand(sql, cn);

        cm.Parameters.Add(new
            SqlParameter("@quantity", SqlDbType.Int)).Value = quantity;
        cm.Parameters.Add(new
            SqlParameter("@inventoryID", SqlDbType.Int)).Value = itemId;

        cn.Open();
        int i = cm.ExecuteNonQuery();
        cn.Close();
        if (i==1)
        {
            tx.Complete();
        }
        return Convert.ToBoolean(i);
    }
}
```

Here the TransactionScope is declared within the C# using statement. The TransactionOption enum has three values: Required, RequiresNew, and Suppress. These are a lot like the transaction options available in COM+. They can affect the transactional behavior of your method in the context of any transaction that exists in the call stack calling the method. In other words, with the setting of Required, if a transaction already exists, the work this method does will participate in that transaction; otherwise, a new one will be created.

The syntax of the TransactionScope simplifies the semantics of transaction management so much, that it's easy to miss it entirely unless you look closely. Here's the code that's managing the transaction for this method.

```
...
using (TransactionScope tx =
        new TransactionScope(TransactionScopeOption.Required))
    {
      ...
      if (i==1)
        {
            tx.Complete();
        }
...

    }
```

Here are some things `TransactionScope` does for you:

- Any statement appearing within the brackets of the using statement will be done within the transaction.

- Any connection created in this block will be enlisted in the transaction.

- If an error occurs within the `using` block, the transaction will be automatically rolled back.

- The check of `i==1` is basically a check of "are you happy with the work?" If yes, then call `Complete` on the transaction for your portion of the work.

- Every step of the call stack must call `Complete` for the transaction to be committed.

How is the transaction managed under the hood? This depends on the database you're connecting to. SQL Server 2005 supports lightweight PSPE transactions. So if this code connects to SQL Server 2005, the transaction is managed by that provider and is no more expensive than an ADO.NET transaction. Let's contrast this block of code to similar code that does the same thing in COM+.

- The type defining this method does not need to inherit from `ServicedComponent`.

- This assembly does not need a strong name, which it would for registration in COM+.

- No special registration steps are necessary to configure the component within COM+.

- It performs just as well as Enterprise Services if you're using SQL Server 2000, and performs as well as an ADO.NET transaction if you're using SQL Server 2005.

- With SQL Server 2005, the DTC would automatically be enlisted to manage the transaction if any layer of the call stack connected to a different database.

Let's build up a simple call stack to demonstrate the dynamic enlistment behavior of this infrastructure. You'll use the tables shown in Figure 12-1 to mock-up an order entry scenario. (The script to build this database is in `XActionIE.sql` in the `Code12` directory.)

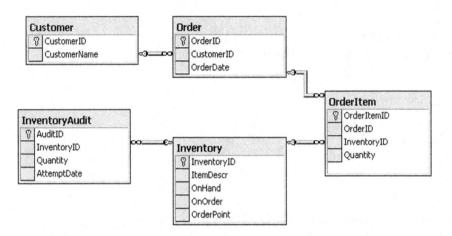

Figure 12-1. *A set of tables to update within a transaction*

So for the sample scenarios, your transaction will be composed of the following steps:

1. Create a new order for the customer in the order table

2. For each order item, decrease the on-hand amount for the item by the quantity being ordered.

3. Audit the attempt to secure the quantity.

4. Create an order item for the order.

If there is not enough on hand for any item in the order, then the transaction should roll back. However, the audits should succeed whether the order is created or not. Here's the method to create the order. (See XAction.cs in the App_Code directory of the Web12 project.)

```
public void AddOrder(int orderId, int customerID, DateTime orderDate)
{
    using (TransactionScope tx =
        new TransactionScope(TransactionScopeOption.Required))
    {
        string sql = "INSERT INTO [Order](OrderID, CustomerID, OrderDate) "
                   + "VALUES (@orderID, @customerID, @orderDate)";

        SqlConnection cn = new SqlConnection(connStr);
        SqlCommand cm = new SqlCommand(sql, cn);

        cm.Parameters.Add(new
            SqlParameter("@orderId", SqlDbType.Int)).Value = orderId;
        cm.Parameters.Add(new
            SqlParameter("@customerID", SqlDbType.Int)).Value = customerID;
        cm.Parameters.Add(new
            SqlParameter("@orderDate", SqlDbType.DateTime)).Value = orderDate;
```

```
        cn.Open();
        cm.ExecuteNonQuery();
        cn.Close();
        tx.Complete();
    }
}
```

The method to create a new order item follows (also in XAction.cs in the App_Code directory of the Web12 project).

```
public bool AddOrderItem(int orderId, int itemId, int quantity)
{
    using (TransactionScope tx =
        new TransactionScope(TransactionScopeOption.Required))
    {
        if (UpdateQuantity(itemId, quantity))
        {
            string sql = "INSERT INTO OrderItem(OrderID, InventoryID, Quantity) "
                    + "VALUES (@OrderID, @InventoryID, @Quantity)";

            SqlConnection cn = new SqlConnection(connStr);
            SqlCommand cm = new SqlCommand(sql, cn);

            cm.Parameters.Add(new
                    SqlParameter("@OrderID", SqlDbType.Int)).Value = orderId;
            cm.Parameters.Add(new
                    SqlParameter("@InventoryID", SqlDbType.Int)).Value = itemId;
            cm.Parameters.Add(new
                    SqlParameter("@Quantity", SqlDbType.Int)).Value = quantity;

            cn.Open();
            cm.ExecuteNonQuery();
            cn.Close();

            tx.Complete();
            return true;
        }
        else return false;
    }
}
```

Notice the first thing that this method does after enlisting in the transaction is to call the UpdateQuantity method (listed previously). If this method fails, it means you're out of stock on the item being ordered, and so this method will not create the order item. It also does not call Complete in this case, which in effect dooms the entire transaction. UpdateQuantity is what calls for the audit. The code creating the entry in the audit table follows (also in XAction.cs in the App_Code directory of the Web12 project).

```
public void AuditItemUpdate(int itemId, int quantity)
{
    using (TransactionScope tx =
        new TransactionScope(TransactionScopeOption.RequiresNew))
    {
        string sql =
            "INSERT INTO InventoryAudit(InventoryID, Quantity, AttemptDate) "
            + "VALUES (@InventoryID, @Quantity, @AttemptDate)";

        SqlConnection cn = new SqlConnection(connStr);
        SqlCommand cm = new SqlCommand(sql, cn);

        cm.Parameters.Add(new
            SqlParameter("@InventoryID", SqlDbType.Int)).Value = itemId;
        cm.Parameters.Add(new
            SqlParameter("@Quantity", SqlDbType.Int)).Value = quantity;
        cm.Parameters.Add(new
            SqlParameter("@AttemptDate", SqlDbType.DateTime)).Value = DateTime.Now;

        cn.Open();
        cm.ExecuteNonQuery();
        cn.Close();
        tx.Complete();
    }
}
```

Here you'll notice that the transaction option selected when creating the TransactionScope instance is RequiresNew. This breaks the work done in this method out into its own transaction. Since you want the audit to persist regardless of the outcome of the containing transaction, this work is done independent from the transaction of the caller. Using TransactionOption.Suppress would have the some effect, except the work done within this method would occur without a transaction at all.

The entire transaction is then managed by this *orchestration* method, which gets handed a hash table of inventory IDs and quantities. (See XActionHost.aspx in the Web12 project.)

```
private void PlaceOrder(int CustomerID,
    DateTime OrderDate, Hashtable OrderItems)
{
    XAction dalTx = new XAction();
    int OrderId = GetNextOrderID();
    bool bSuccess = true;

    using (TransactionScope tx = new TransactionScope())
    {
        dalTx.AddOrder(OrderId, CustomerID, DateTime.Now);
        foreach(int ItemId in OrderItems.Keys)
```

```
        {
            if (!dalTx.AddOrderItem(OrderId,
                ItemId,
                Convert.ToInt32(OrderItems[ItemId])))
            {
                bSuccess = false;
                break;
            }
        }
        if (bSuccess) tx.Complete();
    }
    if (bSuccess)
    {
        lblOutput.Text = "Success";
    }
    else
    {
        lblOutput.Text = "Rolled back";
    }
}
```

This is what you could call the *root transaction object* in COM+. It's the root of the call stack for the entire transaction. All of the work at lower levels in the stack is enlisted within the transaction created by this method (with the exception, of course, of the audit method, which declares its need for a transaction of its own).

The entire call stack breaks down like this (see Figure 12-2).

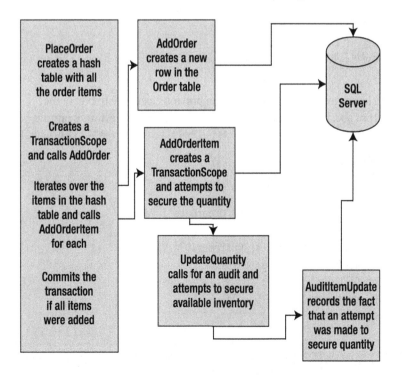

Figure 12-2. *The call stack of your dynamically composed transaction*

Notice that each level in the stack must call `Complete`. If any level fails to call `Complete`, then the entire transaction is doomed up and down all levels of the call stack.

Transacted Types

So far we have illustrated the simplified transaction model for updates of either a single database or many databases, which when you're using SQL Server 2005 will leverage either a lightweight transaction or the DTC. Support also exists for creating your own transacted types, which can affect memory, the file system, or any other resource you need to manage in your application.

Creating your own transacted type involves implementing, at a minimum, the `IEnlistmentNotification` interface. Consider the follow example. Here you move orders from an XML file into the same database you used in the previous example. (See `XActedDomTest.aspx` in the `Web12` project.)

```
private void WOATx()
{
    XmlDocument dom = new XmlDocument();
    dom.Load(Server.MapPath("Orders.xml"));
    XmlNode orderElem;
    XmlNode ordersElem = dom.SelectSingleNode("//Orders");
    int orderCount = ordersElem.ChildNodes.Count;

    for (int i = orderCount - 1; i >= 0; i--)
    {
        orderElem = ordersElem.ChildNodes[i];
        orderElem.ParentNode.RemoveChild(orderElem);
        AddOrder(orderElem);
    }
    dom.Save(Server.MapPath("UnprocessedOrders.xml"));
}
```

The `AddOrder` method leverages the methods from the previous example to create the order in the database. In this case, instead of using the hash table like the previous example, it's using the data read from the XML document. (See `XActedDomTest.aspx` in the `Web12` project.)

```
private bool AddOrder(XmlNode orderElem)
{
    DateTime orderDate =
        Convert.ToDateTime(orderElem.Attributes["OrderDate"].Value);
    int customerId =
        Convert.ToInt32(orderElem.Attributes["CustomerID"].Value);
    XAction dal = new XAction();
    int orderID = XAction.GetNextOrderID();
    dal.AddOrder(orderID, customerId, orderDate);
    bool bSuccess = true;
```

```
    foreach(XmlNode orderItem in orderElem.ChildNodes)
    {
        int itemID =
            Convert.ToInt32(orderItem.Attributes["ItemId"].Value);
        int quantity =
            Convert.ToInt32(orderItem.Attributes["Quantity"].Value);
        bSuccess = dal.AddOrderItem(orderID, itemID, quantity);
        if (!bSuccess) break;
    }
    return bSuccess;
}
```

What happens when you run into an item that's not in stock? The creation of the order and corresponding order items will be rolled back, but you've lost the changes describing the order in your XML document. Your goal here is to have the instance of XMLDocument also participate in the transaction. When the transaction fails, any changes you've made to the tree of elements in the document instance will be rolled back as well.

To do this you'll create a type that extends XMLDocument. The first thing you'll need to do with this type is implement IEnlistmentNotification. Table 12-1 shows the methods this interface requires you to implement.

Table 12-1. *Methods of the* IEnlistmentNotification *Interface*

Method	Meaning in Life
Commit	Called when the transaction is being committed.
InDoubt	Called when the outcome of the transaction is not certain (meaning, in real terms, that it's doomed).
Prepare	Called when the transaction is about to be committed.
Rollback	Called when the transaction has failed and the object should be restored to its original state.

So your responsibility as a transaction supporter is to maintain enough state to track the changes that occur during the transaction, and be able to revert to the original state of the document in the event of a rollback. When the transaction is completed, you should also make appropriate changes to the state of your type to commit any modifications made during the transaction.

Here's the implementation of the IEnlistmentNotification interface. (See TransDOM.cs in the App_Code directory of the Web12 project.)

```
public class TransactedXMLDocument : XmlDocument, IEnlistmentNotification
{
    private string orgXml;

    public void Enlist()
    {
        orgXml = this.InnerXml;
        Transaction.Current.EnlistVolatile(this, EnlistmentOptions.None);
    }
```

```
public void Commit(Enlistment enlistment)
{
    orgXml = "";
    enlistment.Done();
}

public void InDoubt(Enlistment enlistment)
{
    this.LoadXml(orgXml);
    orgXml = "";
}

public void Prepare(PreparingEnlistment preparingEnlistment)
{
    preparingEnlistment.Prepared();
}

public void Rollback(Enlistment enlistment)
{
    this.LoadXml(orgXml);
    orgXml = "";
}
}
```

In this implementation you're tracking the state of the XML document at the point it enters into a transaction using the XML representing the tree at that moment. Any changes made to the tree during the transaction will be reflected in the instance via normal processing that occurs from the base class. Only in the case if the transaction is in doubt or rolled back do you need to take action, and you simply restore the document to its original state by reloading the underlying XML.

This strategy does force your user to call the Enlist method to tie it into a transaction. By calling EnlistVolatile and passing a reference to your instance (via this), you wire your type into the rest of the transaction processing. The transaction infrastructure will automatically call Commit or Rollback when the outcome of the transaction becomes known.

Let's modify the preceding document processing loop to leverage the new transactional functionality of this type. (See TransactedDomTest.aspx in the Web12 project.)

```
private void WithATran()
{
    TransactedXMLDocument dom = new TransactedXMLDocument();
    dom.Load(Server.MapPath("Orders.xml"));
    XmlNode orderElem;
    XmlNode ordersElem = dom.SelectSingleNode("//Orders");
    int orderCount = ordersElem.ChildNodes.Count;

    for (int i = orderCount - 1; i >= 0; i--)
    {
        orderElem = ordersElem.ChildNodes[i];
```

```
    try
    {
        using (TransactionScope tx = new TransactionScope())
        {
            dom.Enlist();
            orderElem.ParentNode.RemoveChild(orderElem);
            AddOrder(orderElem);
            tx.Complete();
        }
        Response.Write("The transaction was written<BR>");
    }
    catch (TransactionAbortedException tex)
    {
        Response.Write("The transaction did not succeed<BR>");
    }
}
dom.Save(Server.MapPath("UnprocessedOrders.xml"));
}
```

Notice you're kicking off a transaction per processed order. Within each of these transaction scopes, you're explicitly enlisting your XML document in the transaction. You then remove the node you're processing from the document tree, and pass it along to the AddOrder method, which shreds it and moves it to the database. If the transaction aborts, the TransactionAbortedExeption is automatically raised, which you trap and report the error to your user. Otherwise you output a message that the transaction was successful.

Since the call to AddOrder is within the scope of your transaction, the entire descent of the call stack participates in your transaction, including all of the code in the instance of XAction that's created in the AddOrder. The one exception again is the audit method, of course, because it explicitly demands its own transaction.

Let's run the following XML through this process. (See Orders.xml in Web12.)

```
<?xml version="1.0" encoding="utf-8" ?>
<Orders>
    <Order OrderDate="5/15/2005" CustomerID="1">
        <OrderItem ItemId="1" Quantity="21" />
        <OrderItem ItemId="2" Quantity="21" />
    </Order>
    <Order OrderDate="5/16/2005" CustomerID="2">
        <OrderItem ItemId="1" Quantity="21" />
        <OrderItem ItemId="2" Quantity="21" />
    </Order>
    <Order OrderDate="5/17/2005" CustomerID="3">
        <OrderItem ItemId="1" Quantity="21" />
        <OrderItem ItemId="2" Quantity="21" />
    </Order>
</Orders>
```

When you start the processing, you'll have on-hand quantities of 60 for both items 1 and 2. This means the first two orders will be processed correctly, and the third will fail for lack of available quantities. The output is shown in Figure 12-3.

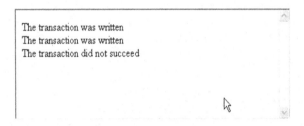

The transaction was written
The transaction was written
The transaction did not succeed

Figure 12-3. *The output of the transaction shredding the* Orders.xml *document*

The UnprocessedOrders.xml document shows you what happened to your document during the process. Since the first two transactions were successful, they have been removed. Notice also that you're processing the orders in reverse of the order they appear in the document, so the last transaction is attempting to process the first order in the document. Even though the line of code to remove the first order was executed, the transaction where it occurred failed, and so the order is restored by the time the document instance is written back out to disk:

```
<?xml version="1.0" encoding="utf-8"?>
<Orders>
  <Order OrderDate="5/15/2005" CustomerID="1">
    <OrderItem ItemId="1" Quantity="21" />
    <OrderItem ItemId="2" Quantity="21" />
  </Order>
</Orders>
```

Here the order is safely persisted, to be processed another day when there are more items on hand.

Summary

Transaction processing was been dramatically revamped in the .NET Framework 2.0. A new lightweight transaction management system has been added to the Framework, and an easy infrastructure for participating in these transactions has been exposed. Transactions use only the resources they need for the work that they're doing. This means that instead of using the DTC for every transaction from the start, transactions are smart enough to realize when they need the services of distributed transaction management, and enlist the DTC only then.

While for now the best support for this is with SQL Server 2005, future versions of the .NET Framework will offer support for transactions with types from System.Collections (for in-memory transactions) and System.IO (for disk-based transactions). For now, you can easily add support for the types you need, as we've showed you for the XMLDocument type.

Index

A

AcceptChanges method, 367

AccessDataSource control, 374

ACID (atomicity, consistency, isolation, and durability) properties, 423

AcquireRequestState event, 35, 38, 41–42

Action attribute constraints, 109

activation, 253

Activation tab, 279

Add element, 51, 53, 360

Add Web Form dialog, 70

Add Web Reference feature, 280

<add> subelement, 174

AddOrder method, 434, 437

AddUsersToRole method, 190

AddUsersToRoles method, 190

AddUserToRole method, 190

AddUserToRoles method, 190

Administrators role, 157

ADO.NET, overview, 321

AdRotator control, DataBoundControl base class, 374

<allow> subelement, <authorization> element, 168

App_Code directory, 79–80, 208

app.config (web.config) file, 33, 51, 55, 62–63, 108, 158, 243, 279

app.config file, 306

Application Center Test tool, 8

Application class, 30–31, 43

Application directive, 43, 46, 50

application server, 272

Application_End event, 43

Application_Start event, 43

ApplicationActivation attribute, 278

appSetting element, 329

appSettings element, 159, 192, 328

AppSettings method, 192

architecture/service orientation, 15–17

ASHX extension, 57

ASMX enhancements, 234

  overview, 210

  version 1.x problems

    custom serialization lacks adequate extensibility, 225–34

    no type sharing across proxies, 210–18

    proxies generate fields and not properties, 218–20

    type fidelity available only for datasets, 220–25

ASMX SOAP Stack, 239

<asp:ChangePassword> declaration, 184

<asp:Login> tag, 179

ASP.NET Framework

  remoting, 276–78

  serviced components, 278

  Web services, 275–76

  Windows Communication Foundation (WCF), 278

ASP.NET Tracing tool, 8

aspnet_compiler command line tool, 81

aspnet_Membership table, 176

aspnet_regiis command line tool, 330

aspnet_regsql.exe tool, 389

aspnet_Roles table, 189

AspNet_SqlCacheRegisterTableStored-Procedure database, 390

AspNet_SqlCacheTablesForChange-Notification table, 389

<asp:PasswordRecovery> scope, 182

ASPX extension, 29

aspx files, code generation of, 71–75

aspx pages, code generation of, 70–71

assembly-level attribute, 262

asynchronous calls feature, WCF, 312

X

forums.apress.com

FOR PROFESSIONALS BY PROFESSIONALS™

JOIN THE APRESS FORUMS AND BE PART OF OUR COMMUNITY. You'll find discussions that cover topics of interest to IT professionals, programmers, and enthusiasts just like you. If you post a query to one of our forums, you can expect that some of the best minds in the business—especially Apress authors, who all write with *The Expert's Voice*™—will chime in to help you. Why not aim to become one of our most valuable participants (MVPs) and win cool stuff? Here's a sampling of what you'll find:

DATABASES
Data drives everything.

Share information, exchange ideas, and discuss any database programming or administration issues.

INTERNET TECHNOLOGIES AND NETWORKING
Try living without plumbing (and eventually IPv6).

Talk about networking topics including protocols, design, administration, wireless, wired, storage, backup, certifications, trends, and new technologies.

JAVA
We've come a long way from the old Oak tree.

Hang out and discuss Java in whatever flavor you choose: J2SE, J2EE, J2ME, Jakarta, and so on.

MAC OS X
All about the Zen of OS X.

OS X is both the present and the future for Mac apps. Make suggestions, offer up ideas, or boast about your new hardware.

OPEN SOURCE
Source code is good; understanding (open) source is better.

Discuss open source technologies and related topics such as PHP, MySQL, Linux, Perl, Apache, Python, and more.

PROGRAMMING/BUSINESS
Unfortunately, it is.

Talk about the Apress line of books that cover software methodology, best practices, and how programmers interact with the "suits."

WEB DEVELOPMENT/DESIGN
Ugly doesn't cut it anymore, and CGI is absurd.

Help is in sight for your site. Find design solutions for your projects and get ideas for building an interactive Web site.

SECURITY
Lots of bad guys out there—the good guys need help.

Discuss computer and network security issues here. Just don't let anyone else know the answers!

TECHNOLOGY IN ACTION
Cool things. Fun things.

It's after hours. It's time to play. Whether you're into LEGO® MINDSTORMS™ or turning an old PC into a DVR, this is where technology turns into fun.

WINDOWS
No defenestration here.

Ask questions about all aspects of Windows programming, get help on Microsoft technologies covered in Apress books, or provide feedback on any Apress Windows book.

HOW TO PARTICIPATE:
Go to the Apress Forums site at **http://forums.apress.com/**.
Click the New User link.